William Denison

Varieties of Vice-Regal Life

Vol. 2

William Denison

Varieties of Vice-Regal Life
Vol. 2

ISBN/EAN: 9783337778996

Printed in Europe, USA, Canada, Australia, Japan

Cover: Foto ©Thomas Meinert / pixelio.de

More available books at **www.hansebooks.com**

VARIETIES

OF

VICE-REGAL LIFE.

VOL. II.

VARIETIES

OF

VICE-REGAL LIFE.

BY

SIR WILLIAM DENISON, K.C.B.

LATE GOVERNOR-GENERAL OF THE AUSTRALIAN COLONIES

AND GOVERNOR OF MADRAS.

'What is that one thing that we shall at this time found our discourse upon?'

'What you will. I will talk of things heavenly or things earthly; things moral or things evangelical; things sacred or things profane; things past or things to come; things foreign or things at home; things more essential or things circumstantial.' TALKATIVE, in *Pilgrim's Progress*.

IN TWO VOLUMES.

VOL. II.

LONDON:

LONGMANS, GREEN, AND CO.

1870.

CONTENTS

THE SECOND VOLUME.

CHAPTER XVI.

PAGE.

New Zealand—Remarks on Responsible Government .   1

CHAPTER XVII.

Arrival at Madras—Landing through the Surf—Body Guard—
The two Government Houses— Native Household—Public
Breakfasts—Durbar—First Evening Reception—Opening of
the N. W. Railway to Naggery—Meeting with the Rajah— A
Mute Dignitary— Incautious Question—Nature of Work at
Madras—State of Government and Army—Letter to Lord
Canning on Army Reduction—Letter on proposed Legislative
Council—Character of Hindoos—Impossibility of Applying to
them English Principles of Government—Railways—Reorganization of Native Army—Suggestions for General Government
of India—Visit to Calcutta—Government House—Large banyan tree—Barrackpoor—Conversation with the Principal of
the Sanscrit College—Return to Madras   .   .   .   25

CHAPTER XVIII.

Public Works Department—Navigation of the River Godavery—
Curious Method of Laying up Native Shipping—Irrigation—
Irrigation Works on the Godavery—Insects—Journey to Salem
—Transits—Thunderstorm and its Consequences—Ride up the
Hills—Coonoor—Accident to Dr. S.—— — Barracks at Wel-
lington—Ootacamund—Shooting Parties—Variety of Game—
We Hunt for a Tiger, and find a Leopard—Makoortie Peak—
Constitution of Councils in India—Remarks on Anglo-Indian
Colonisation   81

CHAPTER XIX.

PAGE

Journey to West Coast—Reception at Beypore—Sedashegur—
Gairsoppah Falls—Bison—Transfer of North Canara to Bombay
—Correspondence on Constitution of Legislative Councils—Gneiss
— Limit of the South-West Monsoon — Mangalore—German
Mission — Smell of the Sea — Its Cause—Steel works—Bessemer
Process—Snake Boats—Wundoor—Inopportune Visit from a
Rajah—Return to the Neilgherry Hills—Proposed Publication
of a Natural History of India—Lady D——'s return to Madras
—Ball at the Banqueting Hall—Prince Azeem Jah—Guindy
Park .   .   . 119

CHAPTER XX.

Treatment of British Officers by the Nizam of Hydrabad—Suggestions on the subject—Cinchona Plantations—New Year's
greetings—Native Aide-de-camp—New Year's Ball—Paper
Chase—Remarks on Proposed Change in System of Land
Tenure in India—Trichinopoly—Tanjore—Visit to the Sixteen Widows and Daughters of the Rajah—Bridge over the
Cauvery—Caste of Thieves—Native Roman Catholic Observance of Good Friday—' Plenty Cry '—Letter to Sir C. Wood
on Registration of Land Titles—Opening of School for Children of Native Servants—College of Civil Engineers—Letter
on Encouragements to Cotton Cultivation—Characteristics of
Mahometan Population — ' King Tom '—Rapacity of Native
Officials—Afternoon Receptions—Jewellery taken at Kirwee—
Journey to the Hills—Holicul Droog—Kotagherry—Rungasawmy's Pillar—Sale of Land—Supply of Horses—Journey
delayed by Bees—Cost of Transport on Railways—Proportion
of Rainfall discharged by Rivers—Chupatties   .   .   . 151

CHAPTER XXI.

Sail round Cape Comorin—Adam's Bridge—Pagoda at Ramiseram
—A Royal Pilgrim—Preparation of Sea Slugs for the Chinese
Market—Landing at Tuticorin—Mangosteens—Mode of Selling
Pearls—Pearl Lime—Tinnevelly—Durbar—The Great Zemin-
dar—Missionary Training School—Night Journey to Nagercoil
—Passage of a Swollen River—Arrival at Trivandrum—State
Visit from the Rajah—Illuminated Road—Dinner with the
Rajah—Metropolitan of the Syrian Church—Visit to the Ra-
nees—Departure from Trivandrum—Night Voyaging on the

PAGE.

Back Water—Fairylike Scenes—Quilon—Illuminated Garden
—Alleppey—Visit from Armenian Merchants — Missionary
work among the Slave Caste—Laterite—Cochin—Visit from the
Rajah—Boating extraordinary—Curious Fishing Nets—' White
Jews of Cochin '—Visit to the Synagogue—Return to Ma-
dras   195

CHAPTER XXII.

Reorganisation of Board of Works—Irrigation—Native Guests at
an English Wedding—Waste of Flood Water—Simple Mode of
Determining the Quality of Soil—Objections to Reorganisation
of Madras Native Army—Characteristics of Hindoo Architecture—Cost of Irrigation works—Journey to Mysore—Birthday
of the Rajah—Dinner at the Palace—Visit to the Zenana—
Seringapatam—Curious Bridges over the Cauvery—Tomb of
Hyder Ali and Tippoo Saib—Tippoo's Summer Palace—Falls
of the Cauvery—Oossoor—Land Assessment—Journey to Bellary and Kurnool—Mowing Match—Tumuli—Return to Madras—' Master looks beautiful '—Burst of the North-East
Monsoon—Wreck of the ' Punjaub '—Effect of Competitive
Examinations   .   .   .   224

CHAPTER XXIII.

Death of Lord Elgin—Assumption of the Office of Governor-
General—War on the North-West Frontier—Arrival at Cal-
cutta, and first days there—Proposition to the Council to Re-
scind their Order for the Withdrawal of Troops from the Frontier
—Protest of Sir Charles Trevelyan—Minute Embodying the
Reasons for the Proposition—Forward movement of Troops—
Successful Result—Political Agents at the Seat of War—Ob-
jections to the Removal of Local Corps from the Control of the
Central Government—Gallant Conduct of Ensign Sanderson—
Etiquette at Calcutta—Appointment of Sir John Lawrence to
the Governor-Generalship—House of a Wealthy Hindoo—Re-
marks on the General Working of the Supreme Government in
India—Ganges Canal—Breeding of Horses for Military Pur-
poses   289

CHAPTER XXIV.

Return to Madras—Opinions as to Origin of so-called Flint Weapons—Water Rate— Finance – Machinery   Want of Survey of

PAGE

Frontier – Irrigation Works - Want of Statistical Information
– Death of Captain Glover—Cinchona Plantations—Action of
Forests on Rainfall - Toilsome Walk after Sambur—Killing a
Tiger—Letter to the Maharajah of Travancore — Irrigation
Company - Visit from Todas and Koters - Wynaad—Native
Archery —Return to Guindy   Cyclone at Masulipatam—Letter
to the Rajah of Travancore   .   .   326

CHAPTER XXV.

Financial Suggestions—Baptism of Native Christians—New Year's
Ceremonies—Visit to 'The City of Bali'—Cattle Show at
Addunky—Vizagapatam—Roman Catholic Female School—
Evening Party at the House of a Native—Ganjam—Chilka
Lake—Aska—Sugar Factory—Wild Boy of the Woods—Ro-
man Catholic Cathedral at S. Thomé—Grave and Relics of St.
Thomas—Threshing-Match, Natives *versus* Threshing Machine
—Madras a Good Winter Residence for Invalids—Prince Frede-
rick of Schleswig-Holstein—Festival of the Mohurrum—Ban-
galore—Lall Bagh—Madras in July and August—Poinciana
Regia—Mysore Carpets—Native mode of Making up Chintz—
Cyclone—Experiment with Mongoose and Snakes—Visit to
Cuddapah—Farewell Fête by the Mahometan Community—
Departure from Madras   370

CHAPTER XXVI.

Concluding Remarks   .   .   .   425

INDEX   .   .   .   441

Directions to Binder.

Map of Tasmania   .   .   **To face** *Title of Vol. I.*
Map of Southern India   .   „   *Title of Vol. II.*

VARIETIES

OF

VICE-REGAL LIFE.

CHAPTER XVI.

NEW ZEALAND—REMARKS ON RESPONSIBLE GOVERNMENT.

So MUCH has been heard of New Zealand of late years, that I feel justified in bestowing a short chapter upon it, for the purpose of elucidating the action of English ideas of ' *responsible government* ' when applied to a mixed community such as that occupying the northern island of New Zealand.

My position in Australia gave me many opportunities of acquiring information as to the state of the islands. I visited Auckland in 1857, when I was called upon to give an opinion as to the mode of dealing with some political movements of the Maories. After the first war broke out, at the end of 1859 or beginning of 1860, I was applied to by the Government of New Zealand to send troops to help them out of a difficulty into which they had plunged themselves, and I was kept constantly well informed as to the state of affairs on the island, both during the first and second wars. I say thus much for the purpose of showing that I do not speak without some knowledge of facts, though I was not in a position to exercise authority, or to do more than give advice when asked.

Before, however, I plunge into the subject of colonial politics, I may as well give a sketch of our relations with the Maories, or natives of New Zealand, which will, in point of fact, amount to a brief abstract of the history of the country for the last thirty or forty years.

The first white settlers, if such they can be called, were traders, who furnished the natives with European articles at exorbitant rates, and who occasionally, with a view, *perhaps*, to a permanent settlement on the island, took, in exchange for their commodities, tracts of land from the chiefs of the different tribes.

These men were followed by the missionaries, who found, at a very early period of their teaching, many, among a notoriously wild and savage population, who rewarded the toil and the risk which their teachers underwent, by a change of life and conduct most marked and complete. It is said that the missionaries took advantage of their position to acquire large tracts of land; this may have been the case in one or two instances, but most certainly the great body of the missionaries were in no way liable to such an imputation; they devoted themselves to their duties as preachers and teachers, and in a very few years produced a very marked change in the habits of the people. The success of the missionaries, as evidenced by this change in the natives, soon attracted a set of land speculators; a species of land shark almost as great a nuisance on shore as his namesake is at sea; and to these succeeded a company, the New Zealand Land Company, which, set on foot by wealthy and well educated people, having, it is believed, a sincere wish to benefit the country, ended by becoming, through the mistakes of their agents, a land shark on a large scale. The evils

arising out of the action of the different classes of settlers,
all talking to the natives of their anxiety to benefit them,
and all, with the exception of the missionaries, doing their
best to defraud them in the purchase of the only article
they had to sell, viz., their land, became so great, that the
Government was obliged to interfere for the purpose of
bringing the country under the dominion of some sort of
law.   Accordingly, the natives were induced to acknowledge the supremacy of Great Britain, and to recognise
Queen Victoria as their Queen.   The New Zealand Company got out of a mass of difficulties by transferring to
the Government, for a consideration, the whole of the
land which they had purchased from the Maories, together
with their obligations; and a stop was put at once to all
purchases of land from the natives by private parties, by
an agreement on the part of the former to sell land to
nobody but the Government.   A Governor was then
appointed, and matters went on as quietly as could be expected, for a time.   Of course there were occasional
movements on the part of the natives of a hostile character,
for it could hardly be expected that each individual chief
would be inclined to defer to the acts or opinions of the
majority; now and then a white man would be cut down,
and perhaps *eaten*; now and then questions would arise
as to the price paid to the Maories for land; but on the
whole, matters began to arrange themselves in a manner
which bade fair to secure peace between the two races,
and increased prosperity to the island.   The Maories
turned their attention to agriculture, and showed themselves sensible of the value of several European inventions
for economising labour; they erected mills, purchased
and navigated small coasting craft, and proved themselves
to possess qualities which admitted of extensive development; while there is every reason to believe, from the
reports of the active and zealous Bishop Selwyn, that
Christianity was exercising its best influence upon them,

and modifying, in a most satisfactory manner, their habits
and principles of action.

Matters were in this hopeful state when some evil
spirit prompted the Government to apply, to a colony so
very peculiarly constituted, the principles of what it chose
to term *Responsible Government*, but which has shown
itself to be a Government composed of persons altogether
irresponsible to either Queen or Parliament.

Under such prompting, it is hardly to be wondered at
that a scheme was devised, which, splitting up a scantily
peopled colony into five or six districts, gave to each of
these an elective Governor or Superintendent, with an
elective Legislative Council and Legislative Assembly;
while an abortive attempt was made to retain a sort of
central authority in the hands of the Governor appointed
by the Queen, who, with another Legislative Council and
Legislative Assembly, and an Executive Council composed
of officers selected from the majority of the so-called
Parliament, was to maintain order among these most incongruous elements of a body politic. The whole scheme
was, in fact, a wretched parody of the constitution of the
United States; and, as our American brethren altogether
ignored the red man, and placed him beyond the pale of
the constitution, so the Government, while professing to
recognise the Maories as subjects of the Queen, gave
them no place in the Government, treated them as aliens
and outcasts,—handing them over *practically* to the
tender mercies of the Legislature, composed of European
settlers; while *theoretically* the Governor was supposed
to have plenary power in matters in which the natives
were concerned.   It is altogether beyond the scope
of my subject to allude to the squalls and tempests
in these petty legislatures, to the efforts of the local
Governments to override the central authority, to those
of the latter to maintain its dominant position; neither
need I allude to the class of persons who have been

placed in authority by the voice of their fellow-citizens; what I wish to show is the effect of this most absurd experiment upon the relations between the Maories and the white settlers.

I must premise that the great mass of the Maori population is settled in the northern island; that it occupied some rich tracts in the centre of the island, and was in possession of by far the largest portion of the soil, though many million acres had been alienated, and were in the possession of white settlers, or of the Government.

The central island contains a large area of land clear of timber and fitted for pasture; while there were not above a couple of hundred natives scattered over the whole island. The settlers have availed themselves of these advantages, have turned their attention to sheep and cattle farming, and have been rapidly increasing in wealth; while those on the northern island, being shut in by land occupied by the Maories, and limited to the amount which they have been able to purchase from the Government, have been compelled to look to agriculture as the only means of employing their labour and capital; and in this pursuit they have found active competitors amongst the natives. The natural effect of this has been to generate a feeling of envy and jealousy among the white settlers towards the Maories, a disposition to look upon these as the main obstacles to the increase of their wealth, and a desire to sweep these obstacles away by fair means or by foul.

This, which, under the former system of government, might have been kept in proper subordination, soon became an active working principle when the election of superintendents and legislative bodies gave to the white population the means of working out their views in what may, by a figure of speech, be called a constitutional way; that is, by the use of tools which the Government had most unwisely placed in the hands of persons not fit to be trusted with them. Of course the gift of these

weapons was accompanied with various sapient expressions of confidence that they would never use them
except as men and Christians; but there is an old Scotch
proverb, 'fules should na hae chapping sticks,' and the
effect of handing over these to such people was very soon
seen.

The different legislative bodies expressed strong
opinions as to their right to legislate for—meaning of
course, against—the natives; and as these, daily improving
as they were in knowledge of their own interests, could not
but be sensible of the spirit which actuated the legislature,
a feeling of jealousy of white interference naturally sprung
up amongst them, and gave rise to a variety of schemes,
which, if met by the Government in a spirit of conciliation,
would have either passed away, or have been so modified
as to produce wholesome results.

It will be remembered that when the Maories agreed
to become British subjects, they engaged to sell their land
to the Government only. Advantage was taken of this
concession by the Government, which, purchasing the land
from the natives at merely nominal prices, such as from a
penny to sixpence per acre, resold it to the white settlers
at ten shillings, and appropriated the proceeds as part of
the revenue of the colony.

Again, all articles imported, whether for Maori use or
for that of the white population, pay duty at the port of
entry, and the proceeds of the customs, as well as of the
land, were appropriated by the white Legislative Assembly,
in which the Maories had no voice, either as electors or
elected. Out of this general revenue a small portion was
appropriated to pay certain officers acting as agents in the
Maori districts, but who, looked upon from a Maori point of
view, might be considered more in the light of authorized
spies than of friends and protectors. Can it be, then, a matter
of astonishment that the Maories, a remarkably acute and
intelligent race, should feel that advantage had been

taken of their position by the Government, that they had been deluded into a bargain in which the whole advantage accrued to the white population, that they were treated, not as fellow-subjects, but as aliens and intruders? They did feel this, and it led to a resolution which was pretty generally adopted by the chiefs, their natural leaders, that they would not sell any more land to the Government. They did not propose to break the agreement which they had made, or to sell land to others, but they determined to retain that which still remained to them, as the sole guarantee for their existence as a people. Seeing, too, how little the Government cared or did for them, and sensible of the benefits which would accrue to them from unity of action among themselves, they took the very natural step of electing a single chief as their representative, and the very foolish step of calling him King.

This was the state of things when I landed at Auckland in September 1857. I found the Government in a state of alarm at the movement on the part of the Maories; it had evidently formed a wrong estimate of their powers of endurance, and had never contemplated the possibility of united action among them. The stoppage of the sale of land to the Government was the measure which excited the greatest alarm, for it threatened to dry up a profitable source of revenue. It was true that the Government had still on hand some millions of acres, but the movement on the part of the Maories seemed to indicate that they had gradually become aware of the value of the commodity of which they had the monopoly, and that they were by no means unlikely to raise the price upon the Government, and thus diminish its profits. The question of the election of a King did not seem to affect the Government so much. The newspapers, of course, denounced it as equivalent to rebellion, and commented upon the ingratitude of the Maories in flying in the face of a Government which had been so tenderly attentive to their welfare; but, as the evil was remote, the king not having been elected, and as the effect of the change from several chiefs to one was not fully appreciated, this question shrunk into insignificance in comparison with that relating to the land, which addressed itself directly to their pockets.

These two questions were discussed by the Governor, Colonel Gore Browne, and myself, very seriously. It happened that I landed at the period of an election of the representatives and superintendent of the district of Auckland, and I had an opportunity of seeing the state of political feeling, as indicated by the character of the representatives and the social position of the superintendent : I had also an opportunity of instituting a comparison between the general demeanour of the Maories and that of the white settlers, having had interviews with several of the former, who addressed me through an interpreter, and spoke very reasonably on the subjects of interest under discussion. Under such circumstances, with the experience of several years of the state of feeling in the colonies, I had no hesitation in proposing to Colonel Gore Browne to meet the difficulties of his position by recognising the right of the Maories to be treated as British subjects, and to be placed in a position similar to that of the white settlers ; that is, to have the power of electing their own superintendents, their own councils of advice, and of legislating for themselves in all local matters. In carrying out this scheme, I proposed that the Maori territory should be divided into three districts, over each of which a chief or superintendent should be placed. The Maories might wish to call such person ' king,'—to this no objection need be made ; the whole sting of their proposal to have *one king* would be removed by *giving* them three kings. A small sum, say 300*l.* per annum to each king for his privy purse, and some 20*l.* or 30*l.* to each of the chiefs in his council, would make it their interest to keep on good terms with the Government ; and should any differences arise, it would be much easier to deal with three separate and distinct interests than with one united body. The question of the purchase of land might, I thought, be left, when these steps had been taken, to find its own solution. The Maories would, in process of time, find it advantageous to sell off outlying portions of their districts, and, if a fair price were offered, would, I had no doubt, be quite willing to dispose of these to the Government, and the latter might be content to derive a profit of cent. per cent. upon the money expended on the purchase, instead of attempting to grasp, as had been the case hitherto, at 1000 per cent.

This advice, which circumstances have shown to be good, had, as is generally the case with that which runs counter to the prejudices or supposed interest of those to whom it was given, no beneficial effect. I believe the Governor would willingly have adopted it; but his advisers set themselves to work to devise a scheme by which, without sacrificing any of the profit which they were making by what I can only term, in plain English, defrauding the Maories, they might render nugatory the resolution of the chiefs on the subject of the sale of land.

In New Zealand, as in other countries occupied by separate tribes, the whole territory is divided among these. Individual members, or families, are allowed to occupy specific portions, but the estate belongs to the collective tribe, and cannot be alienated by any individual without permission first obtained from the chief, or the governing body. This rule had remained unquestioned up to the time when the chiefs adopted their resolution to sell no more land; but it suited the purpose of the Government to assume that they could purchase land from individual members of a tribe, without reference to the chief. After a good deal of enquiry, a native was found, a member of a broken clan, who, residing on the west coast, some twelve miles from New Plymouth, had eight hundred acres of land in his possession, to which, irrespective of the tribal right, he could establish a good title. This man, Te Weira, was induced to sell his land to the Government by the promise of a much higher price than had ever been paid for ordinary land ; he was, in point of fact, bribed to transfer his claims to the Government, which wished to try conclusions with the Maori chiefs, not in the courts of law, or with reference to any civil mode of ascertaining the nature of the title to land, but by the sword. This was, in fact, broadly stated by one of the members of the Government, who, in a carefully prepared minute, said, ' An occasion has now arisen in which it has been necessary to support the Government authority by a military force. The issue has been carefully chosen, the particular question being as favourable a one of its class as could have been selected.' The issue had indeed been *carefully selected.* Te Weira, as before stated, was a member of a broken clan, and the Government might perhaps have imagined that it would have to deal with the individual and not with the tribe. This, however, it soon found was not the case. The chief, on hearing of the proposed purchase, gave an express warning to the Government that the alienation of the property could not take place without his consent, which he was not prepared to give. In the face of this, however, the Government hastened on all its preparations for the purchase of the eight hundred acres, and gave directions to their officer in the district to proclaim martial law, in case any resistance was made by the chief to the persons sent to survey and take possession of the land. When the surveyors came on the ground, they were met by a few men and several women ; the latter occupied the attention of the survey party, while the men quietly walked off with the chains and instruments, without committing any assault, or even threatening the white men. The officer in command of the district, however, acting upon the order he had received, proclaimed martial law, and thus plunged the country into a war which cost upwards of half a million, the property at stake being eight hundred acres, worth, at the utmost, 400*l.* Many valuable lives were lost in skirmishes with the natives, who gained in these, and in the defence of their pahs, or intrenched camps, a conviction that their mode of warfare was well suited to the country which they occupied, and would enable them, with much smaller numbers, to prolong a sort of war of skirmishes indefinitely.

The officer who proclaimed martial law so hastily, under the idea, I suppose, that the Maories would be easily frightened into submission, soon found that he had, in his zeal to work out the purposes of the Government, committed a most grievous mistake. He had but a small body of troops at his disposal, and the Maories, being well acquainted with the country, and thoroughly conversant with their own system of warfare, very soon had possession of the whole district, except a small portion close around New Plymouth. He accordingly wrote to the Government requesting reinforcements, and stating that he should not be able to act efficiently without the command of a body of some four or five thousand men. The Government had but two regiments at their disposal, and these were dotted about all over the country. Application was therefore made to me to forward all the troops I could spare from Australia. These I accordingly despatched, after consulting the General in command; and I at the same time wrote to the Governor of New Zealand, reiterating, in a form modified to suit the changed circumstances of the case, the advice I had given to him in 1857. A copy of my letter I sent, with the following despatch, to His Grace the Duke of Newcastle, the then Secretary of State for the Colonies.

Government House, Sydney, June 8, 1860.

My Lord Duke,—When the Governor of New Zealand applied to me for assistance in the difficulty which had arisen between his Government and the Maories, he sent, for my information, a sort of manifesto drawn up by Mr. Richmond, one of the members of his Executive Council, a copy of which I transmitted to your Grace with my despatch dated April 12 last.

In my correspondence with Col. Gore Browne, I alluded to the exposition of the policy of the Government contained in this document, and I received from him a more formal document, a copy of which I herewith enclose, drawn up by Mr. Richmond, as the mouthpiece of the ministry at Auckland, explanatory of the opinions entertained by the advisers of the Governor of the state of the relations between the Maories and the white population.

In a private letter to Col. Gore Browne, a copy of which I take the liberty of forwarding herewith, I have commented upon the document put forth by his advisers, and have, at the same time, sketched out a course of policy which would, as it appears to me, remedy many of the evils which have arisen out of the anomalous system hitherto pursued toward the Maories.

If the present state of relations between the two races is allowed to continue, outbreaks like the present will recur periodically; demands will be made for military assistance, with which it will be difficult to comply; and claims will be made upon the Imperial Treasury which will not be willingly responded to, and which, if entertained, will only serve as precedents for similar demands from other colonies.

A change, therefore, in the mode of dealing with the native race in New Zealand is urgently required, and I

trust that, in bringing, as I have, my views of the character of this change before the Governor of New Zealand,
and in submitting them to your Grace, I shall not be
deemed to have meddled presumptuously in a matter
with which I have no concern.

I have, &c.

W. D.

Letter enclosed in the foregoing :—

To his Excellency Colonel Gore Browne.

Government House, Sydney, May 16, 1860.

My dear Gore Browne,—The mail having closed, I am
now at leisure to look into and discuss the contents of the
printed document which you sent me, containing the
expression of the views and opinions of your responsible
advisers on the present state of Maori affairs.

I do not think that you can have derived much information from this document. The views and opinions of
your responsible advisers are, to all appearance, confined
to these : first, that they ought to have something to say in
the discussion of questions having reference to the natives
(of whom, I may observe by the way, they are in no way the
representatives); and secondly, that, as they are unable to
defend themselves, England should step in to help them.

With reference to the first of these opinions, I may
observe that the collision between the races would have
been precipitated, had the settlement of questions affecting
the Maories been left to the white men, who have a
direct interest in obtaining the principal article which
the native has to dispose of, namely, his land. With
reference to the second opinion, every one will, of course,
admit that the mother country is bound to defend the
colonies, and to help them out of difficulties ; but there
yet remain these questions : against whom are they to be
defended ? and what is the nature and extent of the
assistance to be afforded？ Mr. Richmond's paper, how-

ever, opens up a much wider question than was, I think,
contemplated by him and his colleagues; nothing less,
in fact, than that of the whole policy of the Government as regards the Maories; and to this I will now
address myself, taking as correct the statements made of
the facts relative to the establishment of the Presidency
of Potatau, but exercising my own discretion as to the
admission or rejection of the inferences, whether as to
the motives which have influenced the natives in their
movement, or as to the results which are likely to flow
from it.

The fact, then, which appears to be established, is the
willing assent of a large proportion of the Maori race to
the establishment of some system of government among
themselves.

Mr. Richmond passes over very lightly the causes which
have induced a people consisting of clans or septs, analogous to those which used to occupy the Highlands of
Scotland, to forget their old feuds, and to unite together
for a common object.   He says little or nothing as to the
origin of the wish on the part of the Maories to subvert
the Queen's authority over the northern island, and but
little more as to the foundation of their wish to prohibit
all further alienation of land to the Crown.   Might not,
however, the movement have its origin in the conviction
of the natives that their position as nominal subjects of the
Queen, while it brought them under a variety of limita-
tions, preventing them from selling their land to private
individuals, and subjecting them to taxation at the hands
of the white population occupying the seaports, did
absolutely nothing for their benefit, and was the means of
preventing the introduction of more wholesome social
arrangements, having a tendency, as administered, to
retain them in the position of isolated savage tribes,
instead of assisting to raise them to the rank of a people?
With regard to the alienation of land, might there not

exist a well-founded distrust of a Government which, while it will not permit the sale of land to individuals, does, by holding out inducements which few savages are able to resist, acquire the article which the Maori has to sell at a very low rate—say from sixpence to a shilling per acre— which article is instantly retailed to the white man at ten shillings per acre? The fact is that Mr. Richmond's letter is based on the assumption that New Zealand is a colony of white people, with whom, unluckily, there happens to be mixed up a portion of the native race, strong enough to make itself respected. His policy, and that of his colleagues, would lead to steps which, if they were backed up by England, would in a short time annihilate the Maori race, and permit the occupation by the white man of the rich land yet in native hands, upon which, for years past, greedy and longing eyes have been cast. My view, however, of the Maori is very different. He is a subject of the Queen, and, as such, is entitled to have his rights respected, his feelings considered; he has shown an aptitude for civilisation which ought to be encouraged; his efforts to raise himself in the social scale should be assisted. If this policy were carried out steadily and consistently, all causes of disaffection would soon be done away; there would be an end to all this petty warfare, which, while it causes a large expenditure of money, results in nothing but an aggravation of the feeling of hostility between the races. The Government, it is true, would be abused by certain classes of the white population; the land speculators might grumble; but I feel convinced that the prosperity of the colony, and the happiness of the people, would be promoted by such a change of system. You may say that all this is utopian, that it supposes a state of things which cannot exist; but this would be to beg the question. You may, however, very fairly ask, by what means is it proposed to work out such a reorganization of society? You may recollect that,

when I was with you in 1857, we were talking of the
policy to be adopted towards the Maories, and I then
suggested that your legislation should be based upon the
positive fact that the inhabitants of the colony consisted
of two distinct races, whose amalgamation, however
desirable it might be, could not be expected to take
place for very many years. My opinion now is much the
same as it was then, and the late occurrences have only
served to give greater precision and distinctness to that
which was, in 1857, more an instinctive feeling than a
carefully formed opinion.

You have now, as a fact, the establishment of something
analogous to a general Government among the Maories,
a recognition on their part of the necessity of some para-
mount authority. This is a step in the right direction ; do
not ignore it ; do not, on the ground that some evil may
possibly arise out of it, make the natives suspicious of
your motives by opposing it, but avail yourself of the
opportunity to introduce some more of the elements of
good government among them ; suggest to them the
necessity of defining and limiting the power of the person
who has been selected as chief or king (I should not
quarrel with the name), of establishing some system of
legislation, simple, of course, at first, but capable of being
modified and improved ; but do not attempt to introduce
the complicated arrangements suited to a civilised and
educated people; recognise publicly and openly the
Maories, not merely as individual subjects of the Queen,
but as a race—a body whose interests you are bound
to respect and promote, and then give to that body
the means of deciding what those interests are, and of
submitting them, in a proper form, for your consideration.

This, you may say, will be very well for the future, but
how will it affect the issue of the present quarrel between
the Government and the Maories? It appears to me that

it will have a most material operation upon the combinations of the Maories. If Potatau and his abettors are made aware that there is a prospect of obtaining by legitimate means a recognition of their position, and an acknowledgment of their rights, they will hardly be induced to plunge into a contest in which they must inevitably be worsted; they will withdraw from the present struggle and leave you to deal with Kingi and his immediate adherents, while these, when they find themselves unsupported by the other tribes, will speedily be brought to submission. The first effect, of course, of the new system of policy will be the cessation of purchases of land from the Maories; they will decline to sell; and, were I in your place, I should be in no hurry to buy.

In proportion, however, as the Maori gets more civilised, will his appetite for gain overpower his nationality, and he will be found, in a short time, quite willing to part with his land to purchasers who will give him a better price for it than his native friends. I do not, therefore, believe that the prohibition of sales to the Government would prevail for any length of time, in case the latter can be persuaded to give the full value for the land; but you will have to give up your present practice of purchasing land at a cheap rate from some of your subjects, and of retailing it at high rates to others: in fact, you must show yourself impartial, and if circumstances compel you to limit the power of the Maori to sell to any but the Government, the latter must give him the full market value of his land, less, of course, the cost of survey, &c.

I do not think that you would have much difficulty, under such circumstances, in arranging for the cession or the purchase of a certain amount of land round New Plymouth, in order to get rid of the anomalous state of things produced by the mode in which the Government has purchased land in isolated patches, to which there is no access except through land belonging to the Maories. I ought to apologise for giving you my 'views and opinions' as to a matter of which I have but a partial knowledge; but thinking that these views and opinions are more clear, and based upon sounder principles, than those of your responsible advisers. I give them to you for what they are worth.

There is no question but that the common and ordinary way of dealing with the differences between the white man and the Maori would be to treat the latter as a rebel; to pour in troops, regardless of expense; and eventually to sweep away a race occupying land of which the white man professes to be in want, though he has millions of acres of which he can, or does, make no use. This, however, is a very costly mode of dealing with such a matter, to say nothing of its immorality and injustice. The Imperial Government will have to pay a high price for the land, which, after having purchased it with its blood and treasure, it hands over to the colonists to sell for their benefit. While, then, the ordinary course of proceeding will be found both immoral and impolitic, that which I have sketched out will be conducive to the best interests of the Government and the people, and, as such, I commend it to your consideration.

Believe me, &c.

W. DENISON.

The first war terminated, after a large outlay in money, by the restoration of the land purchased from Te Weira to the tribe. I do not suppose that Te Weira restored the bribe given to him, so that he, the traitor, was the only person benefited; but as no steps were taken to establish the relations between Her Majesty's Maori subjects and the white settlers upon a footing which should give to each equal rights, and secure the weak from the oppression of the strong, another *casus belli* was soon trumped up, and a war of races commenced, which, after costing several millions, terminated, of course, in the defeat of the weaker party, and in the passing of an Act, by the white legislature of New Zealand, confiscating a large amount of Maori property, which Act has, I believe, been accepted by the Government in England as the sole solution of the question at issue. It would seem, however, that the Maories are not inclined to accept this solution; they are carrying on a desultory war in various parts of the country, setting at defiance the ill-constituted colonial force opposed to them; and the result of ten years' strife, which a little judgment and a small sprinkling of honesty might have prevented, has been the outlay of a large amount of money, the loss of many valuable lives, both English and native, the loss of character on our part, the destruction of a fine race of people whom we were bound to protect, and the return of those that remain to the heathen practices from which the efforts of the missionaries had converted them.

I confess that my sympathy has been all along with the Maories. I have looked upon them as free men struggling bravely against fraud and oppression, and I cannot but think that we have lost more in character than we have gained in power or security, by the course we adopted.

A few words illustrative of the action of the system of government which, by a figure of speech, has been termed 'responsible,' will be an appropriate winding up of the account of the fourteen years of my life as Governor over and among bodies of people differing in origin, but, with trifling exceptions, European in type: thenceforth I had to deal with people born, bred, and nurtured as Asiatics, carrying with them unmistakeable evidences of their origin, and of the permanency of the habits and modes of thought transmitted from father to son for two thousand years and upwards.   Let us first deal with the appellation ' responsible.'   The legitimate inference to be deduced from the peculiar epithet applied to a form of government which has, of late years, been introduced pretty generally throughout our colonial empire, would seem to be that, under all former systems of government, Governors and their subordinates were altogether *irresponsible*, or, at all events, if responsible at all, to an authority at such a distance, and so little likely to be influenced by any representations from the people of the colony, as to render the Governor pretty well master of the situation, and able to do very much as he chose.   Was this, however, the case ? I do not deny that, in the early times of the colonies, power was placed in the hands of the Governor without much security against the abuse of it ; but, most certainly for the last thirty years and upwards, both Governors and their subordinate officials have been held much more closely responsible for their actions in all those colonies where not nominally responsible, than in those where the government has been constituted upon a very indifferent imitation of the form existing in England.

There are many precedents of the recall of Governors in former times ; and in the earlier portions of this narrative will be found several instances in which I held the officers of the Government, *from the highest to the lowest*, responsible for the non-performance of their duties ; and by stern reprimands, and even by dismissal from office, made them understand that they had duties to do, and that there was a superior authority over them whose business it was to see that these duties were performed, and who had not only the power, but the will, to inflict such punishment as the nature of the offence might seem to deserve.

It is clear, then, that neither the Governor nor his sub-

ordinates were, at that time, '*irresponsible.*' ، The change,
therefore, which has been made, *if it be not merely a name*,
should have been towards a system, in which a stricter
responsibility than heretofore would be enforced. Let us
see what it has been in Australia. Parliament, instead of
passing an Act, as had usually been the case, defining the
system of government to be henceforward adopted in the
Australian colonies, gave to the legislatures then existing
the power of manufacturing constitutions for themselves.
It seemed to think that these small communities, differing
very much from each other in their origin and antecedents,
would have such an accurate conception of their present,
and such a correct anticipation of their future wants, as
would guide them towards the formation of that most
difficult piece of mechanism ' a constitution,' adapted to
meet their wants, and to lay the foundation of a prosperous future.

It is hardly necessary to say that these anticipations
have not been realised. The colonists, naturally enough,
wished for a government analogous to that of the country
which they had quitted, but they forgot, as we ourselves
are too apt to do, that a government adapted to the habits
and feelings of a people cannot be manufactured in the
closet of a politician, like a coat in the shop of a tailor,
and fitted at once on the body politic. In adopting the
ultra-democratical costume in which our cousins in
America have clothed their government, they overlooked
the very many circumstances of their position and habits
to which this costume was unsuited. They did not fore-
see the difficulties which would necessarily arise out of the
undefined relations between the two houses of the legislature. Neither, would it seem, did the Government at home
trouble itself to consider the probability or possibility of
such difficulties, or reserve to itself the power of stepping
in to remedy or remove them. It adopted at once the
various patterns of governments submitted, differing, as

they did, from each other in the most remarkable way. It accepted the very peculiar federal scheme sent home from New Zealand, also the constitution of New South Wales, where the Upper House was composed of nominees of the Crown, as well as those of other colonies where the Upper House was elective; there being in some cases a qualification for members, in other cases none; and the result, to say the least, has not been satisfactory.

In New Zealand there have been for the last ten years wars between the Maori subjects of the Queen and the white colonists, which have cost England many millions, have established a contest between the races, and, as far as can be seen at present, have aggravated the evils out of which the war originated. In Victoria there have been differences between the Legislative Council and the Assembly which bade fair, at one time, to put a stop to all legislative, as well as executive, action. In Tasmania, the Government, being the representative of the House of Assembly, proposed to relinquish all indirect taxation, to allow tea, sugar, tobacco, to enter duty free, on the plea that these were necessaries of life to the poor, and to provide for the expenses of the Government by the levy of an income tax of 1s. 9d. in the pound; that is, to compel the rich to pay all the expenses of government, the distribution of these payments to be determined by the representatives of the poor. In New South Wales attempts have been made more than once to swamp the Upper House, in order to secure a majority therein for the then existing ministry, while the police has been reduced to such a state of inefficiency as to be unable to compete with the lawless border population of cattle-stealers and bush-rangers.

In point of fact, instead of being a form of government the members of which are held strictly responsible for what they do, or what they leave undone, I can only describe it as one in which nobody is practically responsible for anything; and the use of the term 'responsible' is but one of the hundred instances in which, of late years, a phrase has been made to do duty for a purpose utterly at variance with its real meaning, the practical effect, whatever may have been the intention of the sponsors, being to deceive. I say 'deceive,' because the name does in no way represent the character, or the action, of the Government. The theory, of course, is, that ministers are responsible to Parliament, and Parliament to the electoral body; but as ministers are but a fractional part of the majority of Parliament, the chance of their being held individually responsible for anything they may do is very remote. We will suppose, however, that the electoral body is dissatisfied with its representatives, and elects others holding different opinions; the result is that A, B, and C make way for X, Y, and Z. These latter, then, enter upon office, knowing little or nothing of the details of the business which they have to superintend, and for which they are, theoretically, responsible. To whom are they to look for information and advice but to the under-secretaries, the permanent holders of office? and to whom are these to look for information as to the thousand details which must constantly come under consideration, but to the chief clerks through whose hands all the papers pass, to whom they are referred, who have at their command the whole of the information which is necessary to enable secretary or under-secretary to form any satisfactory judgment as to the subjects upon which they are called upon to advise or act? The practice is unobjectionable; it is better by far that the business of government should be carried out by its own officers, who can be punished if they act amiss, than by speculative theorists, who cannot be punished for the errors they preach, or made subject to the faintest shadow of responsibility; but the appellation is most objectionable. In no sense of the word is the Government, or an individual member, responsible for anything which it, or he, may do ; and the men who in reality conduct the business of the Government are exonerated from even the faint shadow of responsibility which is supposed to operate upon the members of that Government.

CHAPTER XVII.

ARRIVAL AT MADRAS — LANDING THROUGH THE SURF — BODY GUARD — THE
TWO GOVERNMENT HOUSES — NATIVE HOUSEHOLD — PUBLIC BREAKFASTS —
DURBAR — FIRST EVENING RECEPTION — OPENING OF THE N. W. RAILWAY TO
NAGGERY — MEETING WITH THE RAJAH — A MUTE DIGNITARY — INCAUTIOUS
QUESTION — NATURE OF WORK AT MADRAS — STATE OF GOVERNMENT AND
ARMY — LETTER TO LORD CANNING ON ARMY REDUCTION — LETTER ON
PROPOSED LEGISLATIVE COUNCIL — CHARACTER OF HINDOOS — IMPOSSI-
BILITY OF APPLYING TO THEM ENGLISH PRINCIPLES OF GOVERNMENT —
RAILWAYS — REORGANIZATION OF NATIVE ARMY — SUGGESTIONS FOR
GENERAL GOVERNMENT OF INDIA — VISIT TO CALCUTTA — GOVERNMENT
HOUSE — LARGE BANYAN TREE — BARRACKPOOR — CONVERSATION WITH THE
PRINCIPAL OF THE SANSCRIT COLLEGE — RETURN TO MADRAS.

Extract from Journal.

Guindy Park, Madras, February 10, 1861.

DEAREST ——,—I am afraid, with all the other matters I
have now on my hands and thoughts, I shall not be able
to give you a very connected history of our doings since
I last wrote; but I should like to try, for I feel I have
much to tell. I closed my last letter at Galle, but, as the
ship was all in a mess and bustle, coaling, and our own
servant very busy packing up our things, ready to go on
board the other steamer,* W—— and I determined, when
evening came on, to go on shore, and take a little walk;
and it proved a very interesting one. The place is not
particularly pretty, but it was the first *really eastern* town
we had ever seen; so every object was a picture in itself.
It was like coming into a new world; everything was so
like what we had seen before in pictures, and so unlike
to what we had ever seen in real life. The next morning

---

* The 'Arracan,' Indian Government steamer, which had been sent down
to Galle to meet us, and bring us on to Madras.

(Friday) we went on board the 'Arracan,' government steamer, which was clean and comfortable, but slow, and we arrived here just before daylight on Monday morning. The time of arrival had been pre-arranged and calculated upon, as far as might be; because all the authorities, troops, &c. were to be out to receive W——, and they could not well turn out, nor could we land, during the heat of the day. Almost as soon as it was light, therefore, our landing had to be effected, and it was in itself a novel and curious sight. Some of the members of W——'s new staff came on board, and carried him off in a large boat, manned by native rowers, whose dress was a sort of white *shift*, bordered with blue, and slightly fastened in at the waist, leaving the arms and legs bare. This big boat was attended by four catamarans, each propelled by two nearly naked natives; these are supposed to be in attendance in case the big boat should upset in the surf, for there is no pier or landing-place,* and one has to come on shore on the beach, where the surf is sometimes very high. As soon as W—— landed, he was received in form, and drove off, surrounded by his body guard (a body of native troops, in a rich uniform of dark blue and silver, with a curious red shako, surmounted by a silver knob) to the Fort, to be sworn in, a salute being fired from the Fort as he landed, and another as soon as he had taken the oaths. Then the big boat came back for us, one or two of the staff having waited to escort us. The rowers sang a sort of monotonous song as they pulled, and as soon as we got into the surf, down rushed a crowd of swarthy, almost naked figures, some to seize on the boat and drag it through the surf; some carrying chairs supported on poles, into which we mounted, one in each, and were carried through surf and sand to where carriages were waiting for us, umbrellas being held over our heads the while, for the sun was up by that time, and it

* A pier has since been constructed.

was already getting very hot. Then we drove away to
the Government House in Madras, our town house, where
we breakfasted, and remained during the day; and, in
the cool of the evening, drove out to this place—our
country house—about five miles from Madras, where, for
the present, we remain. Oh! I wish I could describe to
you the curious new world we seem to be living in; the
change of hours and habits; the look of Oriental luxury and
magnificence about everything, and the strange appearance
of our household. Both the houses, here and in Madras,
are charming; so large, so cool and airy, that we have
none of us felt the heat at all since we have been
here: indeed, we sometimes feel almost inclined to be
cold, and occasionally shut a door, or stop a punkah,
rather to the surprise of C——, who, notwithstanding his
longer experience, feels the heat much more than we do.
But then we must remember that this is still winter, and
perhaps you will not wonder at our *cool* feelings when
I tell you that my bedroom has twelve windows and doors
in it, besides a punkah, and the other rooms in proportion. As to the household, I can hardly attempt to
describe it; no pen and ink description could really do
justice to the native servants, with their very picturesque
appearance, and very strange ways and habits: the swarm
of butlers and footmen formed quite a spectacle on our
arrival here, as they stood in two rows on the door-steps,
in their white dresses and turbans, and scarlet and gold
scarfs, to welcome us. The scarlet and gold scarf, as far
as I can make out, appears to be the livery, marking the
peon, or footman; for there are one or two others,
elderly men, and evidently dignitaries, who wear the same
white dress and turban (or rather cap, for it is not quite
of the usual turban shape) but no scarf, and whom I take
to be servants out of livery. All the male servants belonging both to house and garden, consisting of these aforesaid butlers and footmen, cooks, dubashes, bearers,

'mateys,' and I do not know what besides, are paid by
Government, and so are also one or two dreadful looking
harridans, who make the beds, and do that portion of
housemaid's work which is not done by the men. Altogether there are two hundred and five servants kept for us
by Government; in fact, each man does so little in
India, that it is necessary to have a great many to get
through the work. I suppose thirty Englishmen, or less,
would do the work of the whole two hundred and five;
but then their wages would be larger; and, moreover, the native servants find their own board and
lodging. This latter is simple enough to a good many of
them, who sleep about on mats, in the passages and
verandahs; so that as you go to your room at night, you
pass along a sort of avenue of sleeping figures, with their
turbans off, and lying beside them, but otherwise apparently dressed much the same as by day. The stable
servants we pay ourselves, and so we do two ' ayahs,' who
have been hired to assist in the nursery, ' Sarah ' and
' *Minette*,' as I at first understood the name, and as we,
somehow, continue to call her, though I find her real
name is Menachee. These two women are profuse in
ornaments; wear large earrings, bracelets, things like
bracelets on their ankles, and rings on nearly every
toe! in addition to which ' Minette,' who is evidently the
most given to dress of the two, wears a sort of gold patch
on the side of her nose! How she keeps it on is a mystery
that we have not yet fathomed.

To F. G. Denison, Esq.

Guindy, February 26, 1861.

My dear Frank,—I must write a few lines by this mail,
if it be only to give you an idea of the sort of place we
are living in, and to enable you to contrast it with the
Government Houses at Hobart Town and Sydney. We
landed here on Monday; and, after being sworn in at the

Frt I proceeded to Government House. I was very much struck with the dimensions of the building, the luxurious mode in which all the arrangements were made, and the way in which the sun was kept from the walls of the building, while provision was made for the circulation of air in every direction. In order to keep off the sun, there is a verandah fifteen feet in width round every story; or, rather, the external wall of the house is composed of three ranges of columns, while the interior wall, being fifteen feet within this external inclosure, has windows, corresponding with the space between the pillars, looking into this verandah, and also as many openings in the back and side wall as possible. Each bed-room has a dressing-room and bath-room attached to it. Then as to servants, the house is full of them. There are no bells, but you have nothing to do but to call 'Peon,' and a man is at your elbow at once. There are men, too, always at hand, night and day, to work the punkahs—a broad sort of fan, hung from the ceiling, which moves backwards and forwards, creating a pleasant current of air. The wages of all servants are ludicrously small, varying from three rupees and a half, or seven shillings, to ten rupees or twenty shillings, per month, for which sum they find their own food. They have 'godowns' or huts outside, where they wash, eat, and have their food cooked; indeed, as we afterwards found, many of them sleep at their own houses, or in these godowns; and those lying about in the passages are chiefly those who are to relieve each other at the punkahs, or be in readiness for any other duty during the night. When we drive, two horsekeepers run one on each side of the carriage; when I ride, the horse's servant (or rather one of them, for each horse has a man and a maid to attend upon him) runs after me: I cannot venture out into the garden or park but a man is sure to see me and rush after me with an umbrella. All this is to me rather a bore; but I suppose I shall get used to it; there

are advantages as well as disadvantages attendant on it.
Our life is rather peculiar: we get up in the dark, about
five; throw on some clothes, and sally out for a walk or a
ride, as the case may be; come in, not later than half-past
seven, have a bath, wash and dress; read or write till
half-past nine, when we have prayers, and breakfast; sit at
home, working under a punkah, till half-past four, when
the sun is low enough to allow us to go out without risk;
ride or drive till seven; dine at eight; leave the drawing room about ten or half-past. A curious life, is it not?
It seems, however, to agree with us. You will see your
mother, I hope, on her way home; she leaves this on
March 20. God bless you, my dear boy.

Your affectionate Father,
W. D.

Extract from Journal.

Guindy, March 4, 1861.

Dearest ——, I hope this letter may only precede me by
a few days, as I ought, if all goes prosperously, to be in
England almost any day after April 21. We have
remained quite quietly since I wrote last, William going
into Madras on Friday, for the Council, and to have a
public breakfast. This, it seems, is a weekly affair; but
it is an exclusively masculine meal, so that I shall never
have anything to do with it. The object is to enable the
Governor to see and talk to officers and others in a
familiar manner, without the trouble of sending a formal
invitation; anybody who chooses to put his name down
in the aide-de-camp's book comes to breakfast as a
matter of course; and any one who wants to see W——
on any matter of business peculiar to himself, has only,
at the time that he puts his name down, to say that he
wishes to do so, and he has his interview after breakfast.
Last week there were, I believe, ninety people at breakfast; but, fortunately, all the ninety did not want to
speak with him afterwards. This week he is, if all be

well, to hold a durbar, or a sort of levée, at which the natives are presented.

March 11.—The durbar went off very well. The boys were allowed to stand behind William to see what was going on ; and one of the native dignitaries, on being told that they were W——'s sons, came up and kissed both their hands, to their great astonishment, and gave them a couple of limes. I should mention that, as nobody ever addresses a superior without the form of making a present, this fruit is the established representation of a gift. Last Friday I went in to Madras for my first reception : this was a much more formal affair here than it was in Sydney or Hobart Town. There, on my arrival, I merely announced in the papers what days I would receive visitors, and at what hours, and they came in just like ordinary morning visitors. Here, however, it was to be in the evening ; so everybody was in full evening dress, and each person was formally marched up the room by an aide-de-camp, and introduced to me as I stood at the upper end of it. In short, it would almost have amounted to a Drawing-room, but that, when once the introductions were over, the formality ceased ; people then sat down, or walked about the rooms as they liked, or went away ; but the majority stayed, and very amusing it was, I dare say, to them, watching the other arrivals ; but it was terribly stiff formal work for us ; and poor W—— groaned over it, *sotto voce*, whenever he could : but even he was better off than I was, as he had met a great many of the gentlemen before at his breakfasts, &c., whereas I knew nobody. It is said to have been one of the fullest receptions that has ever been seen here, and I did not feel much the wiser at the end of it, though I had been doing my best to remember names and faces. And now good-bye, dearest ; in the midst of heaviness of heart at leaving W——, it is a bright gleam to think that this is my last letter to you.

To W. E. Denison, Esq.

Madras, March 13, 1861.

My dear Willy,—Your mother leaves this next week
with the children. It will be a sad breaking up of the
family; I shall feel the absence of all most bitterly. Your
mother and baby, I may hope to see again in the
autumn, but from your other brothers and sisters, as from
you, my dear boy, it is a long parting. I can only re-
concile myself to it by repeating that it is for the good of
you all. Happy will be the day when I shall again have
you all round me, should God permit me this pleasure on
earth. I am picking up small bits of information from
day to day, which will enable me to apply an Asiatic coefficient to European formulæ as to labour, materials, &c.
I got a wrinkle this morning about brick-making. Here
the expensive article is fuel, in England it is labour; here
labour is as nothing, the price being but one shilling per
thousand for preparing bricks for the kiln. By the way,
you may as well take a hint from me, and note down from
day to day anything in the shape of a ' fact' which comes
across you; stow these away, and they will turn out
to be useful some time or other. I have put a strong
mark against the word ' fact:' you will have hundreds of
statements made and opinions broached; but before you
record anything as a fact, and put it away in your treasury,
make certain that it is worth recording—that it is *true*.
I feel certain that, in discussing Indian railway projects,
the difference between the Englishman and the Hindoo
has been overlooked, or at all events under-estimated.
Here the people cannot comprehend a change—they dislike it; in England, on the contrary, it is one of the peculiarities of our character that we are always changing:
here everything goes on as it did in the time of Abraham;
with us there are few of our habits which will admit of
being traced very far back. Then again, we, having

convinced ourselves that the change we have made is an improvement, are most anxious to force a similar change upon others ; we overlook the difference of circumstances, climate, wages, power employed, &c., and we must needs force upon others contrivances or adaptations suited to us and our mode of working, but not to the people whom I have here.

I went the other day to open the North-West Railway, or rather the first section of it, and took a large party with me.   We started at seven o'clock, and proceeded for thirty-six miles over a country apparently as flat as a pancake, but in reality rising about four feet per mile.   The horizon ran into the sky, as it does at sea, and there was hardly a tree or a house to break the uniformity of the scene, or to indicate the presence of man ; yet the whole of this great plain showed evidence of the expenditure of a great amount of labour upon it.   Wherever water could be got to it, there it was levelled, water-channels made, the fields terraced ; but there was nothing living visible : it gave me quite a melancholy feeling to look over this great expanse of waste.   After thirty-six miles, however, we began to get a glimpse of a range of hills : these gradually assumed visible shapes, and of a very marked and peculiar character.   They were composed of gneiss ; as indeed, I believe the larger part of the Peninsula of India to be ; and when we came near them, they seemed to have been denuded of every scrap of soil, this having been washed down to form the surface of the narrow valley up which the railway was taken.   Much of the gneiss was disintegrated, but hard blocks were left standing, which assumed all manner of forms, and were piled up on each other as if placed there by man.   We stopped at a distance of sixty miles from Madras, in this narrow valley, where the ground began to rise rapidly ; and there we found tents pitched and a comfortable breakfast awaiting us.   A large elephant, gorgeously painted

and clothed, was pacing up and down in front of the
tents, and this I found had been sent by a neighbouring
Rajah, who wanted to know when he could pay me a
visit.   We were much too hungry to postpone our meal,
so I told the messenger that I would receive the Rajah in
about an hour.   Accordingly, after breakfast, carpets were
spread in front of the tent, chairs placed, and people collected, for we heard a great noise of a drum and horns,
announcing the advent of the Rajah.   First came the
aforesaid elephant, then some men blowing horns, then
others leading several horses richly caparisoned, then a
great crowd of people, in the midst of whom we espied
a large palanquin, or sort of open couch, gilt and ornamented, the pole by which it was carried being made
into the form of a huge snake, painted and gilt.   I had
got my lesson from the collector of the district ; so, as soon
as the Rajah got out of his palanquin, I moved forward
to the edge of the carpet to meet him (it would not have
been etiquette for me to defile my feet by putting them
on the bare earth), took him by the hand, and led him to
a seat.   I then had to speak to him through an interpreter ; I had picked up some facts relating to his habits,
family, &c., which formed the basis of my talk, but I
never saw an attempt at conversation so received.   He
looked straight forward, never turned his head towards
me when I spoke to him, never uttered a word in answer,
but two servants repeated my questions and answered for
him.   I, as you may imagine, very soon got to the end of
my budget, and then, being very tired, I said to the collector, 'How am I to get rid of this fool?'   It was an
incautious question, asked under the impression that none
of the natives would understand it ; but a grin on the
faces of some of the Rajah's attendants betrayed that
their comprehension had been greater than I either expected or desired.   The collector told me that all I need
do was to get up, shake hands with him, and express a

hope that I might see him again on some future occasion, which I did (with some qualm of conscience, for I never wished to set eyes on him again), and we got rid of him and his train. Shortly after we went back to Madras, arriving there rather tired. God bless you, my dear boy.

Your affectionate Father,
W. D.

The foregoing letters will have described our arrival at Madras, and the first impressions made upon us by the marked change of place, of climate, and of people.

The change in the character of the work thrown upon the Governor was not less marked and peculiar. Even under ordinary circumstances, there would be much requiring thought and study, in order to enable a man who had been dealing generally with Europeans to adapt the experience of his former life to the new set of circumstances which present themselves daily in the East; but in 1861 matters were still more complicated by the change made in the relations between the people and the Government by the abolition of the East India Company. The Government was, in fact, in a sort of transition state. The East India Company had transferred its whole system to the Crown, and the latter had assumed it, by the mere substitution of the name of the Queen for that of the Company; but the relation between the Government and its agents, civil and military, must be very different when the head of the Government is the Queen, from what it is when that head is a corporation like the East India Company; and the changes necessarily consequent upon this transfer of authority threw a much greater amount of responsibility upon a Governor than he would have been subjected to in less stirring times. He had not only to make himself acquainted with the system which had been in operation, and to ascertain what had been its effect upon the people, but he had also to study the probable action of the changes which must necessarily take place, on the people, and on the agents of the Government, both civil and military. He had, in fact, to carry on, mentally, a sort of double process; to ascertain *what was*, and make up his mind as to *what ought to be;* and this had to be done with reference to a state of things, I might almost say, without a parallel in history. I felt, of course, the weight of the responsibility thrown upon me. My experience as Governor, however, stood me in good stead; I had passed through a somewhat curious apprenticeship in Australia for about fourteen years; and though the people whom I was now called upon to govern were very different from those of Australia, yet I had the same Government at home to refer to, and the tools I had to work with—at all events those with whom I had principally to deal—were Englishmen. It is quite true that these Englishmen were placed under circumstances so totally different from any that existed elsewhere as to make it a matter of necessity to study the action of such circumstances upon their mode of looking at their duties, as well as upon the character of the work done; but still they were Englishmen, and it was quite possible, with regard to most of them, to ascertain what might be expected from them. It was different with regard to the native servants of the Government; as to these, their name was Legion : nearly all the actual work of the Government was carried out by them, under the direction and superintendence, it is true, of Europeans; but all that could be said of the natives was, that their work would be done in a slovenly manner, unless a constant and close superintendence was exercised over them.

The actual state of things, so far as regarded the European civil servants of the Government, was as follows. They were, as heretofore, divided into two classes, ' covenanted,' and ' uncovenanted.' The former entered into certain specific engagements with the Crown, just as they had previously done with the Company ; while the Crown, in consideration of this, bound itself to grant them certain advantages, which, practically, conferred upon this class of its servants the monopoly of all offices of importance, while it promised to each a retiring pension of 500*l.* per annum, after a given number of years' service, compelling each, at the same time, to purchase an additional 500*l.* per annum by the payment of a certain percentage upon his salary. Among the uncovenanted servants were distributed a proportion of the offices of emolument ; but many, even of these, were reserved for the officers of the army, who, when not occupied in military duties, were made use of in a number of ways, though they were considered liable to be called upon to rejoin their regiments, should these be sent on active service. Such a state of things struck me as very anomalous. I could quite understand that the East India Company, standing in such a peculiar position with relation to the native states, would feel itself compelled to maintain a large military force, and therefore a greater number of officers than it could find profitable employment for in time of peace, and would be glad to avail itself of the services of some of these supernumeraries for the performance of civil work. This mixture of civil and military work would naturally cease to be a necessity when the army assumed its proper and fixed relation to the services which might be demanded from it, and when the work of the civil servants became clear and defined. One of the first subjects, therefore, to which I turned my attention was the determination of the strength of the military force requisite to secure the Presidency of Madras from attack from without, and from mutiny within. The reduction of the military expenditure was pressed upon me by Sir Charles Wood, in one of his first letters. The fact was that the mutiny had acted most injuriously upon the finances ; first, by lessening the receipts, and, next, by enhancing the expenditure—

especially the military expenditure.   Troops had been poured into India from England and the colonies, while large bodies of irregular native troops had been organised; the outlay, too, upon stores, camp equipage, means of transport, &c. &c. had been enormous.   Now that the war was over, it became a matter of the greatest importance to bring the expenditure within the limits of the revenue, and, in order to this, to look carefully to the state of all our establishments, and specially to that of the military force, for the purpose of deciding upon its strength and constitution, and of arranging for its distribution in such a manner as to give the Government the means of handling it most effectively.

In the following letter to Lord Canning, I gave a sketch of the course which I was about to pursue at Madras, and pressed upon him the adoption of a similar scheme for the rest of India.

To Lord Canning.

Madras, March 7, 1861.

My dear Lord,—Will you allow me to give you a short outline of my views as to the reduction of the military force, and as to the establishment of a system which, by proportioning the strength of the troops in any given locality to the probable (or, under a proper arrangement, I might almost say, possible) demand for their services, would not only, I feel certain, enable the Government to make an immediate reduction in the native army, but insure it against any possibility of such an outbreak as has so lately taken place?

I start upon the assumption that we must look upon ourselves as holding the country by the sword.   It is quite true that we ought, and also do, use every effort to make the people contented and happy; but differing as they do from us, in colour, in religion, in habits, we cannot imagine that they will ever identify themselves with our

Government as a whole, or feel an interest in maintaining

We must, therefore, *always* have a force at our disposal sufficient to resist, not only any attack from without, but any attempt at combined action, in such a case, from within.

Looking at the subject as a military man, and supposing myself called upon to consider the question with a view to determine the minimum force with which I could fulfil all that ought to be demanded from such a body, I should, of course, first strive to ascertain the position and strength of the force with which I might possibly have to contend ; and, beginning at Cape Comorin, I should work my way up gradually to the northern frontier, carefully noting, as I went on, the character of the population, especially of that of the quasi-independent states included within our territory : their means of action, the best positions in which it would be possible to place a military force for the purpose of keeping them in awe, the character of that force, which would, of course, have to be adapted to that of the country in which it is to act, &c.

When this military survey of the country was completed, it would be seen how it harmonized with existing arrangements ; and it would be a matter for the consideration of the Government, whether some modification might not be made in the proposed arrangements, even though such modification might involve some addition to the minimum strength. Political considerations might, I can imagine, make it desirable to maintain a force at a particular place, or to increase that force beyond what would, under ordinary circumstances, be required. We will suppose this done ; that the Government has before it all the data necessary to enable it to determine the strength and description of the force required for the whole of India ; and that, with a due reference to the quality of the troops, it has decided upon the number of the infantry, cavalry, artillery, engineers, &c. which it requires. Ought this force to be

divided into three? ought there to be any longer an army
for Madras, another for Bombay, another for Bengal? I
should say, certainly not. The whole force should compose 'Her Majesty's Indian Army;' should be under one
head, under one system of management; care being, of
course, taken that, under this system, no offence should be
given to the peculiar tenets or prejudices of race or
caste: the object to be kept in view should be the *mixture*
of various races, not, of course, in the same regiment, but
in the different corps d'armée or divisions, so as to give the
European element, in all cases, a decided preponderance over the native element of any one section or
race. You have now before you the despatches relative
to the amalgamation of the European portion of the
Indian Army with that of the Queen; would it not be
wise to avail yourself of the opportunity of forming the
native armies of the different Presidencies into one united
army, pretty much upon the same principle as has been
suggested for the European portion of the force; that is,
to select a portion from the armies of each Presidency,
numbering the regiments, 1, and perhaps 2, Bengal; 3,
Madras; 4, Bombay, and so on? Before, however, you can
do this, you ought to have a military report, such as I have
alluded to; and so far as regards this Presidency, I will
endeavour to collect the materials for such a document. I
may observe that, if you call upon a General officer for
such a statement, you will be almost certain to get an
over-estimate of the strength required. An officer is,
naturally enough, anxious to have at his disposal a force
sufficient to make success a *certainty*; and he will not
bring down his demands to the minimum. In calling,
therefore, for such a military survey of the country, I
should combine information from various sources. I
should make the collectors and political agents report
as to the number and character of the population, and
the force which might be brought against us.

I should call upon the officers of engineers to report as to the state of the roads, and generally as to means of communication, facilities of transport, character of works of defence, forts, means of crossing rivers, &c. When all this is before the Government, it will then be time to submit it to the Commander-in-Chief, or a board of General officers (though I object to a board, as frittering away responsibility), to determine the amount of the force required at the head-quarters of the different divisions or brigades. A summary of these would give the total strength necessary, which, I feel certain, need not exceed 150,000 men. I have Sir Patrick Grant's authority for saying that the force applied for by Bombay is far in excess of the wants of that part of India, and I have my own positive conviction that the amount stated by Sir Patrick Grant as necessary for Madras is far in excess of our wants. By withdrawing troops from points where they are merely required for show, and centralizing forces upon the frontier of ticklish neighbours, we might always be ready to strike the first blow, and to make that blow an effective one. I need hardly say that proper provision should be made for transport of stores, ammunition, &c. An army which is not in a position to move at short notice is of little or no use : two thousand men who can move at once will be more useful in quelling disturbances, or checking any attempts on the part of an enemy, than ten thousand who cannot move for a month. I send you these remarks for what they are worth.

Yours very truly,
W. D.

The course sketched out in this letter was carried into effect throughout the territory of Madras, and special reference was made to those portions of the Peninsula in which, though not subject to the Government, the Madras army formed the staple of the military force, for the purpose of ascertaining the opinion of the authorities as to the feelings of the people towards ourselves, and their capability of exhibiting these feelings in action, whether they were favourable or unfavourable. As a general rule, the feelings of the Mahometans were said to be unfavourable; and it is easy to understand why this should be the case, when we call to mind the fact that we have reduced the Mahometan from the position of a conqueror ruling over a subject people, to that of a man on a level with his former subjects. In the territory of the Nizam, for instance, where this petty Prince is, it may be said, entirely dependent upon us for his existence, we are most cordially hated; and the only guarantees we have for his good conduct are the dread of the consequences sure to follow on an outbreak, and the wisdom of his minister, Salar Jung. He is fully aware of the weakness of his master's position, who, although nominally ruler over a population of some fifteen millions, would, should he provoke us, be moved upon by troops, concentrated in and about his territory, attacked in front, flank and rear, and very soon destroyed.

To Lord Canning.

Madras, March 7, 1861.

My dear Lord,—My hair stood on end when I heard that I was likely to be visited with such an infliction as a Legislative Council. I went back, in thought, some twelve years, to the time when I was struggling with a body, similarly constituted, in Van Diemen's Land; and all the annoyances and discomforts, all the bitter party and personal quarrels which emanated from this legislative body, came vividly before me.

To deal, however, with the question more seriously; do you not think that to admit, in a country constituted like this, which we may fairly be said to hold by the sword, the smallest edge of the wedge of representation, is a fatal mistake—fatal, I mean, in its eventual result, not its immediate? It will be said, of course, that a nominee Legislative Council is not a representative body ; and this, in one sense of the term, is true : but it is intended to appear as such. The men who are placed in it, not being officers of the Government, are supposed to represent the different sections of which society in India is composed. Their appointment is a practical admission that the Government is not competent to perform all the work which is demanded from it, and is therefore obliged to call for aid *ab extrâ*. As the Government admits its own weakness, the Council soon begins to assume that its presence and aid are essential ; that legislation cannot proceed without it ; that it is not a mere council of advice, but the legislative element in the Government. The next step is to insist upon its freedom from control ; the next, that it be representative in fact. All these are phases which I have *witnessed* myself ; they are not mere theoretical deductions from any abstract idea of the constitution of man, or at all events of the variety, Englishman ; though I believe that they might be very correctly deduced from the nature of the animal, as well known to us. If, then, we are ever to gain wisdom from the past, or are justified in reasoning from what has been to what will be, we have a right to do so in this instance. There are thousands of motives which impel people to follow the course which I have sketched out ; there is but one to withhold them, and that is genuine public spirit, guided by the wisdom gained from a careful study of the past. In how many men will you find the two joined?

You may, perhaps, say that the die is cast, that a legislative system has been in operation some years, and that it would be impossible to revert to the old system. It would be difficult, I admit, but by no means impossible, *in India*. Besides, it would not be necessary to revert to the old system. The transfer of the government from

the Company to the Crown affords a cover under which
changes may be made without creating any great feeling.
I gather from your letter that it is intended to give up
some portion of the control which the central Government
has exercised over the different Presidencies; to place
these, in relation to the central Government, something
upon the footing on which the States of the American
Union (*did*) stand to the federal government at Washington.
Under such a scheme, with the exception of matters in
which the *whole* country is interested—such as military
defence, customs duties, postage, relations with foreign
States, &c.—all legislation would be local. You might
thus retain your general legislative body, composed of
members sent from the different Presidencies, limiting its
action, and calling it together only when there is something for it to do; while in the Presidencies the work of
local legislation might go on, without the intervention of
such a body as a Legislative Council.

It appears to me that the whole scheme proceeds from a
misconception both of the wants of society in India, and
of the best mode of supplying these wants. The Government and country will owe you much, if you can in any
way neutralise the ill effects which are likely to be produced by it. A Legislative Council is, as a tool, calculated
to do European work, I might almost say, only English
work; and is therefore altogether unfitted for India.

I have been but a fortnight here; I have, however,
found out, already, that the general principles which apply,
with some degree of plausibility, to Europeans, require
very extensive modifications when applied to Asiatics.
It is said that men are the same everywhere; that they
have the same senses, passions, affections; that they are
actuated by the same motives; that the inducements to
action vary only in degree, not in character. There
cannot be a greater fallacy than this, or one more mischievous when reduced to practice. Men are men, I admit:

they have the same number of limbs, framed according to the same pattern; their senses are the same in kind, if not in degree. I admit the truth and beauty of Shylock's appeal, and his claim to a common humanity; but when it is sought to apply this principle of the unity of race to regulate the condition of man as a social being, and as a reason for constructing the social edifice according to one pattern, and that our own, I object most emphatically. All men are, I believe, descended from the original Adam; but God, in His wisdom, has modified their physical characters, adapting them to the particular climates under which they exist. We admit—indeed, it would be absurd to deny—the physical difference between the European and the Asiatic; why, then, in the face of all experience, are we to assume an identity of mental constitution?

Why should I have a Legislative Council at Madras? The population of the Presidency consists (I am speaking by guess, but believe myself to be under the mark) of 20,000,000 of natives, and, in addition to the servants of Government, somewhere about 20,000 whites; the latter number I believe to be far in excess of the actual amount. Of the whites, very, very few contemplate making this country their home; they look to a return to England as the end and object of their being; they have few or no local ties: what right have they to claim to be represented in a Legislative Assembly?

If this small portion of the community be abstracted, are there any who wish for a system of representation? When I say, ' wish,' I mean who have a desire to go into the Council for the object of benefiting the country at large? Very few indeed! I do not believe that it ever enters into the mind of the Asiatic that he could, or ought to, assist in legislating for his fellow-men; or that these have a right to an opinion which would lead to action opposed to the views of their rulers. For centuries upon centuries the inhabitants of all the low country in India

have been ruled over by others: they are content to be
so. Why should we suggest to them motives which can
in no way conduce to their happiness—which, indeed, they
are incapable of comprehending ; which, if they eventuate
in action, may, perhaps, produce some good, but certainly
a much larger proportion of very bitter fruit?

Even in England, where these institutions have grown
with our growth, and are almost a part of our nature, we
find that their effect is not purely for good.   Party feelings split up society into hostile sections, act upon the
happiness of families, rend asunder very many ties, and
in no way conduce to the development of that spirit of
brotherhood which ought to prevail among us.   If this
be the case with us, why should we try to force upon the
Indian people an institution the evils of which are certain,
but the good only contingent upon the wisdom of an
uneducated people?   To tell you the truth, I have for a
long time been convinced that, of all the mischievous
delusions which prevail in England, and among the
English, that which traces social evils to legislation, or
believes that they are to be remedied by legislation, is the
most mischievous.   By it we are tempted to look without
us for the cause of an evil which has its abode in our own
hearts; we seek to remove by external actions, by
pharisaical observances, that which can only be remedied
by a change within us ; and we cry out for reform, or we
go on passing ' Acts to amend Acts,' legislating against
every varied external phase which the internal evil
exhibits, till the complication becomes a much greater
evil than that which it is sought to remedy.   However,
I am making, what I commenced as a letter, an essay upon
the principles of government ; so good-bye.

Yours very truly,

W. D.

I was not satisfied with making this appeal to the Governor-General; but I wrote to the Secretary of State, reiterating the arguments addressed to Lord Canning, and pointing out the special absurdity of any attempt to introduce the principle of representation into an Indian community.

The remarks, however, made in the letters to Lord Canning, and in those on the same topics to the Secretary of State, elicited a variety of comments. I was told, with reference to the question of reduction and redistribution of the military force, that the old Indian officials objected to the concentration of the army; that their wish was to have the country divided into circles with an English regiment at the centre of each; their plea being that a regiment so placed would act as the centre of a large area of '*contented submission.*'

Of this area the collector, or head man of the district, would be the chief authority, and he would be naturally inclined to maintain a system which placed at his disposal (to a certain extent at all events) a military force for his assistance and protection, and which insured for him, in an out-of-the-way place, detached from European society, a body of gentlemen with whom he could associate. These old Indian officials, moreover, seem to have forgotten that the new police—which was rapidly extending its action throughout India, and which, in 1861, was, in Madras, thanks to the energy of the officer placed at the head of it, already well organised and efficient—was intended to perform many of the duties which had formerly been improperly thrown upon the military. Among these was, specially, the duty of watching over the internal peace of the country, and enforcing that ' contented submission ' to the law which can only result from the conviction that the representatives of the Government, in the shape of policemen, are always close at hand and ready to act. The circle over which a regiment can exercise its influence is but a small one; its action, like that of gravitation, diminishes as the square of the distance from head-quarters; while that of the police, quartered in every village, is spread over the whole district, and is continuous, and therefore efficient.

With reference to the Legislative Council, I was assured by the Secretary of State that the idea of a representative system had never entered his head; and, indeed, I do not believe that he thought of the scheme as involving such a consequence. Others, however, took a different view; the people of Madras understood it as involving the principle of the representation of classes; and the Eurasian, or half-caste, population petitioned the Government to nominate a person whom they recommended, as their representative in the Council. Their claim was of course disallowed by me, and they were told that they had altogether mistaken the object of the Government in constituting the legislative body, the members of which were selected solely with reference to their capacity to assist the Government with their advice. I felt, however, at the time, that the first step had been taken, and that my reply to the petitioners was an evasion.

Others, too, appear to have imbibed the same notion as the Eurasians. Mr. Laing, in his speech introducing the budget in 1861, alluded to representation as visible in the distance; others too, high in office, have talked of our position in India as being that of schoolmasters sent there for the purpose of teaching the Hindoos to govern themselves; while an 'East Indian Association' in England has adopted 'responsible government' as one of the blessings it proposes to confer upon the Hindoos. Such schemes, however, argue on the part of their framers a disposition so to fix their eyes upon an impossible future as to ignore both the past and the present: had they not closed their eyes to the past, they would have seen that a very large proportion of the qualities and habits of men are hereditary ; and that when there has been but a scanty infusion of fresh blood, the stamp of race is indelible. They would have seen that the Hindoo of to-day is the genuine descendant of the Hindoo of two thousand years ago, in habits, character, modes of thought ; and that he has never admitted, or even dreamed of any Government but an autocracy. Had they not ignored the present, and closed their eyes upon their own experience, they would have confessed that all attempts to train the Hindoo, to induce him to adopt European habits or modes of thought, have been most signal failures.

It is a curious fact that while we, in the two centuries, or thereabouts, during which we have been dealing with the Hindoos, have made no appreciable change in the conduct or motives of the body of the people, they, the soft and apparently yielding people, have impressed their stamp upon us, and have had a very injurious action upon the European character.

To Lady Charlotte Denison.

Government House, Madras, March 29, 1861.

My dear Sister,—I am writing against time, as the steamer from Calcutta arrived yesterday, and the mail is made up at nine o'clock. Our habits of early rising, however, give me some hours in a morning, and I am devoting this to letter-writing to-day, instead of to a walk.

By the time you get this, L—— will have arrived in England with five of the children. I put her on board the steamer on the 21st, but had I anticipated the bitterness of the parting, I should, I think, have hesitated to accept the appointment of Governor. It is the great penalty attached to service in India that it breaks up all family ties: it separates *often* husband and wife, *always* parents and children. We have not yet fairly settled ourselves here ; there is some doubt whether it would not be advisable to give up the house at Madras for public offices, and to take advantage of the opportunity of purchasing the house of the late Bishop on the Neilgherries, making that the second residence of the Governor. The cooling down we should get on the hills would enable us to withstand the heat of the low country, which in the winter is not excessive. The great complaint against the weather here is its uniformity. You know exactly what it will be from day to day, the only variation being the character of the wind, which, when it blows from the southward, or is what is called an 'along-shore wind,' is damp and unrefreshing. Day and night the thermometer shows much the same: you cannot dispense with the punkah.

The relation in which we stand to the people of India is a very peculiar one; I do not think that it has its parallel in history. We are not conquerors who, after a time, amalgamate themselves with the people whose country they occupy; we are not like the Spaniards in America, who reduced their subjects to the condition of slaves; we occupy a most anomalous position, and I am very much afraid that the transfer from the Company to the Government will be productive of many difficulties, among which the constant meddling of the House of Commons, and the consequent absence of anything like fixity in the system of administration, will be one of the greatest. People will reason about the inhabitants of India as if they were Englishmen, or rather, as if by subjecting them to a cut and dried system of education, as it is erroneously termed, they might become Englishmen at last. To this I entirely demur. I do not think that national characteristics are to be thrown over as unworthy of consideration; but, even supposing the theory to be correct, they ought to begin at the beginning, and to work the Indians through the whole course of training, from the Heptarchy. Instead of this, these theoretical Solons apply to a people who may, so far as political learning is concerned, be said to be in their infancy, the principles by which the grown-up man is governed, and, of course, the result is very much what it would be were I to put my little George into a pair of my buckskin breeches and top boots, and send him into the hunting-field. Have you ever read the first Napoleon's correspondence with his brother Joseph? I imagine not, for, as it deals very much with military questions, it would not interest you; but there are some very shrewd observations, which apply with full force to us as governors of India. Joseph was expressing his anxiety for the comfort of his Neapolitan subjects, and his wish to make himself beloved by them; and Napoleon, pointing out to him the peculiarity of his position, as a king thrust upon the people against their will, and supported altogether by a foreign military force, asked him how he could expect that his subjects would, all at once, give him credit for his good intentions. 'No,' said Napoleon, 'govern them: insist upon submission; show them that you are their master. You may then relax, if you like, the reins; but you must not think to govern by love for many a year.' Here we are exactly in the position of Joseph; we have thrust ourselves upon these people; they have no affection for us; our colour, our habits, our religion, our principles of action, are altogether opposed to those of our subjects. How can we imagine that they will look upon us otherwise than as usurpers? Since I came here, I have had a much higher opinion of the indomitable energy of the Anglo-Saxon than I ever had before; and yet I have always set him up pretty high: but to see, in India, a mere handful of English keeping in subjection upwards of 120,000,000 of natives, and doing it without any apparent effort, is really a thing to be wondered at. If, however, we presume too much upon our moral strength, and begin to say to the Hindoo, 'Take your share of the property; I trust the administration to you,' we shall find ourselves very soon tripped up, and shall have a desperate struggle to main-

tain our ascendency. Yet this is what we have a tendency
to do : we are talking of applying what people choose to
call ' the great principles of our system of government ' to
a people as utterly unfit to appreciate or apply them as a
child at the breast. However, I will not bore you with
politics ; though, as these matters are now pressed very
much upon my attention, it is natural that I should let a
little escape occasionally. I had no idea how closely
these people pack themselves, till yesterday, when S——
and I, in our morning's walk, passed through a portion of
the town just in rear of Government House. This was a
mass of low huts, six feet high to the eaves, each range
forming a quadrangle, into which the houses opened. The
lanes were about twelve feet wide, and the houses as close
as they could pack. Swarms of men, women, and children, were about ; the houses themselves appeared clean, as
also the court-yard, but the alley was awful. There is no
fall to carry off the drainage, on water to flush the gutters,
and my only wonder is that fever and cholera do not
sweep away thousands and tens of thousands annually.
This suburb was occupied by Mussulmen, who are said,
with what degree of truth I know not, to be the dirtiest part
of the population. I am going to test my engineering knowledge in devising a scheme for the drainage and cleansing
of the town : many have tried their hands at it, but
hitherto the difficulty arising from the low level of the
town, and the flatness of the country, has, together with
the expense, put a damper upon every scheme.

Seeing that I began my letter by saying that I was
writing against time, I have, I think, done pretty fairly.

Your affectionate brother,

W. D.

To Colonel Harness, R. E.

Government House, Madras, April 14, 1861.

My dear Harness,—I am sorry to hear from you that you do not anticipate success in your endeavour to improve the character of the instruction given at Chatham to the young officers of the corps. Now I do anticipate a good deal. In all institutions of this kind, I look a good deal more to the head of the institution than to the system. It is too much the fancy of the present day to think that men are mere machines; that a certain routine can be carried out with young men or boys, by which (to a great extent irrespective of the people who administer the system, and carry its details into practice), a perfect *homunculus* is turned out, fitted either to lead an army, or govern a state. Now all my experience contradicts this, and tells me that a good system badly administered, or rather administered merely as a system, is far inferior in its results to an indifferent system worked by a man who is in earnest. Now my reason for thinking that you will produce a good effect is a conviction on my part that, in the first place, you are in earnest; and, in the second, that you have sympathies with the young; that you are not old in mind, though both you and I are getting on in years. Take, then, my advice, my dear fellow, and go straight ahead, in the line you mark out for yourself; work upon the young men by the influence of example— by bringing the stores of knowledge, which you have accumulated during the thirty five years we have been alongside each other in the corps, to act upon their minds; stimulate their appetite for every sort of information; do not bind them down to the 'narrow gauge' of purely professional study, but let them work on the 'broad gauge' of general science; and you will turn out good officers and useful men, I will answer for it. You have read, I dare say, some of Hugh Miller's works; do you recollect his advice to his fellow workmen? It is, I think, in the first chapter of his 'Old Red Sandstone.' He says, ' do not seek happiness in what is misnamed pleasure; seek it rather in what is termed study. Keep your conscience clear, your curiosity fresh, and embrace every opportunity of cultivating your minds.' I could not give better advice to a young officer than Miller did to his brother masons. So much for your encouragement; so work away in hope, and in faith.

Now as regards myself. I had never before been in any but European society; here I find myself dropped into one which is, I may say, altogether Asiatic, for the number of Europeans is too scanty to act even as leaven to the mass; they can only be looked upon as the thin, very thin, upper crust of the pie. I had not been here a week before I found that all my European experience required an Asiatic coefficient to enable me to apply it properly. I have hitherto done but little, having occupied myself in reading up papers, and making myself acquainted with the people and their doings, in order to enable me to get data for my Asiatic coefficient. I am beginning, however, to see my way. One of the first things which I have had to consider has been the railroad question; and the conclusion which I have come to is, that the Government here has acted hastily in undertaking a great system of railroads; it has never gone quietly and calmly into the consideration of the character of the railway communication applicable to India, but has allowed itself to be led away by analogies between the state of things in India and in England, which have no real existence. I am afraid, too, that the companies, certain of the five per cent. interest upon their capital, which is guaranteed to them (a much larger interest than they can get in England), will, while lavish in their expenditure of capital. take but little trouble to develope the traffic, but will allow it to jog on so long as it will pay its working expenses. The scheme was commenced without the necessary data, with nothing but vague promises of possible future advantages, and in these promises, military and civil matters were heaped together into a most incongruous mass, no one thinking it worth while to attempt to separate the two, or to disentangle the complicated web. I have here before me a line from the east coast at Madras to Beypore on the west coast. The only reason I have ever heard for going down to Beypore, which is a mere open roadstead, is the substitution of Beypore for Madras as a place of call for the Peninsular and Oriental steamers. With this misty vision before it, the Government has constructed 400 miles of railway, 200 miles of which are through a poor country, which can contribute little or nothing to the traffic; and, with the most perverse ingenuity, the line passes at a distance from every single town on this route, which might possibly have furnished a little passenger traffic. I will deal with other matters in subsequent letters. I hope you will catch a sight of my wife before she leaves England. Yours affectionately,

W. D.

The question of the strength of the army required to maintain our supremacy in India was very soon complicated by a proposal on the part of the Government at home to *reorganise* the *native army* (which, in Bengal, and to a certain extent in Bombay, had been disorganised by the mutiny), on a footing altogether different from that which had prevailed before in these two Presidencies, and which did, at the time, prevail in that of Madras. I think, from the tone of Lord Canning's correspondence with me, that he must have made the original suggestion, and supported it on the ground of economy; but I do not believe that he had the most distant conception that what he proposed to apply to a fraction of the body would be made at home the ruling principle for the organisation of the

whole army. The subject was brought under my notice
incidentally, while the despatches containing the scheme
were under consideration at Calcutta, and I wrote to Lord
Canning, asking him to give me an opportunity of expressing my opinion upon the scheme. The two months
which I had spent at Madras had given me an insight into
the general condition of the country and the feelings of
the people, which put me in a position to discuss subjects
connected with the military occupation of the country
with much more effect than I could have done had I
gone up to Calcutta soon after my arrival. I had now
formed an opinion upon the facts before me, and what I
wanted was to ascertain whether the state of things in
Bengal and Bombay would harmonise with that opinion.
Lord Canning kindly asked me to come up to Government
House ; and I accordingly put myself on board the mail
steamer, and landed at Calcutta on April 29. As the whole
scheme had been concocted in England, I might have
spared myself the trouble of remarking upon it. I
submitted, however, the following memorandum to Lord
Canning, which he returned with the notes appended to
it in his own hand-writing, showing that he was in no
way responsible for the impracticable and hopeless form
in which the scheme was sent out. To these notes I
appended some remarks, and I forwarded the whole to the
Secretary of State.

*Memorandum on the Reorganisation of the Indian Native
Army.*

NOTES BY LORD CANNING (SIGNED C.)   REPLIES TO NOTES (SIGNED W. D).

The native army at present consists of three distinct
bodies, the armies of Bengal, Madras, and Bombay.
Each of these is constituted of cavalry and infantry in
various proportions, and may be said to have an organisation peculiar to itself, which is due, perhaps, in some
measure to traditions of the army itself, but to a much

greater extent, to the peculiar habits and customs of the
people among whom it does duty, or from whom it is
recruited.   This threefold form has sprung naturally from
the peculiar position in which the East India Company
was placed.   Its settlements at Calcutta, Madras, and
Bombay being separated from each other by wide tracts
of country, occupied, in many instances, by natives either
actively or passively hostile, each was compelled to
provide for its own defence by the maintenance of an
efficient body of troops, which was gradually, by the
extension of territory, magnified into an army.   This,
however, can no longer be pleaded as a reason for maintaining three distinct armies.   The British territory
(meaning by that the districts over which the Government exercises a direct control) is so united, the communications from one part to another so comparatively easy,
that the necessity for a separate force for each Presidency
has manifestly ceased.

Such an anomaly as an army under three distinct
commanders-in-chief should be put an end to as speedily
as possible.   The effect of such a system is to increase[1]
expense by multiplying staff appointments—to diminish
the efficiency of the troops by rendering concert[2] between
the different commanders-in-chief a matter of necessity.

[1] Quite true.—C.

[2] I doubt this.   It is physically impossible that a commander-in-chief in
India can hold his charge for more than a few years (even if his command
were not restricted, as now, to five years), and could any man in so short a
time acquire such a knowledge of a necessarily heterogeneous army, and of
the enormous and diversified country over which it is spread, as to enable
him to dispense with careful concert with the general commanding in parts
of the country with which he has not become acquainted ?   The substitution
of lieutenant-generals for commanders-in-chief in each of the three Presidencies, and of a single commander-in-chief for all India, is quite practicable,
and there is something to be said in its favour : but it will not enable the
commander-in-chief to act with much less of concert than at present.—C.

His lordship grants all I ask.   The lieutenant-general is in fact a
general of division under the *orders* of the commander-in-chief.   The
concert I allude to is that which involves the necessity of agreement, not
the mere asking of advice.—W. D.

There are also many minor evils to which it is unnecessary to allude, but which will present themselves at once to any military man. Economy, therefore, and efficiency, would be consulted by the union of the three distinct armies of Bengal, Madras, and Bombay, into one body, which might be styled 'Her Majesty's Native Indian Army.'

While, however, I am quite prepared to recommend the fusion of these three armies into one, I am by no means disposed to admit that it would be wise to adopt such an unity of system with regard to the three elements of which this army would be composed, as would in any way tend to lessen the feeling which makes the soldier cling to the recollection of the past, and gives him an interest in the honour of the corps to which he belongs. Neither should I propose to adopt any uniform system of enlistment, &c. On the contrary, I should retain every existing privilege and every existing[1] tradition. even, if possible, to the number and designation of the regiments ; and I should strive to make the change merely a substitution of one commanding officer for another, and of Her Majesty's Indian Army for the Bengal, Madras, or Bombay Army, as the case may be.

Having thus determined the name and style of the army, the next point to be considered would be its strength : and in order to decide this, it would be necessary to determine the relation which should obtain between the

---

[1] It will be very difficult to retain these when the armies are, even nominally, fused into one. The rivalries and jealousies of the three armies have been shown to have their use. Would the same spirit of wholesome antagonism to the mutinous Bengal army which animated the armies of Madras and Bombay in 1857, have shown itself so readily if all had been taught to consider themselves of one army? Nobody will say so.—C.

This antagonism is principally a matter of feeling among the officers : I believe it obtains but very partially among the men, and as the men were the mutineers, this feeling could have had but little effect in restraining them from joining the mutineers. In Madras, the peculiar privileges granted to the men and their families had a great influence on their conduct.—W. D.

Native and European element in the force provided for the defence of India.

Everyone will admit that it would be impossible to depend upon the Native Army alone for the defence of the country even against aggression from without ; but wide differences of opinion exist as to the proportion which the native troops should bear to the Europeans acting with them. It is not necessary that I should attempt to decide upon the proportion with any exactness ; it must be finally determined by discussing the character of the forces required at different points to meet any possible, or, rather, probable, contingency—but, as an approximation, I may say that the European element ought not to bear to the native a less proportion than that of one[1] to two.

Before, however, we can come to a satisfactory opinion as to the strength of the whole force, English and Native, which would be required for the maintenance of our supremacy in India, we ought to possess a good military report upon the whole country, coupled with remarks upon the character of the people, the amount of force[2] which might under any circumstances be brought against us, the state of the communications,—the means of procuring food,[3] the facilities for transport[4], &c., &c., &c. : without such in-

[1] Too large.—C.

[2] The amount of disciplined, or quasi-disciplined, force in the employ of native states we know. The amount of undisciplined men, but possessing arms, who might rise in a general rebellion, no report could give us.— C.

This may be known, but it has not formed an element in any general scheme for the maintenance of our supremacy.—W. D.

[3] The available food in any district varies so enormously with seasons, that no report two years old would be trustworthy.—C.

The supply varies from year to year according to the season, but the quantity of land under crop remains pretty nearly the same— or is subject to similar variations—and this, with a knowledge of the character of the previous season, would give all the information required.—W. D.

[4] This knowledge is very necessary. The Bengal commissariat can give it pretty correctly for this side of India.—C.

If the commissariat can do this, it will do more than any commissariat ever did before.—W. D.

formation a general officer would not be able to decide as to the position of his troops, or to make proper arrangements for concentrating them in case of necessity.

I have already arranged for the collection of data upon which a military description of the Madras Presidency may be founded, and if similar data can be furnished from the other Presidencies and provinces, the task of drawing up the complete report will be comparatively easy. It should, however, emanate from one person, and that person an officer of experience.

When the absolute force required for the defence of the country has been settled, the difference between the European element and the whole force will give the strength of the Native Army. There are two considerations which must have a great influence in determining the strength of the European element; the first is the number of men which England can, without injury to her other important interests, maintain in India; the second is the number of these expensive troops which India can afford to pay.[1] I have, however, an intimate conviction that the result of a proper military report upon the whole

But upon the above points I should be sorry to see the Government or the commander-in-chief leaning upon any report of a few years old.

The elements upon which it must be founded are, in Central and Upper India especially, constantly fluctuating.

That which we are most deficient in is military topographical knowledge of Central India, Rajpootana, and some parts of our own old provinces. We do not even know the number or strength of native forts, or the fords of the rivers, or the passes through the hills—as they ought to be known.—C.

All this shows the necessity of such a military report as I have sketched out; upon such a report the local changes could be easily noted.—W. D.

[1] Even when we have ascertained these two points, we must take a third into consideration.

The most probable and most serious danger which awaits India is a stoppage, perhaps a withdrawal, of its supply of English troops in a European war. We must, therefore, so deal with our native army, and with native interests and feelings, as to give us the fairest hope of obtaining support from that quarter when the time of pressure arrives.—C.

I consider that in such a case we should lean upon a very slight reed: indeed, we ought not to speculate upon its support.—W. D.

of India, will show that a large reduction can be made in the existing force, both European and Native, and, therefore, a corresponding diminution of our military expenditure.

I will now proceed to consider the important question of the organisation of the Native Army. I approach this subject with some diffidence, for my residence in India has been too short to enable me to make myself thoroughly acquainted with the details of the existing organisation; my position, however, has placed at my disposal a vast heap of official information, and I have received from many sources much information, both oral and written, bearing upon this important question.

I may premise that I consider the maintenance of a really efficient army to be the only guarantee which we can have for the permanence of our authority in India.

I feel quite certain that, beneficial as our system of government may be to the natives of India, however much we may strive to convince them of the honesty of our intentions towards them, of our wish to place them in a position of complete equality with the European before the law, the feeling of the native is that we are interlopers, that we have acquired by force or fraud, and retain, by the power of the sword, countries which had for very many years been governed by an hereditary race of princes; and I am equally certain that the whole mass of the community would rise [1] against us if they dared, and would submit to

---

[1] I do not go this length, though I admit that we cannot trust the *mass* of the community anywhere.

I am sure, however, that we can operate upon the masses so as to diminish greatly the chances of danger from them: not by elevating or favouring them to the prejudice of the grades above them, amongst which their natural leaders and instigators will always be found; but by reversing this policy (which has been the policy of later years), and by so dealing with the gentry of the country as to convince them that their material and social interests are *actively* cared for by us—in other words, by giving them power and position, and by showing them that we look upon a native gentleman of

a really grinding tyranny on the part of a native authority, in preference to the mild control we exercise over them.

An army, therefore, we must have, to protect us from enemies from without and traitors from within. This army must be composed, probably to the extent of two-thirds, of native troops, and the question which we have to consider is one which involves :—

1. The consideration of the character of the individuals whom we seek to enlist.

2. That of the military organisation to which these men should be subjected.

As regards the character of the individual soldier, I assume, of course, that it is by no means desirable that the army should be composed of such a preponderating number of men belonging to any one of the various tribes or sects by whom India is peopled as would give to that tribe or sect any, even the most remote, chance of establishing its superiority over the European portion of the army.

It would seem, therefore, desirable that men should be enlisted from every district[1] in India, in order to insure as

property and family as something more than a coolie. When the chiefs and gentry begin to feel that they may lose a great deal, and can gain very little, by substituting any other rule in the place of ours, I shall have little fear of the masses. Even fanaticism will gradually give way before plain and sure material interests.

I grant that this policy is not so applicable to Madras, where a native gentry is an unimportant element, as to Upper India: but wherever such a class remains, or can be re-called into existence, it is through their more substantial interests, and, comparatively, greater intelligence, that we must influence all below them. I see no reason why, without any sentimental trust in the effects of generosity, we may not bring every zemindar to the state of feeling which actuated Scindia, Rampore, the Cis-Sutledge chiefs, and some of the Rajpoot chiefs throughout 1857 and 1858.—C.

The fact that in Madras, where the semi-feudal system has but slight root, there was but little tendency in the masses to rise, is a very pregnant one; they had no leaders. Lord Canning seems to wish to raise up leaders, to create a strong feudal body — a policy very different from that of the kings of England (who did their best to break down the feudal system), and I am afraid a perilous one.—W. D.

[1] This could not be done literally;—for there are many parts of this country where the necessary conditions of military service are so distasteful

great a mixture as possible of all the elements of which society is composed. In some instances it might be desirable that the whole of these elements should be thrown into one mass, without respect of caste or sect; in others, it might be advisable to group together into a company or regiment the men belonging to a particular village or district—to give, in fact, to the body, a special locality to which it should look for recruits, and the inhabitants of which would be, to a certain extent, hostages for the regiment,[2]—securities for its good faith and fidelity. This system would, I think, be peculiarly applicable to parts, if not to the whole, of the Madras Presidency.

Other methods of grouping men together will of course occur to officers; but to these it is unnecessary that I should refer, my object being merely to press the adoption, not of any one particular system, but of one, or several, which would secure such a mixture of the various castes and sects as would neutralise any efforts made by one or more to rise against us.

The second subject to be considered is the character of the military organisation to which these men should be subjected.

I address myself to this part of the subject with some hesitation, because I fear that my remarks must assume somewhat of a controversial tone. It is impossible now to deal with this question as an abstract one, having reference to soldiers in general; I must, perforce, contrast the two systems which have been placed in direct opposition to each other[3] in India, 'the regular and irregular.' As, however, I have no local partialities, no feelings which would lead me to give a preference to one system over

to the people, that good and willing soldiers could not be made out of them.—C.

[2] I quite agree in these remarks. No one mode of mixing creeds, castes, and local classes can wisely be prescribed as a universal rule.—C.

[3] The placing of these two systems in opposition to each other, or as alternatives, is an English blunder, and a very serious one.—C.

the other, the judgment which I may form will be, whether correct or incorrect, at all events unbiassed, and as such I submit it for what it is worth.

The 'regular' organisation is based very much upon that of our European troops. To each regiment there is a lieutenant-colonel, a major, a certain number of captains, lieutenants, and ensigns, and these are all Europeans. In addition to these, each company has a native officer having the rank of captain, and another having the rank of lieutenant. The non-commissioned officers, of whom there is a full proportion, are all native.[1] This is substantially the organisation of those armies to whom all our success in India is due ; it is analogous to the formation of every European army ;[2] it carries out that which is an acknowledged military maxim, that the officers should bear a certain proportion to the men ; the only difference being that an inducement is held out to the better behaved men of the regiment to strive for distinction, inasmuch as there are rewards for good conduct in the shape of commissions, to the extent of two to a company.

I cannot but think, then, that this system of organisation has much in its favour. It is based upon acknowledged principles,[3] it has succeeded in action, has precedents in its favour, and holds out rewards for good conduct of a kind peculiarly attractive to a soldier.

It may, of course, be the case that a regular regiment

[1] Not exactly. In Bengal it has been the rule to have a European sergeant, and to allow him to take command of the *commissioned* native officers, when parading or mustering the regiment. It is an atrocious practice.—C.

I perfectly agree with Lord Canning. It is an atrocious practice, and yet one to which Bengal officers cling tenaciously.—W. D.

[2] I doubt whether any army in the world can present such an anomaly as that of allowing the junior European ensign to take precedence of the older commissioned officers, because they are not European. But this is unavoidable so long as native *commissioned* officers are retained ; and it is difficult to get rid of them without incurring other evils.—C.

[3] Except as regards the position of the commissioned native officers.—C.

may be in a bad state of discipline, may misbehave itself before the enemy ; but it will be found in nearly every instance that this misconduct was not the result of organisation—not from having too many officers, but too few. It is very often the case that a large proportion of the officers of a native regiment have staff appointments, and consequently that the discipline becomes lax, because there are not a sufficient number of officers to superintend it. Surely the best remedy for this would be to compel a certain number of officers to join their regiments, not to diminish the number doing duty.[1]

A regiment on the '*irregular*' system consists of a body of men commanded by an European officer, having under him a second in command, an adjutant, a surgeon, and two officers with indeterminate duties,—six in all.

The men of these irregular regiments receive a certain daily allowance, which is calculated to cover all expenses of food, clothing, arms, accoutrements, transport of stores and camp equipage, &c.[2] They have their own native non-commissioned officers and regimental officers, but the peculiar organisation of each individual body is very much dependent upon the fancy of the officer who may be placed in command. The advantages which this system is said to hold out are—1st, economy ; 2nd, efficiency.[3]

---

[1] But it must not be supposed that a regular regiment can be turned into an irregular one by simply reducing the number of European officers. The relations between the Native and European elements are radically different in the two systems.—C.

The less possibility then of making the transformations alluded to in the Gazette of April 22, 1861.—W. D.

[2] There are other important peculiarities. Companies, troops, and squadrons are commanded and led in the field by native officers *alone*.

Native officers do not rise from the ranks to the same extent as in regular regiments, but come in at once as officers; and are, very many of them, sons of chiefs and gentlemen of high birth, and sometimes of fair fortune.

They are allowed, and often required, to bring a certain number of troopers into the regiment from their own dependents.—C.

[3] And, 3rdly, the opportunity, almost the only which we have, of giving congenial and honourable employment to the cadets of the respectable and influential families of the many parts of India where the feudal system is

With regard to economy, it is evident than the six officers of the irregular regiment must cost much less than the twenty-six officers of a regular regiment. It may also be possible that, taking a particular regiment, the amount paid to the soldiers and native officers, as a consolidated allowance, is less than the amount which is disbursed in various ways before the regular regiment can be brought into line; but this advantage will be very much diminished, if not done away with, so soon as the whole army is framed upon the irregular system. Any arrangement which presupposes the absence of a commissariat establishment must[1] involve a system of living upon the country, which implies the plunder of the inhabitants, their consequent hostility, and all the evils which follow necessarily such a state of things.

So far as I have been able to learn, the expense of the irregular regiments on service has not been inferior[2] to that of regular regiments. Without, however, laying any stress upon this, I would observe that even under the system proposed by General Jacob, who considered four[3] European officers to be sufficient for a regiment, there must of necessity be a large surplus of officers unemployed, from whom a selection might be made of those whose talents fitted them for employment as officers of irregular troops.

---

still cherished. No native dynasty has ever neglected to turn that system to account. We have done so, and have no reason to be proud of it.—C.

How many native dynasties have been deprived of their thrones by successful feudal dependents? Is the policy a wise one? I doubt it.—W. D.

[1] The regular regiments have no commissariat establishment (in our sense of the term), and an irregular regiment, if properly commanded, does not plunder or oppress the people more than a regular—or even than a European one.—C.

[2] There will be found to be a considerable difference. Colonel Balfour can furnish the details at once.—C.

There are not, as yet, data sufficient, as I do not want estimates, but payments.—W. D.

[3] If the four were immortal I dare say Colonel Jacob would be right: or if a vacancy could at once be replaced by a fit officer found elsewhere. The object of increasing the number to six is, partly, to make sure that a regiment shall never be at a loss for an officer capable of stepping at once into

These officers must be paid, and they ought to be employed upon such duties as might give them a knowledge of native character, and of the mode of dealing with men. The cost of the reserve of officers must, therefore, be set against the saving arising from the diminution of the number of those actually serving with the regiment.

It may, however, be true, though I should be unwilling to assert the fact positively, that the 'irregular formation' is cheaper than the 'regular;' unless, however, it can be shown to be superior in other respects, I should consider this but a very poor reason for making so sweeping and startling a change in our military system.[1]

The next claim made in favour of the 'irregular organisation' is that the regiments under this system are more efficient than the regular regiments.

This, however, is stated too broadly, and requires, in the first place, explanation, and, in the second place, proof.

Is it intended by this to affirm that a regular regiment, deprived of 18 out of its 24 officers, and compelled to furnish itself with all those articles for which it formerly looked[2] to the commissariat, would, from the very fact of the change, become more efficient than it was before?

If this is not intended, then the efficiency of the regiment is not due to mere organisation.

If, however, it be intended to affirm that a regular regiment, commanded by an inefficient officer, will be very much improved by being placed under the supervision of an active, intelligent and zealous officer, who has full power to reward and to punish, I am quite prepared to admit the correctness of such a statement; but it has

the discharge of the essential duties which are concentrated in the three (or four) senior officers.—C.

[1] I quite agree.—C.

[2] Is this so in Madras? Is the system of regimental bazaars not the same as in Bengal?—C.

yet to be shown that the same officer would not have produced precisely the same beneficial effect upon the discipline of the regiment under its old organisation.

The truth is, that the form has little or nothing to do with the efficiency or inefficiency of the regiment. The 'regular' system, worked by an active and zealous officer, will turn out troops as[1] good, or even better than the 'irregular,' for there will be a large European element in the former; and even in cases where the actual commanding officer is inefficient, there is a chance that, among the 24 officers belonging to the regiment, one or more will stand out to whom the native troops will look, and whom they will willingly follow.

The 'irregular' system is based altogether upon the supposed qualities of the officer in command. Should he have peculiar qualifications, be active, zealous, fond of his duty, have a knowledge of the mode of dealing with natives, he will manage his regiment well; should he, in addition to these qualities, have those military instincts, as they may be termed, a quick eye for ground, a perception of the weak or strong points of the enemy's position, or his own, he will lead his troops well during war, and secure for them and himself the credit which is given to success; but it is absurd to imagine that such men are common, or that it is in the power of the Government, or any

---

[1] The systems are so different that this can hardly be safely predicated. Of two officers, equal in professional ability and acquirements, the one who has an aptitude and liking for dealing with natives, and who has pleasure in moulding and training them into something better than he finds them, will make a good irregular commandant; whilst the other, with no such tastes, will make a bad one—although he may be a very fair lieutenant-colonel of regulars, with whom he has little personal contact. It is the same in the civil service. The man who makes an excellent secretary or judge at a Sudder station, may be quite unfit to be a commissioner of a district in a non-regulation province—and *vice versâ.*—C.

I quite agree—but then the two men are not *equal* to begin with. Give the same qualities to the lieutenant-colonel of a regular regiment, and he will make them felt.—W. D.

one, to select out of a large batch of officers the man, the proper man, for such a responsible position.[1]

The truth is, that the work of the army, as the work of the world at large, must be done with the ordinary tools which are placed at our disposal; by no system of examination, by no tests which we can apply, can we hope to make certain of securing a man so peculiarly constituted as one who would develope the advantages claimed for the irregular system by General Jacob; and that, therefore, is the best organisation which, demanding from those who are called upon to work it out no very extraordinary talents, does yet afford a scope for the development of such talents;—which, while working out satisfactory results from men of an average capacity—men who are acted upon by the ordinary inducements of interests and ambition such as are exhibited in the mass of mankind —does offer sufficient inducement to men of the higher degree of talent and mental power.

It is true that the 'irregular' system does hold out to the ambitious man, and to him who feels that he is possessed of qualities which fit him for command, inducements far superior to those which can be offered by the 'regular' system, and it is desirable that opportunities should be offered to such men of bringing themselves forward; but it is no way desirable that the army should be so organised as to induce a constant struggle among the officers for opportunities of exhibiting their qualifications for command. Where one commands many must *obey*, and place must be found for those who, conscious of no particular power of mind, go on their path steadily, doing that which they feel to be their duty to the best of their ability; and I confess that I have a higher opinion

---

[1] I entirely agree. The men are not common, and it is not easy to pick them out.

Hence one of the advantages of adding junior officers to the irregular regiments, although there may be no distinct duties requiring their presence.—C.

of him who does his duty because it is his duty, than of him who, actuated by[1] a restless ambition and love of distinction, is always pressing forward into the front rank, and who too often in the pursuit of this shadow sacrifices his truth, his honour, and his conscience.

The fact that the principle of the 'irregular' system is based upon the selection of officers, is to me one of the strongest objections to it. Who is to be the judge of the qualifications of an officer? The Government? What means has the Governor-General, or anyone in authority, of ascertaining the peculiar qualifications of so many officers? This principle of selection becomes, under ordinary circumstances, but another name for jobbing; and unfair preferences, to an extent to which the regular system affords no opening, will be exhibited daily.

The injury done by this is not to be measured by the damage done to the service by the promotion of incompetent individuals, but for every such individual improperly promoted dozens are injured, dozens feel that they have been unfairly dealt with, and a bitter feeling is engendered which is most injurious to the service.[2]

On a careful consideration of the subject, with special reference to the existing state of things in India, I am decidedly of opinion that the 'regular' organization is that best fitted to work out satisfactory results.

---

[1] One of the chief charms which the irregular service has for those officers who are fit to take it up is the feeling that their individual character tells upon the natives, and especially upon those of a higher class, far more effectually than in the regular service.

This is a great attraction to those men, who are the very best servants that England can have in India.—C.

It is the charm of commanding instead of being commanded.—W. D.

[2] There are great evils in corps d'élite in any circumstances. But the advantages of an irregular service (which as regards its officers must be a corps d'élite) are so great that it is worth while to face those evils.

As to an irregular system without selection—and selection from a large field—it cannot subsist.—C.

Why, then, attempt to constitute the whole army upon this system?—W. D.

I am, however, by no means disposed to deny that bodies of men organized upon the irregular system may form a very useful addition to the regular army. My objection applies to the establishment of a system under which the whole army is to be transmuted into a set of irregular bodies, to the commanding officers of which it is proposed to entrust powers far greater than any now given to colonels of regiments, and the abuse of which power may produce effects of a most dangerous character.

I believe that the opinion which I have here expressed will be borne out by a very large majority of the officers both of the European and Native Army. I cannot, of course, expect that those who, like General Jacob, have founded a system, or who have been instruments in working it out, will admit the correctness of my inferences.[1] They have a natural tendency to attribute to the system itself the results which are in fact the product of their own energy, determination, and mental power. Much, however, as I respect and admire such men, I cannot admit that they are to be looked upon as the best evidences in their own cause.

For my own part, I cannot but consider the extensive experiment now about to be made as fraught with great danger to our Indian Empire. I believe that it will be looked upon by a large portion both of the officers and men with distrust and dissatisfaction; and I believe it to be altogether uncalled for by any circumstances connected either with the state of the army itself, or with our financial position. W. T. DENISON.

In my memorandum to Lord Canning, I alluded to the anomaly of having three distinct armies in India, under three different commanders-in-chief. My reasons for

---

[1] There is great force in this. But, as I have already said, the scheme of substituting the irregular system for the regular system, instead of leaving it as an off-shoot, is mainly an English scheme.—C.

pressing the amalgamation of these three armies into one
were purely military and administrative; and when, on
political grounds, it was decided to retain the three, as at
present, distinct, I said no more on the subject. With
regard, however, to the reorganisation of the native army,
the case was quite different. I, reasoning partly *a priori*
from general military principles; Lord Canning from
experience of India, and a knowledge of the habits of the
people; the commander-in-chief from military experience
in India, had all arrived at the same conclusion, that the
scheme was a great mistake. I felt myself bound, therefore, to bring the subject before the Government again
and again; and I am bound to say that, during the course
of my residence in India, I had many opportunities of
representing the vices and absurdities of a system which,
while it is, in principle, altogether dependent upon the
power of selecting well-qualified officers for command,
does, by the very mode in which it is worked out, render
such selection impossible. In writing to the Secretary of
State on this subject, I could not avoid remarking
upon the difference of the views taken by me and by
himself. He looked at the question as a civilian, I as
a soldier; he had decided to make an experiment upon
a large scale, and to reconstruct an army upon a novel
footing, with but the minimum of military experience,
and but indifferent military advisers. I, feeling certain
that the experiment must fail, that it was wrong in
principle and most clumsy in detail, did not hesitate to
tell him so. I was certain that it would injure the tone,
and destroy the efficiency, of the army; and I pointed out
in 1861, that a portion of the scheme by which it was
proposed to allow the old officers to die off, or to retire
till the number present was reduced to six for each
regiment, would be impracticable, for that the whole army
would, so far as officers were concerned, be composed of
majors and lieutenant-colonels, while there would be no

subalterns to fill up the gaps occasioned by death or retirement.

My visit to Calcutta, which took place in May, made me much better acquainted with the working of the general Government than I could have been had I reasoned from the facts which came within my own cognisance as Governor of Madras. I witnessed this working in many matters of detail, as well as of importance, and the impression produced upon me was that it was clumsy in its organisation, and slow in arriving at results. I could quite understand that, when there were two different heads of the Government—the East India Company, and the Queen—acting through the Board of Control, the complex system which, practically, placed the Governor-General and his Council in the false position of representatives of the two heads was almost a matter of necessity; but now that the Queen had become the sole head of the Government, it struck me that the time had arrived for making a change which should place matters upon a more satisfactory basis. As Governor of Madras, I had already found the action of my Government much impeded by the interference of the Governor-General in matters of detail which ought never to have come before him; and I had the less hesitation, therefore, in submitting my recommendations to the Secretary of State. The outline of this recommendation was as follows. The Governor-General should be placed in a position analogous to that of the President of the United States: on him should rest the sole and entire responsibility of managing all correspondence with States not under our control. He should have the sole control of the army and navy: he should—with the advice of a legislative body, to which I will allude hereafter—have the power of imposing customs duties and of regulating the foreign trade of the country. The post-office should be subject to him, telegraphs, railways (except such as are of a purely local character), and generally, all matters in which more than one Presidency is interested should be placed under him. He should be assisted, not checked, by an Executive Council composed of a sufficient number of officers to do the work of the different departments; but it would not be desirable to hamper him with too many advisers. These advisers, or the Executive Council, might be formed into a Legislative Council or *Senate* by the admission of one or two representatives from each Presidency; and it would be well worth consideration whether this Council might not be extended by dividing the country into blocks of more manageable size than those which form the existing Governments; and placing all these, as regards their relation to the general Government, upon one and the same footing. By changing the present Council into a Senate, consisting of public officers and representatives of the different Presidencies or provinces, the necessity of admitting any but public servants as members of the Legislature would be avoided.

Such was a sketch of the constitution of the general Government which I submitted to the Secretary of State. With regard to the local Governments, I thought that the best form would be something analogous to that originally in force in the colonies; namely, a Governor, appointed by the Queen, and responsible to the Secretary of State; and an Executive Council, composed of the heads of departments, with the power of obtaining information and advice from people interested. Such a Government might undertake all the legislative as well as the executive work, looking to the fact that the main body of the people are living under their own laws, and would be far better pleased to remain as they are than to be hampered by laws prepared by people ignorant of their manners, habits and wants. I was too well aware of the working of the anomalous legislative bodies composed of officers of the Government and nominees holding no appointment, save the honorary one of member of the Legislative Council, and therefore altogether irresponsible, to wish for their assistance.

The final change which I wished to see in the machinery of the Government of India was the abolition of the ' Council of India.' The gentlemen composing this can only give the Secretary of State the record of their past experience; they dream of the India of the present day as that of their youth; they can give no information which cannot be obtained in a much more perfect and correct form from the local authorities in India; their advice is disregarded by the Secretary of State when it does not harmonise with his own views, and is merely made use of by him to shelter himself from the responsibility which ought to devolve upon him of thinking out and deciding questions submitted to him from India; questions, I may say, which would be, in most instances, better dealt with by a fresh mind than by a body constituted like that of the Indian Council.

To Children in England.

Government House, Calcutta, April 30, 1861.

My dear Children,—I must send you a joint letter, for I have not time to write one to each of you. You will have heard of my voyage up here, and will have seen my rough sketch of this house. The dining-room occupies the whole centre of the house, is upwards of a hundred feet long, and must be sixty feet wide. It has two rows of columns to support the upper floor, which is the ball-room; it is paved, as well as the drawing-room (which is a long gallery running across one end of the dining-room), with grey marble, and looks very magnificent. The Governor-General's body-guard are dressed in scarlet, and have jack-boots coming up above the knee; but they do not, I think, look so soldierlike as my body-guard at Madras.

I went one day with Lady Canning to the Botanical Garden, which is on the opposite side of the river. We drove down our bank for a couple of miles or thereabouts, and found our boat waiting for us; pulled across to the landing-place at the Garden, and wandered about for some time, quite unconscious that a thunderstorm was coming up. This burst upon us on a sudden, and we had to run for shelter to the house of the superintendent, where we waited some time till the rain ceased. The wind, however, blew heavily, and we had some difficulty in making our way across the river in our barge, which exposed a long side to the wind: we got across at last, however, and drove back to Government House.

On Sunday I went to church with Lord Canning. The church at the Fort looks well inside, and was well filled in the morning, but there were very few in the evening. I saw *such* a banyan tree in the Garden; it spread over nearly two acres of ground; the great stems which it sent down were covered with creepers, and the effect was as if you were walking under a grove of large trees. It is, I think, hotter here than at Madras; hitherto, however, at about six o'clock in the evening heavy clouds come up, sometimes with thunder and lightning, and sometimes with a gale of wind which brings up dust like a ' brick-fielder' at Sydney. Captain Glover and I went out riding yesterday evening; it was very hot indeed; and to make matters cooler, Glover had a hot, fidgety chestnut horse, which, when it began to canter, got its head up and pulled vigorously. The absurdity was, after all, that we had taken horses which were not intended for us, but which the native servants, who seem to think it necessary to give such an answer as they think will be acceptable, assured us were intended for the ' great Sahib Governor and his officer,' while they were, in fact, horses belonging to the General and his aide-de-camp! I took a short walk this morning through a garden on the side of the road leading by the river bank, and came across a Burmese pagoda. The woodwork was most elaborately carved, and had been brought from Burmah; the stone, or rather chunam, foundations were made by an artist brought over for the purpose. At each corner was a large sphinx with one head and two bodies, and these were backed up by two great alligators on each side.

May 3.—Yesterday was a very hot day, and yet I had to go out at four o'clock, first to visit the Museum of Geology, which was very well arranged; then to the Agricultural Society's rooms, where I saw all sorts of machines for cleaning cotton, and a variety of textile fabrics: there was some beautiful stuff, very like silk, made of the fibre of nettles. After this I went to the Asiatic Society's Museum: their collection of shells is a very indifferent one: they have a magnificent collection of birds and animals, but so crowded together, for want of space, that I could see but little of them. I walked into one room where there was a table covered with stuffed monkeys in all sorts of attitudes; they really looked, in some instances, as if they were asleep. I had good accounts, per telegram, from Madras yesterday. God bless you, my dear children.

Your affectionate Father.

To Lady Denison.

Government House, Calcutta, May 4, 1861.

Dearest,—I finished yesterday my memorandum on the organisation of the native army, and am going to give it to Lord Canning, while I send a copy to Sir Charles Wood. Lord Canning spoke highly to me of Sir Robert Napier,[1] who was promoted for his services in the mutiny, and I had a long talk with Napier on the subject of the reorganisation of the army.

I was about to drive with Lady Canning yesterday,

---

[1] Now Lord Napier of Magdala.

when a violent thunder-storm burst upon us. This cooled
the air, and I was more comfortable yesterday evening
than I have been since I left King George's Sound.

Barrackpoor, May 5.—We came to this place yesterday. Barrackpoor is on the bank of the Hooghly, fourteen miles above Calcutta. The road to it lies generally
parallel to the river, over a country perfectly flat ; the
road itself being quite straight for at least ten miles out
of the fourteen. It is said that Lord Cornwallis proposed to
build a house here, the duplicate of the one at Calcutta,
and to have a road quite straight, with an avenue of trees,
from one to another. The Directors, however, put a
stop to this. The present house stands about fifty yards
from the bank of the river, and is built to look down
a long reach of it. The park is well laid out, planted with
very ornamental trees, and has an aspect of neatness and
tidiness about it, such as I should be glad to see at
Guindy.

Calcutta, May 6.—I started from Barrackpoor at half-
past five, and here I am at half-past seven, but my baggage and servants will not be here for three hours. I sent a
copy of my minute to the Commander-in-chief, who says
it is excellent—sound, true, and practical. I am going to
send it to Sir Charles Wood by this mail, and I am, at
the same time, writing to him on the subject of the
government of India generally, which I want to see
transformed into something having more of a federal
character than the existing Government. My wish, however, is to define and limit the power of the Governor-
General, and also those of the Governors of the different
Presidencies ; and I am also anxious to see the country
subdivided into more of these separate provinces. At
present, a large portion of India is under the direct administration of the Governor-General ; that is, it is handed
over to Residents, who are practically omnipotent. I want
to have these Residencies transformed into Governments,

with well-defined duties on the part of the Governors.   I
feel certain that the change would be both beneficial to
the country itself, and economical ; but it would be, I
imagine, unpopular at first, for these Residencies are high
prizes to the men in the civil and military services.

I dined with the Engineers last night ; we sat down
about fifteen altogether, and had a good chat over all sorts
of matters.   My health was proposed by General Napier
after dinner, as that of a brother officer who had worked
himself up to the top of the tree ; and I, in reply, expressed
the pleasure which I felt in being able to look upon men
who had been my friends, as now, by the amalgamation,
my brother officers also ; and assured them that I should
always do my best to promote the interests of the corps.

May 8.—We had a large dinner here yesterday—seventy
people—among whom I made acquaintance with the
Principal of the Sanscrit College.   I talked with him about
the mental capacity of the Hindoos.   He corroborated all
that I have heard elsewhere as to their memory, but seemed
to think lowly of their mental power.   The only two original works which have proceeded from the Hindoo mind
are, first, a mathematical treatise on Maxima and Minima
—which is Sanscrit to you—and, secondly, a novel, illustrative of Bengalee life, something after the style of Dickens.
He tells me that a Pundit strictly confines himself to one
book; not one subject, but to *the book* which is supposed to
illustrate and explain the subject ; so that, as you may
imagine, the chance of improvement is small.   The teacher
keeps reading this book till he gets every word implanted
in his memory, and he then teaches that which he knows;
namely, as much as his book tells him.

May 11.—Peninsular and Oriental steamer ' Simla.'   I
parted with Lord and Lady Canning, not only as good
friends in the ordinary acceptation of the term, but very
cordially.   I had nothing to say yesterday, for I was almost
too hot even to think.   I tried to read the fifth volume of

Macaulay, but, to my astonishment, fell asleep. It must have been sympathy which made me do so, for, looking along the deck, I could see nothing but faces of people in various stages of somnolency.

May 13.—We are nearing Madras, but I am afraid we shall not get in till too late to land. This will be a bore. However, it is all right, I have no doubt.

Yours affectionately,
W. D.

CHAPTER XVIII.

PUBLIC WORKS DEPARTMENT—NAVIGATION OF THE RIVER GODAVERY—
CURIOUS METHOD OF LAYING UP NATIVE SHIPPING—IRRIGATION—IRRI-
GATION WORKS ON THE GODAVERY—INSECTS—JOURNEY TO SALEM—
TRANSITS—THUNDERSTORM AND ITS CONSEQUENCES—RIDE UP THE HILLS
—COONOOR—ACCIDENT TO DR. S—— — BARRACKS AT WELLINGTON—
OOTACAMUND—SHOOTING PARTIES—VARIETY OF GAME—WE HUNT FOR A
TIGER, AND FIND A LEOPARD—MAKOORTIE PEAK—CONSTITUTION OF
COUNCILS IN INDIA—REMARKS ON ANGLO-INDIAN COLONISATION.

To Captain Clarke, R.E.

Madras, June 8, 1861.

MY DEAR CLARKE,—Since my arrival here in February, I
have been to Calcutta, where I stayed twelve days with
Lord Canning, talking over a variety of matters. I am
very glad that I went there, for, had I not done so, I could
not have got such a correct idea of the system of Indian
government as I have thus picked up. I have now
dropped quietly into my seat, and am setting steadily to
work.

I am busy at present upon two knotty questions—the
constitution of the Public Works Department, and the
reduction of the Army.

The Public Works Department was transferred from the
Revenue Department to the Engineers some years ago, in
accordance with the recommendation of a Commission
composed of men unconnected with the department.
These Commissioners worked out a very pretty theoretical
scheme, showing a gradual chain of responsibility from
the overseer up to the chief engineer, and a beautiful system
of accounts and checks, by which the Government was to
be able to tell, at any instant, what works were going on,
how they were advancing, what they had cost, &c., but,

as this scheme supposed that every man was perfectly
master of his part, it, of course, broke down in practice.
The system of accounts was so elaborate, and so onerous,
that, practically, the Government paid a shilling to avoid
the risk of being cheated out of sixpence.   Then, again,
the Commission included, under the head of Public Works,
all the little village tanks and roads, with which the country is covered, and of which tanks upwards of ten thousand,
on an average, require some small repairs annually.   To
throw such works upon the Public Works Department was
absurd ; it would be just as reasonable to compel the
Board of Works in London to take charge of all the
parish roads in England.   This subject has taken up a
good deal of my time, for I have been forced to read up
a mass of papers ; and, even now, though I see clearly the
mistake committed by Lord Dalhousie in adopting the
report of the Committee as a whole, I find great difficulty
in scheming out a plan which may work satisfactorily.
The principal complaint made against the existing department is the cost of superintendence : this upon an outlay
of 700,000l. amounts to 170,000l. or nearly 25 per cent ;
but it must not be forgotten that this is not only engineers'
superintendence, but contractors', and manufacturers' as
well, for the department is obliged to manufacture its
own bricks, burn its own lime, &c.

The reduction of the army, too, is a question I am
about to take up seriously ; and I have called for information which may enable me to apportion to each district, or
military division of the country, such a force as may be
sufficient, in connection with the police, to keep everything
quiet internally, as well as to repel any attack from without.   I feel certain that, when I have gone carefully into
this, I shall find that half my present force will be sufficient for all the wants of Madras.   So much for politics.
I must now give you an idea of the country and the people.
Calcutta is a fine-looking town : it is called the City of

Palaces, but this is a misnomer. The so-called palaces are built of the most rubbishy brickwork, covered over with plaster or chunam; in fact, the place is rather a sham, and, were we to leave the country, half a dozen years would bring the whole to its original state of mud. I must say that the works of the natives put us to shame: their public buildings are constructed of granite or gneiss carved in the most elaborate way: they must have expended an enormous amount of labour upon the work. Madras, as a town, is not to be compared with Calcutta; the population is larger, but there are fewer white people. The natives pack together like ants, in the smallest possible houses, built of mud, generally. The effect produced upon an European by the aspect of things in a native village is a conviction that no forethought has been expended upon the plan or arrangements of the buildings: these are dotted about most confusedly; and this, together with the dingy, muddy exterior of the buildings themselves, gives a rubbishy aspect to the whole place. The people—with some good qualities, such as affection for parents and relatives, whom they feel bound to support—are an indifferent lot: they are cowards and liars, abject in their submission to those above them, and bitter tyrants to all those over whom they can exercise control. I am afraid that there is a sort of maudlin feeling in England that they have been a fine people at one time, but have been reduced to their present state of prostration by misgovernment; and that, by good government, as we choose to term it—meaning thereby a system utterly at variance with every Eastern idea—we shall raise them again to their proper place in the scale of nations. I look upon this as a mischievous delusion. The mass have remained as they are for a couple of thousand years, and two thousand years more will not change them, or make a white man of an Hindoo.

Yours very truly,

W. D.

Some of the first matters pressed upon my attention by the Secretary of State, after my arrival at Madras, were those connected with the improvement of the character of the cotton sent from India, and the increase of the amount exported. The war in America had cut short the supply from the southern States; the pressure in consequence brought upon our manufacturers, and the distress and misery among the working population in the cotton districts of England, made the Government willing to listen to any scheme, showing a shadow of plausibility, which was brought under its notice. Among these schemes were two as to which reference was made to me.

The first of these was a plan for making the river Godavery navigable. It was said that the interior of the Peninsula was full of cotton fields, only wanting an outlet to the coast to freight any number of ships for the English market. This outlet was supposed to present itself at the mouth of the Godavery, a stream pouring into the sea the water of several rivers having their heads in the Western Ghauts, and therefore delivering, during the south-west monsoon, an enormous body of water. The Government, under the advice of Colonel Sir Arthur Cotton, had availed itself of this supply of water to irrigate a large portion of the delta at the mouth of the river; and some four or five hundred thousand acres had already been brought under cultivation, while it was proposed to increase this amount to nine hundred thousand or a million acres.

Rough sketches and estimates had been made of the cost of the works required to make the river navigable during a portion of the year, and the Government, under pressure from England, had somewhat hastily accepted these plans and estimates, and had already commenced work at some distance up the river. I was in no respect inclined to believe that a river, such as the Godavery was described to me, could be made navigable for a distance of four hundred miles for the sum stated in the estimates ; but I was unwilling to express any opinion upon the scheme till I had seen the river, and had a conference with the engineer. Shortly after my return from Calcutta, I made arrangements for a trip to Coconada, a township, rather than a town, at the mouth of the Godavery ; and I proposed to push up the river as far as I could, in order to enable me to see with my own eyes the state of the lower portion, and to form my own judgment of its capabilities.

The next scheme pressed upon me was the formation of a harbour at Sedashegur, on the west coast of the Peninsula, a little south of the Portuguese settlement of Goa. It was supposed that the cotton grown on the plains of Dharwar, which are above the Ghauts, and about eighty miles distant from Sedashegur, would find an easier outlet from that port than from Bombay.

Here, again, the scheme—which embraced the making of a road through a feverish jungle for eighty miles, rising some two thousand five hundred feet, the formation of wharves, landing places, &c., the probable construction of a breakwater in deep water, to shelter the harbour from the sea brought in by the south-west monsoon — was undertaken upon the loosest possible data. The slightest inspection of the plans and soundings was sufficient to convince me that the difficulties which would be encountered were enormous, and that, when everything had been done to form the harbour, there would be little or no traffic to justify the outlay.

The work, however, had been commenced ; that is, men were employed in making the road up the Ghaut, but no definite plan had been submitted to the Government, nor had it the most distant conception of the probable cost of the work which it had been forced to undertake.

In the meantime complaints had been made by those interested in the cotton supply, that the Government of

Madras, in whose territory Sedashegur was situated, had
not pushed on the work of road-making with sufficient activity; and it was suggested to the Government
at home that the territory in connection with the
harbour, including a large portion of the district of North
Canara, should be transferred from Madras to Bombay,
on the ground that the proximity of the Government of
that Presidency would enable it to exercise a more
efficient superintendence over the work. It was in vain
that I pointed out the objections to the transfer of a
people living under one system of government to another
differing altogether in all the details of local management;
the pressure brought upon the Government at home was
such as to override all local considerations. I determined,
however, to visit the place as soon as the south-west
monsoon had blown itself out, and in the meantime to
content myself with directing the engineers to push on
the work which they had already in hand as quickly as
possible.

The following letters will explain the state of things on
the Godavery in the summer of 1861.

To F. G. Denison, Esq.

Madras, July 16, 1861.

My dear Frank,—Since I wrote to you, we—that is S——
and I, your uncle, and others of my staff—have had a run
to the north to visit the Godavery, which, after draining a
large section of the central part of the Peninsula, runs into
the sea at a point about two hundred and fifty miles north
of Madras. We embarked on board the ' Dalhousie,' a
Government steamer, which, owing either to bad coals or
a foul bottom, could make but little way, and we were
thirty-six hours making two hundred and fifty miles with
the help of steam, the south-west monsoon, and a current
of upwards of a mile per hour. The heat was dreadful
below; on deck, by means of a double awning, we

managed to keep ourselves comfortable ; but my attempt,
on the first night, to sleep in my cabin was a fatal mistake :
I was nearly melted, and had to get up in the middle of the
night, and finish my nap on a chair on deck. All the rest
slept on the deck as a matter of course, S—— and her
maid having a sort of tent of flags made for them. The
Godavery has made for itself a delta, extending about
thirty miles in depth, and it keeps pouring an immense
quantity of mud into the sea during the south-west monsoon ; so that the (so called) harbour of Coconada is pushed
farther to the north every year. We had to anchor about
two miles from the shore ; and, as it was quite calm, a small
canal steamer came to take us from the ' Dalhousie.' As
we had but little time to spare, I, instead of landing at
once, pushed up the Coringa river (one of the branches or
outlets of the Godavery) for some distance. This I found
to be one of the harbouring places of the native craft ;
there were about seventy or eighty vessels, varying from
two hundred to six hundred tons, all laid up in dock in a
curious manner. The shore is quite low and flat, so a
sort of ditch is scooped out of the silt, big enough to allow
the ship, when quite light, with only lower masts on board,
to enter. As soon as she is well in, a dam is made across
the mouth of the ditch, and water is pumped in from the
river till the vessel floats high enough to get her keel
above low water. She is then temporarily shored up, the
water allowed to flow out, any repairs which she may require are executed ; and then the earth is banked up
against her, and the shores withdrawn, so that she looks
as if she was growing out of a potato ridge. But what a
set of sailors they must be to lose the use of their vessels
for six months in the year for fear of the monsoons? Do
you recollect in the account of St. Paul's voyage to Rome
it is said, ' for sailing was now dangerous, because the fast
was now already past '? Here, after June 15, the south-
west monsoon is supposed to blow, and no native vessel

likes to keep the sea. In point of fact, the natives are doing now exactly what their fathers have done for the last two thousand years; and I have no doubt that if we could transport ourselves back to the time of St. Paul, we should have seen ships planted on the banks of the same river, and in the manner I have just described. The dodge of raising the vessel by pumping in water may be of some use to you hereafter, so lay it up in one of the pigeon-holes of your memory, to be in readiness when you want it. We went from Coconada, up one of the irrigating channels, in a small steamer, to the head of the delta. The people were all employed getting in their paddy or rice crop, the floods in the Godavery having supplied water enough; so they were, what they call ploughing, in the water, with a sort of wooden implement dragged by two bullocks, which merely scratched the surface of the ground, tearing up the weeds, and leaving the entrance clear for the water. After this was finished, more water was admitted, and the women were turned in to dibble in the paddy plants, which had been grown in a sort of forcing ground, or seed-bed. They were stooping down under a vertical sun, with hands and feet in the water and mud, while a man stood on the narrow embankment with his feet dry, seeing that they did their work. We were glad to get on board the 'Dalhousie' again, but we were sixty hours making our way back to Madras.

Your affectionate Father,
W. D.

To W. E. Denison, Esq.

Madras, July 15, 1861.

My dear Willy,—Our trip up the Godavery was interesting, though not very pleasant. I saw a good deal, and learned a good deal. We have been dealing with this river for the last sixteen years, have used it to furnish water for irrigation, and are now thinking of doing something to keep the silt out of the harbour, and to enable us to get up the river, and use it as a means of internal communication.

The irrigation works have been skilfully constructed: the great anicut, or dam, which crosses the river at the head of the delta, for the purpose of raising the water to the level required for irrigation, is a stupendous work. The river at the point where this had to be placed is four miles wide, divided into four channels; and these four have a total water way of two miles and a half. The bottom of the river is of shifting sand, and the time for working did not exceed seven months in each year. Yet, in the face of these difficulties, and of the risk of damage by the floods, which rise during the monsoon from twenty to twenty-five feet or even more, the dam was completed, with sluices and appendages, in three years, and has required but little repair since. Here and there it has been necessary to fill in rough stone, so as to maintain the apron in rear of the dam, or at places where the action of the flood has scoured away the sandy bottom; but there has been no accident of importance for years. The dam is composed of two stout walls parallel to each other, and some fifty feet apart. Each of these walls is founded upon 'wells.' In England we should use wooden piles, but timber is scarce and dear in India, and these wells are a common and convenient foundation. A brick well about three feet in diameter and six or eight feet deep, is built on a curb of timber, and is sunk into the ground gradually by excavating the earth or sand inside. When this is done, another is placed alongside of it, a space of about six inches being left between the brick rings of the two. The whole line of the foundation is thus filled with wells, two or more rows being used in proportion to the thickness of the wall; and these are packed with rough stone or concrete, and make a set of stout legs upon which the heavy weight of a building may rest securely. The friction of the large surface of the brickwork, and the broad foot of the well filled with concrete, effectually prevent any settlement from the mere pressure of the mass; all that has to be guarded against is the action of the water washing away the sand from underneath and between the wells. This was especially to be dreaded at the dam of the Godavery, for, in the first place, the river was raised twelve feet; and, in the second, there was, during flood time, a rush of upwards of twenty feet of water over the dam, which bid fair to carry everything away; however, an apron of rough stones, both above and below the dam, has prevented this. The most serious action took place when there was an eddy close to the junction of the dam with the wall containing the under sluices. Here the water worked, in a very short time, a hole thirty feet in diameter, which swallowed up some thousand tons of stone. We went up the river about sixty miles beyond the head of the delta, getting well into the heart of the mountains, and through a narrow gorge, about five miles in length, where the river, previously half a mile in width, is reduced to two hundred and fifty yards, the mountains rising 2,500 feet above it on both banks. These hills are covered with jungle, bamboo, and fine tamarind trees at bottom, teak and other timber higher up. Their appearance struck us, at first, as very picturesque, but, in a little time, the sameness of form and colour became oppressive, and we began to crave for some evidence of life, for the small huts of the natives were too few in number, and too small, to give any character or break to the landscape. These native villages occupy the small valleys or, rather, gorges opening on the river, and are poor and miserable-looking; there is hardly any appearance of cultivation about them. The people earn their living, I was told, by felling teak and bamboos, which they float down the river in flood time. The teak is heavy, and is supported by a raft of bamboos. Tigers are so numerous in these jungles that every village is surrounded by a good bamboo fence or stockade, about ten feet high, for the protection of the people as well as of their cattle. The Government gives a premium for tiger and cheetah skins, at a rate sufficient to induce people to hunt these animals. When we were at Coconada, a hunter brought in to the collector three tiger skins (male, female, and cub), and also a cheetah or leopard skin, for which he received about sixty rupees. I examined his gun, and such a weapon you never saw : it was so thin at the muzzle that it was split in various directions ; it had a miserable flint lock, and was fastened to the stock in all sorts of ways, the original holdings having given way. I honoured his courage much, in trusting his life to such an instrument. I should have been afraid to fire it off, and should never have dreamed of confronting a tiger with it. Good night, my dear boy.

Your affectionate Father,

W. D.

Miss Denison to F. G. Denison, Esq.

Madras, July 15, 1861.

My dear Frank,—Papa tells me that he has given you an account of our visit to the Godavery, and all the scenery, business, &c. of our little tour. I have only, then, the little miseries to enlarge upon, and among these the insects are the most prominent. Such a place for these I never saw. The gentlemen of the party went from Coconada to Dowlaishwaram by day in a steamer, Lady Cotton, Rosalie, and I following in a canal boat. We started about dusk, and as soon as the sun was fairly down, out came cockroaches of all sizes in swarms. When tea came, I climbed up on the roof of the cabin to be out of their way, and I would not have a candle for fear it should attract them ; but by the starlight I could make out myriads of little black things careering in and out of my plate, which, as you may suppose, rather damaged my

appetite. How we were to sleep was the question in my
mind; but, to my astonishment and relief, about ten
o'clock they all disappeared, retiring, I suppose, for the
night. We sat in the cabin for some time after this, and
only saw one or two of patriarchal size, wandering about
as if to see whether all their children had gone to bed.
I had no idea they kept such early hours, and treasured
up the fact for my comfort in future, for, as Spreadborough
says, 'I can't abide varmint.' Our experience in insect
habits, however, was by no means over. The next day
we passed Dowlaishwaram; in the day time I found only
some many-footed crawling creatures on the walls of my
room, and a good many ants on my floor, but in the
morning, when I woke, I heard a regular drip, drip, on
the floor, and imagined that rain was coming in; but
when I got up, I found that a swarm of large ants had
come in by the hole in the wall through which my
punkah rope went, had crawled along the rope for a
certain distance, and all dropped on the floor at the same
spot, luckily about two feet or so from my head. The floor
was quite black with them in a round spot about two
feet across, from which lines radiated in every direction.
I got away, however, without being bitten, dressed in a
hurry, and went off, nearly sick, from finding at the last
moment the decomposed remains of a great crawling
animal in the water-bottle I had been using. The climax
came the next night. We steamed up the river very pleasantly, looking about all the day for deer, peacocks, and
alligators, all of which we were told were plentiful either
on the banks or in the river, but of which we only *fancied*
we saw one alligator. We anchored at night in a narrow
gorge, with steep lofty banks, but no sooner had we lighted
our candles than we found ourselves in the very midst
of a tremendous swarm of winged creatures of various
kinds, chiefly white ants; they flew into the candles,
dropped into our tea, and buzzed in our hair; they dropped

their wings and crawled over us, looking like nasty little
grubs of some kind, for they have not the shape of ants ;
it was lucky that they have not the pugnacity of ants,
or they would have been the death of us. We passed
but an uneasy night, and, to add to our discomfort, the
only water for washing was that which we got from the
river, and as this was in flood, it brought down such a
quantity of mud that we were obliged to let it stand to
settle for a time, and then had to skim it carefully, so as
not to disturb a sediment of about two inches thick at
the bottom of the bucket. We were right glad to get on
board the ' Dalhousie ' again, for this was, when compared
with our small steamer, a perfect palace.

Your affectionate Sister,
S. M. D.

To Major-General Sandham.

Madras, July 14, 1861.

My dear Sandham,—Thanks for your letter : I am
very glad that you met my wife in town. I am anxious
that she should see as many of my old friends as possible, that she may give me an account of their appearance, and assure them that they are not forgotten. Do
you know that it almost makes amends to me for the
absence of my wife to find that she has had such a kind
and cordial welcome from everyone, and that she so
fully appreciates it? Her letters show how happy she has
been ; she will bring back with her a host of remem-
brances of kindly feelings and expressions, which will
serve her to feed upon during the remainder of her stay
in India.

I have just returned from a trip up the Godavery, where
works have been carrying on for several years for the
irrigation of the delta. These consist of a dam, some
four miles in length, at the head of the delta, which
raises the water into the irrigating channels. I could

see but little of the dam itself, as the water was going three feet six inches over the crown, but I got sight of the wing walls, sluices, and locks. These were all plainly and solidly built; they had been lucky in finding good lime pretty close to the work. The arrangements for dredging the irrigation channels, into which the river brings an immense quantity of silt, the repair of steam-tugs, &c., has made it necessary to establish a large work-shop at Dowlaishwaram, close to the dam; and the sappers, who were originally sent up to assist in the work, have their head-quarters there. I did not visit the barracks; it was too hot to venture out during the day; but I shall come up later if I can, when the river is lower, and have a better look at the works. There are four companies of sappers at head-quarters, and ten altogether; but their organisation is an imperfect one, and will require revision. At present they are under the command chiefly of officers of the line, with a few young officers of engineers inter-spersed. From Dowlaishwaram we pushed up the river about sixty miles, as I wished to form some idea of its prospects as a means of internal communication. It certainly is a fine stream, bringing down a body of water about a mile in width at twenty miles above Dowlaishwaram. What will it do when the water is twenty feet over the dam instead of three or six? Imposing, however, as the river now seems, it is for six months and upwards, a mere bed of sand, having a shallow stream about two hundred yards wide meandering about it, at the rate of about a thousand yards per hour, more or less; so that for those months all navigation, either up or down, would be impossible, unless one could bottle up some of the flood water, and let it out during the dry season. I think I must send you a copy of my memorandum upon the reconstruction of the Indian native army. In the opinion of nearly everyone to whom I have spoken, not excepting Lord Canning, the attempt to transform all the native force into ‘Irregulars’ will be a complete failure. Of course the captains, who look forward to be *selected* and placed in command of regiments, are rejoiced at the prospect of promotion ; but every man who is capable of analyzing the details of the scheme, and who has moral courage enough to express an unfavourable opinion of a proposition emanating from the Government, says that it will destroy the army instead of improving it, and that it will be accompanied with great risk to our supremacy in India. For my own part, I do not in the least comprehend what the staff corps is to do, or how it is to provide means for *selecting* the regimental officers, when there is nobody left to select from ; and no one has been able to enlighten me as to this.

Remember me most kindly to Mrs. Sandham and all old friends.

Yours very truly,
W. D.

My visit to the Godavery, and the enquiries which resulted from it, showed me very clearly that the whole project had been hastily got up, without due thought or consideration ; that it had been paraded before the merchants and cotton-manufacturers, as an easy and cheap means of bringing down to the coast the (supposed) enormous produce of Central India ; and that the Government, pressed by the manufacturing interest in England, and deluded by the promises held out to it by the engineers in India, had plunged hastily into the scheme, more, I imagine, with the wish of stopping the mouths of people in England, than with any definite idea of the mode in which a system of internal navigation of 450 miles in length could be completed. I soon found that the engineers had but a very slight knowledge of the state of the river ; they had a general survey, or rather sketch, of the whole, and were aware of the existence of three prominent difficulties, in the shape of rapids, to be overcome, and of one of these rapids there was a middling survey; but their plans partook of the vagueness of their knowledge: they were the hasty suggestions of an inventive mind, pressed to devise some mode by which the two parties interested in the completion of the undertaking could, if not be satisfied, yet have a glimmering of hope held out to them. It was proposed to surmount the special difficulties mentioned above, in the ordinary manner, by making canals round the rapids, with locks to enable the up traffic to ascend the river, while it was supposed that the down traffic would be able, for several months in the year, to shoot the rapids. It was also proposed to retain a quantity of the rainfall of the south-west monsoon in the valleys of the rivers discharging themselves into the Godavery, and to let this water free during the dry season, for the purpose of keeping up such a supply in the river as would secure a depth of three or four feet of water in the shallow parts, and thus enable the traffic to continue during a part, at all events, of this season of drought. I sent for the engineer, and had several interviews with him; I carefully examined all his plans, and listened to all he had to say in support, or in explanation, of his schemes. The plans were evidently framed on very insufficient data; there were no proper surveys or levels of the river; the information respecting the amount of labour available or procurable, the cost of this labour, the quality, quantity, and price of materials, were all vague and indefinite; all, in fact, was purely hypothetical. I also differed in opinion with the engineer as to the general principle to be adopted, my feeling being that it would be more advisable to make the river navigable in the ordinary manner, by turning it into a set of pools or basins, by means of dams from distance to distance with a set of locks at each dam to lift the vessels from the lower to the upper pools, than to plunge into a scheme the expense of which, though apparently much smaller than that of the more perfect plan, could never be estimated, and the success of which was dependent upon the establishment of large reservoirs of water at the heads of streams running through a country not belonging to us. I came also to the conclusion that we had no sufficient data to enable us to form the slightest reliable approximation to the probable return from the traffic up and down the river.

The investigations which I made led to a long correspondence between myself, the Secretary of State, and the Government of India, but nothing very definite resulted from this. I requested to be relieved from the responsibility of superintending, nominally, a work beyond the limits of my own Government, and eventually the charge was transferred to the Commissioners of the Central Provinces. I have lately heard that the work is very much in the state in which it was some six years ago ; that but little more is known of the river itself, or of the probable traffic ; that the estimates have gone on gradually increasing. In fact, the Godavery navigation must be classed as one of those loose suggestions which an engineer, strong in the conviction of his own power to overcome difficulties, is apt to press upon a Government or a company. These, when money is cheap and labour plentiful, may be successfully carried out ; but they had better be postponed till capitalists can be found willing to speculate upon possible, but improbable, returns.

Yours, &c.

Miss Denison to F. G. Denison, Esq.

Ootacamund, August 12, 1861.

My dear Frank.—We left Madras on the 26th of last month, for the Neilgherry hills. We had a special train as far as Salem, a pretty little town two hundred miles from Madras, where we arrived about two o'clock, rather hot and terribly dusty, and drove to the house of the Collector (chief magistrate and general great man) of the district, passing under triumphal arches and strings of leaves hung across the street. Papa, the children and I were lodged in the house; Dr. S——, his daughter, the private secretary, and an aide-de-camp, in large comfortable tents, pitched in front of the house and joined to it by covered passages, decorated very prettily with banana leaves and boughs. We remained there three days, as papa had to pay a visit to the Shevaroy hills, a sort of resort for the people of Madras in hot weather. We drove through the town the evening of our arrival, amidst the shrieks and groans (for their attempt at a cheer always was a sort of yell) of several thousand natives. Of course papa had to stop at one place to put on an immense necklace and bracelets of white and pink flowers, very prettily made, but not becoming, and smelling too strong to be pleasant. Papa went the next day up to the Shevaroys, where he slept in the house of a coffee-planter, returning early the following morning, and before we started for the hills he held a durbar in a tent in front of the house. In the afternoon we started on the railway, which took us up to a place called Sunkerrydroog, about twenty-five miles from Salem, beyond which it was not as yet ready for traffic. There we found our 'transits' waiting for us, and a crowd of coolies whose business it was to transfer our baggage from the train to the transits; but their work seemed light, or they made it so, for Mr. V—— saw four of them each take up one pith tumbler (covered cases of pith, each holding a large tumbler of iced water); put it on his head and march off with it, quite satisfied that he had his fair load.

You will ask, perhaps, what a 'transit' is? It looks like a bathing-machine, but is a two-wheeled carriage on springs. It is difficult to get into, at least with a crinoline, as the door is behind, at a good height from the ground, and the bed, which fills up the whole inside, comes up to half the height of the door. Once in, however, it is fairly comfortable when the roads are good, but, as they are not generally in very good order, the shaking is something awful, and the only mode of securing any comfort is to surround oneself with pillows, and give oneself up to be tossed and shaken like dice in a box. We started off, papa leading, but we had not gone far when a heavy thunderstorm burst upon us. I became very uneasy about my poor parrot, which was in front on a sort of box-seat, and was getting very wet. The little birds I got in, cage and all; but poll's cage was too big to come through the opening. Of course the stupid creature would not understand what I wanted, or appreciate my motives; and it was only after a long struggle, and getting very wet, and a good deal bitten, that I pulled him out of the cage, and got him into the transit, looking very draggled and sulky. My bed, too, got wet in the struggle. I had not long finished my battle with the parrot when I found myself stopping, and was told that the thunderstorm had filled a nullah or water-course, and changed it into a torrent, which they were afraid to cross. Of course there was a great deal of yelling and noise, in the midst of which I heard Mr. B—— order my driver to try the stream, and in we splashed. We soon stopped, however, turned round and came out again. Papa had apparently got through the place before the water rose, but the rest of us were in our transits, on the brink of this muddy stream, looking rather disconsolately at each other. It would have been amusing had I not been a little uneasy about the result. The torches were flaming and smoking, and throwing odd gleams of light on the trees, and on the faces of the drivers and bullocks. I could make out through the clatter that our gentlemen wanted some of the natives to try the depth of the stream by wading in, but this they were not at all willing to do; but, after a time, I saw Mr. B—— himself wading in, followed at some distance by a frightened 'mussaulchee' or torch-bearer, whom he was in vain beckoning forward. After a time I heard a splash and a sort of struggle, and Mr. B—— was, I believe, nearly carried down the stream. This, however, did not seem to disturb him much, for I saw him in a few minutes coolly sauntering back to his own transit, affording a most complete illustration of the difference between the Englishman and the native. We were now rather in a mess, I thought; we had fifty miles to go, and had only done seven or eight. Papa had got over the stream, and would not know what had become of us. The roads were heavy with the rain, and four miles an hour is the utmost to be got out of bullocks at the best of times. However, the storm passed over, and the stream ran down as fast as it rose, so that in about an hour or so we were able to get across. We found papa waiting for us at a place called Bowany, where the road crosses both the Cauvery river and the Bowany, by two fine bridges. Both streams were running full, and the sight, even by night, was fine. Papa had been in for more than two hours; he had got his writing-case out, and was writing away very philosophically, feeling pretty certain that we should come up. We had some tea at this place, and then pushed on, getting to our bungalow at about nine o'clock, where we stopped during the heat of the day. We started again about two P.M. and by eight o'clock reached Coimbatore, a distance of twenty-four miles, where we put up at the house of the Collector. I must send you the account of our journey up the ghaut in my next letter.

Your affectionate Sister,

S. M. D.

The same.

Ootacamund, August 15, 1861.

My dear Frank,—I must take up my parable from Coimbatore, where my last letter brought us. We stayed there that night and the next day, and it was arranged

that we should set off in our transits at ten o'clock at
night, so as to reach Metapolliam in time to get up the
Coonoor Ghaut before the sun got hot.   There was, however, a large dinner party.   Then we, that is the ladies,
had to change our dresses before starting, and we were
just thinking of retiring to do so, when we were suddenly
summoned to prayers.   I am afraid we were not quite
well disposed for this, as we were in a hurry to start.
However, there was no help for it, and we all knelt down
in rather an improper frame of mind, to follow, if possible,
a lengthy extempore prayer.   Dr. S——, whose uncon-
cealed appreciation of personal comfort is one of the
most amusing things about him, was particularly put out,
for, being taken by surprise, he unfortunately placed himself in a corner, out of reach of the punkah, and between
the heat and the desire to get on with our journey, his
impatience for the end of the proceedings became irre-
pressible, and vented itself in a sonorous Amen, to which
he gave utterance at every pause in the prayer, by way
of a hint that it was time to conclude.   We got off, however, at last, and went on in our transits to a place called
Metapolliam, where there is a bungalow.   Here we put on
our riding habits, as well as we could by the light of a
tallow candle stuck in a bottle, and went on again about
five miles to the foot of the ghaut, where we found our
horses waiting.   The ride up is charming, though it is
steep towards the end, and was hot; but the scenery is
beautiful, and the delight of feeling a fresher breath of air
at every turn, and seeing the hot glaring plains further
and further below and behind, is something only to be
appreciated after some months' experience of the Indian
hot season.   We reached the top of the ghaut, at about
ten o'clock, nearly a couple of hours later than we ought,
and were kindly received by Mr. and Mrs. Arbuthnot,
who occupied a cottage beautifully situated on a hill looking down the ghaut.   No description could give you any

idea of the character of the scenery, so I shall not attempt
it.   We remained at Coonoor till Saturday afternoon.   On
Friday we had a very pleasant ride to a point called
Lady Canning's seat, from which there is a beautiful view
up, down, and across the ghaut.   We made our way back
to Coonoor by a different path, and Dr. S—— had the
most terrible-looking fall I ever saw.   He was riding a
large, clumsy, ewe-necked horse, and as we were going
along a narrow path on the side of a steep hill, he stopped
to gather a flower.   His horse backed just as he stretched
out his hand for this purpose; its hind legs went over a
high bank of stone which supported the road, and it fell
backwards.   Dr. S —— was thrown, luckily, clear of the
animal, but both rolled down the face of the hill for some
thirty or forty feet, and it seemed to me that the horse
rolled over him.   I was terribly frightened, thinking he
must be killed.   Papa, however, and Uncle Charles were
off their horses in a moment, and scrambled down to him,
and found him a good deal shaken and bruised, with a
cut on the back of his head.   It was a great mercy that
the side of the hill happened to be covered thickly with
shrubs, which broke his fall.   It took four people to get
him up to the path again, the hill was so steep ; Uncle
Charles and papa supported him, one on each side, while
two others helped to pull them up.   The horse was not
injured at all.

On Saturday afternoon we started with a large caval-
cade to ride over here.   General B—— and his staff and
several officers accompanied us, while others met us as
we approached Ootacamund, and escorted us to our new
home, which is comfortable, and cool enough to require
fires always in the evening and pretty often during the
day.

Your affectionate Sister,
S. M. D.

To W. E. Denison, Esq.

Ootacamund, August 11, 1861.

My dear Willy,—S—— will have given you an account of our movement from Madras to this place. We are here perched up about 7,500 feet above the sea, almost at the southern extremity of the northern portion of the backbone of the Peninsula, upon a sort of buttress. We drop down at least 6,000 feet to the plain, which extends about forty miles to the point where the mountains rise again, leaving a distinct gap in the chain, of not more than twelve hundred feet in height, and of which the railway has taken advantage. The hills to the south of this gap are from five to six thousand feet above the sea, and continue nearly to Cape Comorin. On my way from Coonoor to this place, I went to visit a large range of barracks, intended to contain a thousand men; these were built for a regiment of European infantry, and were occupied, when I went there, by a battalion of the 60th Rifles. The barracks were placed here, not that there was any need of a regiment on these hills, but because it was a healthy place. The consequence is that a sum of 180,000l. has been thrown away altogether. I have stated that I have no occasion for a regiment at this place, and the result will be that the barracks will either be left to go to ruin, or be converted to some purpose for which it is not well fitted. All these mistakes are the result of our departmental system. We throw more responsibility upon the heads of the military departments than they can or ought to be made to bear, and we do not hold them responsible for failures. Here military considerations have been absolutely ignored, and all that the proposers of these barracks have looked to is the health of the soldier— a very important thing, no doubt, and one to have every attention paid to it *at the place where the soldier is wanted;*

but which ought not to influence, except in a very
secondary way, the selection of the position where he can
be made most available.

Your affectionate Father,
W. D.

To Mrs. Stanley.

Ootacamund, September 1, 1861.

My dear Mrs. Stanley.—We have, as my date will show,
fled from the heat of Madras, where the temperature
varied from 82° at night to 98° during the heat of the
day. The effect of the change of temperature upon the
children is very marked; they have picked up both flesh
and colour, and are twice the boys they were a month
ago. It is different, however, with our servants; we are
obliged to treat them as exotics, to clothe them warmly,
and watch over them as hot-house plants; and, after all,
they look miserable and pinched. It is by no means
uncommon to find several very ill from a change to the
hills from the warm plains. Here we have many English
flowers and vegetables, and a few fruits; yet, by riding
twelve miles, I can place myself in the midst of pine-
apples, nutmegs, cinnamon, &c., in a tropical climate.
The south-west monsoon blows heavily against us, bringing with it a steady drizzle, and sometimes heavy rain;
but the great mass of the rain discharges itself on the
west face of the hills, where from 120 to 180 inches is
the average downfall in three months, while here we do
not get more than 60 inches. We have our gallop every
day, in spite of the rain, sometimes after jackal, sometimes
merely exploring. Luckily the ground is covered with a
strong coarse turf, upon which there is no fear of slipping;
the roads, where this is cut away, are very greasy and
slippery.

I am working at various matters connected with the
Government and the people; but I have a hard fight with

the authorities in England. They will insist that everything which is good for Englishmen must necessarily be
good for the rest of the world ; that men are men, whether
they are black or white. Men they are, it is true, acted
upon by the same passions as ourselves, but acted upon
in a very different manner. Then, again, the whole
circumstances of the country are in direct opposition to
those which obtain in England. Here labour is ludicrously
cheap : it is better, that is, cheaper, in many instances to
employ men instead of bullocks, though these cost but
little. Steam is useless here, as I can do everything
cheaper by hand. Then, again, if people get money, they
do not speculate with it, or dream of a savings-bank ; they
purchase jewels and ornaments. Wilson and Sir Charles
Trevelyan thought that if money were made cheap, people
would change their habits, and speculate like Englishmen.
I am by no means certain, by the way, that this tendency
to speculate is an unmixed good ; however, good or bad,
it is an entire delusion to fancy that the Hindoo would
follow our example ; the habits of 2,000 years are not so
easily got rid of. The adhesiveness to old customs is one
of the circumstances which presses most forcibly upon an
European when he comes to this country. We, who
change our habits almost every month, cannot conceive
that tenacity of purpose which makes people here cling
to what they have been used to, without the least reference
to the appropriateness of the tool, or whatever it may be,
for the purpose to which it is applied. It is most
interesting to look at the inner life of these people, and
compare the existing state of things with what the Bible
tells us was the condition of the East 3,000 years ago.
The women go to the well to draw water, they grind the
meal in the same hand-mill which was used in the time of
Moses ; no one appears to have ever dreamed of a machine
which would cleanse or grind all the meal wanted for the
supply of the village. The corn is threshed or trodden

out by bullocks; they have jewels in their ears and noses as described by Ezekiel. Yet these people, so tenacious of their customs, we believe will change their habits all of a sudden! I am altogether incredulous. We flatter ourselves that they are so pleased with our system of government that they would prefer that we—aliens in colour, language, customs, religion—should reign over them, rather than one of themselves. Bosh! How should we like King Mumbo-Jumbo, with 100,000 Africans, to set up his throne in London, and domineer over us? Certainly, if they are unlike us in many things, they are like us in this, that they prefer their relations to strangers.

Yours very truly,
W. D.

To Miss Hornby.

Ootacamund, September 6, 1861.

My dear M——,—My letters to L—— are now directed to meet her on her way out. I shall, therefore, give you a sketch of our proceedings here, in order to keep up the connection between my journal to her, and hers to you. Tell the Admiral that, as I was ordering some guns for myself from Nixon, of Newark, I have told my brother to get an additional double-barrel for Willy. You may think that an order for guns, in the plural, is rather excessive; but were you to see the mode in which we issue forth, your surprise would cease. We go out in parties of from six to twelve, each man having with him a couple of shikarries or huntsmen; or, if he cannot afford this, he has two gun coolies, or common labourers, to carry his guns, that is, generally, a double-barrelled gun and ditto rifle. We proceed some miles on horseback to our ground, having sent on before us dogs, beaters, guns, &c., and, above all, some luncheon. When we have large covers to beat, we employ eighty to a hundred beaters, and twenty or thirty dogs, if we can get them. Still you

may say, why so many guns? We have, in the first place,
a variety of game : we have a chance of hares, jungle-
fowl, peacock ; and these we must fire at with shot. We
have sambur or elk, jungle-sheep (another kind of deer)
and ibex, and perhaps bison ; for these we want ball. We
have also a chance of a tiger, or a leopard, and for these
we want several balls. For instance, the day before
yesterday, I went out early, rode about eight miles,
wounded a sambur, shot a hare, missed a black monkey.
The party came home with one deer, one hare, and one
monkey. As we were riding homeward about six o'clock,
we were stopped by a 'Burgher,' or one of the agricultural
community, who, with frantic gestures, pointed to one of
his oxen, which, he said, had just been killed by a tiger.
There was the ox lying dead by the side of a brook, but
where was the tiger? He had gone into a small patch of
jungle, from whence he would issue at night, and make
his meal comfortably. We had no guns, it was late, and
we were riding home fast, so there was nothing to be done
but to promise the man to come out early the next morning, and finish off the tiger, who would probably gorge
himself so as not to be desirous to go far after supper.
Eight of us accordingly started early yesterday morning,
got to our ground pretty quickly, and, after a good deal of
consideration, took our places in pairs, so as to command
all the ground around the jungle. The tiger had, as was
expected, dragged the ox into the jungle, and, having
gorged himself, had sneaked off to a quiet spot to digest his
supper. The place was pointed out to us by the owner
of the ox, who had been on the watch all night, and had
no intention of allowing the brute who had taken such
liberties with his herd to get off scot free. We began to
beat the jungle ; a number of natives with drums threw
stones into the jungle in front of them, and the dogs beat
all the bushes, but no tiger made his appearance. The
ox was found, which turned out to be a yearling, of which

the tiger had eaten the hind legs and the sirloin. We then looked about, and conjectured that he had travelled about a quarter of a mile over a hill to a small jungle ; and accordingly proceeded to beat this. After a short time out dashed a leopard, at which no fewer than ten barrels were fired.   These turned him back into the jungle, and he foolishly went up a tree, from which he was dislodged by a ball, or rather half-a-dozen. He then took refuge in a patch of jungle covering the two sides and bottom of a small nullah or ravine—it was not more than thirty yards square —and from this he would not move. That he was alive was very evident, for he damaged some dogs which ventured too near him, and made himself heard occasionally by a savage growl. The question was how to get at him ? We tried to fire at the spot from whence the growls came, but this produced no effect. We then tried to set fire to the jungle, but it would not burn.   At last a Colonel H——, who showed more pluck than the rest of us, went down, with two shikarries in front of him, to open the bush and enable him to get a sight of the leopard.   He caught a glimpse of him, and fired a ball ; this was replied to by a roar, which frightened the shikarries, who, jumping back, upset Colonel H—— and ran over him, setting a number of others running also : they all thought the animal was after them.   Another shot, however, from a shikarri whose eyes were better than ours, finished the animal, and we brought him home in triumph.   We were obliged to have him watched, or the Burghers would have cut off his whiskers and claws as amulets.   We also brought in an old wild boar which was shot afterwards.   The leopard is much smaller than the tiger, but is said to show more fight when wounded ; and I can testify to the fact of the unpleasant sound of his roar when near ; for I was crossing the nullah, in order to see whether I could not look down upon him from the other side, when I heard a roar apparently not a yard from my ear.   I was up the opposite bank in an instant. This is a long explanation of the necessity of having several guns. I do not intend, however, to get in the way of either tiger or elephant.

September 8.—Tell the Admiral that I killed a fine sambur yesterday; a fellow much larger than a red deer. I sat for two hours waiting patiently while the dogs and beaters were working down a large cover; and at last my shikarri touched me, and pointed to a spot, whispering 'Stag sare!' I saw nothing at first, but at last I made out a pair of horns moving about; after a little time the stag moved forward eight or ten yards, and I then fired a little below what I guessed to be his head, and hit him in the chest. He plunged round, and I gave him another ball in the hind quarter; he got about fifty yards into the wood, and there the shikarri came up with him and finished him. I brought his head home; he looked a monster when on the ground. I am going off to-morrow for two or three days to a distant part of the district, coupling business with pleasure. But this letter must go. Best love to you all.

Your affectionate Brother,
W. D.

To Miss Hornby.

Ootacamund, September 28, 1861.

My dear M——,—Since I sent off my last letter to you, I have had a mixed exploring and shooting expedition, of which I must give you an account. We started early on Monday, 23, and rode to our camp, stopping occasionally to beat the sholas or woods near the line of march. We got to our camp about four o'clock, and found everything prepared. I had a subaltern's tent, and, in order that you may form some idea of how subalterns are treated in India, I will give you a sketch of it. It was a marquee eighteen feet square in the inside, with a closed passage between the outer and inner tents, four feet in width.

In this, my bath was placed, my baggage stowed away, and my servants lodged. Inside the tent there was room for a bed, table, dressing-table, three or four chairs and arm-chairs, &c; the whole must have been a load for at least three camels, so you may imagine what a train must follow an Indian army. On Tuesday morning we were up early, and on horseback before six o'clock, in order to be at the top of Makoortie Peak before the mist from the low country rose. We rode up the valley of the Pykara river for two or three miles, crossing the stream several times. We then began to ascend a spur by a series of sharp zigzags, and were able to ride up till within about three hundred feet of the top of the peak. Here we had to dismount, and clamber to the top, which was literally a peak, going sheer down on one side to the depth of seven or eight hundred feet, and sloping rapidly to the right and left, as well as on the side by which we ascended. The view from the top was indeed glorious : to the right, that is, over the precipice, we looked down, 1,500 feet, into a dark valley, on the opposite side of which rose a peak to about the same height as that on which we stood, having a background of mountains in the distance. To the front—that is, facing westward—we had in the foreground the two other peaks composing the summit of Makoortie, which means three-peaked : beyond these the eye dropped at once into the low country of Malabar, more than 6,000 feet below us. This was covered with alternations of forest and glade, had hills of peculiar shapes rising up from the general level, was dotted about with white fleecy clouds floating three thousand feet below us ; and, in the distance, though hardly visible at the time, was the sea, some seventy miles away. We turned to the left, and there was a total change of scene. We looked first over some green slopes descending steeply, and these led the eye down into a deep and almost black chasm, beyond which rose the scarped sides of a range of hills nearly as high as that on which we stood, with spurs projecting from them at intervals, the spaces or gorges between these being of the darkest purple, brought out more strongly by the contrast between this background and the light fleecy clouds floating halfway up the slopes, or the white threads of waterfalls pouring down into the black abyss below. I never saw such a magnificent scene before. The peak where we stood is held sacred by the Todas, one of the hill tribes ; from the highest point the soul of the defunct Toda, accompanied by those of the buffaloes sacrificed by his friends and relatives, is supposed to take its last flight, where to I cannot say. The jump is a grand one. Three of our party commenced sketching this scene, but it is one to which pencil and brush can hardly do justice. We had our breakfast at the base of the actual peak, and intended to return by another route to the point where we began to ascend, but the mist came up so thick from the low country that we were glad to get into the zigzag path by which we came up.

My brother and I started the next morning early to look after some ibex ; and after a long stalk, I was deluded into going down a steep hill, at the bottom of which our shikarries had seen a herd. The going down was easy enough, though, as we had to keep out of view of the animals, we had to slip down on our backs. At last I was planted behind a rock, and there, not twenty yards from me, was an animal like a horned sheep, lying on a flat rock. I fired, of course in a hurry, and missed him ! fired the second barrel as he darted off, and missed him again ! Just fancy, all this labour for nothing ! and just fancy the intense disgust of the shikarri ; but, above all, picture to yourself my face when I looked back, and saw the hill up which I had to clamber, rising 1,500 feet above me ! I was thoroughly beat before I got to the top, and was only too glad to get on my horse and ride home. We returned here on Thursday, and found the children

with colour in their cheeks, and fat and well. I shall
keep them up here till November 1, that L—— may have
a chance of seeing them in good looks.

Your affectionate Brother,

W. D.

To Lord Elgin.

Ootacamund, October 3, 1861.

My dear Lord,—Will you allow me to congratulate
you on your appointment to the Governor-General-ship of
India, and to express the gratification which it will be to
me to work out in the Madras Presidency those general
political arrangements which you may consider best suited
to the peculiar condition of this great empire?

I trust that you will, on your way to Calcutta, stop at
Madras, and afford me an opportunity of talking over
with you sundry subjects, as to which my views differ
from those of my predecessor; and with reference to one
of which at least (the location of Europeans in India), I
am almost afraid that I am at issue with the Government
—I mean as to the policy of encouraging the settlement
of Europeans in India. I am aware that there is a great
demand, at present, for the introduction, as it is termed, of
British capital and British science—two very useful articles,
certainly, and if they could be introduced without the in-
cumbrance of the owners it would be very well; but the
fact is, as soon as you encourage the settlement of any number of them, they, as was the case with the indigo-planters,
get into trouble with the natives, and then call upon the
Government for assistance. I have a number of coffee-
planters in the hills, and Sir C. Trevelyan, after listening to
their complaints, ordered that the whole country should be
surveyed, that large sums of money should be expended
upon roads, looking upon it as a step in the way to
what he termed Anglo-Indian colonisation. The result of
these measures has been an outlay considerably in advance

of the receipts from the coffee planters, who only pay to the Government two rupees per acre upon the area under crop. Should any outbreak occur, these men will be a source of weakness instead of strength to the Government ; I shall be obliged to send troops to protect them, and thus weaken the force disposable for active operations. There is another point of view from which I wish you to contemplate the settlement of Europeans in India. My experience has shown me that the first step taken by settlers in a colony is to demand assistance from the Government, while the second is to claim political privileges ; that is, to insist upon representation. I firmly believe that, with a few scattered people, dotted about here and there, engaged in mercantile speculations, these claims might safely be ignored, but when we have them by hundreds—when the Manchester Cotton Association multiplies its transactions, and sends agent after agent to India—when we have irrigation companies, railway companies, &c. &c., we shall be flooded with Englishmen in no way under control of the Government, and shall find it difficult to withstand claims which will be pressed upon the Government by members of the House of Commons, some of whom may be political fanatics, but others who will merely wish to make political capital for themselves out of any question which may be mooted ; but, whether fanatic or trading politician, each and both will be perfectly ignorant of the state of society in India, or the operation of the measures which they advocate upon the Indian people, the millions whom we fancy we are about to leaven with our very minute particle of English yeast. I have written more at length than I intended, and must apologise for troubling you ; but I have always liked to have the views of different minds upon any given subject, and I have dealt with you as I should have wished to be treated myself.   Believe me, yours very truly,

W. DENISON.

In the summer of 1861, I received a copy of the Act of Parliament making regulations for the establishment of the Council of the Governor-General and of the Governors of the Presidencies; it was, of course, too late to do aught but record opinions; and this I did in a letter to the Secretary of State, bringing forward again my objections to these heterogeneous legislative bodies, composed partly of officials and partly of nominees.

I pointed out also to Sir C. Wood, that the Act had been framed with such ingenious perversity as to limit, or I might almost say nullify, the power of the local councils to deal with local matters; while it yet afforded them an opportunity of dealing with subjects of a more general character; so that there would be soon in existence four bodies, three local and one general, each of which would have power to legislate separately upon the same subjects.

Towards the end of 1861, I had to bring before the Secretary of State some correspondence between the Government of India and that of Madras, curiously illustrative of what I had said a few months before, showing how possible it was for a local legislature to take a view altogether different from the Council of the Governor-General on a given subject, and that a subject of importance.

Some papers were forwarded to me by the Governor-General, having reference to the sale of waste land, and to the redemption of the existing land revenue or rent, at a certain number of years' purchase. I believe the subject was pressed upon the Government by English capitalists, who were at that time anxious to invest their money in land which would, they believed, yield them a large interest when cultivated with cotton, sugar, coffee, &c.; but with this I had nothing to do. I was, however, directed to have a bill drawn up, giving effect to both these measures, and it behoved me to consider the subject

carefully. Now the question of the redemption of the
land revenue had been referred to the Government of
Madras in 1859 by Lord Stanley, and had elicited a
distinct expression of opinion that such redemption would
be unadvisable. I, too, had been thinking over the
subject very carefully in connection with a proposal of
Colonel Baird Smith to make the existing *money* assessment perpetual, and had arrived at the conclusion that
it would be decidedly unwise to sell the assessment; that
is, to enable the ryot to turn his *leasehold* into a *freehold*.
In the teeth, however, of this conviction, I was directed
to bring in a bill, to the principle of which both I and the
members of my Council were opposed. I could, of course,
only send the bill back to the Governor-General with a
statement of our objections, and call the attention of the
Secretary of State to the necessity of defining, more strictly
than had been done, the sphere of action of the different
legislative bodies and Governments. Some two years
afterwards, further experience of the tendency of the
Councils to take different views of the same subject
led to a proposal, on the part of the Governor-General,
that all attempts at legislation should be submitted, in the
first instance, for his consideration and approval. This
would have rendered the local legislation a mere non-
entity, and the proposal was not acceded to; but the
very fact that such a proposal was made is sufficient to
show that this specimen of the collective wisdom of the
nation was by no means faultless.

While I was on the Neilgherries, in 1861, several complaints were brought before me by the coffee-planters in
Wynaad, a district at the top of the Western Ghauts, but
about three thousand feet below the Neilgherries. The
burden of these was the want of means of communication. The settlers required access to the table-land of
Mysore, on the one side, as from it they procured both
labour and the means of feeding that labour; to the sea-

coast on the other, as from the ports on that coast they shipped their produce for England and elsewhere.

These complaints, while I did my best to aid and advise the planters, led me to look closely into the general question of ' Anglo-Indian Colonisation,' and to consider whether it was wise or not to encourage it. The term ' Anglo-Indian Colonisation ' is one of those high-sounding phrases which, as my experience has shown me, are generally used to cover an attempt to deceive either individuals or the Government. In the present case, the object was to deceive the Government. There was no attempt at ' colonisation,' properly so called ; the English capitalists who invested their money in indigo and coffee plantations were in no proper sense of the word colonists, but merely men seeking a profitable investment for the money lying dead on their hands. The bait held out to attract the Government was the idea that, by giving to such persons facilities for the investment of capital in these undertakings, a nucleus would be formed, round which might be gathered an European population, a population upon whom dependence might be placed in case of any difficulty or outbreak like that of 1857.

I questioned the wisdom of this policy, for I could not shut my eyes to the fact that these detached plantations would be an element of weakness, and not of strength ; that, instead of helping the Government and banding together to maintain themselves, the Government would have to detach troops to secure them from insult. It is true that the introduction of European capital into a country like India, where money is dear, would be a great advantage, and the active brain of the European would also be of use ; as soon, however, as the owners of capital and brains congregate together, there is a tendency, among Englishmen, to corporate action ; and this in India, and other countries analogously situated, shews itself, not in joint exertions for the improvement of the district, but in pressing upon the Government claims for special consideration ; for large outlays of money from the general revenue for making roads, &c., and for diminished payment of rent or land assessment. My predecessor had encouraged these Anglo-Indian colonists, had reduced the assessment in Wynaad, had set on foot a survey both of land and titles, in order to simplify to them the process of purchasing land from the natives ; he had also, at the Neilgherries, established a *quasi*-corporate body, for the purpose of spending, not their own money, but that of the Government. I had to check this tendency, as leading to a wasteful expenditure of public money, and as giving help to those who needed it least.

Another objection to the extension of Anglo-Indian colonisation was, to my mind, the tendency on the part of Englishmen to claim for themselves political privileges analogous to those which they possessed in England. Demands are made for ' representation,' for what they choose to call their inherent rights as Englishmen ; and these claims find supporters in the House of Commons, where few members give themselves the trouble to enquire whether the existence of such rights is consistent with the peculiar tenure by which we hold possession of India. They look into these questions with reference to the claims of A or B, and neglect the rest of the alphabet ; and they never dream of enquiring what took A or B into a country where he must have been aware that he could not claim any political status.

After thinking over the subject very carefully, the conclusion I came to was, that it would be unwise to encourage the introduction of any number of Europeans unconnected with the Government, and still more unwise to give to these stray sheep any special political status. The natives we can govern in the true sense of the word ; they will not ask to be allowed to govern themselves, and if they are foolish enough to make such a request, there is a very ready and correct answer, ' You are not able to do so.'

This answer, however, cannot be made to English mer- chants or planters; they have a natural tendency to insist upon having something to say to the Government of the country in which they reside, and when they once get astride upon their political hobby, they lose all considera- tion for the road on which they ride, or for the other passengers travelling along it. The following extract from a letter of Bishop Heber to Charles Wynn, dated March 1, 1825, will corroborate, to a certain extent, what I have said above.

' The indigo-planters are chiefly confined to Bengal, and I have no wish that their number should increase in India. They are always quarrelling with and oppressing the natives, and have done much in those districts in which they abound to sink the English character in the natives' eyes; indeed, the general character of the lower order of Europeans in India is such as to show the absurdity of free colonisation.'

I can fully bear out the testimony of Heber, and I am quite certain that the effect of inducing the English to settle largely in India will be most prejudicial to the peace, and I may say also to the prosperity, of the country, as this must be dependent upon the quiet submission of the people to the Government, which can never be the case where there is a perpetual blister in the shape of grumbling settlers irritating the body politic.

CHAPTER XIX.

JOURNEY TO WEST COAST—RECEPTION AT BEYPORE—SEDASHEGUR—
GAIRSOPPAH FALLS—BISON—TRANSFER OF NORTH CANARA TO BOMBAY—
CORRESPONDENCE ON CONSTITUTION OF LEGISLATIVE COUNCILS—GNEISS
—LIMIT OF THE SOUTH-WEST MONSOON—MANGALORE—GERMAN MISSION
—SMELL OF THE SEA—ITS CAUSE—STEEL WORKS—BESSEMER PROCESS—
SNAKE BOATS—WUNDOOR—INOPPORTUNE VISIT FROM A RAJAH—RETURN
TO THE NEILGHERRY HILLS—PROPOSED PUBLICATION OF A NATURAL
HISTORY OF INDIA—LADY D——'S RETURN TO MADRAS—BALL AT THE
BANQUETING HALL—PRINCE AZEEM JAH—GUINDY PARK.

To W. E. Denison, Esq.

Calicut, October 9, 1861.

MY DEAR WILLY,—We left Ootacamund early on the
morning of the 7th on a trip to the west coast. We
breakfasted at Coonoor, went down the ghaut in the
afternoon, getting into our transits at the bottom, and
reached the Collector's house at Coimbatore about half-past
eleven at night. We left Coimbatore the next morning,
having to go about four miles to the station, and we started
by train at half-past eleven for the west coast. The road
for about twenty miles was over a very bare country;
to the south there was a brown plain extending some
forty miles to a range of hills which form the continuation
of the Western Ghauts; to the north, at a short distance,
rose a very marked and peculiar range of hills, varied
both in form and colour, but exhibiting very scanty
evidence of the presence of soil. The rock of which these
are composed is gneiss, tilted up at a very high angle, the
sides being smooth and bare, while in the crevices, where
the edges of the strata collect the water, there is soil and
moisture enough to nourish a few bushes.

The railroad was not complete to the west coast; we

had to pass over a break of about seven miles in bullock transits, which delayed us a good deal, but we got to Beypore about half past six. There we were welcomed with the usual display of lights, flowers, &c. We had to drive about ten miles to Calicut, where we were to take up our abode with the Collector. We crossed the river on a sort of raft composed of two canoes lashed together; the platform forming the raft being very gaily and tastefully decorated with chains of flowers, bright-coloured elephant's trappings, and tassels of cocoa-nut leaves twisted into various shapes. We landed among a crowd of the native population, a mixture of Moplas (Mahometans) and Nairs (Hindoos), and, getting into our carriages, found the road, for the whole distance to Calicut, crossed at every fifty yards with festoons of flowers, banana leaves and fruit, &c., while the whole population turned out, some running by the side of the carriages, with torches of dry cocoa-nut leaves, which they swung in a most reckless way amongst each other's legs and light cotton or muslin garments, others performing all sorts of antics. As some fell out, others took their places, and the effect was that of a continuous crowd for nearly ten miles. I had no conception that the Mahometan, whom one is apt to consider a very staid, sober person, could cut such capers as some of the Moplas did. To-day I have had the principal officers of the district with me; to-morrow I have a durbar, when the natives are to present themselves. We embark to-morrow evening on board a Government steamer, which is lying off Calicut, and sail up the coast to Sedashegur, which we expect to reach on Saturday.

Your affectionate Father,

W. D.

To F. G. Denison, Esq.

Sedashegur, October 12, 1861.

My dear Frank,—We embarked at Calicut on the 10th, the vessel, a small Government steamer, lying about a mile and a half from the shore, in five fathoms water with a very muddy bottom. We had a pleasant run up here of about thirty-six hours, sea calm, sea breeze decently cool. We got here before daybreak. All was clear outside the Heads, but as soon as we passed these we plunged into a sea of fog, through which we had some difficulty in finding our way to the anchorage. The 'Feroze,' which is to take us back, was lying in the bay, as also a surveying vessel, which had been left here during the whole of the south-west monsoon, in order to test the capabilities of the place. The captain of this craft did not speak in high terms of the comfort or safety of his position. Sedashegur is a sort of bay formed by the projection of Carwar Head, a bold promontory extending about two miles beyond the general line of the coast. There is deep water—that is, from four to five fathoms—close along the north side of Carwar Head, the ground of which rises a hundred or a hundred and fifty feet pretty steeply. I fancy that at some no very distant period Carwar was an island, for the land connecting it with the coast is quite low; indeed, it is nothing but a sand bank rising a few feet above the sea, and planted with cocoa-nut trees. There are a few islands to seaward, but these are too small to afford shelter to vessels against the action of the south-west monsoon, or to break in any way the heavy sea which rolls in upon the coast for the three or four months during which this lasts. The captain of the surveying vessel had anchored as near the north shore of Carwar Head as he could, but the wind veered about, sometimes eddying through the gap between the head and the main land, sometimes getting northing

into it, and whistling round the head, bringing with it a
nasty short sea which broke about a cable's length outside
of him.   Had his ground tackle failed, he must have gone
on shore ; for he could not have weathered the islands outside.   As it was, he had held out ; but he told me that two
vessels coming in before the gale, and luffing up to get
into the anchorage, had been caught in the trough of the
sea and gone bodily on shore.   I had reported against the
attempt to make this place a harbour upon the sight of
the plans which were sent to me.   I am glad, however,
that I came here, and have satisfied myself, on the spot,
that this opinion was a correct one.   S—— and I are living
in a chupper, or cottage run up with bamboos and cocoa-
nut leaves ; the front is open to the sea breeze, and it is
much cooler than a tent.   The rest of the party—consisting of Commodore Wellesley, the Hon. Mr. Frere,
and two of the staff of Sir George Clerk, the Collector,
Mr. Fisher, and his daughter, and my own companions
—were similarly accommodated, or had tents ; while one
large tent, looking out to seaward and open to the sea
breeze, was our sitting and dining room.

Gairsoppah Falls, October 17.—We left Sedashegur
on the 14th, in the middle of the day, and ran down the
coast. about forty miles to the mouth of the river, which
runs into the sea at Honore, where we arrived about four
o'clock.   We sent off our servants and baggage at once,
proposing to follow in the evening, and to pull up the river
about twenty-six miles during the night ; but when it
came to the point, the boatmen objected to cross the
surf in the dark, so we could not start till the morning.
We got off about five o'clock, and found no surf to signify ;
and, on seeing the river, I was very glad that we had not
lost such beautiful scenery by going up during the night.
There was pretty ground on the banks, partially cleared in
places, and dotted about with cocoa-nut trees ; while from
time to time we caught a sight of a high range of hills in

the distance. We stopped to breakfast in a cocoa-nut grove, and quenched our thirst with fresh cocoa-nut milk, which was cool, and by no means bad when mixed with a little sherry. We found the boats rather hot, notwith-standing the protection of a sort of after-cabin ; but about ten o'clock the sea breeze caught us up, and enabled us to make use of a sort of square sail, both accelerating our movements and cooling us. We reached the end of our navigation about one o'clock, landing at the site of a village, the inhabitants of which had some years before been swept away by fever. We there found ' muncheels,' or hammocks, slung upon bamboos, ready for us, and as we had no wish to remain longer than necessary in a place with such a character, we started at once. The mun-cheel is fairly comfortable when you are once in, but the getting in is a feat requiring no inconsiderable agility. The hammock is slung so near to the pole that sitting is impossible, and one has to wriggle in sideways and lie prostrate. There is a sort of cover to keep off the sun, and one is carried by four men, who are relieved by four others from time to time, eight being the number attached to each muncheel. These men carried us up the ghaut, a distance of twenty miles, with a rise of 1,800 feet, in little more than six hours ; and we got to our bungalow and tents, just above the falls, by eight o'clock, having stopped for half an hour on the way to have some tea, and rest our bearers.

We got on our arrival as good a sight of the falls as the light of the moon would admit of ; but next morning early we went across the river above the falls, and break-fasted under an arbour which had been constructed at a spot from which there was a glorious view of all four falls. The main, or ' Rajah ' fall, drops clear 820 feet ; the next, or the ' Roarer,' rushes down a sloping crevice for about 250 feet, and then drops into the pool which receives the water of the main fall. The third, or the

'Rocket,' is, if anything, a little higher than the main fall, but it does not carry such a body of water, and is broken against rocks. The fourth, or 'La Dame Blanche,' is split by projecting rocks into several little streams, which fall gently in wreaths of mist.

In the height of the monsoon the whole four falls are merged into one, and a grand sight it must be to see a body of water at least 300 yards in width precipitated into such a deep chasm. Below the fall the river is squeezed in between rocks, and must be a boiling cauldron during the wet season. The rock over which the river tumbles is a hard gneiss, tilted up at a high angle; the stratification is very marked, and here and there the water finds a soft bed, as in the case of the 'Roarer,' and works its way along it. It is difficult, if not impossible, to get a sight of the falls from such a distance as would enable one to form any idea of the height; one is obliged to look at them from a point so near that, whether one looks up or down, the foreshortening does away with the idea of height or depth. We were discussing the propriety of attempting to descend to get a sight from below, and were almost inclined to make the attempt, in spite of what we heard of the leeches which swarmed among the wet grass and shrubs, when the account of a herd of bison, at a distance of two miles, settled the question for us, and induced us to get our guns and start off in search of them. The two miles kept extending till they reached five, and the herd of bison diminished, till it got to one solitary bull. However, we got up to him at last, and having posted our party so as to ensure a shot to some one, the men began to beat. After a time the bison came out, about a hundred yards from me, and about fifteen from V——, my aide-de-camp. I fired and missed him, but V—— fired both barrels, and certainly hit the animal hard. He managed, however, to keep on his legs, and got off for the night at all events; though, as some men were set upon his track, they may come up with and finish him. Bisons are said to have been seen twenty-one hands, or seven feet, high in the withers; but I do not think that ours was above fifteen hands; I could only see a sort of brownish-grey mass as big as a horse when I fired. We got back to the bungalow about six o'clock, very tired. In the evening we let down some blue lights and bundles of blazing straw in front of the large fall, which lighted it up beautifully.

Your affectionate Father,
W. D.

To Sir George Clerk.[1]

Sedashegur, October 15, 1861.

My dear Sir George,—I must steal an hour or so from Sunday to write to you upon certain matters connected with this place, and upon one or two other subjects which I have discussed with Frere. I am sorry that you were unable to meet me here, and still more that you are in the hands of the doctors. I feel certain that a few weeks in the Neilgherries would set you up, and should I not be there, my house, &c., is quite at your disposal. From Beypore now you can reach Coimbatore easily in one day; the next day would take you to Ootacamund. Nothing would please me more than to think that you had benefited by such a trip.

Now for Sedashegur. You will have heard from the commodore and from Captain Fraser the *facts* relative to the silting up of the harbour, and to the character of the wind and sea during the monsoon months. A personal inspection of the place has convinced me that it would be most unwise on the part of the Government to commence any large works under the idea that this might be made a place of great traffic. In the first place, the engineering difficulties are of a character which it would be impossible to surmount, unless at a cost far exceeding that

---

[1] Governor of Bombay.

which a Government would be justified in incurring; and, in the second place, the traffic to and from this place, shut in as it is by mountains, would necessarily be very limited. A few ships would carry off all the exportable produce, and fewer still would bring to this place all the articles which the people in the back country consume. Mr. H—— is one of those men who, in dealing with large concerns, cannot condescend to the minutiæ of arithmetic; and is disposed to think that Dharwar cotton will come down in quantities sufficient to freight a fleet; but a little consideration will show the fallacy of this. An acre of cotton will yield, perhaps, fifty pounds of clean cotton; that is, forty-five acres will produce a ton, 45,000 acres will load a ship, 450,000 acres will load ten ships. Now it may be, though I doubt it, that Dharwar will yield this quantity; but when the cultivation extends over such an area as this, the chances are that it will be found cheaper to take a portion of the produce to some other port. In fact, each shipping place on the coast is the receptacle of the produce of a section of country varying in size in proportion to the facility of transport. I have had a long talk with Mr. H—— as to the wants of the company, and the best mode of meeting them; and I will see that these are at once provided for; that is, if they are in any way reasonable. Now as to the arrangements for the transfer of this district, or a portion of it, to Bombay. This, as I told you before, is strongly objected to by the members of my Council, and since I have been on the spot, and have heard the reasons which have been urged in favour of it, I confess I am quite disposed to agree with them. Nothing, it appears to me, would justify such a severance of the relations which exist between the people and those to whom they have been accustomed to look up, but some very special necessity; here there does not appear to be any necessity at all. Mr. H——, it is true, says that his communications with the Government will be facilitated if Bombay is to be his place of reference ; but I cannot think that the convenience (if indeed it be a convenience) of a single merchant or firm is to overbalance the wishes and the convenience of the population at large : besides, as I said to Mr. H——— yesterday, what communication can the members of a Manchester firm have to make to the Government? I have hundreds of merchants dotted about the country, and they never find it necessary to bother me with their private affairs. I am afraid that Mr. H———, big with the idea that he is the representative of the Cotton Supply Association, will be delivered of a variety of crude schemes based upon the principle of encouragement to cotton, that is *protection*, very much at variance with those which were advocated by his principals when they fought *against* protection. The further he is from the seat of Government the better, for the Government at all events.

Now as to the Legislative Council. I had written ' representative,' I suppose as a sort of foreshadowing of that to which these legislative experiments would tend. I talked over with Frere and my principal secretary the replies to be returned to the queries submitted by the Governor-General. As to the time of meeting, we agreed that December, or thereabouts, would answer our purpose ; we decided that the Council should not sit permanently, but be called together when wanted ; we sketched out some of the general rules or standing orders, and came to an understanding as to the number of members, &c. There are, however, one or two matters as to which I should wish to have your views. Frere thinks that you are in favour of the introduction of natives, but he does not profess to speak with authority. My idea is that the introduction of the native element can do no good, and may do much harm. Frere advocates it under the idea that, as the natives must rule the country some time or another, we had better begin to teach them to do so. I take quite the contrary view; we have won the country by the sword, and I see no reason why we should not retain it by the same means, and govern it. As to inducing the natives to carry on the government under our supervision, I should, I confess, have a very much lower opinion of them than I have (and I have by no means a high one) were they to submit for an instant to our rule, did they see any chance of getting rid of it. So while I would train and educate them, I would not put power into their hands, or trust them beyond what is necessary. I do not want, therefore, to have a native in my Council. He may be able to speak English, but he cannot divest himself of the idea that he is not in his place, that he is only there on tolerance, that, in fact, his presence as a *quasi*-representative of India is but a sham. The next question is as to the admission of the public to the consultations. I am decidedly opposed to this. Give, if you like, full reports of proceedings; but I do not like to change the character of our deliberative body, and to make it a sort of debating society; neither do I think that it would harmonise with the position of a Governor, were he to discuss questions with his Council under the eyes and in the hearing of the public. Constituted as the Council will be, especially if natives are admitted, the colloquial form of discussion will be by far better suited for the conduct of business than that which will prevail if the public are to be present, and men speak, not to the president, but to the editors of newspapers. I think these are the main points at issue at present. It is so desirable that we should act together, and upon one principle, that I should be glad to meet your views if possible; so pray let me know them. Trusting that this will find you in better health,

Believe me, yours very truly,

W. D.

The result of the correspondence relative to the transfer of North Canara to the Bombay Government was that the greatest portion of the district was so handed over, and the works for the conversion of the bay into a harbour, and a safe shipping and landing place for goods, were undertaken by that Government energetically. Mr. H——, too, as the representative and agent of the Cotton Supply Association, selected the spot as a sort of head-quarters, and commenced his share of the work at once. He got land from the Government on the shore of the bay, as he did not like the idea of the additional mile or so of road, &c., which would have been required to take the cotton to Carwar Head by the side of the deep water; he got out machinery for cleansing and packing cotton, and he began to erect the necessary buildings; but, as might have been expected, the two parties at work upon the joint scheme soon found that their interests did not harmonize. Mr. H—— and the company wished to get a rapid return for their outlay; the Government, finding itself called upon to complete a much larger undertaking than it had calculated upon, and to finish it off rapidly, began to suspect that it had been made a cat's paw of. It found that the revenue of the district which had been transferred from Madras was but a mere trifle when compared with the outlay it was called upon to make, and it began to question the propriety of most of the details of the scheme, and, inferentially, the wisdom of the plan itself. Fevers of a very malignant character decimated the labourers brought in to make the road up the ghaut to the high land of Dharwar, and, under the influence of these various causes, the works progressed but slowly. It was found that, owing to Mr. H——'s preference for the main land, a long jetty was required to enable the cotton to be placed even on board boats, so that when I left India in 1866, the work so energetically talked of and arranged in 1861 was as yet in its infancy, and I am

led to understand now that the buildings and machinery
of the association have been sold for a very moderate sum
—in fact, for next to nothing.

To Sir Roderick Murchison.

Gairsoppah Falls, October 17, 1861.

My dear Sir Roderick,—I want your solution of the
origin of 'gneiss.' Here I am at the edge of a magnificent fall, 820 feet in one sheer pitch. At present there is
not a great deal of water in the river, and there are four
distinct falls, besides a few subsidiary driblets ; but in the
monsoon, when the river above is full, there must be a
body of water three hundred yards wide, pitching head-
long into a chasm of the depth above mentioned. The
rock is gneiss, tilted up at a high angle, hard and angular
in appearance, but the water has found soft parts here
and there ; and in several cases it runs in crevices which
it has worn for itself. Now the rocks forming the mass
of the Neilgherries are also gneiss, but there they are in
many cases soft, almost in the state of clay, with veins of
broken quartz here and there, the quartz being angular,
not as if it had been subject to the rolling action of water.
There are, of course, masses of a harder material ; but
where deep excavations are made, the state of the strata
is such as I have described it. Now what was the primi-
tive state of gneiss—hard or soft ? if the latter, how has
it been hardened ? I came, above the falls, upon a dyke
of hard blue stone about two feet in width, crossing the
line of stratification ; and this seemed to be altered at the
edges where it was in contact with the gneiss. The
latter, however, appeared to have acted on the dyke,
not the dyke on the gneiss. The scenery about here is
beautiful ; the hills angular in outline, as might be expected ; below the hills—that is, between them and the
sea—there are numerous low, flat-topped hills composed of
' laterite,' a sort of vesicular material aggregated by iron,

of which it contains a large quantity; so large, indeed, as to admit of its being worked as an iron ore. When exposed to the air, the surface of the laterite is hard, but a little below the surface it is soft enough to be cut by a pickaxe, and in this state it is quarried extensively as a building material, being easily wrought into any form, while a short exposure to the air hardens it to about the consistency of a middling brick. I am writing hastily, as I am continually on the move, which must be the excuse for this short interrogatory letter.

Yours very truly,
W. D.

P.S.—On coming down by the railway to the west coast we passed through a gap in the Western Ghauts, about forty miles in width and 1,200 feet above the sea. The Neilgherries rise 8,500 feet to the north of this; the Anamullays 6,000 or 7,000 feet to the south. The space between is a brown dry plain. After passing over about twenty miles of this, on a gradual descent, we, all of a sudden, plunged into the richest possible tropical vegetation, there being no change in the soil. On enquiring into the cause of this, I was told that the line of the jungle marked the limit of the south-west monsoon; but why the monsoon should stop there I cannot tell. People informed me that a quarter of a mile was the amount of disputed territory between moisture and drought; that I might stand at one place, and get but a slight sprinkling of rain, while a movement westward of a hundred yards would bring me into a tropical downfall. I have seldom seen anything which struck me as more remarkable. Why should not the wind sweep the rain up the plain, seeing that it has brought it thus far? I am dealing in questions, but, in point of fact, these apparently trifling queries are most difficult to answer.

To Colonel Davidson, C.B. Resident, Hydrabad.

Mangalore, October 19, 1861.

My dear Sir,—I have only just received your letter of
September 30. I have been on the move ever since the
beginning of this month, which accounts for the delay.
Many thanks for the papers you have furnished, illustrating
the proceedings which you are taking to give to the
ceded districts the full benefit of the railroad, and the
Godavery navigation.

I trust I have not explained myself badly as to the
question of the Toombuddra Anicut. I quite concur with
you in the opinion that the claim to utilise the water of
the river for both banks is fair and reasonable; we have,
it is clear, no right to make use of the land of another
proprietor without giving him compensation, or advantages in return; it was a conviction of the correctness of
this principle which made me draw a parallel between
the works on the Godavery and those on the Toombuddra.

You will, long before this, have received an official communication from the Government of Madras, inclosing
plans, &c., of Captain Haig's proposed road round the
barrier as a temporary expedient. This will be partly on
the Nizam's territory, and it will be advisable that his
permission should be obtained for its construction.

I will take care that you are kept fully informed as to
the works which are projected, their object, cost, time of
completion, &c.

I can quite understand the incapacity of the Nizam to
comprehend the principles of political economy. I have
no doubt that he would object to *exports*, as tending to
raise prices; but he would be open, *perhaps*, to the argu-
ment that the improvement of the navigation would tend
to cheapen *imports*; and would probably jump at the
idea of raising a revenue from them by the imposition of
duties. I do not expect any assistance from the Nizam

in the construction of the Godavery works ; all that I want
is permission to work in his territory, which work, however,
would involve a right of exit and entrance, and also a
right to consider the works, when complete, as my own.
I will illustrate my meaning by submitting a case. It is
necessary to cut a canal round one of the barriers or
rapids, and this can only be done with advantage on the
territory of the Nizam.

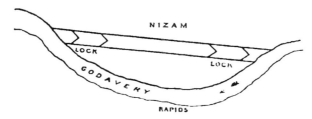

Now we must not only have his leave to construct this,
but it must be transferred to us in property ; in fact, we
ought to have the whole of the land between the canal
and the river in order to secure ourselves from difficulties.

I will not, however, trouble you more on this subject
at present ; I have only written for the purpose of explanation. I will take care that everything is communicated
to you which can either affect the Nizam, or the ceded
districts, feeling certain of your co-operation.

Believe me, yours very truly,
W. D.

To Miss Hornby.

Mangalore, October 19, 1861.

My dear M———,—We left the Gairsoppah Falls on the
17th, in the afternoon, having been very well pleased
with our visit. I should have liked very much to have
had a good sketch of the place, but I do not believe that
such a thing could be made so as to give any conception
of the height of the fall. We went on the morning of
the 17th to a spot opposite the main fall, and about a

hundred or a hundred and fifty feet below the top, but we could not get any conception of the depth below us. There were flocks of pigeons flying in and out behind the fall; they had their nests in the crevices of the rock, I suppose, but they must have had very damp beds. We went down the hill in muncheels, as we came up; and, to our great satisfaction, found that the collector had pitched tents at the landing-place, and provided a capital supper for us, to which we did great honour. We embarked at ten o'clock at night, and got to the mouth of the river about four o'clock A.M. We had some difficulty in inducing the boatmen to face the surf, though there was a fine moon; however, we managed to screw them up to make the attempt, which succeeded, for there was not even a shadow of a break in the rollers, and we got on board before six o'clock, and were soon under way. We reached this place about half-past four P.M., and the collector came off to tell us that there was no surf; we got into the river, therefore, without a wetting, and as the tide was low, we were carried in tonjauns to the landing-place. Nothing can be prettier than the towns on the west coast: the streets are clean and well kept; everything looks tidy; and the houses stand back from the street, and are hidden among the cocoa-nut trees, except here and there where one peeps out, looking most picturesque. S—— and I are residing with the Judge, and are very comfortable. There is a broad space in front of the drawing and dining rooms, some thirty feet in width, open on three sides; a sort of magnified verandah, which is used as a drawing-room whenever the weather is fine—that is, for eight months in the year. Then I have a good sitting-room, opening into a verandah on two sides, and into my bed-room at the end, while S—— and her maid occupy the rooms next to me. I held a levée to-day for the European population, consisting principally of the officers of the two native regiments quartered here; and the Roman Catholic Bishop, who has resided here for thirty years, and some German missionaries were also introduced to me. We visited the establishments of these last; they have a sort of industrial school or manufactory here, and at other places along the coast. I could not understand that, as a proselytising establishment, they were very successful.

Your affectionate brother,

W. D.

To W. E. Denison, Esq.

Wundoor, October 23, 1861.

My dear Willy,—We left Mangalore on the 20th, pretty early, and reached Cannanore in the evening. During the whole of the distance we were nearly poisoned by the smell of the sea. I was at first disposed to accuse the captain of having his hold filled with bilge water, but when I took up my position just abaft the paddle I was compelled to admit that it was the sea which stank most abominably. At Cannanore I was told that this was always the case after the south-west monsoon. The quantity of fresh water poured into the sea, from a long line of coast upon which from 120 to 180 inches of rain fall in three months is the mode of accounting for this; the sea becomes nearly fresh water, the salt-water fish are killed, as also the sea-weed, and the water, under the action of a tropical sun, becomes very offensive, till it is mixed with the general body of sea water, and resumes its saltness. We saw thousands of dead fish floating on the sea, and the shore was covered with them. There is a small fort at Cannanore, built by the Dutch, which serves to contain our military stores for this side of India; it wants a little doing to it on the side of the sea, but would keep out any number of natives. The barracks, however, are on the level land outside of the fort, which is occupied by an ordinary guard. We left Cannanore on Monday evening, and got to Beypore early on Tuesday morning; landed at once, and, after breakfasting at the railway station, went up the river to inspect some iron works, at which the Bessemer process has been tried with success. The manager had everything prepared for us, and a furnace full of metal nearly melted, so that I had the pleasure of seeing the whole process. The metal was run from the furnace into a huge ladle; this was swung by a crane to a large pot, and the metal allowed to escape into this by a small opening in the side. As soon as the metal began to flow into the pot, the blast was turned on, acting through about a dozen $\frac{3}{4}$-inch blast pipes, the lines of direction of which were tangents to a circle of about twelve inches diameter in the centre of the pot. The effect of the blast was to create an intense flame, first of a blue, and then of a red colour, which, I was told, showed that the oxygen was combining with the silica and the phosphorus in the metal; then the flame got white, and after ten minutes the blast was stopped, and the metal run into moulds, being in the state of steel, that is of iron combined with a certain proportion of carbon. I was told that 100 lbs. of metal from the furnace would give 80 lbs. of steel, while by the old process of puddling, &c., the produce would have been only 70 lbs. of wrought iron, and the cost much greater. I was very much pleased with the intelligence of the manager, who was doing his work entirely with natives. After lunching at the iron works, we started up the river in 'snake boats,' being long wooden canoes pulled by five men forward, and steered, as well as aided a little, by two paddlers aft. In the middle of the vessel there was a sort of cabin, long enough for two people to lie at full length. We pulled about twenty miles up the river against the stream, and arrived shortly after sundown at a place called Ariacode, where a bungalow had been got ready for us. The boats' crews amused themselves by singing, and I could gather that their songs had some relation to me, for I heard the word Governor pretty constantly, accompanied by a shout of laughter. We started early in the morning, and pulled some seven miles further up the river, where our horses had been sent from the hills to meet us, and rode seven or eight miles to a place called Wundoor, where we found a bungalow and tents pitched for the accommodation of the party. The weather was oppressively hot, and we felt ourselves altogether unfit for any exertion.

In the midst of our listlessness, we were horror-struck at the announcement of the approach of a Rajah. He did not, however, stay long. He made S—— a present of two pea-fowls and two wild pigs; to me he gave a young bison, which I have left with the collector, who will try to rear him, and if he succeeds I shall send him to the Zoological Society. The Rajah had with him a fine elephant, and we tried to verify on him the statement that twice round the foot is equal to the height at the withers; but the animal thought, I suppose, that he was going to have a chain put round his leg, for he began to scream, and backed under a tree in order to knock off his mahout; and, failing this, he set off in a sort of wild canter, roaring and screaming. The mahout, however, had slipped off his back and held on to a chain round the neck of the animal, and very soon got into his seat again, and, by a proper exercise of a very unpleasant weapon, like a short and sharp boat-hook, brought him to his senses, and made him walk quietly away. We had intended to have remained at Wundoor, and shot elephants, &c., for a couple of days; but my private secretary was unwell, having an attack of fever; the weather was very hot, and the game a long distance off; so we decided not to wait, but to push on as fast as we could. Accordingly at two o'clock this morning we got into muncheels, and were carried to a small hut at the foot of the Sispara Ghaut. There we again met our horses; and a ride of twelve miles, during which we rose 6,000 feet, brought us to the bungalow at the top of the ghaut, where we found our camp pitched, and ourselves cool and comfortable, having exchanged the vapour bath of yesterday for an atmosphere where we were glad of a fire.

The hut at the foot of the ghaut is but a poor place; no one can live there, it is so feverish; it is fenced in, at about ten feet from the walls of the hut, by the strongest possible fence, in order to keep out the wild elephants. The posts are twelve inches square, and are let deep into the ground, and the horizontal bars are of corresponding dimensions. The elephants have, notwithstanding this, made more than once an attempt to get into the place. Some time ago a gentleman and his wife were coming down the ghaut in palanquins, and were met by a wild elephant. They had but just time to escape into the jungle before the animal was upon them, and it broke the leading palanquin to pieces. I heard one shortly after we left the hut, crashing through a sort of cane brake below me; but I made S——, who was with me, push on as fast as possible, and did not wait to reconnoitre the animal. We got to Ootacamund on the 27th, and found all well. God bless you, my dear boy.

Your affectionate Father,

W. D.

To Miss Hornby.

Ootacamund, October 28, 1861.

My dear M——,—The heat of the weather, the illness of my private secretary, and the wish to get to Ootacamund on Saturday, so as to have a quiet Sunday there, induced us to push on more rapidly than we had intended. We got to the top of the ghaut on Thursday, rode on Friday eighteen miles to the Avalanche Bungalow, and coming in on Saturday morning, found the little boys quite well. I hope to be able to show them to L—— in no way the worse for their nine months of India.

I find that at Madras and elsewhere, where there are schools for natives, the first effect produced by education is to destroy all belief in their old religion. On asking some clergymen engaged in the work of instruction whether they thought it wise to knock on the head the old belief before they attempted to substitute a better, I always got a reply in the affirmative. Now I am in doubt as to this. It seems to me like casting out the evil spirit and leaving the house empty. Substitute the principles of Christianity for those of Brahminism, let the strong man eject the weaker, and all will be well; but I am afraid that the disbelief in their own gods is not likely to be succeeded by a belief in our Saviour. The result is more likely to be a confidence in self and a love of self, which will produce as great, or greater, evils than a faith in Brahma. It strikes me that the difficulty we have to encounter in our attempts to turn the heathen to Christianity is the absence in them of a conviction of sin. Of course, unless there is this, there can be no possible conception of the value of our Saviour's sacrifice: they need not a Redeemer. Our first efforts, therefore, ought to be to convince these people of their sinfulness; not of the general sinfulness of man, but of their own individual sinfulness. When this is once done, then follow repentance and faith, and the heart is open to receive all the promises of the Gospel; without this, faith, being a mere belief in certain facts, is void.

We had a curious exhibition of the docility of the elephant at our camp at Sispara. Seven of these animals and sundry camels had been sent to convey our tents. It appears that it is the practice, at a certain time of day, to wash the elephants, and to give them an allowance of jaghêry (coarse sugar) and spices: this was done just below our bungalow, and S—— and I were looking on. One of the elephants, *a female* (showing the usual perversity of the sex), refused to lie down and be washed. In vain did the mahout drive his pointed weapon into her head, or pull her ear with the sharp hook; she only grumbled, and in the end gained her point, for she had the chatties of water poured over her, and her skin rubbed or holystoned with cocoa-nut shells, as she stood. The docile *male*, on the contrary, quietly laid himself down when he was told, and rolled himself from one side to the other as he was directed, without making any resistance; he now and then tried to raise his head, but was stopped at once by a pull at his ear.

I have had very kind letters from people in New South Wales and Van Diemen's Land. It is a great pleasure to find that we are remembered with something of an affectionate feeling, and that people are willing to give us pleasure even now, when I can neither benefit nor injure them. It is one of the greatest pleasures that I have, connected with the past, to think that I have secured many friends, and have made hardly a single personal enemy; and that I have secured this without compromising my duty in any way.

Your affectionate brother,
W. D.

To Lord Canning.

Madras, November 10, 1861.

My dear Lord,—Dr. Cleghorn was with me yesterday, and handed me the enclosed letter from Dr. Hooker to himself on the subject of a work on the botany of India. I had received a letter about this, by the last mail, from Sir William Hooker, and had written to him, suggesting that he should bring the matter in a positive form before the Government of India, when I would do my best to forward an undertaking of so beneficial a character. Dr.

Hooker's letter does this, and, as no time should be lost in commencing so extensive a work, I do not hesitate to bring it before you, even in this informal shape, in the hope that you may be induced to adopt the scheme, and to communicate officially with Dr. Hooker, so as to enable him to commence his work at once. His proposition is that he shall receive from each Presidency 100*l.* for each volume as it is completed and published; that is, practically, the Government of India is to pay 300*l.* for each volume, such volume to contain the description of some 1,200 to 1,500 species, and to be the work of a year. In fact, Dr. Hooker asks for 300*l.* per annum while he is thus engaged. This is a very trifling sum for the hire of the services of such a man, especially as the Government only pays for work done; and it is only because Dr. Hooker has other sources of income that he is able to make such an offer. This is to be the only remuneration to Dr. Hooker; but in order to enable the publisher to print the book, the Government will have to pledge itself to take a hundred copies, at a price not exceeding twenty or thirty shillings per volume, according as it is printed on small or large paper. I do not think that I need say more to induce you to take up the scheme. In Australia, the different colonies have combined, though they are separate and distinct political bodies, for the publication of a work on the Australian Flora; and it would be a disgrace to India, which is under one head, to be left behind by a few isolated communities dotted on the coast of that great country. While I am on the subject of natural sciences, will you allow me to allude to Dr. Jerdan's work on the zoology of India? He has sent to me, asking me to move the Government to subscribe liberally; that is, to take a good number of copies: but it appears to me that, as the work includes the whole of India, territories as well as presidencies, it should be set on foot by the general Government, the copies being distributed among the

different Governments as published. If, however, you
think that each Presidency should act for itself, I should
be quite willing to move the Government of Madras to
purchase or subscribe for fifty copies, or even more. Dr.
Jerdan says, in his letter to my private secretary, that he
has received every encouragement from you, and I should
be glad, I confess, to find that you had worked out
for India a problem which I failed to solve in Australia ;
namely, the publication by the Government of a natural
history of the country. With Hooker for the botany,
Jerdan for the zoology, and Oldham for the geology, you
will have nearly embraced the whole range of natural
history. You only want an account of the fishes (which
Dr. Day might furnish) of the invertebrata and the
insects ; and these will no doubt be taken up by competent hands, as soon as they see that the Government is
disposed to assist in such an undertaking.

Yours very truly,
W. D.

Extract from Journal.

Government House, Madras, November 12, 1861.

Dearest M——,—I cannot remember whether it was
to you or L—— that I wrote from Galle, but it does not
much signify. We got in there about the middle of the day
on Thursday, and, as it was blowing fresh from the south-
west, which always sends a heavy sea into the harbour of
Galle, I, and most of the other passengers, went on shore,
to spend a quiet night at the hotel. Cingalese hotels are
not first-rate in point of comfort, but still they are infi-
nitely better than the ship in a rolling sea, and the quiet
sleep at night was very refreshing. The next afternoon
we went on board again, and steamed off; the sea still
high, but less heavy than it had been, and gradually going
down. Moreover, I had had a cordial in the shape of a

telegraphic message from W——, intimating that he and the children had all just got safely from the hills; and this good account of them, up to the present time, put me in such good spirits that I cared comparatively little for the roughness. As soon as we had ' turned the corner,' round the south coast of Ceylon, we had the sea with us, and ever since our voyage has been smooth and pleasant— an unspeakable blessing, for there was something so un- usual in this south-westerly wind breaking in on the ordinary career of the north-east monsoon, that people had an idea that the strange change was the forerunner of an approaching hurricane. We arrived here yesterday morning. Before we came up to the anchorage, W——'s boat was seen putting off through the surf, and just as the anchor dropped he was alongside. You may imagine what that meeting was between us, after our long separa- tion; and you may suppose that the greater part of the day, after this, went in talk; and I did not attempt to touch my letters till to-day, though they must go to- morrow. So now I must end, in great thankfulness for having been brought to the end of my sea troubles, and for having had such a prosperous meeting with all here. Much love to all.

To Major-General Sandham.

Madras, November 23, 1861.

My dear Sandham,—Here I am back again at Madras after a three months' run on the hills, which has been to me like a run at grass to an old horse; it has set me up again, and been of the greatest benefit to my children. Here I cannot keep myself cool, there I was glad of a fire all the day long; here I cannot take exercise without being almost dissolved, there I could walk up and down the hills after deer all the day. I had some very good sport after a variety of game. Woodcock and snipes are now abundant, but I came down before they were fully

in; but there are two species of deer, the sambur, a large
fellow, bigger than a red deer, and the jungle-sheep,
which is about as heavy as an antelope, but not so high
in the leg; then there are hares everywhere, ibex on the
mountain precipices, elephants and bison occasionally,
and, to add to the zest of a shooting party, you have a
chance of seeing a tiger or leopard, and now and then a
bear. I have killed samburs and hares; had a shot at a
tiger, also at a bison; was present at the death of a
leopard; and was unpleasantly near to an elephant when
I was coming up the ghaut at the back of Calicut. I
heard the brute crashing through the jungle about a
hundred feet below me. These risks add to the excitement
of shooting, but they are, practically, but small, fractional
parts of a risk. The other day I was out deer-stalking on
the hills; I had just caught sight of two deer, and was
setting off to get the wind of them, when my shikarri, or
gamekeeper, touched my arm, and said, 'Tiger, sare;' and
there, true enough, at about five hundred yards from me,
was a monstrous fellow, stalking quietly along by the side
of a brook. I got very excited, and when the shikarri
said, 'Want shoot tiger, sare?' I said, unhesitatingly,
'Yes!' and off we set. Our object was to cross a brook,
and then, climbing up a steep bank on the opposite side,
to head the tiger, before he could get into cover. In
doing all this, I had time for deliberation, and it occurred
to me that I was rather a fool for attacking a tiger on
foot and single-handed. However, it was too late to turn
back, so I had to make up my mind to do battle; and,
as I had a double-barrelled rifle and gun, both loaded
with ball, I thought I might, if my gun-carrier stood by
me, give a good account of the animal. My nerves were
not strengthened by seeing the shikarri, when we came
near the top of a slope, lift himself carefully on his toes
and peer over the ridge to see whether the tiger was
coming up on the other side; I was, however, *quitte*

pour la peur. The tiger had probably winded me, and not being hungry, had taken himself off into the wood. In addition to shooting, we have capital fun riding after jackals on the hills; these are covered with good sound coarse turf, and there are many jackals about, and if we get near enough to slip a greyhound at them, we have a good rattling gallop. I am getting from Australia some harriers, and kangaroo dogs, a powerful description of deer hound, and hope to have good sport next year; the harriers will push the jackals out of the cover, and giving tongue, we shall be able to ride up to them. The bottoms of these valleys are generally boggy, so we have either to ride round the heads of them, or to make for known passes. Ladies, however, manage to join in our sport. I have made a trip up the west coast from Beypore to a little south of Goa : on my way back I visited a magnificent waterfall ; the principal pitch is 820 feet ; this was measured by an officer of the navy, who passed a rope across the chasm and swung himself into the middle while he let down a plumb line into the pool below. Nothing is more deceptive than looking down at a fall, I should not have put this at more than 400 feet.

Lady Denison got out safe on the 11th ; pray remember us both to Mrs. Sandham, and believe me,

Yours very truly,
W. D.

Extract from Journal.

Guindy Park, November 24, 1861.

Dearest M——,— We came up here yesterday, and now that we are settled here, I hope to be able to recommence my letters in the journal form. I paid a visit on Tuesday to some of the native schools ; and my morning there resulted in an impression that, if I wished to be of any use, either in the schools, or any thing of the sort, I must know something of the language : so I have made

enquiries for a teacher of 'Tamil,' which is the prevailing
language here.

November 27.—This morning W—— had his usual
weekly public breakfast, but had it, for the first time,
here, instead of at Madras. There was something in the
aspect of all the arriving carriages, which put me in mind
of the old 'public days ' at Knowsley, when we as children
used to stand at upper windows to see the carriages come ;
but with a great difference ; for Indian carriages, at
least those in which people go about in the day time, are
very unlike English ones, as they all have to be closed up
with venetians, and white covers, and outside blinds, and
all sorts of contrivances to keep off the sun ; and the
running horsekeepers, with their dark faces and bare legs,
are very unlike English footmen. I have had my first
lesson in Tamil this morning : a very ungainly looking
language it is, though not an ill-sounding one.

December 6.—I believe I wrote you word that W——
has had a slight attack of fever ; nothing of consequence,
but it came at an unlucky moment, when we had on
hand the great ball, properly belonging to the Queen's
birthday, but which we had postponed till this cooler
season, and which took place yesterday. W—— was
much better, but still not able to leave his room ; so,
at a quarter before six in the evening, S—— and I
started for Madras, and dined at the Madras Government
House, in company with Mr. Morehead, the senior
member of council, who was coming to personate W——
at the ball, one or two other guests, and the staff. At
about a quarter past nine, Mr. Morehead and I, followed
by these dinner guests, made a formal entry *into* and
march *up* the Banqueting Hall, which was already pretty
well filled, chiefly with Europeans, but a fair sprinkling
also of East Indians and natives. This Banqueting Hall
makes the handsomest ball-room I ever was in : well
lighted, and well filled, it looked beautiful; and outside

it was illuminated, I suppose to please the public eye, for
the natives are very fond of illuminations, fireworks, &c.
Some half an hour after the ball had begun, a hasty scuffle
out of the ball-room on the part of Mr. Morehead and the
aides-de-camp announced the approach of Prince Azeem
Jah; and here occurred a dire misfortune: for His
Highness is very tenacious of his honours, and for days
beforehand his 'private secretary' had hovered about
Government House with endless negotiations and arrangements as to the manner of his reception: he seemed
always to have an idea that it was intended to slight his
dignity; and when, in the afternoon, it had become
necessary to inform him that W—— was ill, and would
not be able to receive him in person, he evidently received
the message with some distrust, and was all ready to
believe that the illness was assumed for the purpose of
slighting him: so, I suppose, he was not in the best of
humours to begin with; and, unluckily, he did not send
forth the announcement of his approach as soon as he
ought to have done; so poor Mr. Morehead, hurrying out
as soon as he heard he was coming, had only time to
reach the top of the stairs, where he met the Prince
coming up, instead of being, as he should have been, at
the bottom of the stairs, ready to receive him when he
alighted from his carriage. This, of course, aggravated
the original annoyance of W——'s absence: the Prince
appeared, as the gentlemen afterwards told us, 'as sulky
as a bear;' his private secretary came and wrangled with
Mr. B——, and the whole course of explanations had to
be gone through again. However, all this was behind
the scenes: I suppose the Prince was content with vent-
ing sulky looks on the staff, for he entered the ball-room
very amiably, leaning on the arm of Mr. Morehead, who
brought him up to me. Oh! the difference between my
idea of an Eastern prince and the sad reality! I saw only
an elderly man, in a tumbled and rather dirty white

muslin dress, with an ordinary looking scarf or shawl round
his waist. Into this was stuck a handsome dagger, but not
one morsel of jewellery or ornament of any kind had he
about him. In fact, he looked *shabby*. After him walked
ten or a dozen of his suite, all dressed much like himself,
in dirty white muslin gowns and scarfs, and looking in-
finitely less well got up than our own native servants do.
However, he was very civil to me: he was introduced,
and sat down by me on my own particular sofa, and we
said civil things to each other through the medium of an
interpreter: and I really flatter myself that I rather
mollified him, for he absolutely relaxed into a smile once
when he asked whether I intended to *dance*, and I told him
in reply, that we considered that, when we had grown up
daughters, it was time to stop dancing ourselves. You
should have seen the sort of quick, amused glance that
the old man turned upon me, as though he would have
said, 'Quite right: it *is* high time!' Conversation with
him was, however, rather a burden: and it was a great
relief when he took his departure. If I had not mollified
him, I suppose Mr. Morehead did: for they parted with
an *embrace*; and I could not help thinking that W——
had an escape of that, at any rate. The rest of the ball
went off very well, except the supper, with the appearance of which I was not at all satisfied: this came of
trusting things to our native head man, Cowajee: but it is
mortifying to one's vanity to start with a failure, in one's
first début on a new stage.

To Lady Charlotte Denison.

Guindy, December 21, 1861.

My dear Sister,—I must anticipate Christmas, or I shall
never get my letters finished in time for the mail, and wish
you every happiness: mirth, perhaps, dies out as advancing years take the spring and elasticity of youth out
of us; but happiness, I think, grows and increases, till it
is perfected when we are taken away from this world. I

have been hard at work during my leisure time in writing comments upon the Essays and Reviews. I began the work, at first, more for my own satisfaction than with any idea of publication, just, indeed, as I did with Buckle's work on Civilization; but somehow or other it grew upon me, as I kept reading and commenting, and it struck me that comments by a layman, and by one whose professional studies had given him a knowledge of physical science, and whose tastes had led him to the study of natural history in its various branches, and to some metaphysical reading, might have far more effect than the more professional and conventional view which would probably be taken by a clergyman; so I am going to print my comments here, and will send you a copy. I take a very strong view of the conduct of the individual writers, and of that of the collective body : their work, however, is but a réchauffé of the old objections, deistical and atheistical, which have been so frequently brought against the Bible, with a little fresh sauce distilled from the bones of the fossil world brought to light by the geologists. However, you will read it and judge for yourself; that is, you may read it if these are subjects which interest you. My faith, thank God, is too firmly fixed to be moved by such attacks as these : to others, however, they are suggestive of doubts which cling to and harass many a conscientious mind; and it is one of my great objections to the work that it is not in any way prompted by the love of truth; it does not seek to prove anything, to make the present happy, or the future full of hope; it merely brings forward difficult points as suggestive of objections to the truth of scripture, without attempting to solve or explain one of them; and without establishing any plausible theory in place of that on which it has cast a doubt. However, I am writing an essay, not a letter.

I have moved out from Madras permanently, and am going to make this place my home. It is far pleasanter than our Madras house ; here we are in the country, in

the centre of a park, with plenty of deer of two kinds,
and of antelopes skipping about; a good garden which
may be made almost perfect when I get water, and plenty
of ground to gallop over. I have got L—— a horse, so she
and S—— can be companions of my rides. What political
moves are likely to take place? We hear all sorts of
rumours of changes, either partial or total, of the ministry.
I do not like the course which has been pursued with regard
to India, either in respect to the army or to the general political arrangements. The Government has rushed hastily
into changes of system, under the idea that if the principle
be good, the details would work themselves out; it took its
principle for granted, whereas it was essentially unsound,
and therefore every attempt to bring the details into har-
monious action does but plunge us more deeply into the
mire. The worst of these great political changes is that
they cannot be remedied; you cannot say, 'The experiment
has failed, and we will revert to our old system;' you have
made the plunge, and you must get through the bog as
best you may. It is an old Whig hobby to substitute an
entirely new system for an old one which seemed to want
mending; instead of acting as a sensible man would do
whose coat pinched him, that is, send for the tailor to
remedy the particular defect, they must needs order a
new coat, which, instead of having only one fault, would
probably have a dozen. It is true that the necessity of
remedying these gives rise to much ingenious speculation;
all the political tinkers must needs try their hands upon
the social kettle, and all sorts of changes and modifications
are proposed. I, however, have lived long enough, and
seen sufficient of society under various phases, to have
convinced myself that change is a great evil in itself, and
requires strong reasons to justify it. I have written a
curious letter to you; however, it represents the state of
my mind at the instant, so I must let it go. I am writing
to E——, so good bye. Your affectionate brother,

W. D.

CHAPTER XX.

TREATMENT OF BRITISH OFFICERS BY THE NIZAM OF HYDRABAD—SUGGES-
TIONS ON THE SUBJECT—CINCHONA PLANTATIONS—NEW YEAR'S GREET-
INGS—NATIVE AIDE-DE-CAMP—NEW YEAR'S BALL—PAPER CHASE—
REMARKS ON PROPOSED CHANGE IN SYSTEM OF LAND TENURE IN INDIA
—TRICHINOPOLY — TANJORE — VISIT TO THE SIXTEEN WIDOWS AND
DAUGHTERS OF THE RAJAH—BRIDGE OVER THE CAUVERY—CASTE OF
THIEVES—NATIVE ROMAN CATHOLIC OBSERVANCE OF GOOD FRIDAY—
'PLENTY CRY'—LETTER TO SIR C. WOOD ON REGISTRATION OF LAND
TITLES—OPENING OF SCHOOL FOR CHILDREN OF NATIVE SERVANTS—
COLLEGE OF CIVIL ENGINEERS—LETTER ON ENCOURAGEMENTS TO COTTON
CULTIVATION — CHARACTERISTICS OF MAHOMETAN POPULATION—'KING
TOM'— RAPACITY OF NATIVE OFFICIALS — AFTERNOON RECEPTIONS—
JEWELLERY TAKEN AT KIRWEE—JOURNEY TO THE HILLS—HOLICUL
DROOG—KOTAGHERRY—RUNGASAWMY'S PILLAR—SALE OF LAND—SUPPLY
OF HORSES—JOURNEY DELAYED BY BEES—COST OF TRANSPORT ON RAIL-
WAYS—PROPORTION OF RAINFALL DISCHARGED BY RIVERS—CHUPATTIES.

To Lord Canning.

Guindy, December 21, 1861.

MY DEAR LORD,—I spoke to Laing when he was here about two matters of much importance to which I wish to draw your attention. In the first place, as regards Mysore. The Rajah is very anxious to have the handling of the balance in his treasury, and all the management of his own territory. Would it not be as well to concede this to him upon the specific condition that he does not adopt any one as heir to his territory? or at all events under the distinct understanding that no successor to the territory will be recognised by the Government after the death of the present Rajah? In the second place as to the Nizam's contingent. Are you aware that the treatment encountered by British subjects, officers and others, who may chance to visit Hydrabad, is such as would not be tolerated for an instant in any other part of the world?

They are ill treated, spit upon, and run the risk of their
lives unless protected by an escort.   Is a man who has
so little control over his own subjects fit to be entrusted
with a force, in the shape of a contingent, nominally ours,
but in reality his, not one of whom would be found to act
against him should either he or his friends, by their con
duct, compel us to exercise some gentle military pressure
upon him?

What I want to see is the substitution of a Madras
force instead of the contingent; and the erection of such
a citadel within cannon shot of Hydrabad as would
cover our treasury and military stores, and keep the city
in awe.   A small place with a trifling garrison would do
this.   A company of Artillery, and 400 men, would in
case of necessity hold the place, and destroy Hydrabad.
Pray think of this.   I do not wish to disband effective
regiments while I can get rid of such rubbish as the contingent; and I want to secure our position at Hydrabad,
which, at present, as every officer who knows it will tell
you, is badly arranged and most insecure.   By the erection of a citadel, the whole of the force, except 500 men,
would be rendered disposable, while the 500 would secure
the stores, treasure, ammunition, etc., form a safe base for
our operations, and smash Hydrabad if occasion called
for such an exercise of force.

Yours very truly,

W. Denison.

Lord Canning altogether declined to adopt the suggestions contained in the foregoing letter, and the ground of
his objections to the course proposed will be seen in my
reply to him, which was as follows :—

Guindy, January 7, 1862.

My dear Lord,—I think you must have altogether mistaken my meaning with reference to the Nizam.   I am
perfectly aware that he is, within his own dominions,

theoretically, an independent sovereign ; though you must allow me to observe that his independence is, as I say, purely *theoretical*, for we, for our own purposes, that is to secure ourselves from the risk of attack by his turbulent subjects, and him from having his throat cut by them, maintain two distinct bodies of troops in his territory. It was because I did and do thoroughly recognise his position, and ours, that I made the suggestion contained in my letter, and which I cannot conceive to be otherwise than just as well as politically expedient. You say, ' I confess I am at a loss to understand upon what principles of policy or right you advocate cutting and carving our relations with the Nizam after the fashion suggested in your last letter.'

Now the only suggestions I made were two. 1st. That the ' contingent,' a force which we are bound by treaty to maintain, should be composed of Madras troops, owing allegiance to the Queen, instead of men, who, although paid by us, and maintained for our purposes, would at once, did occasion serve, turn their arms against us.

2nd. That the fort required for the security of our depôt of arms and ammunition, our treasury, and the women and children following the camp, should be placed in such a position as, while it answered the above purposes, would also keep in awe the inhabitants of Hydrabad. I don't think that there is much cutting and carving in this.

The contingent is a force borne on our army list, and is enumerated as one of the bodies of troops under the control of the Government of India in the resolutions of that Government bearing upon the reduction of the native military force : so, in point of fact, my proposition was merely to the effect that one body of our troops should be substituted for another, and that the force upon which least dependence could be placed should be disbanded.

You say, 'A treaty is a treaty, whether it be with a strong power or with a weak one.' Granted (though, by the way, we have been very apt in India to put our own interpretation upon treaties); but it was because the treaty, as was distinctly explained to me by Mr. Temple, made no mention of the character of the troops, but merely specified their number, that I considered, and do still consider, that we should be fully justified in substituting troops whom we can trust for those upon whom we can place no dependence.

In my second proposition, as to the site of the fort which must be erected at or near Hydrabad, I merely expressed a military opinion, which I believe to be essentially a sound one.

You say, 'I can understand picking a quarrel with the Nizam, and taking his possessions from him.' This, however, in my opinion, would be neither just nor politic; and it is precisely because I do not wish that any occasion should arise to compel us to take such questionable steps, that I am anxious to see our relations with the Nizam placed on such a sound footing as would lessen the chance of such an occurrence. Now the maltreatment of the Queen's subjects by a prince, or the vassals of a prince, holding friendly relations with us, would be likely at any time to call for explanations and apologies which might lead to war.

The treatment to which Englishmen are now subjected at Hydrabad would not be tolerated for an instant in Europe. Why should it be submitted to in India?

Believe me, yours very truly,

W. DENISON.

Plans of works for the security of our arsenal and stores in the vicinity of Hydrabad have been called for since the date of this correspondence, but all those which I have seen have been of too slight a trace, and far too extensive an outline. They would require a large force to maintain them, while our main object should be to cover what requires protection and security with works which could not be carried by storm, though defended by but a small force ; and to leave as large a proportion of the troops as possible available for active operations.

Of the facility with which a quarrel can be picked with a native prince, the war with Abyssinia, or rather with King Theodore, is a curious and pregnant instance. Now the Nizam has a large and compact territory, with some fifteen millions or thereabouts of bigoted subjects, over whom he can and does exercise but a very limited control. He is an ignorant man in every sense of the word, specially ignorant in matters of government ; and he is led by our obsequious conduct to him, to form an erroneous estimate of the position in which he stands with relation to us, and an exaggerated idea of his own importance. We can have, in point of fact, no guarantee for peace with him but the life of his minister Salar Jung, a very weak security ; or a well-founded fear of us, and I should be disposed to pursue a line of policy which would cultivate a wholesome dread of our power.

Our East Indian policy has led us generally to truckle to the strong, till, as Lord Canning observes, we could pick a quarrel with him and deprive him of his territory, while we never hesitated to bully the weak. It is time that we should assume a more dignified position ; that we should spare the weak, and make the strong fear and respect us.

To Lord Canning.

Guindy, January 7, 1862.

My dear Lord,—I saw Dr. Anderson on his way down from the Neilgherries, and heard what he had to say. I infer from this that he considers Darjeeling a more favourable site for cinchona plantations than the Neilgherries, and he may possibly be right; he speaks, however, a little too dogmatically when he asserts, as I gather from your letter, that not only is there *no promise* of success at the Neilgherries, but that success is impossible; this can only be decided by experiment. The sites where we are making our experiments were selected by the man who brought out the plants, who knew their habits, was well acquainted with the climate, soil, and other conditions connected with the growth of the plants, and it is fair to believe that he was not gratuitously deceiving the Government. 'Who shall decide when doctors disagree?' Why, quiet, sensible men who have no hobbies to ride, no theories to maintain. I consider myself to be one of these impartial persons, and my opinion is that experiment is the only test which can possibly be applied to decide the relative quality of the two sites. Let Dr. Anderson have a plantation, by all means, at Darjeeling; but as we have already incurred all the expense of building houses, clearing land, &c., it would be as well that we should ascertain by direct experiment whether our horticultural prophet is not as much to be depended on as Dr. Anderson.

Extracts from Journal.

Guindy, January 2, 1862.

Dearest M——,—On Monday we went to dine with the Chief Justice, and here I saw a new Indian custom; for at his gate we were met by four men with lanterns in their hands; and though we had the carriage lamps lighted, and therefore did not need their assistance, they ran with these lamps in front of us all the way up to the house.

Yesterday (New Year's Day), as I emerged from my own room in the morning, I found myself waited for by a whole troop of the native servants, with nosegays and limes to present, and a great garland to hang round my neck ! This was their New Year's greeting, and they had strewed flowers about the floors, and hung them up in various places. After breakfast we had a visit from a functionary of whose existence I had never been aware before, viz. William's native aide-de-camp. He came, however, very grand in full uniform, also bringing garlands and nosegays with which he adorned me, and the two English aides-de-camp. We bowed and smiled our thanks, and looked very absurd with great garlands hanging round our necks. To-day is fixed for the great official New Year's Ball : there are two of these annual balls here, one on the Queen's birth day, and one at the New Year. We are just preparing to start for Madras for it, as it is given in the Banqueting Hall, and therefore we are going to dine at the Government House there.

January 3.—Our New Year's ball went off very well. Prince Azeem Jah was in such high good humour that he stayed to supper, and in the course of the evening invited us to be present at his son's marriage.

We have had some rain during the last two days : a great blessing, for there was beginning to be great alarm at the want of it ; and for the last two or three Sundays we have had in all the churches either the prayer for rain, or that against famine and scarcity ; for the terrible thing in this country is, that if we miss the usual amount of rain at the monsoons, it is not, like a bad harvest in England, merely a matter involving a troublesome rise in prices, bearing, perhaps, rather heavily on the poor. Here it amounts to actual starvation and death amongst the native population ; and, do what you will to relieve them, many die before supplies can be obtained. I am afraid the rain has not yet been sufficient to avert the threatened danger, but it looks as if there might be more.

Guindy, January 20, 1862.

My dear J——,—The Bombay steamer must have broken down between Suez and its port, for although we heard an account of the death of the Prince Consort, yet the official intelligence, which should have come by that route, has not reached us, and we have, in fact, no authentic news later than December 10 or 11. This is annoying on several grounds; but we must now wait patiently for the mail *viâ* Galle, the telegram from which we may expect in a day or two. I am most anxious to know how the poor Queen has stood the shock. Now that her children are growing up and leaving her, she would feel the want of some one to lean upon very much. Here we are going on as usual; the weather, warm during the day, is beautiful about sunset, and if we could have the English twilight, nothing could be more delicious than the soft cool breeze from the sea.

I have just been practising rifle-shooting. I have given a cup to be shot for by the members of the Rifle Club, of which I am patron; the butt is in the park here, and several men come all the way from Madras (six miles) to practise: the firing commencing at a little after six in the morning, so that they must be up before five.

I have sent E—— a set of Indian agricultural tools, which contrast curiously with our perfect implements. There are, however, among them the rudiments of our drill and horse-hoe, the principle of which is almost identical with that adopted in England, the execution, however, being rude; but then the whole lot, consisting of plough, harrow, drill, horse-hoe, leveller, spade, sickle, bill-hook, &c., only cost me, I think, about 2*l*. 7*s*. 0*d*.

Yours affectionately,

W. D.

Guindy, February 20, 1862.

My dear William,—We had to put off our Christmas tree owing to the death of the Prince Consort, the news of which cast a gloom upon society here ; but two days ago we gathered the children together, had jugglers to amuse them, then, after dark, some fireworks, and after that the usual tree and presents. The children were all young, hardly one above nine years old, and most under seven. We sent them away highly delighted. Yesterday we had a ' paper chase ; ' my private secretary and an A. D. C. having reconnoitred a line of country, rode off at half-past four on horseback with saddlebags full of paper ; about half-an-hour afterwards a party of ladies and gentlemen started from Government House, and in about ten minutes we hit upon the scent and commenced our running. At first our horses were so fresh that we kept overriding the scent ; my horse, an old steeple-chaser, nearly pulled my arms off ; the foxes gave us some very cunning checks, which delayed us a good deal, but at last, after fording a river, and having a good gallop for an hour and a quarter, we ran them into the park at Guindy. There were two slight accidents : one of the ladies' horses came down in getting over a ditch : I, however, was close by, picked her up and caught her horse, and, as she was not hurt, she was soon up with the rest. Another horse came down in a sandhole and gave his rider a roll, but no harm was done. Sport of this kind does good in a variety of ways : it is good for one's health in the first place, and it shows people I look after their pleasures as well as their interests.

I think I mentioned to you the stinking sea between Mangalore and Cannanore ; I told the same tale to Sir Roderick Murchison, suggesting an enquiry into the circumstances, and asking whether this might not account for some of the phenomena of Palæontology, as, for instance, the alternation in layers of sandstone of deposits of fossil fish and molluscæ. On the west coast we might expect to find the annual deposit of mud brought down by the monsoon smothering thousands of the fish and shells of those seas, and in course of time this would become a bed of fossiliferous sandstone. I heard from Sir Roderick not long ago, and he said that Lyell had taken a note of the circumstance. As soon as you get your commission, you should join some of the societies which deal with questions of natural science; you will find among the members both useful and amusing friends.

February 25.—I rode yesterday, for the first time, my grey horse which I bought at Sydney; he is a cross between an Arab horse and an Australian mare, of which I have had several, and all good. I dare say you recollect two very powerful horses of this breed, belonging to the mounted orderlies at Hobart Town. Sinbad, for that is his name, came up to the door with two men at his head, for he is apt to go off with a sort of plunge before one gets fairly into the saddle; however, he was quiet enough with my weight on his back.

This is your birthday; my dear boy, may God bless you and give you many happy returns of it; happy they will be, whether many or few, if you strive to please Him, and act under a steady and abiding conviction of His presence.

Your affectionate father,

W. D.

The Government of India, pressed by people at home who had visions of turning India into a sort of colony by the encouragement of what they termed Anglo-Indian colonisation, took up the idea of selling its waste land, and then, deluded by the hope of getting some capital into its hands, went a step further and proposed to sell the assessment or rent; that is, practically, the land from which more than one-half of its revenue is derived, at twenty years' purchase. A reference was made to the Government of Madras by that of India, requesting an expression of opinion as to the applicability of this to the various districts of Madras.

My opinion was decidedly adverse to the whole scheme. I pointed out that a permanent money assessment gave to the ryot an advantage to which he could have no claim; that the value of money had been steadily decreasing for several years past, and that the landlord had a fair claim to the benefit arising out of the rise of prices; this indeed would be the only means by which he could escape the difficulties arising out of the fixed character of the payments made to him, and the ever-varying but steadily increasing price of labour and commodities.

I objected altogether to the powers proposed to be given to the ryot of redeeming his annual rent by the payment, at once, of twenty years' purchase; not that I thought that many would be foolish enough to sacrifice capital which would pay them, at the ordinary rate of interest, some twelve per cent., and invest the same in land returning five per cent., but on the ground that no Government ought to be trusted with the power of expending its capital.

My reasons, however, did not bring conviction to the Governor-General, and a series of resolutions was sent down to Madras relative to—1st, the sale of waste land, in perpetuity; 2ndly, permission to redeem the existing assessment by a single payment of twenty years' purchase. These resolutions, in a modified form, and with a change from twenty years to twenty-five as the standard rate at which the rent was to be bought up, were approved by the Secretary of State, and an Act in accordance with them was passed by the general Government. The effect produced has, however, in no way realised the expectations of those who advocated the change: no large amount of land has been purchased, Anglo-Indian colonisation has not increased to any extent, and the amount of capital produced by the sale of assessment has been very trifling.

In discussing the cause of the great rise of prices during the last ten years, Sir Charles Wood, in estimating the effect of the discovery of gold in California and Australia in cheapening money, or raising prices generally, put this at about five per cent. The returns, however, from the revenue board of the prices of various descriptions of grain for a long series of years shewed that the average price of a given measure of paddy for the years from 1801 to 1852 was 14 pence; while for the years from 1853 to 1858 the price of the same measure was $21\frac{1}{2}$ pence. I brought this fact under Sir. C. Wood's notice, and put it to him whether such a marked and rapid change did not seem to indicate a greater effect of the gold upon prices than he had stated. I pointed out to him that we should, if these high prices continued, have to raise the pay of our troops, of our police, and generally of all the servants of Government whose salaries were contingent, in any way, upon the price of food, and that it was for this reason that I insisted so strongly upon the establishment of a corn instead of a money rent or assessment.

To Mrs. Des Vœux.

Trichinopoly, March 12, 1862.

My dear J——,—I came here to open the South of India Railway, which has been completed so far (eighty miles) from Negapatam on the East Coast. The railway authorities wished to make some display, and I was desirous to please them, though, in so doing, I have plunged into one of the hottest places in the Madras territory. Trichinopoly was once the head-quarters of the Nabob of the Carnatic ; it stands on the banks of the Cauvery, one of the sacred rivers of the Hindoos, and the whole country around is under irrigation (the water being

taken from the river for the purpose), producing, consequently, three crops in the year. Rice, sugar-cane, cotton,
&c., &c., all grow luxuriantly.

There is a curious rock, rising abruptly out of the flat
alluvial soil, close to the banks of the river, to a height of
about 400 feet; the top of this is crowned by a large
pagoda, to which the ascent is by a fine range of granite
steps, deeply worn by the action of the naked feet of the
thousands of worshippers. The entrance to the pagoda is
a passage with walls of granite or gneiss, having square
columns from distance to distance, all made of single
blocks of the same hard stone, while the capitals, cornices,
corbels, &c., &c., are most elaborately carved in all sorts
of fantastic forms in the highest relief. I must say that
these people beat us out and out in the solidity of their
structures, and in the amount of labour and taste dis-
played in their decoration.

We stopped at Tanjore on our way here. This was the
seat of the government of an old Mahratta dynasty, and
in default of direct male heirs has been '*annexed*' by us.
As to the wisdom of the absorption I have no doubts; as
to the honesty of it I have many. However, the question
was settled by Lord Dalhousie many years ago, and all
I have now to do is to distribute the private property
among the several heirs or claimants, giving as liberal a
construction as I can to the term '*private.*' This, however, exposes me to a variety of modes of solicitation.
I had yesterday to visit the wife, or rather wives, of the
late Rajah. I was met at the door of the palace by six
or seven great bearded fellows, who claimed to stand in
some relationship to the Rajah, and who consequently
embraced me, going through the motions of kissing me
on both cheeks; two of the oldest then each took a hand
and led me up a sort of narrow back staircase, only wide
enough for one stout person like myself, till at last I
found myself seated in front of a curtain, with here and

there holes in it, behind which, I was told, the sixteen
wives of the late Rajah were assembled. I had then to
listen to the eloquence of the senior widow, who, through
an interpreter, tried to persuade me to recognise the
adoption, by her, as the successor of the Rajah, of a fat
youth who was sitting by me. I had no sooner escaped
from her, by expressing my intention to do whatsoever
the Queen told me, than I was pounced upon by a man
who had married the Rajah's only daughter. He carried
me off to another range of apartments, and after some
discussion as to whether I was to see the Princess or not,
the husband evidently wanting to exhibit her, the Princess
being unwilling to show her face, and I being utterly
indifferent, it was decided that she was to be behind a
curtain. She spoke English, and, having been well
tutored, addressed me as her father and grandfather,
and asked me whether I was not prepared to fulfil the
promise, made to her by Sir Charles Trevelyan, of putting
her on her father's throne. To this I was, of course,
obliged to make the same sort of evasive answer that I
had given to the other princesses. The husband, however, thinking that I might be influenced by the sight of
beauty in distress, just as we were taking our leave,
pulled up the curtain, and exhibited the princess in the
shape of a young girl gorgeously dressed, arms, neck,
and legs covered with gold and jewels; and my firm
conviction is that he wanted me to salute her on both
cheeks. I, however, backed out of too much familiarity,
and kissing her little henna-tipped fingers very respect-
fully, took myself off. It is odd that these people should
not yet have learned how little store we set upon all
these observances; it is, perhaps, due to the way in
which we enforce their customs upon them when they
come to call upon us. We insist that a native shall take
off his slippers, and approach us either with bare feet or
in English shoes and stockings. I am disposed to treat

these as matters of indifference, but my advisers insist upon the necessity of adhering to them.

13*th.* Yesterday I drove down to look at the bridge over the Cauvery, which consists of thirty-two arches of fifty feet span, while that over the Coleroon, another branch of the same river, has thirty-eight arches of the same size. These seemed to be gigantic works, and so they are, but the former only cost 9,600*l.*, and the latter only 11,000*l.*, so cheap is labour here. The river, at this time of year, is merely a broad bed of sand, over which runs a shallow stream of water not ten yards wide, but during the south-west monsoon it rolls down a large body of water, as you may imagine from the width of the two channels.

This morning I was up at five, and at a quarter before six was on the parade-ground, watching the movements of four regiments of infantry (three native and one European) and a battery of artillery (European). From thence I went to visit the hospital and barracks. The heat here I found very trying, but the health of the troops is not bad; in fact, mere heat does not do one much harm, unless one is exposed to the direct action of the sun, or unless there is matter upon which the heat can act to generate unwholesome gases. I have invested some money in Trichinopoly work. The natives are capital workmen in gold and silver, and, what is more, they work cheaply. In gold an addition of one-fourth to the actual value of the gold itself generally covers the cost of workmanship, indeed always, unless the pattern is new and elaborate; for instance, a bracelet, if it contains gold to the value of four pounds, would cost five pounds. The value of the gold is tested by experts, who compare the colour of the gold used with that of standard specimens, both being rubbed on a touchstone.

There is a custom in Trichinopoly, and I believe pretty generally throughout the South of the Peninsula, which will rather astonish you. There is a caste of ' *Thieves*,' of which the Rajah of Poodoocottah is the head; and, in Trichinopoly, every man who has anything to lose maintains a 'Thief,' not for the purpose of stealing other people's goods, but of securing his own. His paid thief guarantees him against loss by theft; in fact, his wages are a sort of black mail paid to the caste. We are going to try to break this down by means of our new police, but we shall have some trouble in doing so.[1]

16*th.* I left Trichinopoly on Friday morning at seven, ran down by rail to Negapatam, where the company had provided a sort of breakfast and luncheon in one, and, as the whole white population of Trichinopoly and its neighbourhood were invited, we had a large party. The usual toasts were given, and the usual speeches made, and at two o'clock I was on board the steamer making my way to Madras, where I arrived in twenty-two and a half hours. I found all well, and was delighted to be back in this comparatively cool temperature. Lord Elgin looked in upon us on his way to Calcutta; he stayed with us a couple of days. He was very amusing, having seen much of the world, having much to tell, and being able to tell it well. All well here.

Your affectionate brother,

W. D.

Extracts from Journal.

Guindy, April 15, 1862.

Dearest M——,—Yesterday morning brought us a couple of guests in the persons of Mr. and Mrs. Bowring: he was Lord Canning's private secretary, and has just been appointed Chief Commissioner of Mysore; that is, he is, practically, governor of the country. They will stay with us until they can make their arrangements for going up to Bangalore, which is the head-quarters of the Government, the Rajah residing at Mysore.

---

[1] See Note A at the end of the chapter.

17th. We have been to church this morning (Good Friday), and hope to get to the little seaside church of St. Thomé in the evening, for there it will be quite cool and pleasant. I am a little curious as to the observance of Good Friday amongst the native Roman Catholic Christians : our old woman servant, Jenny, as we call her (her real name being, as I afterwards discovered, Chinnee), told Spreadborough last night that she and her daughter and grandchildren were all going into Madras to-day to church ; and she added, ‘Plenty crying to-morrow.’ ‘Crying, Jenny!’ said Spreadborough, ‘what for?’ ‘Oh, yes!’ said Jenny, ‘all cry in church; fishermen, everybody cry, plenty cry!’ This looks as if they thought it a matter of course to make a great wailing and lamentation on Good Friday ; but I am afraid they do not understand much about it. However, with their very small knowledge of English, and my still smaller acquirements in Tamil, it is impossible, as yet, to have anything like conversation with them ; and the more I see, the more I marvel how missionaries ever do get on—how they make their first steps, I mean, towards acquaintance with, and instruction of, the people ; and instead of exclaiming, as some people do, at the slowness of missionary progress, I only wonder that they have got on so well, and done so much as they really have.

.   .   .   .   .   .

To the Right Hon. Sir Charles Wood.

Guindy, April 10, 1862.

My dear Sir Charles,—I am glad to see that a Bill for the registration of titles has been introduced in the House of Lords. When I was in New South Wales the subject attracted my attention, and I placed myself in communication with the registrars-general in South Australia and New Zealand, in both of which colonies Acts had been passed dealing with the subject of the registration of titles to land, and simplifying very much all the proceedings connected with the transfer, &c., of real estate. The lawyers, of course, complained because their business was lessened, all, or nearly all, transfers of land being made through the registrar; but the benefit to the public was very great. In this part of India we have the means of establishing a similar or analogous system : the registrars in the collectorates, with a trifling modification of form, would probably answer all our purposes. I have written to Sir George Grey, asking him to send me a full report upon the system in force in New Zealand, and should I see my way to the introduction of something of the same kind here, I shall bring the subject officially before you.

I don't like the tone which the House of Commons is taking with reference to the colonies. The resolution relative to the share of the cost of the defence to be borne by a colony is very vague, it is true, but it will, of course, be interpreted by the colony in the worst sense. I hold that the mother country and the colony have a joint interest in maintaining the connection ; and that the cost of defending the colony against attack from without should be shared equally between the two. I should like you to look at a despatch of mine on this subject, dated August 14, 1856. We are in the habit of looking at these matters in England from our own point of view, and of forgetting that the colonists also have feelings and opinions as to both the rights and the obligations of the mother country.

Yours very truly,
W. D.

To Colonel Harness, R.E.

Guindy, May 14, 1862.

My dear Harness,—Many thanks for your letter : it touches upon several objects of great interest to me, both as a member of the corps and as Governor of Madras, and

I will deal with these in their order. I have always maintained that the inspector-general of fortifications should make a point of knowing the qualifications of his officers, and thus be able, when applied to by any department of the Government, to supply an officer competent to do, and do well, the particular work required. Science in all its branches, art in its various applications, should find representatives amongst us; and I think it will be one of your privileges to develope this idea among the young officers under you at Chatham. I should not attempt to tie them down too strictly to any particular routine. Of course there are certain subjects with which they must be thoroughly acquainted, certain things which they must be able to do; but, apart from these, I should encourage the widest scope of study, I should open the door to an unlimited area of research. All physical science, every branch of natural history, all the arts and their appliances, are open to you; and I should be glad to see individuals taking up in *earnest* particular branches of study, and should afford them every assistance, with a special reference to the benefit which would result to the corps. Your library, your museum, your observatory might offer subjects of interest to many, and lead them to particular fields of observation. With reference to your museum, I send you a copy of some instructions which I caused to be published in Australia, and have republished in India; if you can get officers to take even a trifling interest in such subjects, you might soon have a magnificent collection of specimens. If you will give me an idea of the character of your museum, I will lend you a helping hand both as regards Australian and Indian specimens. I can send you specimens of timber from India; Ward can send you the timber of Australia; Mould could send specimens from New Zealand. Then I could get you from Australia geological specimens illustrative of the coal-fields there; I could do the same for you from hence. I could send you

specimens illustrative of the natural history of India, &c.
I have looked into some of the papers you sent me, and I
think they are likely to prove useful : at all events it is a
good thing to get a man to put his ideas in writing, for he
finds by this how vague and indefinite they often are.   I
have been thinking of trying to discuss, on general principles, the effect likely to be produced upon the attack
and defence of fortresses by the improvements which are
taking place in artillery, and, generally speaking, in
weapons of offence and projectiles.   Has any one taken
this up ? It is a subject which ought to be discussed carefully, now that we are talking of spending so much money
on fortifications.   I feel, I must say, rather ashamed of the
panic which has led the people of England to rush so
hastily, and unadvisedly, into such an outlay.

I think you exaggerate the probable amount of traffic on
the railroads. You say ' endless hackeries, piled with stacks
of cotton,' &c., &c.   Now, translate this cotton into bales
and tons, and you will find that it will go but a little way
towards maintaining a railway. A million bales would give
but 250,000 tons; in fact, as the cotton in the hackeries
is compressed, it would not give above half this, or 125,000
tons for freight ; and this, at our rate of 13 pice per ton
per mile, would give about 800*l.* per mile for each mile
gone over. However, we shall soon see what the result will
be on our railway, for on the 12th, that is two days ago,
we opened the whole length from Madras to Beypore.

Yours very truly,
W. D.

To Children in England.

Guindy, June 2, 1862.

My dear Children,—A climate where the thermometer
ranges from 83°, as it now is, to 91°, is decidedly unpleasant, and takes all energy out of one. However, it
does not seem to disagree with us otherwise. . . .

I went the other day to the Normal School, to give the prizes, both to the boys of the practising school, and the pupils under instruction as masters. They were mostly natives; some of them seemed very well up in their work, and they were especially quick in their geography. We went this morning at half-past six, to open our new school for the children of the native servants and others, just outside the gate leading from the park to the race-course. There was an old building there, which had been put up by Lord Harris as a school, but it was out of repair. Now, however, it has a new thatch, new mats round it, floor made good, benches ditto, and the whole looked very tidy. We found fifty children and upwards candidates for admission, and we opened the school by a very few words of address from myself, and a prayer, read in Tamil by the schoolmaster, who is a native Christian. One of the native inspectors of schools helped the schoolmaster to classify the children, which involved, of course, an examination of each. Some could read fairly in Tamil, and had made some progress in arithmetic. They had been at a school near, in Sydapet, and professed to come for the sake of better instruction, but I strongly suspect that the true motive was an expectation that something would be got out of the Governor Sahib. I must be careful as to any system of rewards, or I shall have all the children from the surrounding schools streaming in upon me.

On Friday I went to distribute prizes at the College for Civil Engineers, in the Chepauk Palace.[1] The object of the Institution is to train soldiers, and others, fitting them for the subordinate appointments in the Department of Public Works, such as overseers, &c., and it seems to answer very fairly. When I left the college, I found myself in the midst of a dust storm, which is equivalent to a thunderstorm elsewhere; only here, instead of rain falling,

[1] The Chepauk Palace is the palace of the old Nabobs of the Carnatic, now occupied as public offices.

dust rises. There was very fine lightning, but it was so
far off that the thunder was poor in comparison to that
which we used to hear at Sydney.   .   . .

The school mentioned in the above letter, which was
opened by us chiefly for the children of our native
servants, was nevertheless soon attended by several others
from the neighbouring villages. The attendance was
irregular, at least amongst the younger children, but the
school contained, throughout our stay, an average of from
thirty-eight to forty children ; a very small proportion,
alas ! of the numbers belonging to the servants of our
household ; and those that *did* continue to attend were
almost exclusively boys. Female education is, as might
be expected, little cared for by native parents ; we never
had more than four or five girls in the school, and these
soon left us, with one sole exception—a Roman Catholic
child, by name Elizabeth, a niece of our head butler ; and
she, chiefly, I believe, by the force of her own will, continued a regular attendant at the school up to the time of
our leaving Madras. We admitted children of all persua-
sions, though the school teaching was, of course, based on
what we felt to be of most importance—instruction in the
Christian religion. A difficulty had been felt in some
mission schools, with respect to a suitable prayer to be
used daily on opening the school ; our schoolmaster
solved this by commencing, every day, with the Lord's
prayer alone; and this, though pre-eminently *the* Christian
prayer, was never found to provoke any cavil or opposition from either Hindoo or Mussulman parents. The first
hour each day was devoted to religious instruction,
beginning with an easy catechism used in mission schools,
and compiled somewhat on the principle of Dr. Watts's
First Catechism, and going on to the Bible itself, as the
children became more advanced ; but it is painful to see
how little impression seems to be produced by all this.

The children, with the naturally good memory which characterises the Hindoo, soon became proficients in Bible history; they could answer questions, and repeat all the principal facts as to the creation and fall of man, our Lord's life on earth, death, resurrection, &c., quite as fluently as English school children could have done; but it was all repeated just as any other lesson would have been, without, apparently, the slightest approach to any realisation of these things as actual truths. I believe they had the general impression which appears to me to prevail among the Indian natives, that all religions are good, one not better than another; and I could not but feel that they would have learned and repeated anything about Brahma and Vishnu with exactly the same amount of appreciation.

The instruction given at the school, both religious and secular, was at first entirely in Tamil; but we found such a desire prevailing among the natives that their children should be taught English, that we soon established English as part of the routine for the upper class, who made rapid progress. A small fee, the same as that usually established in mission schools, to the amount of two annas (threepence) a month! was paid by each child in addition to the schoolmaster's regular salary. We established this regulation at the recommendation of those more experienced in native schools than ourselves, and the advice was undoubtedly good: the native parents appreciate the school more if they have to pay for it, and it must surely be well, in a moral point of view, for a child to feel that he owes his advantages of education, in part at least, to his father. Moreover the rule entails the minor advantage of making it the schoolmaster's interest to keep up the numbers of the school, and to induce continuous attendance there.[1]

_____

[1] See Note B at the end of the chapter.

Guindy, June 3, 1862.

My dear Sir Charles,—Have you looked into Money's book upon Java? I am reading it carefully for the purpose of getting at the arithmetical fallacy which I am convinced must lurk at the bottom of the comparison between Java and India. How the labourer, the farmer, and the Government are each and all to enrich themselves out of a crop which often ruins a private individual, it is difficult to imagine. I take it that the enrichment of the labourer is a figure of speech, meaning, that he manages to live, without the power of laying by a farthing, the forced labour at the disposal of the Government being the power which sets the machine in motion. Without, however, discussing this, have you thought at all about the culture system as described by Money? I do not mean that part of it which makes the Government the great dealer in produce, but that which empowers the Government to advance money to persons about to commence any undertaking likely to be profitable. The two great wants here are capital and brains : the Government could supply the former at all events. This has been done in Java by an advance of money on the part of the Government to any person willing to devote himself to any kind of manufacture or cultivation, the Government repaying itself by taking the whole or a portion of the produce at a fixed price, and running the merchants' risk. This would, of course, be out of the question in India generally, though it is done with reference to opium, and, to a certain extent, with salt ; but I do not feel quite so certain that advances of money might not be made to encourage cotton-planting in the present peculiar state of the trade. Capital is, as I have said, the great want, and the charge made for interest is so enormous, that a man who begins with a mortgage on his farm is very soon ruined. As regards cotton, no man but a gambler would be willing to invest capital in a scheme which might be rendered unprofitable at any instant by a change in the political relations of the sections of the United States! (rather a bull this). Government, however, is anxious to bring about a state of things in India which will relieve the country from the risk of being caught napping again, and of having so large a proportion of its population thrown out of work. Government, then, must run some risk ; it cannot cultivate itself, but it can make it the interest of others to cultivate, and content itself with a share of the proceeds.   I throw out this merely as a hint.   Should you think it possible, or, rather, should the Government be willing to make a trial of the scheme, I will go more fully into details.   The principle is objectionable, but if you can once swallow this, there will be no difficulty as to details.

Yours very truly,
W. D.

To Lady C. Denison.

Guindy, June 11, 1862.

My dear Sister,—I was present last week at the examination of the children of a Mahometan school, and met there a large proportion of the Mussulman gentry, the former conquerors and rulers of India.   They contrast favourably in external appearance with the Hindoo, are men of more powerful frame, and better features; and there is an appearance of power about them still ; but when the children were examined, the tables were turned. The Hindoo is quick and intelligent, and his mind appears to be at work ; but the Mussulman is slow, heavy, and hardly shows any mental activity.   It is difficult to say whether this proceeds from natural causes ; that is, from the constitution of the animal ; whether it is the result of their religious creed, which merges into fatalism ; or whether it arises from that sort of contempt for intellectual cultivation which seems, oddly enough, to have come upon the Mussulman within the last four or five centuries. In the time of the Crusades the literature and sciences of the world were in the hands of the Eastern nations ; now there is not a remnant of this visible.

16th.—'King Tom,' the barber, has just been to cut my hair. A barber is proverbially a talkative animal, and King Tom is no exception to the rule. He speaks English, and I got from him casual remarks as to the feelings of the people, their wants, fancies, &c., which are useful. To-day, after enquiring the price of rice, condition of the working class, health of the town, &c., I got him to talk about the produce of land, the mode in which it is shared between the Government and the ryot ; and from that we naturally got to the illegitimate claims made upon the cultivator by the subordinate agents of the Government. These are, first, the tahsildar, who is responsible to the collector for the rent of a district called a talook, consisting of several villages ; he is a sort of land agent. Second is the sheristadar, or accountant in the office of the collector ; he keeps the accounts, and comes between the tahsildars and collector, and I should have called him No. 1. Nos. 3, 4, 5, 6, &c. are a swarm of subordinate bloodsuckers, who prey more or less upon the ryot. The tahsildar is a magistrate, a man of weight and power locally ; he lives upon the people : they give him rice, grain for his horses, cut his grass for him, and, in fact, supply his household. In addition to this, there is, according to Tom, a regular black mail levied—a sort of assessment per acre, which is divided among the sheristadars, tahsildars, and subordinate leeches in different proportions. Now all this is very probable ; they are a gift-loving and a gift-giving people ; but it is a practice liable to gross abuse, and I should be glad to break the neck of it : but it would require a long time, the cordial concurrence of all the

European officers, and hard work on their part, to overcome the tendency.

Your affectionate Brother,
W. D.

To Mrs. Des Vœux.

Guindy, June 16, 1862.

My dear J——,—We have had some rain at last: a
rattling thunderstorm brought down a deluge last night,
which will, I hope, cause the grass to spring, and give
food for the deer, who have been reduced to browse on
the trees. The contrast between the bright green of the
trees which have got their new leaves, and the brown
ground about them, is very marked. I am cutting away
several of an ugly species of palm, and am planting
clumps here and there, in order to fill up the space left
vacant, and relieve the eye from the monotony of the
brown ground.

I have established a system which seems to work very
well and to give much satisfaction. L—— used to have a
visiting day once a week, as had been the usual practice
hitherto; and people came between eleven and twelve,
sat for ten minutes, and drove back, some three or four
miles, in the very heat of the day. Now we have the
visiting hour at five in the afternoon, and instead of
sitting in-doors, we have chairs placed in the shade of
the trees, the band playing under a tent at a short distance; targets for those who wish to practise archery,
croquet for others. People get their afternoon drive, have
music, see each other, have some amusement, get ices and
refreshments, and accomplish a visit at the same time,
without the formality of a regular call. This bids fair to
be a very popular move. I have always found it advisable to bestow a little thought upon the amusements of
our society.

During the mutiny a portion of the army took the

town of Kirwee, inhabited by a Rajah, who was foolish enough to imagine he could hold the place against us. The spoil in jewels, gold, and silver was very great, and much discussion has been going on as to the claims of different parties to share, and these have not yet been decided. In the meantime, however, the jewellery has been sold at Calcutta, and agents from all the native princes have been bidding against each other, till the prices paid are far in excess of the intrinsic value of the articles. The curious thing is how a petty prince could have collected such a mass of jewellery; but the truth is that an appetite for jewellery and personal ornaments prevails in India, and, I should say, generally in the East. Every woman has rings in her ears and her nose, necklaces in the plural number, armlets, bangles, &c., &c.; the commonest labourer spends his money in this unproductive way, and his superiors show him the example. The quantity of money thus locked up is incredible, and the loss to the country from this unproductive mode of dealing with earnings is immense. The artisan or labourer hoards his wages and buys a ring or a silver girdle: the Rajah hoards his revenue, probably cheats his creditors, and buys all sorts of useless baubles. You would have been astonished at the sight of the tables in the palace at Tanjore, covered with every kind of useless absurdity, from jewellery down to the lay figures seen in a tailor's shop, dressed in the fashion of the day. The sale at Calcutta has set free a lot of rupees which have been hoarded for years. I see that some gold mohurs, a coin worth about 1l. 10s., but which has become scarce, have been sold for ornaments, at from 4l. to 6l. each. I am about to start for the hills in a few days. God bless you.

Your affectionate Brother,

W. D.

To W. E. Denison, Esq.

Coonoor, July 1, 1862.

My dear William,—Here we are at the top of the ghaut, about 6,000 feet above the level of the sea, with a corresponding decrease of temperature. In Madras the thermometer ranged from 82° to 90°; here it stands pretty steady at 68°. We made our journey easily enough, travelling through from Madras to Coimbatore, 300 miles, in the night, provision being made for the children in the shape of beds, as well as for your mother and S——, all of whom slept very fairly. The next night we left Coimbatore at eight o'clock, and got to the foot of the ghaut at six A.M., having stopped for an hour to clothe the children and ourselves for the change of temperature: some of the party rode up the hill, the children were taken up in tonjons. We have been staying with Mr. and Mrs. Arbuthnot for three or four days. We are about to move to a house at a place called Kotagherry, about twelve miles from this place and eighteen from Ootacamund, the climate of which will be better suited to the children than that of Ootacamund, where I imagine the monsoon is blowing hard. We had a pic-nic party yesterday at a place called Holicul-droog, an old fort belonging to Tippoo, situated on the scarped end of a spur of the hills, the road to it passing over narrow saddles easily defended, while the fort itself occupied the whole area of the spur. Tippoo used it as a state prison, I believe; as a fortress it is useless. You will often hear unprofessional men, when they see a scarped rock, express an opinion that such a site would be a capital one for a fort, the truth being that for most of the objects of a fortress it would be useless. The difficulty of access is in many instances a disadvantage, and is always coupled with a corresponding difficulty of egress; while a few men properly placed would shut up the garrison, and soon starve it out. Our ride was a trying one. I was glad that your mother stayed at home. We had incessant clambering, and, starting at nine, we did not get back till five. I saw in the journal of the United Service Institution a paper by Captain Tyler, R.E. on the effect of the modern rifle upon siege operations. He seems to think that the attack will be facilitated by the improvement in cannon and fire-arms generally. I am disposed to think that the advantage would be with the defence. When a place has its scarps properly covered, so that no breach could be made, unless the batteries were placed on the covered way, the improvement in fire-arms would tend to prolong the time required for the siege, and most certainly to render it more destructive to the assailants. In a fortified place arrangements might always be made to secure cover, and a steady fire from a very few guns upon the head of a sap would make it impossible to carry this on by day. I have had letters from officers in New Zealand, which do not speak hopefully of the state of things. It is an awkward country for regular troops : the fern grows six feet high, and very thick, so as to give perfect cover to the natives. We committed a great folly in going to war at all.

Your affectionate Father,
W. D.

To Lady C. Denison.

Kotagherry, July 3, 1862.

My dear Sister,—We have taken up our resting-place here for a month, as being warmer and more sheltered from the monsoon than Ootacamund, and therefore better for the children. This is ‘ the hill of the Koters,’ the head-quarters of a sort of mechanical tribe of the hill-folk, specimens of whom I saw last year at Ootacamund. We had an easy journey, as we were able to make use of the railway for 300 miles. The house in which we are residing was occupied by Lord Dalhousie, Lord Harris, Lord Elphinstone; in fact, it has been the refuge of all the Governors. It does not offer much accommodation, but, such as it is, we find it comfortable enough.

I hear rumours of all sorts of reverses and successes in America, and I am looking rather eagerly for positive accounts from thence, as affecting us out here. The Manchester people have squeezed the Government at home, and the pressure has been transmitted to us; cotton has been the universal cry; there has consequently been an increased amount of cotton cultivation, the ryots having been stimulated by the promise of higher prices than usual. Should, however, any change in America throw open the trade with the Southern States, down will go prices here, and hundreds of merchants will be ruined. A little forethought might have brought the cotton trade into a steady, wholesome state; now it has all the aspect of gambling; while, should a reaction take place, the natives will be more suspicious than ever of our motives, and more unwilling to adopt our ideas or carry out our suggestions. However, we must do our best to induce a change of system, but the process will be a very slow one. What annoys one most is the folly talked and written at home on these and similar subjects. People in England have a mania for legislation, and seem to think that moral as well as social evils can be cured by law. They forget that law is but the exponent of the opinions and wants of the people, and that it is utterly hopeless to legislate in a manner contradictory to their opinions and wants. They would legislate in London for India just as if they knew as much of it as they do of Kent; and this, be it recollected, is not the fancy of the ignorant, but of the educated portion of the community: the ignorant man merely repeats that which the educated and semi-educated thrust upon him through the medium of the newspapers. I have asked G—— to give an article in his Review upon the use and abuse of language. Since education has become more general, language has been unfairly dealt with—men learn words, not as the representatives of ideas, but as tools to be used for certain purposes, generally for my-tification.

Your affectionate Brother,

W. D.

To Mrs. Des Voeux.

Kotagherry, July 13, 1862.

My dear J——,—The view from our present habitation is beautiful. I am sitting in a library opening into a broad verandah, which runs the whole length of the building. In front of the verandah is an English garden full of flowers, running down the hill, and looking into a beautiful valley, closed in by green hills to the right and left. Beyond this we look down into the low, flat land of Coimbatore, differing altogether in colour and aspect, reflecting from its brown surface the hot rays of the sun, some 6,000 feet below us. Beyond this again, at a distance of some forty miles, a range of hills is seen, about 6,000 or 7,000 feet high ; while to the right hand we catch sight of the outlines of the Neilgherry escarpment, broken into all sorts of forms, and variously coloured. Last week we went out to see whether we could get any shooting, and we decided to combine sport with a sight of Rungasami's Pillar, a sort of pinnacle of rock which is one of the wonders of the hills. We had but indifferent sport. I, however, killed a jungle-sheep (a small kind of deer), and a young pig, which, by the way, we found very good, roasted as a sucking-pig. Our trip to the pillar gave us a hard day's work. I rode out with L—— and S—— to the camp to breakfast. L—— was tired, and wisely remained in camp, while S—— and I and the rest of the party went first to try for some deer over roads or tracks which you never would have conceived to be practicable for horses. We got no deer, and had to work our way up hill to the Peak, where our luncheon had been sent. It certainly is well worth a hard ride to see the pillar, which is a thin pinnacle of gneiss rising up from the steep side of a hill to the height of at least 500 feet. It is separated from the escarpment called the Peak by a gap of 100 or 150 yards in width; but this is not the most beautiful part of the picture. Standing on the Peak, with the pillar in front and in the foreground, one looks down into the Mysore ditch, as it is termed—a sort of chasm, separating the table land of Mysore from the hills. The opposite side of this ditch was formed of variously coloured hills, broken into peculiar forms, making a most beautiful picture. We had to make our way back to camp after luncheon, and had then to ride home, which we reached about six, not a little tired.

We have done little but take scrambling rides about a rough country, over tracks which would make you shudder to look at. S—— and I narrowly escaped yesterday from passing the night in a native village. We were trying to get home by what we imagined to be a short cut, and at half-past five found ourselves going down hill at six miles from Kotagherry, when we luckily met a party who told us that we could not possibly make our way in that direction. We had therefore to turn to the right-about and ride hard, for we had a dinner party; and we managed to get home by seven o'clock, quite wet through, for it rained hard all the way back.

Your affectionate Brother,

W. D.

To the Earl of Elgin.

Kotagherry, July 15, 1862.

My dear Lord,—There are one or two matters now before you as to which I wish to say a few words. 1st. Sale of land. Lord Canning's resolutions have gone into such detail, that they appear to have pledged the Government to a fixed price throughout India, and this fixed price has reference altogether to the character of land in Bengal, 2½ rupees and 5 rupees being the prices stated. Now with us in Madras the value of land is actually reversed; that which is to be sold for 2½ rupees is very much more valuable than that which is to be sold for 5 rupees. Neither of these prices, however, represents the value of land in districts where Europeans are likely to purchase it. Coffee land, for instance, on the Neilgherries is sold for 30 rupees per acre, subject to our assessment of 2 rupees per annum. This is land covered with jungle, and which, according to Lord Canning's resolutions, would be sold, out and out, for 2½ rupees, or one-tenth of its marketable value. This, however, is not the worst feature of the scheme. By putting so low a price on the land, jobbers are induced to come in : they purchase for the mere purpose of selling again, so that, by establishing such a low maximum, you neither secure settlers, nor promote their interests : you merely pander to the capitalist, who puts the money into his pocket which ought to go into that of the Government, and which might be expended by it in making roads and opening the country. What I object to in the resolutions is, 1st, the fixture of a maximum price without the guarantee of auction ; 2ndly, the establishment of one price for all India, without any reference to the character of the soil or the nature of the crop ; 3rdly, the power given to any purchaser to lock up a quantity of land equal in amount and contiguous to that which he has purchased for a given number of years. There are other modifications of detail which might be made, but to these it is unnecessary to allude.

The second subject which I wish to bring under your notice, is that of the supply of horses required for remounting the cavalry and artillery. In a despatch from Sir C. Wood, he alluded to the plan of breeding horses for the service, and I think Sir Hope Grant has a fancy for the establishment of a stud in this Presidency. Now, my

Australian experience in horse-breeding is, that even there, where the mares have an unlimited run over capital pasture, the system is, comparatively, unprofitable; that a large number of weedy brutes are bred, which would not be fit for either cavalry or artillery, and whose sale would not cover their expenses. If this be the case in Australia, where there is good pasture, what will it be here, where for four or five months in the year we have none? It is absolutely necessary that the mare, both while she is with foal and while she is suckling, should have good and abundant pasture; otherwise the foal is never fully developed, and becomes a poor stunted animal. Then, again, the foal as a yearling should have plenty to eat, or it is stunted in its growth. Now, here, at all events, we should be obliged to feed both mare and foal with gram, or some food specially cultivated for them, and the cost of this would seriously enhance the price of a five-year-old. I shall be able to give you some idea soon of the cost of our horses. It is very desirable that some simple system should be established, which might, should a large demand for horses arise, be capable of development. This, it is evident, cannot be the case with a stud; indeed it could only be done by multiplying the regular markets for the supply of horse stock: a few hundred extra horses from each of these markets would not have much action upon the price. I have an offer, which I have accepted, from an Australian breeder, to deliver horses in India, subject to the approval of the Government at landing, for 55l. per horse, the breeder or importer taking the whole risk of shipment, &c., so that the Government gets a good horse for 55l. and is subject to no risk. Others would be found, I have no doubt, to undertake to deliver horses at Calcutta and Bombay on about the same terms.

Yours very truly,

W. D.

Ootacamund, August 3, 1862.

My dear Sister,—We moved over from Kotagherry on the 1st, sending the children some twelve miles in tonjons to meet the carriage, as Kotagherry is inaccessible to vehicles on wheels; while we rode a shorter, but very pretty, new bridle road, which is cut out of the hill side for most of the distance of eighteen miles. We sent spare horses and our luncheon forward to a sort of half-way station in a wood, and took L—— that distance in a tonjon. We had just established ourselves comfortably and commenced our luncheon, when two aides-de-camp, who had been sent to look after the horses, came rushing back, followed by a swarm of bees, and we had to beat a hasty retreat, leaving our luncheon behind us. L—— and Dr. Sanderson were both stung, and eventually we had to retreat about a quarter of a mile before we could feel secure from attack. It seems that some of the horse-keepers had seen a large set of combs hanging to the trees near the road (this is the usual position of the comb of the wild bees), and had appropriated them, starting the inhabitants in search of vengeance and a new home. We were delayed by this upwards of two hours. We first tried to make fires along the path, advancing gradually, pushing each fire about twenty yards on beyond the last. However, when we got near the main body of the bees, they mustered in too great force to allow us time to make a new fire, so we had to retreat. The side of the hill was too steep to permit us to venture off the path, and as our attempt to drive the bees from their position had failed, I rode back about a quarter of a mile to see whether I could not get down the hill by some other route. I had made up my mind to make the attempt, when I was told that the bees had gone off in a body, and that the road was clear, so we succeeded in passing the defile. These bees are different from ours;

they are shorter and fatter, with yellow bodies; they leave, however, their stings behind them, as I had to extract some from those who had been wounded.

I have been looking over the book which you sent me, or, rather, have been reading it with great interest and pleasure. The difficulty which I have always had in appreciating the feelings of those who press ' the Church' upon us almost as a substitute for Christ, is the conviction that religion must, in the first place, be personal and individual; whereas they would almost reverse this, and make the Church, that is the multitude, teach and form the individual. God's Holy Spirit operates upon the heart of the individual, makes it loving and trustful; the soul, thus acted upon, looks around for sympathy, and finds it in those whose conduct shows them to be subjected to the same influence; man is thus added to man, and a Church is formed; but a Church is nothing abstracted from the individuals who compose it. *The* Church (I use here the definite article) has its ministers, and its machinery for teaching; and of course the young, and indeed the old also, are dependent upon this for instruction, but not for holiness—not for that which God alone can give. I have given you a long explanation of my reason for liking Goulburn's work: it deals with personal religion, and this, I feel sure, is, and ought to be, the first step to be taken by the individual, and pressed upon him by the teacher.

Your affectionate Brother,
W. D.

To Colonel Harness, R.E.

Ootacamund, August 10, 1862.

My dear Harness,—I got your letter yesterday. I think you have over-estimated the quantity of goods likely to come by the rail. You must recollect that in this country the cost of conveyance by the usual bullock bandies may be put at 3d. to 3½d. per ton per mile. This is not a heavy charge. In England, before railways were constructed, the cost upon the turnpike-roads was from 9d. to 10d. During the dry season here, the peasant, having nothing for his bullocks to do, or indeed for himself, is glad to avail himself of any opportunity of earning something, so he goes upon the road. As he must maintain his cattle and himself, any money which he may make is almost clear profit. At present we charge 1½d. per ton per mile by the rail, but I doubt whether this covers the cost of transport. I must send you, when I get back to Madras, two papers on railways, which I read to the Royal Society at Sydney. In these you will see, fully stated, my views with regard to these expensive constructions in particular countries.

I have had a curious incidental confirmation of some facts relative to drainage, &c., which I deduced from experiments made in New South Wales. This may be useful to your young officers. The Irrigation Company, which is bringing water from the Toombuddra River into the Pennaar, and making a canal for navigation as well as for irrigation, proposed, as a part of their scheme, to make a dam 200 feet high across the outlet of a valley in Mysore, to collect therein the drainage of a large extent of country, and to pass this water down the canals, during the dry season. The scheme was submitted to me, and I asked to be informed—

1st. As to the area of country the drainage from which was to be intercepted.

2nd. As to the number of inches of rain falling upon this area.

3rd. As to the proportion of this rain which ran off to the outfall.

I got at the time but a very vague reply to questions one and two, and the reply to question three was that three-fourths of the rainfall was discharged pretty speedily by the river. I told the engineer that the result of my experiments showed that the proportion in Australia was between one-fourth and one-fifth ; and I directed the engineers in different parts of the country to make some experiments to determine this proportion for the Madras territory under varied circumstances. I have as yet got no returns which can be relied on ; but a short time ago I got a proposal from the Mysore Government to construct a dam across the very river which the Irrigation Company intended to make use of, and to employ the water to irrigate a portion of their own territory. With this scheme I got tables showing the actual discharge of the river, the area of drainage, &c. Now the facts were as follows : The area of drainage was 400 square miles, or 256,000 acres. The discharge of the river during nine months 320,715,286 cubic yards, or $\frac{320715286}{256000} = 1253$ cubic yards per acre ; that is, the amount coming to the outfall from each acre would be equal to about 9·3 inches in depth over that area. I have not the actual measurement of the rainfall, but I shall be under the mark if I put it at from 36 to 40 inches during the rainy season ; so that the actual discharge is pretty much as my experiments in New South Wales testified, namely, between one-fourth and one-fifth of the total quantity falling. Of course, when there is a steady down-pour, as in the monsoon on the west coast, and when the hills are bare and precipitous, this proportion will be exceeded ; but I think that the proportion of one-fourth might be taken in calculations for drainage, and one-fifth for those relating to the supply of water.

Yours very truly,
W. D.

To Sir C. Wood.

Ootacamund, September 13, 1862.

My dear Sir Charles,—I have heard from two sources that the natives in the northern parts of the Nizam's territory are beginning to send about chupatties, or cakes, as they did before the mutiny. This would seem to be something analogous to the fiery cross in the Highlands. The process appears to be as follows. Cakes are sent to a village, with instructions that they are to be thrown to the dogs, and that other cakes are to be prepared and sent on to the next village. The suggestion, or warning, or whatever it may be, circulates in this way throughout the country without attracting much attention. My feeling is that we are dealing with these people too much according to English principles. We attribute to them feelings which would operate upon us, but which have either no action, or a very different action, upon them. I do not believe that, with perhaps a few exceptions, they care one farthing about the justice, as we term it, of our dealings with them, and for the security, we say, that they enjoy. All that they remember—and their memories are very good—is that we have come in as aliens and intruders, have ousted their native rulers, sometimes by the strong hand, and sometimes, between you and me, by very dirty processes. We must not expect gratitude or affection from them, and must be prepared to deal with them, should they be foolish enough to break out a second time, just as their native rulers would do ; that is, to show but little mercy, to act thoroughly upon their fears. Leniency, they, as well as other savage or semi-civilised nations, regard as a proof of weakness.

Yours very truly,

W. D.

To Mrs. Des Vœux.

Ootacamund, September 11, 1862.

My dear J——,—The more I see of the state of things in this country, the more earnestly do I wish for alterations and reform ; yet the growth of abuses has been so natural and so gradual, each step having been almost a necessary consequence of the preceding one, that it is difficult to know where to begin, and, having begun, equally difficult to know where one is to stop. Many matters come before me which involve a consideration of the treatment dealt out by us to the great men of the land in former times, and which impress me with the conviction that we acted towards them most nefariously; but, were I to attempt to grant redress to the children of these, where could I stop? I should have to give over a large slice of the Madras Presidency to others who, ignorant and full of native prejudices, would bring back a state of things which, if not passed, is, at all events, passing away. I have made up my mind, therefore, not to attempt to redress hereditary injustice, but taking what happened before my time as a *fait accompli*, to be careful that no complaint is made against me. The evil, however, is not merely in the injustice committed, but in the generation of ideas and principles in the servants of Government which lead them to advocate such injustice—to do evil that good may come; and I by no means exclude myself from the number of those upon whom this influence acts. In looking to these crooked paths, we neglect the simple and straightforward way by which good is sure to be done; that is, we neglect to train or educate the people. You must not think when I use the hackneyed phrase *educate*, that I mean mere mental training, mere teaching to read and to write. I lay much more stress upon that sort of training by the eye, that exhibition before the people of the results of education upon ourselves, that proof of the benefits of civilisation of which Christianity is the main element, which it is so desirable to introduce. However, I have given you too large an allowance of grumbling; so good-bye.

Your affectionate Brother,
W. D.

NOTE A.

I subjoin an extract from a series of notices sent to the Rajah of Poodoocottah by one of his creditors ; the whole letter having been eventually sent in to the Government, in the form of a complaint against him.

'Take notice of sale, Maharajah Rama Chundra Tondimon Bahadoor, Rajah of Poodoocottah,

'That, on and after the 10th of December, in the year one thousand eight hundred and sixty-one, unless the sum of rupees (28,200) in full is previously sent by you to my house, as intimated in my last notice, sent to you under open cover, dated 1st November, 1861, your second wife, son, and daughter, begotten of her, will be put up conjointly, and nominally sold to the highest bidder, in my Receiving Hall, in satisfaction of the claim in question, of which you will receive notices from time to time.'

After two or three repeated notices, at different dates, of nominal bids for the Rajah's wife and children (probably intended as stinging insults ; for, of course, no real sale could be attempted), the document concludes as follows :—

'But should you, Maharajah Rama Chundra Tondimon Bahadoor, of Poodoocottah, fail either to send down the above-said amount, or your second wife, son, and daughter by her, within the 25th inst., *Know you for certain* that my old shoes or slippers will be issued and sent to you, to compel and demand of you to fulfil the terms of this condition ; for you must bear in mind that you are not supposed to trample upon the rights and liberties of others with impunity, when you yourself wish and expect your own rights, liberties, and privileges, accorded you, as an ally, to be respected.'

It is evident from the above that the reception of a creditor's old shoes or slippers is looked upon as a greater degradation than the sale of wife and children ; for, in a former part of the document, after one of the notices of nominal auctions, it is tauntingly remarked, that it will now be seen whether Rama Chundra is '*even willing to submit to the shoes or slippers,* rather than act the part of a prince.'

NOTE B.

On the occasion of a Christmas examination at our little school, about a year and a half after its establishment, we were requested to listen to a Tamil song, composed by the schoolmaster, and sung by his pupils; and this 'schoolmaster's song' eventually became an annual Christmas performance. The sound of the tune, when delivered with the true Tamil twang, and falling off into a sort of nasal groan at the close of each cadence, was, as a friend of ours present on one of these occasions remarked, 'like vocal bagpipes;' and I subjoin a translation of the song given at the last examination, which is worth preserving, in its way, as a specimen of Orientalism, and a proof that our schoolmaster, though a Christian, and really, to all appearance, conscientious in the discharge of his duties, yet could not divest himself of the ordinary tendencies of the Asiatic in contact with his superiors.

(TRANSLATION.)

THANKSGIVING.

D E V A R A M.

Praise the feet of the All-adorable—Bhagaván is indeed a beautiful rule given by the high Tamil Pundits; but the voice of the genuine Gospel—Science revealed by the Glorious One—bids us to keep to His matchless feet that that Mary had kept as 'One thing is needful.'

PORTUGUESE TUNE.

(1) Ever cheerful DENISON—the Representative of Her Majesty the Queen Victoria, whose constant care is universal preservation. Like the great mystery of life, whereby the physical nature is sustained by the beams of the bright sun, is our Royal Supporter and Auspicious Parent.

(2) The Sun of Righteousness is Jesus our Lord, who on that
    day (of crucifixion) had wiped off our shame, is even
    to this day our own dear friend; He is the prime cause
    of the Universe and our great Preserver.

(3) (In) the maternal bosom of the benevolent Lady DENISON
    is our livelihood and our prosperity now and for ever-
    more.   The Honourable Anglican Lady is our sup-
    porting stay.

ANOTHER.

(1) The first cause, The Gracious Order, The Sun of Righteous-
    ness, The Light of Love, The Grand Teacher of man-
    kind.

(2) May the little School of Governor DENISON of the Presi-
    dency of Madras be blessed, and may its glory shine to
    the relief of many a little one.

(3) O King of Heaven, grant us improvement in learning
    and sound wisdom, and save us from all evils in this
    life.

(4) O God of Angels, The Holy One worshipped by man-
    kind, grant that possessors of the Truth may long live;
    give us wisdom to seek thy feet and to attain Eternal
    life.

DEVARAM.

May the Gracious God continue His blessing to the Institution
established by Mother Lady DENISON in 1862, and cause its
usefulness to extend on.

CHAPTER XXI.

SAIL ROUND CAPE COMORIN—ADAM'S BRIDGE—PAGODA AT RAMISERAM—
A ROYAL PILGRIM—PREPARATION OF SEA SLUGS FOR THE CHINESE
MARKET—LANDING AT TUTICORIN — MANGOSTEENS — MODE OF SELLING
PEARLS—PEARL LIME—TINNEVELLY—DURBAR—THE GREAT ZEMINDAR—
MISSIONARY TRAINING SCHOOL—NIGHT JOURNEY TO NAGERCOIL—PASSAGE
OF A SWOLLEN RIVER—ARRIVAL AT TRIVANDRUM—STATE VISIT FROM
THE RAJAH—ILLUMINATED ROAD—DINNER WITH THE RAJAH METRO-
POLITAN OF THE SYRIAN CHURCH—VISIT TO THE RANEES—DEPARTURE
FROM TRIVANDRUM — NIGHT VOYAGING ON THE BACK WATER — FAIRY-
LIKE SCENES—QUILON—ILLUMINATED GARDEN—ALLEPPEY—VISIT FROM
ARMENIAN MERCHANTS—MISSIONARY WORK AMONG THE SLAVE CASTE—
LATERITE—COCHIN—VISIT FROM THE RAJAH—BOATING EXTRAORDINARY
—CURIOUS FISHING NETS—' WHITE JEWS OF COCHIN '—VISIT TO THE
SYNAGOGUE—RETURN TO MADRAS.

To Mrs. Des Vœux.

Coimbatore, October 11, 1862.

MY DEAR J——,—We got here at five this morning, and our journey did not commence prosperously, for we had not got three miles from Ootacamund before it began to pour. L—— and I were in a carriage, but the rest of the party, who were riding, were wet to the skin ; luckily we had dry clothes for S——, and she and L—— and I went down the ghaut in tonjons. We got into our bullock transits at half-past eight P.M., and arrived here, twenty-six miles, at half-past five in the morning. We met a man going up the ghaut who had been nineteen hours going the same distance.

13*th.*—Off Cape Comorin. We ran down by rail in three and a half hours from Coimbatore to Beypore. The first half of the distance has a very peculiar character ; on one side you look out on a bare brown plain, while on the other the eye dwells upon a curious range of hills most peculiar in form, colour, and structure. Lower down again you plunge into the low land of Malabar, well clothed with timber, rich and well cultivated. At this time of year the people were employed in the fields, and everyone had either an umbrella, or a hat equivalent to an umbrella, made of palm leaves, about 2 feet 6 inches or 3 feet in diameter, with a centre part to fit on the head. I was told that the men with umbrellas were the aristocracy of the country, while those with umbrella hats were the lower or working class, many of whom were slaves. They were working in the paddy fields (paddy is growing rice, or rice in the husk), some reaping, some planting, some preparing the ground for a second crop. They always get two crops off the ground, and in several instances three. We found the steamer waiting for us about two miles from the shore, and we got on board by five o'clock, and were very soon under weigh. We stood down the coast all that night, sighted Cochin, Alleppey, and Quilon, and when I awoke this morning, pretty early—for I slept upon deck on account of the heat—I found that we were abreast of Cape Comorin. There are some hills in the vicinity which make a bold termination to the Peninsula, but there is a gap between these and the southern end of the long range of the Western Ghauts.

Paumben, October 14.—This is, speaking generally, a part of the reef connecting India and Ceylon, called Adam's Bridge, across which he, according to tradition, stepped when he went to visit the eastern portion of his inheritance. More particularly, Paumben is the channel which we are deepening and widening for the accommodation of the native trade between India and Ceylon. We arrived at our anchorage this morning, having stopped for a pilot at Tuticorin. On the island of Ramiseram, off which we anchored, there is a pagoda of great note; it forms the southern termination of a

great Brahminical circuit, commencing at Benares; and
during the new moon as many as 5,000 pilgrims pay
their devotions to the idols, wash off the dust of their
journey in the sea, and after that follow different routes
back to the North, some going up the holy river Cauvery,
while others go round by Cape Comorin and the West
Coast. Last year a Rajah came down as a pilgrim, went
to bathe at the end of the island, and was beset, on
coming out of the water, by a herd of Brahmins, who got
5,000 rupees out of him in exchange for a few rings
made of grass. The distance to the pagoda was too great to
allow of our paying it a visit *en masse;* but two of our
party went ashore for the purpose, and got a good duck-
ing in the surf on landing. They described the pagoda as
being poor-looking externally, but beautifully carved and
arranged within.

Tinnevelly, October 16.—My last sheet was written
at Paumben. I went from the steamer to inspect the
works of the channel, and after a long pull landed at a
small village, where the reef abuts on the Island of
Ramiseram. I was met by the authorities of the pagoda;
they paraded an elephant, a camel, and a body of
dancing girls; they also brought me a present of fruits
and sweetmeats. I had not much time, however, to waste
upon these formalities, as it was getting dark, and we had
a long pull back to the ship, luckily, however, with the
stream. I forgot to say that we stopped on our way to
Paumben at a Chinaman's establishment, where he was
catching and preparing sea-slugs (trepang) for the
Chinese market. The children of the place collect these
for him at low water, and receive two rupees per thousand.
They are large, nasty-looking slugs, about 9 inches in
length and 2½ inches in diameter, striped on the back
with black and grey, and have a white stomach spotted
with black. The mode of preparation is simple enough:
the slugs are thrown (alive!!) into an iron pot, and

boiled for a short time, or rather stewed partially; they
are then put into a hole in the sand of the beach, and
left there for some time to dry and cool; boiled a second
time, and then dried, first in the sun, and after that in a
hut, a fire being kindled on the ground, and the slugs
spread upon a hurdle about 6 feet above the fire. They
sell at Singapore for 13 rupees per thousand, so the man
drives a profitable trade. We left our anchorage in the
evening, and found ourselves abreast of Tuticorin by six
o'clock in the morning, made all our preparations for
landing, and got ashore, after a long and hot pull, by
half-past nine. We were getting short of ice; so, as I
proposed to go back, as far as Cochin, overland, I sent the
steamer over to Colombo for 1,000lbs. weight of that
necessary of life. We landed, of course, in the midst of
a crowd of officials and natives, the latter all standing in
the water, and found breakfast ready, and, to my great
satisfaction, a basket of fresh mangosteens, which had been
sent by a merchant from his garden on the east side of
the Ghauts. Everybody in India speaks of the mangosteen
as the prince of fruits. It is got in perfection at the
Straits Settlements, Singapore, &c., but it grows in particular localities at the south extremity of India. It is a
dark-coloured, round fruit, about as big as an average-
sized apple; the skin is purple, about one-eighth of an inch
in thickness; this is cut through carefully, and when the
interior is exposed it is snow white, and consists of five
or six lobes like those of an orange, one or two of which
are larger than the rest, and contain the seed. The fruit
itself is sweet, slightly subacid, with, perhaps, a *soupçon*
of strawberry flavour; but its coolness, its consistence,
which is slightly mucilaginous, and its slight acidity are its
great recommendations: it is not, however, to be compared to a peach. We went to visit some of the cotton-
pressing establishments; they are driving a thriving

trade. I was told that cotton to the value of 800,000*l.*
had been exported from Tuticorin during the present
year.

Of late years the pearl fishery has been rather productive, and a merchant brought us specimens of several
which had been the product of his speculations during
this year. I say speculations, for the mode of dealing is
as follows. The shells are brought to land, a certain
number are opened, and the character of the pearls determined and made public. The shells are then put together
in heaps containing a given number, and each heap is bid
for separately, the chance of the return being estimated
by the quality and quantity extracted from the sample
lot. Of course there is a great variation in price, but
there has been a fair return to the Government, and we
are now beginning to attempt to breed the animal, which
is not an oyster, but an avicula, a very different animal,
as I shall be able to show you some time or other. The
leading man of the pearl-divers was presented to me ; he
had, as a sort of badge of office, a gold shell with a pearl
inside, a very pretty ornament. We had some shells
brought in and opened, but found nothing but small seed
pearls, and these seemed to be deposited within the
animal, and not to adhere to the shell. The rich natives
have these seed pearls burned into lime, and use this
with their betel nut instead of ordinary lime, a piece of
luxurious folly about on a par with that of Antony. I
had two addresses presented to me, to which I returned
the usual answer. We left Tuticorin after dinner, I——,
S——, and I in palanquins, as the road was said to be bad,
the rest in bullock transits. We sent off our baggage at
two o'clock ; but such roads I never travelled before,
except, perhaps, in Australia. Our bearers were sometimes in water, sometimes plunging through deep sticky
mud, and sometimes in deep drifting sand, but never on
a decent road. It took us ten hours to go twenty-eight

miles. Some of the transits and carts have come straggling
in, but some I do not expect to see for hours. L——
and S—— went on at once to the collector's house, but I
stopped at some distance from Tinnevelly in order to get
myself into a fit state to be seen by the concourse of
people, military as well as civil, who turned out to welcome me. We are at the collector's house, and are very
comfortable.

October 18.—As I am the first governor who has visited
this district, I am made much of. The night after our
arrival we had a display of fireworks; the next day all
the principal natives came to the durbar, or levée. One
zemindar, determined to outshine his neighbours, came
with a procession consisting of five elephants, two camels,
a lot of led horses, two sets of dancing-girls, two bands,
guards, &c. &c. without number. He himself was dressed
in cloth of gold and covered with jewels. We made him
stop, after the rest had gone away, and show us his
various ornaments. Diamonds and emeralds seemed to be
the stones most in request, but they appear to set more
store upon size than on quality; many of the stones had
flaws, and all were badly set. He had a small dagger,
with a sort of guard which covered the back of the hand,
which was one mass of emeralds and diamonds. This
man pays the Government 9,000*l.* per annum, and gets
out of his tenants, I dare say, 30,000*l.* in addition. I have
had addresses without end, and specially a long one from
the missionaries; this is, in fact, the head-quarters of the
two great bodies, the Church Missionary Society and that
for the Propagation of the Gospel.

I went yesterday to inspect a training school where
about 100 children are boarded, lodged, clothed, and
educated, most of whom will eventually become clergymen or catechists, schoolmasters and mistresses. The
place is prettily situated; the ground, though flat, has a
beautiful background in the Western Ghauts some twelve

or fourteen miles distant; these rise up abruptly from the plain, and have a marked and peculiar outline.

October 19.—I inspected the native regiment here at a quarter before six, and gave great pleasure to officers and men by my commendation of their appearance and movements. I visited two schools in the afternoon. All the authorities are anxious that I should see everything, or, rather, I believe, they are anxious to show me as a sort of lion. One old lady, the wife of a missionary, and an active agent in all educational matters, told me that she was holding me up as an example of simplicity of costume to her children, and had pointed out the difference between the Governor, in his plain black coat, and the zemindars, dressed in cloth of gold and covered with jewels. The fact is that I dress simply in this country on principle, to say nothing of comfort. It would be hopeless in me to attempt to vie, in finery, with the humblest zemindar: he in cloth of gold must always make a greater show than I could, even were I to dress in uniform. I, therefore, put on a simple black dress with my star, and I stand out in strong relief to my military staff, and to the gorgeously dressed natives. We go on towards Trivandrum to-morrow. God bless you, my dear J——.

Your affectionate Brother,
W. D.

To W. E. Denison, Esq.

Tinnevelly, October 18, 1862.

My dear W——,—S—— is giving you an account of our journey, so I will confine myself to one or two matters in which I feel a special interest. At Beypore I went to examine a spot sheltered in some measure by a reef, which it was proposed to turn into a boat harbour. The people connected with the railway are, of course, anxious to get anything done which might draw more traffic to the line. I, however, set my face against the

202 VARIETIES OF VICE-REGAL LIFE.

proposed breakwater, on the plea that the shelter given by the reef was quite sufficient to make smooth water inside, and that all we wanted was a sort of jetty from the station, at which boats and small coasting craft could lie and load or unload. We sailed from Beypore to Paumben, rounding Cape Comorin. We found the sea as offensive off Beypore and along the West Coast as it was last year off Cannanore, and I made the captain of the steamer put her head off shore till the evidence of my nose told me that we were in sweet water. At Paumben we are deepening and widening a cut through 'Adam's Bridge.' There is a great traffic by this channel to Colombo in Ceylon, as much as 170,000 tons passing through every year. The reef looks in places like a set of giant stepping-stones, over and between which the water rushes rapidly, for a north wind forces the water into the gulf on the north side, creating a fall sufficient, *they say*, to give a current of six or eight knots; and there is a reverse current when the wind is southerly. When I was there the water was rushing from the north, but 2½ or 3 knots was the full velocity of the current. We have deepened the channel from 8 to 12 feet, and are going to carry it to 14 feet. It is useless to make it deeper, because the water in the channel followed by the vessels which use the passage is not more than that depth. A committee of the House of Commons reported in favour of a deep-water channel, which must have been made farther to the eastward, and would have cost at least half a million; but I see no use in this, the only object being to shorten the voyage, at a certain time of the year, between Calcutta and Colombo, a voyage not made by half-a-dozen vessels.

From Paumben we went to Tuticorin, the shipping port of most of the cotton from the South of India. I went over the stores of two merchants, one of whom was packing cotton with the old screw press, the other with a new patent press which weighed the cotton and pressed it into a bale, at one-half the cost of labour expended in working the screw. The machine, however, was very expensive. The idea of this machine was taken from the bent lever of the printing-press. One end of the lever was fixed at the top of the framework of the press, while the other was connected with the moveable top of the case containing the cotton ; the centre of the bent lever was connected with an arc or quadrant which, being moved, as the patent windlass, by two claws catching alternately on two racks in the edge of the arc, gradually drew the lever into a position approximating to a straight line. These claws were worked by a capstan moved rapidly by twenty men.

October 19.—I had the district engineer with me for a long time to-day. He brought before me a plan by which a large reservoir might be made in the hills, by putting a dam 100 feet high between two ranges of rocky hills, through which gap a river runs. This dam would make a pool, covering an area of 5 miles by 3 miles, to an average depth of perhaps 30 feet ; this would supply water to a tract of country of some extent, and would ensure the whole valley of the river against drought. We then went into the question of roads, and decided what was to be done by the Government, and what by the people. Upon the whole I think the people will be well satisfied with the result of my visit.

Your affectionate Father,
W. D.

Extracts from Journal.

Residency, Trivandrum, October 23, 1862.

My dear M——, —I do not think that I shall ever keep pace in my letters with all I have to tell. This Indian travelling is *so* amusing, and letters are so little able to do justice to the scenes. On Monday evening we left Tinnevelly, and a palanquin journey through the night brought us to Nagercoil, where we were to rest in a bungalow for the day. The night journey was long, very wet and tiring, but nevertheless very amusing. We passed through a native town, where the people were waiting in crowds to see us. Through the darkness we had a glimpse of a large elephant, with smart red trappings, making salaams to us, and the people ran by the side of our palanquins with flaming torches till we got a long way past the town. At another place we crossed the boundary between our territory and that of the Rajah of Travancore, and there was some great official or other sent by the Rajah to welcome W—— to his dominions; but I, unfortunately, had fallen asleep in my palanquin just at this juncture, so I missed the ceremony. I am told, however, that W——, who had also fallen asleep, was roused suddenly, and, only half awake, conscious of a necessity for *some* immediate action, but not quite aware of what the occasion might be, stepped hastily out of his palanquin, just as he was, without waiting to put on his coat and waistcoat, which he had thrown off for the sake of coolness; so, in the midst of a gazing crowd, and of all the 'pomp and circumstance' which the place could muster, there suddenly emerged the great man, in shirt sleeves and rumpled hair, not, I am afraid, for the moment, a very imposing representative of British majesty! Wherever we have gone, all through our journey, we have found all the bungalows at which we stopped prettily ornamented with strings of flowers, and all along the road, crossing over our heads, long strings, with leaves, ferns, &c., fluttering from them. I thought at first that these were feeble attempts at triumphal arches; but I have since been told that they are charms intended to preserve us from the evil eye! We had a long weary day at Nagercoil, for it rained in torrents, and we had nothing to do. The missionaries of the station (it belongs to the London Mission) and their wives called on us in the afternoon, and we went with them to see their schools,

or rather their scholars, for the children and adults of the
different schools were all collected together in the church;
but this was our only occupation, and we were all glad
when night came on, and with it the time for starting
again on our journey, though it still rained as hard as
ever. Now we had to encounter the greatest obstacle to
our travels; we had a river to cross; and everybody said
that this would be so swollen from the rain, that we
should find it very difficult, probably impossible, to cross
it, as there were none but native boats, which, if the
torrent was strong, were likely to be swept far down the
stream before they could reach the other side. At all
events we were told that it would be quite impossible to
cross it in the dark; so our palanquin journey that night
was only to take us to a bungalow on the bank of the
river, there to wait till daylight, and then cross, if possible.
We got to our bungalow about two o'clock in the morning,
rested there for three hours, and with the first of the daylight went down to the river. Imagine my horror, when
I and my palanquin got there, at being told that W——
and Dr. Sanderson had gone off first in the boats to try
the passage. It was just like my good man to try it himself first; but nevertheless I wished he had not, and
remained in a great fidget, for intervening trees hid the
boats from our sight. The Dewan Peishcar, or official
whom the Rajah of Travancore had sent to welcome
W——, and to assist us on our journey, and who was
among the party waiting on the bank, apparently thought
that now, in a moment of anxiety, it behoved him to dis-
tinguish himself. Accordingly, with an air of great
gravity and preparation, and as if about to take a very
important step in our behalf, he came forward, and, leaning on the shoulder of one coolie, and carefully sending
another before him to sound the depth, he solemnly
stepped into the water, about half-way up to his knees, and
there stood till the boat in which W—— had gone was

seen returning—a sign that he had got over safely.
We were a little astonished at the importance he seemed
to attach to this step, when compared with the smallness of
the result; for it was difficult to see what good effect the im-
mersion of his fat legs could have on our progress; but it
was impossible to mistake the expression of self-compla-
cency with which he stood there, as if now he really had
helped us over the whole difficulty ; and, sure enough, he
afterwards sent in a claim for some reward, on the ground
of his distinguished services during our journey ! It was a
great relief to see W——'s boat come back safe, and we
addressed ourselves to our crossing in good heart. S——
and I were to go in our palanquins, which were to be
hoisted into the native boats, and which took up so much
room that only one gentleman was to go with each, the
remaining gentlemen following in other boats.   After all
the stories we had heard about the difficulty of crossing,
we got over the river as peacefully as possible : it had
overflowed its banks, and was very wide ; but though
the stream was strong, there was no torrent to sweep us
down, or anything of that sort ; and in due time we got to
the other side, and went on in our palanquins for about
twelve miles, to a bungalow, where we stopped for breakfast.   At twelve o'clock we started again, still in palanquins, and came to this place, the capital of Travancore,
which we reached about half-past three.   At the entrance
of the town we were met by an escort of the Rajah's
cavalry, and some of his carriages, into which we got.
The carriage in which S—— and I were was a tolerably well-appointed English-looking carriage, drawn by
four white horses, ridden by two postilions, dressed in
scarlet jackets with *epaulettes*, blue trowsers, and bright
blue caps with gold ornaments ; but, in contrast with
this, the horse-keepers who ran by the side were almost
naked ; and this is generally the way with these Eastern
appointments and equipages—a queer sort of incongruous

mixture of finery and shabbiness. We were followed by
a troop of police peons and a crowd of people; and
thus we came to the house of Mr. Fisher, the English
resident at the court of Travancore. This morning
W—— has held a levée, and I have received the ladies;
and we have had a private visit from an old acquaintance,
Prince Rama Vurmah, the first prince, brother of the
Rajah, who came dressed in dark lilac satin trimmed with
gold.

October 24.—The Rajah paid W—— a state visit
yesterday, and it was an amusing sight. The long drawing-room was prepared for it by having chairs and sofas,
in a long semi-oval, round the room, and we were told off
beforehand to the seats which we were to occupy during
the ceremony. W—— and the Rajah were to sit together
on the sofa at the upper end of the room; I on the nearest
chair on W——'s right hand, and next to me Prince
Rama Vurmah. In the opposite chair, on the Rajah's left
hand, was to sit the Resident, Mr. Fisher, and next to
him S——. All the staff, and the other European gentlemen of the Residency (who all come on these occasions
to meet the Rajah), were to occupy the remaining seats
along the room. Having made all these arrangements,
we went out into the verandah to watch for his coming.
There was a guard of honour posted, and all the different
European gentlemen came dropping in one by one. By-
and-by we heard a salute, the signal that the great man
had started from his palace; but he went very slow, and
it was a long time before the near sound of native drums
announced that he was entering these grounds. The first
thing that appeared was a magnificent elephant; then
came a horse, with a man sitting far back, nearly on his
tail, as boys do on donkeys in England, beating a pair of
kettle-drums; then five or six more led horses; then a
tolerable band of military music; then all the Rajah's
troops, cavalry and infantry, amounting to about 1,800

men; then some discordant native music; and by-and by
the Rajah himself, sitting enthroned on a high state car,
drawn by six white horses, with all sorts of fans and
flags waving about him. After him came the Prince in
an ordinary carriage, and then four or five more elephants;
but I did not see this part of the procession, for we were
called in hastily to take our seats. Mr. Fisher met the
Rajah as he descended from his car by a flight of steps of
green velvet and gold, and handed him up the steps to
the door, where he was met by W——, who offered him his
arm and led him to his sofa, while Mr. Fisher went back
to escort the Prince. All the other gentlemen streamed
in after them, and dropped into their respective seats, and
then began the conversation. The Rajah is about thirty-
two years old, but looks older; stout and portly, with a
sort of jolly, comfortable-looking face. He was dressed in
gold brocade, studded over with emeralds; this dress
was shaped something like an Englishman's dressing-
gown; and on his head he wore a sort of cap, with a
beautiful plume of bird of paradise feathers. He is an
intelligent man, and speaks very good English, and he and
W—— seemed to be getting on capitally, but I had not
time to listen to them, as I was labouring, with great toil
and trouble, to keep up a conversation with the Prince,
who, though he also speaks English well, is shy, and not so
conversable as the Rajah. He also was dressed in gold
brocade, but duly inferior in splendour to his brother.
After about a quarter of an hour of this work, W——,
according to previous instructions, made a sign, and a peon
brought forward a tray covered over with a cloth, on
which were garlands of flowers, one of which W—— was
to put round the Rajah's neck, and two others round his
arms. It was all I could do not to laugh during this
part of the ceremony, it looked so very absurd, particularly
as the large garland, on being put over the Rajah's head,
caught somehow on the back of his cap, and Mr. Fisher

had to come behind him and set it all to rights again. W——, however, kept his countenance admirably. Then another tray of flowers was brought in, with which he similarly decorated the Prince, and then they took their departure. The whole show was the best, and the least *trumpery* I have yet seen in India. The Rajah's state car was really handsome, and so was his dress.

October 25.—Our state dinner with the Rajah yesterday was a fairy-like scene, more like a spectacle in a pantomime than anything in real life. The dinner was to be at half-past seven; so we started from the residency at a little past seven, all in open carriages; for in this climate one can go out in one's evening dress with only a light shawl over one's neck, and that more for appearance' sake than for any need of it. The whole road from the residency to the palace, about a mile and a half, was illuminated by a line of bamboo frames with three rows of lights hung on each; and, as if this was not light enough, there were numbers of men running by the sides of the carriages with torches, and at every turn of the road very powerful blue lights were lighted in succession just as we came up; and really the effect of all this—the blaze of blue light illuminating the thick trees and showing off the carriages, the cantering escort of cavalry, and the crowds of native spectators—was beautiful, particularly at a place where the road passed by a piece of still water, in which all the lights were reflected. The only unpleasant thing was, that at the moment we entered the palace-gates, a salute was fired almost close to our ears. Luckily the Rajah's horses are used to all this sort of thing (we were in his carriage), and minded neither guns, torches, nor the band, and clash of presented arms as W—— arrived. At the palace door stood Prince Rama Vurmah, who offered me his arm, and handed me upstairs to the drawing-room, where we were met by the Rajah, dressed in a dark blue velvet dress, rather hot, I should think,

for this climate, but still very handsome, and in real good
taste, rich, but with nothing gaudy about it. This velvet
tunic reached about half way down his legs, and below it
appeared a pair of white muslin trowsers and bare feet.
He had on a beautiful collar of diamonds, and diamond
earrings ; a white turban with the bird of paradise plume,
and a quantity of little emeralds attached to the ends of
the plume, just to give it weight enough to make it hang
gracefully ;—a gold chain went round his turban, with
some large emeralds hanging in front of it. The dress
was made quite plain, without any trimming or ornament,
except a sort of little wristbands of pearls, which stood out
well on the blue velvet. The Prince was also in dark
blue, but his dress was slightly trimmed with gold lace,
and he wore no jewels, nor any plume in his turban. The
drawing-room was a good room in the shape of a **T**,
furnished as much in English style as an Indian room,
open on all sides, can be ; that is to say, with Brussels
carpet, marble tables, glass chandeliers, some good
alabaster statues ranged along the long part of the room,
and some rather trumpery-looking pictures hanging
against the wall. By-and-by dinner was announced.
The Rajah offered me his arm, and led the way into the
dining-room, which opened from the long straight part of
the drawing-room. The dining-room was a mass of
looking-glass—a long room with pier glasses, not here and
there only, but rows of them all down the sides. The
room was narrow in proportion to its length, but still
wide enough to admit of the servants passing with ease
round the table : it was lighted by a row of glass chandeliers hung from the ceiling, and there were standing
lamps on the table besides.

The dinner was altogether English. The Rajah sat in
the centre of one side of the table, with me on his right
hand and W—— on his left. The Prince handed in
S——, and placed himself opposite us, with her on his

right hand and Mr. Fisher on his left. No natives sat at the table except the Rajah and the Prince. His dewan, or prime minister, was in the drawing-room before dinner and after, dressed in white muslin and gold; but he did not come in to dinner, because it is not etiquette for him to sit down in the presence of the Rajah. Their Hindoo religion does not permit the Rajah and Prince to *eat* with Christians, so they merely sat in their chairs without touching the table, and talked with us while we eat. The Rajah is very conversable.

The table was filled by Europeans, nearly all the English inhabitants of the place, gentlemen and ladies, having been asked to meet us. I made the move after dinner as soon as it suited me, and the Rajah, Prince, and other gentlemen were not long after us. There was to have been a display of fireworks in the evening, and for this we had all to get into carriages and palanquins again, and move from the palace to what is called the durbar hall, which looks into a large square, where the fireworks were to be. A shower of rain, however, came on, and spoilt most of the fireworks. Of course I did not care much for this, for there were quite enough left to show, from time to time, the picturesque sight of the large square with the crowds of natives looking on, a living spectacle which was far more interesting. As soon as the fireworks were over, we took our leave of the Rajah, who accompanied us downstairs to the door, and we returned here with the same circumstance of guns, torches, &c. with which we came.

This morning I have seen a remarkable sight in its way : viz., the Patriarch or Metropolitan of the Syrian Church, who has been to call on W——. These Syrian Christians were once very numerous in this part of India, but they were a good deal oppressed by the Jesuits, under the Portuguese rule, and so they migrated to the hill country, to which they still confine themselves. The Metropolitan's

dress was decidedly hand-ome and ecclesiastical-looking
—a black silk gown, not unlike those worn by our own
clergymen, only more voluminous; a black skull cap, embroidered with gold, and having two black silk lappets or
bands depending from it behind. W—— says that he
seemed a shrewd, intelligent man, and spoke English well.

Extracts from Journal.

Quilon, October 28th, 1862.

Dearest ——,—I must resume my history, but really I
despair of ever keeping pace with the events of this
travelling time, still more of being able to give an
adequate idea in writing of all the scenes which arise
in these Eastern travels : such a succession of pictures ;
such gay spectacles and amusing sights; sometimes with
a strong dash of the absurd, but always with a much
stronger of the picturesque ; so that this journey has altogether been a time abounding in enjoyment. I finished
my last bit of journal with a description of the dinner
with the Rajah ; that was on Friday. On Saturday afternoon we were to pay a private visit at the Palace, for the
purpose of seeing the young ' Ranees,' the Rajah's nieces.
I do not suppose gentlemen in general are allowed to
see them, but W—— was specially invited, and also Mr.
Fisher. We went at five o'clock, and were met at the
door by the Rajah, who took us up to the drawing-room,
and moved about in a quiet, sensible way, without any
attendants or fuss, going out himself to fetch these poor
children, who were not in the room when we arrived.
In they came presently, following him : two girls, one
not quite fifteen, the other eleven ; both small of their
age, and so cumbered with their dress and ornaments
that it seemed almost difficult to them to walk. They
had only a petticoat on by way of lower dress, but were
muffled up in great red shawls ; they had jewels in their
noses, and such enormous ear-rings that they quite drag

the ears down, and make large holes in them; broad,
heavy gold necklaces and anklets, and each one ring on
their second toe. They came up and shook hands with
us, and just said 'Good morning,' and then seated themselves; and this was the extent of our communication;
for, though I spoke once to the eldest, the Rajah answered
for her, as if conscious that she would not be able to do
so, though they have both been by way of learning a little
English. They are both married! but their husbands did
not appear. They were followed into the room by two
little boys, nephews of the Rajah; one eight years old,
the other five. These were dressed, the elder in yellow,
the younger in white satin, a good deal embroidered, and
came in attended by a man servant. The elder might
have stood for the fat boy in 'Pickwick'—nearly as broad
as he was long, and looking stupid and heavy; the younger
was a nice intelligent little fellow, who spoke three or four
words in English very well. After sitting thus for a few
minutes, we rose and took our departure; but it was not
our final farewell of the Rajah, for he paid a quiet visit at
the Presidency that evening, coming in just as we had
finished dinner, without any fuss or parade, except that
W—— and Mr. Fisher went out to meet him, and the
rest of us all stood up as he entered; and then he sat
quietly down, and spent the evening like anybody else.
In fact, he is really a sensible, kind-hearted man; and he
is said to have been very much pleased with W——'s
visit, and to have liked talking over general and useful
subjects with him. The Sunday arrangements of Trivandrum are not agreeable; for, though there is an English
church, there is no clergyman! Two gentlemen, the 'lay
trustees' of this church, are in the habit of reading prayers
and a sermon every Sunday, one of them in the morning,
the other in the evening. This last was at six o'clock,
and we dined as soon as we returned from it: for we
were to set off in the night for our voyage to this place.

This was to be a new mode of travelling : in boats, up
what is called the 'back water,' a succession of rivers,
canals, and lagoons, running parallel with the sea, but at
a distance of from a mile and a half to three miles inland.
Our departure was just the same fairy-like scene that our
drive to the palace was : torches, blue-lights, a very
prettily ornamented tent to receive us, as we got down
from the carriages, and from that an illuminated and
ornamented descent to the boats, and crowds of natives
standing to look on. The torch-bearers ran by the side
of the carriages, sometimes with an attendant carrying a
pot of oil to replenish the flame ; and one of these attendants, close by the side of our carriage, running along,
eagerly gazing at the spectacle, tripped and fell, his
oil-pot breaking with the concussion, and jets of oil
scattering all round him, to the great delight and amusement of the bystanders. The boats are long rowing-boats,
with a sort of poop at the stern, and under it a little cabin,
that just holds two people ; there is a seat on the top of
the poop, where one can sit during the evening and night ;
in the daytime, of course, the sun is too powerful, and one
has to take refuge in the cabin, which is shaded by
venetians. We sat on our poop seat till sleep overpowered us, greatly enjoying the scene—the lovely starlight, the thick trees by the water-side, and feathery-
looking palms, stretching almost into the water, and
showing well in the torch-light ; for torch-bearers continued to accompany us, walking along the banks. Every
now and then we came suddenly upon an illuminated
bridge, or some unexpected demonstration in the way of
illuminations on the banks ; the Rajah having, I believe,
given orders that everything of this sort should be done
in honour of his guests. The rowers made all sorts of discordant noises, and every now and then we stuck in a
shallow place, and then six or eight men, who walked
with the torch-bearers along the banks, all rushed into

the water to the rescue, and, with much shouting and vociferation, helped the rowers to push us off. Yesterday morning we got to a neck of land, where the navigation was interrupted ; but here there were palanquins waiting for us, and we were carried for about five miles, and then got into another and better boat, which brought us here about the middle of the day. Here we are again in a house of Mr. Fisher's, as his residency extends here ; and he and his daughter are accompanying us. This is a military station, and in the evening the band came and played on the water just opposite to the landing-place at the bottom of the garden ; and the scene was more pantomime-like than ever. The garden and steps down to the waterside were illuminated ; blue-lights were burned in barges on the water ; and we sat in a sort of alcove close to the water ; groups of native servants at some distance behind us ; behind them the illuminated garden and steps, and on either side the usual gazing crowd of natives from the town. This afternoon we are to proceed again in our boats to a place called Alleppey, which we hope to reach to-morrow morning.

Cochin, October 30.—Our voyage to Alleppey was not very agreeable, for there came on a thunderstorm, with such violent rain that I was obliged to close the shutters on my side of the cabin, which is not pleasant in this climate, where one wants all the cool air one can get. At Alleppey we were received in the house of a Mr. Crawford, a merchant, the only European resident there. He and Mrs. Crawford were very kind to us, and, in the course of the morning, W—— received a visit from a number of Armenian merchants, who came in, looking gorgeous in long robes (I think silk ones), of various gay colours ; and who brought with them, and presented to us, sundry little bottles of excellent attar of roses. Also, there was some very interesting talk with a missionary clergyman, a Mr. Andrews, who came to call on W—— ;

and who told us about the effect that had been produced
by Christian teaching amongst the poor slave caste in that
part of the country, a race much oppressed and ill treated
by their own countrymen of higher castes, who treat them
like the dirt under their feet. Very ignorant these poor
creatures are, and stupid on most subjects; but they
listen with evident pleasure, and a sort of *surprise*, on
being told of a God who loves and cares for them. They
are not used to be loved or cared for, and this idea evidently finds its way to their hearts, and connects a happy
feeling with their first notions of Christianity. We embarked again in our boats at night, and came on here,
reaching our destination about six o'clock this morning.
This was our last night of back-water navigation, and it
was a glorious one : the stars seemed to stand out from
the sky like great blazing jewels. You must have noticed
this sort of effect in your tropical voyagings, and I do not
think one sees it anywhere but in the torrid zone ; and
the glowing tropical dawn this morning was equally
glorious. This seems a pretty place. We are still guests
of Mr. Fisher, who is Resident here likewise. Cochin once
belonged to the Dutch, and this house is built in a sort of
Dutch Oriental-style, with a verandah, haunted, they say,
by the vexed ghost of some old Dutch governor. We
are to stay three or four days here, and then take our
leave of the Fishers, and go by sea to Calicut.

To Sir Roderick Murchison.

Travancore, October 20, 1862.

My dear Sir Roderick,—I repeated in my last letter a
query which I made last year as to the origin of a
large stratum called 'laterite,' which exists between the
Western Ghauts and the Malabar coast. I have, since
my arrival here, been able to give a partial answer to
my own question, thanks to information obtained from
Mr. Brown, who is in charge of the observatory here,

whose name is well known to those who have made the phenomena of terrestrial magnetism a study, and who is a man of many and varied attainments. With this preface I will tell you what I heard from Mr. Brown. The laterite, as I mentioned, assumes the form of low flat-topped hills apparently weathered at top and washed by the heavy rains of the monsoon. Some twenty miles to the north of Trivandrum, one of these hills comes down to the coast, making a headland, and intercepting the ordinary formation of sandbanks and backwaters which characterizes the whole of the coast to the south of Calicut. Through or round this hill it was intended to make a canal in order to continue the inland navigation parallel to the coast. On my arrival, I enquired from the engineer what was the character of the soil of which this obstacle was composed, and was told that the upper part was laterite, the lower granite, and that between the two were various fossiliferous strata; he added that the cliff was yielding fast to the action of the sea. This seemed to me but an incongruous mass of information, and, in mentioning the matter to Mr. Brown, he at once denied the existence of either granite or gneiss, and affirmed that the rock at the base of the cliffs was a nummulitic lime-stone. I went, therefore, yesterday to the observatory to examine the fossils, and Mr. Brown showed me a section of the strata composing the cliff. I cannot, of course, give you from memory the relative thicknesses of the strata, but the top consisted of sixty feet of laterite; under this were strata of sandstones and clays variously coloured; below there was a bed of lignite, under which was a stratum of clay with nodules of limestone, and under this, near the level of the sea, a bed of limestone containing shells. Mr. Brown calls this a nummulitic limestone, but it hardly appeared to me to have such a number of shells as to deserve the title. I have now given you a sketch of the information I got yesterday. I think it would justify an

appeal to Mr. Brown, who would, I am sure, be glad to give
you every information in his possession.   You might as
well give Oldham, if he is in England, a hint to take up the
geology of the Malabar coast; it would settle the geology
of upwards of 24,000 square miles.   My belief is that the
laterite is one of the latest formations.   I will not, however, attempt to give reasons for such an opinion, which is,
after all, but a mere guess.   Some time ago, when I was
at Sydney, a tailor came to me with a scheme for the
defence of the harbour.   I listened to him very patiently
till he had told his story, and I then asked him whether
he would not think me an intense ass were I to give him
instructions as to the making of a coat?   He cordially
assented to this, but was not disposed to adopt the consequence when applied to himself, that he was equally an
ass for attempting to meddle with matters of which
he knew nothing, or to give advice to an engineer on
questions relating to engineering.   In dealing, therefore,
with experts like yourself, I am content to supply *facts*,
and leave you to draw inferences.

Yours very truly,

W. D.

To Lady C. Denison.

Cochin, October 31, 1862.

My dear Sister,—We arrived here yesterday morning.
At half-past four in the afternoon the Rajah paid his
state visit.   The English Residency, where we are, is situated on a small island, so the Rajah came over with a
train of boats from his palace on the opposite side of the
bay which forms the harbour.   At the end of his procession came one long boat, the rowers pulling very fast,
with a sort of hasty, agitated stroke, as if there was some
need for immense haste, the water apparently coming in,
and the boat sinking deeper and deeper into the water.
At length, when within a short distance of the shore,

down it sank! The rowers, however, sprang to their
feet, and stood upright, apparently upon their sunken boat;
and then it appeared that the whole affair was a regular
part of the programme; the water having been purposely
let into the boat in just sufficient quantity to make it sink
a short way below the surface as it neared the shore.
From his boat the Rajah stepped into a palanquin, in
which he was carried up to the house. His procession,
however, was nothing like so showy or magnificent as
that of his Travancore neighbour. He spoke English
fairly, but looked dirty, and had a ragged half-and-half
beard, which gave him the appearance of not having
shaved for a week. His dress was a green robe, with a
kind of shawl-like pattern upon it, and a collar of mixed
jewels; but it looked tumbled and shabby, and though
some of his attendants took great pains to shake it out
into proper folds as he alighted from his palanquin, the
result was not, on the whole, successful. I got rid of him
in the usual way, after which we pulled about the harbour,
and I went to examine the entrances, where the sea has
latterly been making heavy inroads upon the cocoa-nut
plantations which occupy the ground as soon as it rises a
couple of feet out of the sea. The whole coast was
lined with a peculiar kind of fishing net. It is, in fact, a
large casting net turned the wrong way. It is kept
stretched by two bamboos, and is suspended from the top
of a post, from a bamboo which turns upon this. The net
is lowered and raised by means of this bamboo; it
remains four or five minutes in the water, and is then
hauled up; the fish are turned into a small net by hauling
the point up, and down goes the net again. The whole
circumference of the bay—a distance of eleven miles—was
illuminated last night in honour of my arrival. The Rajah
came to pay me a private visit this morning at half-past
seven. He had a number of grievances which he wished
me to redress, and I felt well disposed to do so with many of

On the morning after the ceremony described in the foregoing letter, we received a visit from two fine, venerable-looking, middle-aged or rather elderly men, who were announced as 'Elias Rabbi' and 'Samuel Rabbi.' They were apparently elders, or persons in authority among the Jewish community of Cochin, and a part of their errand was to invite us to be present that evening in the synagogue at their first sabbath service,—their sabbath, according to the Jewish method of computing time, commencing on the Friday evening. No invitation could have been more welcome; for we had heard of the two singular communities, 'the white and the black Jews of Cochin,' and we were anxious to increase our acquaintance with them. Of the black Jews we had, unfortunately, no time or opportunity to learn anything : whether they are Jewish proselytes from native races, or people of Jewish origin, who, while retaining something of their own faith and religious ceremonies, have, by intermarriage with the natives, lost much of their distinguishing physical characteristics, we could not ascertain. Our two friends, however, belonged to the white Jews; and these, according to their own statement, which is to a great extent corroborated by other records, migrated from Palestine a short time before the destruction of Jerusalem—before the advent of our Saviour indeed, as they deny having taken part in His crucifixion—and have, ever since, continued here as an unmixed race, so careful to preserve the

Jewish blood unmingled, that, when the men cannot find a sufficient number of wives in their own community, they go to seek them from afar, and import those of pure Jewish descent from Damascus, and other parts of Syria and Armenia. Their appearance certainly goes far to bear out this statement: they are unmistakably Jewish in feature, and with complexions so fair as to show that the climate, at any rate, has had no effect on them during the number of centuries through which they have resided here. As sunset approached, we set out in compliance with the invitation we had received in the morning; pulled across the bay, and were met at the landing-place by our friends the Rabbis, and one or two more, who conducted us up some narrow lanes to the house of the chief Rabbi, through a sort of back passage of which we passed at once to the synagogue. In this passage we met the Rabbi's daughter, who was introduced to us by her father, a decidedly handsome woman, of the Jewish type of feature, and richly dressed, with a sort of necklace or stomacher that looked to be entirely composed of gold coins. She, and one or two other women, apparently of the Rabbi's family, accompanied us into the synagogue, and sat, during the service, on a seat just below the pulpit of the reader; and they were the only women that appeared. There was, indeed, at one end of the synagogue a raised and partly closed gallery, that looked as if it might have been intended for women, but it was quite empty; and the two or three above mentioned who were present sat throughout the service, chiefly occupied in gazing at us, listless and lounging in manner, and apparently feeling no interest, and taking no part in what was going forward. With the men it was strikingly different; they were a remarkably handsome race—some of the finest old men I ever saw, and strong, vigorous looking young and middle-aged ones, some with black hair, some with red, and their complexions, as a

general rule, fairer than that of the ordinary Jew in
England. They were dressed in short robes, something
between a tunic and a blouse, of various colours, either of
silk or some less costly stuff, according, I suppose, to
their means; and their manner was peculiarly solemn and
devout. The Rabbis gave us printed papers, containing
the Hebrew service on one side, and an English translation
on the other, so that we were able to follow what was
going on. The first part of the service consisted of
selections from the Psalms, chanted, in a sort of
monotonous voice, by the reader and congregation; then
ensued a solemn pause of complete silence, during which
each seemed engaged in private prayer, moving the lips,
and occasionally bowing the head, but with no sound
audible. Then the reader moved from his pulpit, covered
his head with a kind of white cloth or veil, and, in a
different tone, and standing in another part of the synagogue, commenced reciting a few more prayers, chiefly
intercessory, and with these the service concluded. I do
not know whether they habitually recognise the English
as rulers of the country, or whether it was only in compli-
ment to us: the printed form, with the translation, looks
as if it were habitual; but there was a prayer for the
Queen, and another for me, as Governor; every prayer,
whatever might be its subject-matter, ending with a
petition for the coming of the Redeemer! When the
service was concluded, they asked if we should like to see
' the Ark,' which was a high chest behind a curtain, on
the top of a flight of steps: and which, on being opened,
disclosed five huge rolls of parchment. These, we were
told, were a copy of the Pentateuch, one book contained
in each roll. After seeing this, we left the synagogue,
escorted, as before, by the Rabbis, who accompanied us
to the landing-place, where the boat awaited our return.

To Mrs. Des Vœux.

Madras, November 13, 1862.

My dear J——,—The remainder of our tour was as successful as the portion of which I have already given you an account. We stayed at Cochin till Monday, going to church twice on Sunday. The church is a solid old building, containing monuments of both the Portuguese and Dutch, the former European masters of the place. The Bishop of Madras, who was on a visitation tour, and had arrived at the Residency during our stay, confirmed several young persons. We started on Monday about the middle of the day. The Rajah came to pay us a visit on board the steamer, just before our departure. I showed him the engine, and gave him a brief practical explanation of the mode of working, which, of course, he did not comprehend. When he was gone, we steamed away for Calicut, which we reached early on Tuesday morning, and there I and some of my staff landed, in order to meet a deputation of coffee-planters, while L—— and S—— returned in the steamer to Beypore. I had a very satisfactory interview with the planters, and left them well pleased with the views I propounded. After breakfast we drove over to Beypore, where we met the rest of our party, got off from thence by rail at half-past two, arrived at Coimbatore at six, and got home on the following day.

Yours affectionately,

W. D.

CHAPTER XXII.

REORGANISATION OF BOARD OF WORKS—IRRIGATION—NATIVE GUESTS AT
AN ENGLISH WEDDING — WASTE OF FLOOD WATER — SIMPLE MODE OF
DETERMINING THE QUALITY OF SOIL — OBJECTIONS TO REORGANISATION
OF MADRAS NATIVE ARMY — CHARACTERISTICS OF HINDOO ARCHITECTURE
— COST OF IRRIGATION WORKS — JOURNEY TO MYSORE — BIRTHDAY OF
THE RAJAH — DINNER AT THE PALACE — VISIT TO THE ZENANA —
SERINGAPATAM — CURIOUS BRIDGES OVER THE CAUVERY — TOMB OF
HYDER ALI AND TIPPOO SAIB — TIPPOO'S SUMMER PALACE — FALLS OF
THE CAUVERY — OOSSOOR — LAND ASSESSMENT — JOURNEY TO BELLARY
AND KURNOOL — MOWING MATCH — TUMULI — RETURN TO MADRAS —
'MASTER LOOKS BEAUTIFUL'— BURST OF THE NORTH-EAST MONSOON —
WRECK OF THE 'PUNJAUB'— EFFECT OF COMPETITIVE EXAMINATIONS.

To Colonel Harness, R.E.

Guindy, January 4, 1863.

MY DEAR HARNESS,—A happy New Year to you, and
much success in your efforts to work out good among the
young officers of the corps, intellectually and morally.
The great thing is to unite intellectual and moral excel-
lence : we too often find them disunited, and many seem
to think that the two are incompatible ; but this, I am
certain, is a mistake. That intellectual power brings with
it many temptations is perfectly true: it is like wealth,
of which it is said, 'How hardly shall they that have riches
enter into the kingdom of Heaven ;' but, though intellectual activity does bring temptations in its train, yet it
also, in many instances, provides that which enables one
to resist and overcome ; that is, it brings a more certain
conviction of the truth of God's Word, and of the folly
and weakness of those who pretend to impugn it.   I say
this, as I am fresh from reading that book of Bishop
Colenso, who, being great in arithmetic, has tried to treat

the Pentateuch according to the rule of three; but has forgotten that, in all computations, as well as in all logical processes, you must first be sure of your premises before you multiply the second and third term together, and divide by the first.

I think you were quite right in trying to induce the whole of your young men and sappers to be confirmed, and I am not certain that you were not right in leaving the general questions of faith, &c., to the clergyman ; but I think that I should have taken a more practical, and less doctrinal, view of the matter, and should have said somewhat of the object of confirmation, and of the blessing of that feeling of firm confidence in God as our Father, our Saviour and Redeemer, our Comforter and Sanctifier, ever present and ready to hear and to help us. That is the conviction which makes life happy.

I must not, however, make my letter a confession of faith, but must tell you something of my doings. At present I am at work upon the re-organisation of the Board of Works. In May, 1861, I sent in my memorandum as to the changes which I should wish to make, not in the department, but in its mode of working. I had not had time to ascertain whether its strength was properly proportioned to its work, or not. My minute rested with the two members of Council till November, when they sent in their minutes, recommending that the charge of the Public Works, that is, of repairs, &c., should be intrusted to the Collector. The minutes went home, and the Secretary of State took bits of both; decided to give to the Collector a bit of his old authority, and proposed, in fact, to have two sets of people working in each district. When this order came out, in May, we referred to the revenue authorities, in order to ascertain how they proposed to carry out the views of the Secretary of State, and what sort of help they wanted. We got their answer in November; it was then handed to a commission of

engineer officers, and I have now got all the papers before
me, and am writing my minute. The engineers shew
that the cost of the establishment required by the Collector
will be about forty per cent. of the money he has to ex-
pend ; and they then propose to reorganise this department
so as to produce a saving of upwards of 20,000*l.* per annum.
This slow process of amendment or alteration is but a
type of the working of the Government in India. The
local Governments are slow, very slow ; but then, when
they have made up their minds, they have first to convince
the general Government at Calcutta, and then the
Secretary of State.   Yours truly,

                                                    W. D.

To Sir Charles Wood.

                                    Guindy, February 4, 1863.

My dear Sir Charles,—Do you recollect my assertion
of a principle as to the storage of water—that we
should begin at the outlet of a river and proceed to make
anicuts or dams, until not a drop of water got into the
sea without having been previously utilized for irrigation ?   I have just had a return of the amount of water
passing into the sea at the outlet of the Cauvery ; the
quantity being sufficient for the full irrigation of a million
of acres.   I have also had a scheme submitted for bottling
up a portion of this in some of the gorges of the Neilgherries, sufficient to irrigate 125,000 acres.   The anticipated
cost is 8 lacs ; but double this, and call it 16 lacs, and let
repairs, &c., cost five per cent. on this outlay, and even then
there would be a return equivalent to twenty per cent. per
annum.   I will have the plan carefully examined, and
hope to be able to submit it in a few months, or, rather,
after the next monsoon shall have shown me the amount of
water I can depend upon collecting.   What I want you to
think over is, the advisability of carrying out such works
by *borrowed* money : it is perfectly hopeless to attempt any
large undertaking out of savings of revenues.   The

cost of dawdling over such works, expending a lac or two per annum, would be enormous, and the loss of returns during the period of construction would more than swallow up the interest of the sum which would be borrowed to complete it in the course of two or three years.   Yours very truly,
                                        W. D.

Captain Clarke, R.E.

                              Guindy, February 6, 1863.

My dear Clarke,—I am sorry for your disappointment, but it will probably, nay *certainly*, turn out that the result will be beneficial. I have for very many years made up my mind that God manages matters for us far better than we can do for ourselves, and have given up any attempt to carve out paths for myself. I tried in former years to alter the groove in which I was running, but, *very luckily*, failed in so doing : do you take up the same principle of faith and trust in God, and you will find yourself freed from an immense amount of trouble and anxiety. I send you a couple of copies of a minute of mine on secondary punishment, addressed to the Executive Council of New South Wales : it may be of use to you if you have anything to do with the Commission which is about to enquire into the subject. You will see that we took action upon this minute to the extent of declaring that no remission of sentence was to be permitted for the future. Of course the prerogative of *pardon* remained, and would be used, sparingly, and in special cases only ; but we determined that, as a rule, every man should work out the whole of his sentence, whatever that might be. I feel convinced that the principle is a sound one. The idea of reformation in a gaol is, generally speaking, a delusion ; I can testify to the fact that the men who used to come out to Van Diemen's Land with the best recommendations from the gaol chaplains were, as a rule,

the greatest scoundrels in the lot, and had added hypoc-
risy to the catalogue of their vices. The man who talks
loudly of his reformation, who pleads that he ought to
be let out because he has repented of his conduct, is just
the man who ought to work out his full time; he is a
hypocrite. Were he penitent in truth, he would submit
to the punishment as a just consequence of the crimes he
has committed. The people who advocate the issue of
'*tickets of leave*' in England, appear to have altogether overlooked the fact that '*transportation*,' that is, '*banishment*,'
was *the punishment* inflicted by law; and that the arrangements in the convict colonies were merely police regulations
intended to secure the people from the dangers arising out
of the preponderance of a convict population; the sentence
was very seldom remitted, for free pardons were rarely
issued.

I have now got an opportunity of dealing officially with
the question of the proposed reorganisation of the native
army, and I am going carefully into the whole subject,
taking up, first, its action upon our military position, and
then looking to the political consequences. My views as
to the military part of the subject are strongly backed by
military men; and some of the civilians who advocated
the change of system were startled when I pointed out to
them that the necessary result of the new organisation
would be to sweep away at least 500 European gentlemen
in this Presidency only; these being the men upon whom
alone the Government could place any dependence,
should the natives show any inclination to rise against us.
Good-bye.   Yours truly,
                                                  W. D.

To Sir Charles Wood.

Guindy, March 4, 1863.

My dear Sir Charles,—I have been reading two articles
on the government of India, one in the 'Edinburgh,' the

other in the 'Westminster Review,' the one most laudatory
of Lord Dalhousie (after a sort), the other condemning
him as a public robber.   As usual, the truth lies between
the two, but it seems to me that both are in error when
they begin to deal with the grounds upon which the
policy of the Government of India is made to rest.   The
'Westminster' represents Lord Dalhousie as ready to take
everything he could lay hands upon, by hook or by crook.
The 'Edinburgh' depicts him as without any fixed policy at
all ; but neither seem to refer at all to the state of the
native territories, embraced by ours, as operating upon
the peace and happiness of *our own* people.   The 'Edinburgh' justifies the annexation of Oude on the ground that
the king tyrannized over *his own* subjects.   The 'Westminster,' in its anxiety that a man should be allowed to do
what he likes with his own, altogether ignores the fact
that a man who breeds up a set of banditti upon his estates
cannot prevent them from attacking his neighbours.   We,
for instance, have no right to meddle with the internal
arrangements of the Nizam ; but we have a right to insist
that he should look after his own people, and prevent
them from robbing our tenants.   The country on the
border of the Nizam's territory to the southward is in-
fested by Rohillas—mounted robbers, who take refuge in
the Nizam's territory, and its state is analogous to that of
the Scotch and Welsh marches in times past.   We have
ample grounds for attacking a man who is injuring us,
but a very meagre excuse if we punish him for ' wallop-
ing his own nigger.'

To Captain Clarke, R.E.

Madras, March 10, 1862.

My dear Clarke,—I have had a long talk with Captain
Haig, the engineer in charge of the Godavery, on the
subject of the works proposed for the improvement of the
navigation of that river.   The Government at home,

pressed by the cotton manufacturers in England, who wanted to facilitate the transport to the coast of the cotton supposed to be rotting in the interior of India, rushed hastily into the speculation. The estimate, a very rough one, amounting to 300,000*l.* was accepted without investigation, and the work was commenced. When I visited the Godavery in 1861, I told Sir Charles Wood that I thought Haig's plan was a mistake, that it was an expensive makeshift, and that it would cost at least 1,500,000*l.* to do the work well. I applied to be relieved from the responsibility of the charge of the work, which was then transferred to the Government of Central India. I asked Haig, however, how he was getting on, and was told that wages were rising, that everything was getting dearer, &c. This I interpreted to mean that the estimates would be exceeded, so I put the question to him with reference to the lower dam and locks, which were to have cost 80,000*l.*— 'Will this be doubled?' 'No,' said he, 'I don't think that they will cost more than 14 lacs or 140,000*l.*' I would not mind betting that they do cost upwards of 200,000*l.* Now all this is very much the fault of the Government, which accepts loose statements instead of estimates, and which does not punish the officer who submits these as estimates. I propose to make a great change in this; that is, to hold the chief engineer, whose business it is to investigate thoroughly every estimate, responsible for the plan and the estimates for the work; while I make the executive engineer responsible for its proper execution. In any plan for the improvement of the Godavery, I should take into account the application of the flood water to irrigation. A slight sketch of the state of the river will serve to give you an idea of what might be done in this way.

At 40 miles from the mouth the river is 4 miles in width, including islands, and has at least 2½ miles waterway. During the monsoon, that is, from June till October, an enormous body of water passes down. This may average, for at least thirty days of this period, a depth of 25 feet, or say 8 yards, for a width of 4,000 yards, with a velocity of $2\frac{1}{2}$ yards per second, so that 6,912 millions of cube yards would pass during the day. Now, 5,000 cube yards is an ample allowance per acre for the whole of the season, so that there is a waste of water during twenty-four hours, which would, if properly applied, irrigate thoroughly upwards of 1,250,000 acres, and if this were multiplied by the number of days during which the flood continued, say thirty, the *resultant* would be 37,000,000 acres and upwards. Now the value of water when applied to land varies from $2\frac{1}{2}$ rupees to 7 rupees per acre per annum ; say, on an average, 4 rupees. We therefore allow water to go to waste which would be worth to the Government 120,000,000 rupees per annum, or 12,000,000*l.* sterling, while the value to the ryot may be put at three times that sum, or 36,000,000*l.*

It would cost the Government, say, 1*l.* per acre to construct the dams, channels, &c. that is, 30,000,000*l.*, which could be borrowed at less than 5 per cent., or, say, 1,500,000*l.* per annum ; the Government would clear at least 30 per cent. on its outlay, while the ryot would realise a profit of about one-third of the value of the water to him, or say 10,000,000*l.* annually.

Is not this an enticing speculation ? Yet it is not to any great extent exaggerated, except that it would be difficult to find such an area of ground to be irrigated within our own territory. As a principle, however, we ought not to allow a drop of rain-water to pass into the sea, without having first paid toll and done its duty in irrigating the dry soil of India.

Yours truly,

W. D.

Lady Denison to Mrs. Stanley.

Guindy Park, Madras, March 21, 1863.

My dear Mrs. Stanley,—I hope you will not have felt much disappointed at my long silence, but will have made allowance for circumstances; for I have been fairly overwhelmed with letters, and have never been able to complete all that I wished. Now let me begin by thanking you for your letter of January 31st, entering so warmly and affectionately as it does into our interests, and especially into that great one of dear S——'s marriage. Our bride and bridegroom returned to us a few days ago, after a month's stay on the hills, and are here now; but I am afraid we shall lose them soon, for they expect to start on their homeward voyage early next month. We had some trouble, and a good deal of cogitation, over our list of invitations to the wedding. One element of difficulty was the intense interest which the upper classes of the native population took in the affair; they had been *at us* ever since before Christmas, in the most point-blank way; at one time accosting W—— with, ' Your daughter going to be married; why do you not ask *me* to the wedding?' at another, coming to wish me a happy new year, and taking advantage of the occasion to ask me for an invitation; at others, attacking the aides-de-camp with similar requests. After some consideration, we decided on inviting three or four of the leading natives, and we asked them, just as we did every one else, to meet us at the church, and come here afterwards. In truth, as they were to be there, I was glad that they should witness the religious part of the ceremony, as well as merely the social one; and should see how quiet and sensible a Christian marriage ceremony is, as compared with their own noisy proceedings on such occasions. We had no formal breakfast, but we had the wedding-cake, and some ices, &c., in a tent on the lawn at the side of the house;

and the native guests were most eager to taste the wedding cake, and took very kindly to the champagne, which, considering that they were Mahometans, I thought rather odd; but I believe they somehow persuade themselves that that sort of effervescing liquor is not wine!

To Sir Charles Wood.

Guindy, March 21, 1863.

My dear Sir Charles,—I had no idea till the other day that it was so simple and easy a matter to classify soils according to their quality or productiveness. I had an idea that an accurate chemical analysis was required, but we manage matters in a much more simple manner here. A pinch of soil, less than an ounce in weight, is sent by post from the different localities to the Revenue Survey Office, and being there submitted to the inspection of some sharp-sighted functionary, is shaken up in a bottle with some water, and a rough determination of the proportion between the clay and sand in the specimen is sufficient to settle the class. The simplicity of the plan is evident; the accuracy of the result is not quite so clear. For instance, I got a threshing-machine from America, and being anxious to show its mode of working to the natives, and at the same time to get at some facts as to the amount of the crop upon different soils, I bought some ten or twelve acres of standing paddy, had it reaped and carried to my farm-yard, and there threshed by the machine. In purchasing the crop I got a return from the tahsildar showing the number of the field in the register, its class, its size, the rate of assessment, the estimated crop, the amount I was to pay for this, and the amount due to each man. I was grossly cheated, of course, as to the amount of the crop; in one or two instances the owner (probably a friend or relative of the tahsildar) got three or four times what he ought; but as my object was to get information as to the actual produce per acre, and to work my threshing-machine, I did not grudge the loss of a few rupees. I got more information than I anticipated, for I found that the classification, based upon the simple system of inspection described above, was an entire delusion. I got crops off land rated as 1st, 2nd, 3rd, and 4th class. The largest crop came off a 2nd-class field; the next largest off a 4th-class; and the sixth in the scale was off the 1st-class. The cultivation was the same in all, for it was wet land and fully irrigated. The difficulty I experienced in bringing the quantities into a proper form for comparison has led me to press upon the supreme Government the advisability of looking into our system, or rather no system, of weights and measures; not for the purpose of establishing the *best possible system*, which people will tell you is the decimal, but for that of getting one uniform system for India, and that, one which will harmonise with our English scale. What we require is simplicity and uniformity, while for statistical purposes the scale of our dependencies should admit of easy reduction to our national scale. Hitherto attempts to establish a better system have failed, principally from an absurd fancy on the part of some persons to continue the rupee or tola as the unit of weights. Now the rupee weighs 180 grains, and this cannot be made to harmonise in any way with our standard of weights.

Yours very truly,

W. DENISON.

To Sir Charles Wood.

Guindy, April 8, 1863.

My dear Sir Charles,—The worst feature in our relation with the inhabitants of India is our incapacity to act upon them in such a way as to modify their views, or to introduce any beneficial change of principle or practice. We are teaching them English, but their object in learning it is to get a place under Government. They, as a body, get little or no benefit from their knowledge of English, they do not read our books, and they have a literature of their own. The change, if there be any change, will be very gradual. I only hope that the Government will not put the cart before the horse, and give institutions which the people cannot comprehend, under the idea that they will adapt themselves to the institutions instead of adapting their institutions to themselves. This would be about as wise as it would be to put the father's coat on the child, in anticipation of the time when he would grow up to it. That time will *never* arrive in India. You will never be able to give to the Hindoo the feelings and character of the Englishman ; he belongs to a distinct race. I hold it most unwise to press upon such a people forms, or even principles, which we have, after centuries of labour and toil, made out for ourselves, upon the plea that they are the best possible. Man is not a mere machine, cast in one mould common to all ; his physique is different in different climates, and so are his moral and intellectual faculties. You would not give to the French people English institutions ; at all events, if you were to do so, experience shows that they would not comprehend or work them out. Much less could you venture to give to the semi-savage (for, with all the talk about Indian civilisation, the Hindoo is but an agricultural savage instead of a hunting one) institutions based upon the principle that each man is capable of judging correctly of his wants, and of the means of supplying these.

Yours very truly,
W. D.

To Colonel Harness, R.E.

Madras, June 18, 1862.

My dear Harness,—I enclose a comment upon Huxley's book, in which he strives to prove man to be first cousin to the gorilla. His object is to back up Darwin's modification of Lamarck's theory of development. I have a great objection to all these baseless hypotheses, and am quite content to believe that God made us, as we are told in the Bible, and that He gave us dominion over the beasts of the field, who were also made by Him. We have, by His gift, a right to deal with these as made for our use; but, had we merely arrived at our present position by development, or natural selection, our rule over the animal world would be but an usurpation. I have taken advantage of Huxley's anxiety to further Darwin's theory to have a cut at the foundation of the materialists; for if the gorilla, with man's brain, is but a brute, and has no more reasoning powers than any other animal, it follows necessarily that the formation of the brain has little, or nothing, indeed, to do with man's position as lord of all. I am hard at work upon two matters of some importance. First, the reorganisation of the Public Works Department, which will lead to some modification of the position of the Engineer officers, to the formation of a Survey Department, and, eventually, to a discussion with the home Government of the numerical strength and position of the officers of Engineers. I will send you my minutes when I have fully discussed all the points, but at present the whole matter is so mixed up that I hardly see my way to disentangle the knot. Secondly, the Revenue Survey and settlement. This has been before me some time; last year I dealt with the general question, and decided that the work was done in too costly a manner. Now I have had to go closely into the details, and have arrived at the conclusion that, not only is the work too costly, but that it is so badly done as not to be worth anything, and this implicates the Board of Revenue, and bears upon the general question of the mode of doing business.

On looking over your letter, I see you allude to the mode in which the Engineers are employed in this country, and you ask my opinion on the subject. As long as the Madras Engineers remained as a separate corps, used specially for civil purposes, and only occasionally as military men, I was willing to make such use of them as I could, without thinking or caring much about the principle upon which we were acting. Now, however, I have had this forced upon me. They are, or very soon will be, members of the corps of Royal Engineers, and the rules which guide us in the performance of our duties in the colonies, must apply to India also. The officer of Engineers will receive his pay as usual; he will have some colonial allowance, proportioned to his rank; but, having that, he will not be entitled to any staff pay, such as he gets at present in the Public Works Department. My present feeling is to reduce the number of officers sent out to the number which are required for military purposes, such as command of sappers, &c.; to have, at each divisional command, a company of sappers, and a field officer, and, perhaps, one or two officers on the general staff; to give to these men the charge of the construction and repair of all military buildings: then, as regards public works, if there were any who showed an aptitude for employment in such matters, I should *second* him, as is done in England, and pay him, certainly not more than I pay a civilian, as is the case now, but something which would be a sufficient inducement to him to take charge of the works. These, however, are but rough outlines of my present ideas. I have not licked them into shape at all. I shall, probably, in writing to Sir Charles Wood, recommend him to talk the matter over with you. We cannot move yet, or until we get rid of a good

number of our present men; but the sooner we let it
be understood that the men who now join the corps
will not find the Indian service an exceptional one, the
better.   Yours very truly,
                                                  W. DENISON.

To Sir Roderick Murchison.

My dear Sir Roderick,—An action has been brought
in the Court of King's Bench at Timbuctoo by the gorilla
against the chief of the Fans. I suppose it must have been
in form of a writ of ejectment. I send you the speech
of the counsel for the defendant, for whom the verdict
was given.[1] I have been reading Lyell since I last wrote,
and, so far as I have gone, am not at all disposed to adopt
his hypothesis. He will, of course, say that it is a legitimate induction from facts; but these, if they are facts,
are eked out and supplemented by the imagination; and
Lyell has the advantage of being able to draw upon a bank
—that of time—which honours his drafts to any amount.
I object to his appeal, for I can call it nothing else, on
behalf of Darwin. He says, do not trust to negative
evidence; do not refuse to believe in him, because no
specimens have been found which in any way bear out his
hypothesis. This would be all fair enough if the hypothesis had the slightest basis on fact. I quite admit that
a very small bit of positive evidence is quite sufficient to
overpower any quantity of negative testimony; but we
want this tiny little bit. Darwin has drawn upon his
imagination altogether, and may very fairly be told that,
before we yield assent to any such speculations, we require
to have something like evidence. Huxley is doing his
best to back up Darwin. What I have seized upon is his
admission that the brain of the gorilla is *as perfect* as that
of man. If this be the case, the inference is simple, that

---

[1] This has reference to a pamphlet.

the brain which, in its perfect state, allows a brute to be *such a brute* cannot be that which constitutes the man.

Yours very truly,

W. D.

At the beginning of 1863, we received from the Governor-General a sketch of the mode in which it was proposed to carry out the reorganisation of the native army, and the Government of Madras was asked whether such a system as that submitted could be advantageously introduced into the Madras Presidency.

As the opinion which I had expressed to Lord Canning in 1861 had been confirmed by longer experience of the state of the relations between the Europeans and natives of India, and of the working of our civil and military system, I had not the least hesitation in objecting to the introduction into Madras of the crude and ill-digested scheme which was laid before me. In a minute addressed to the Council, I went fully into all the reasons, military and political, against the measure which presented themselves to my mind. A brief abstract of these will be sufficient to give a clear idea of the grounds upon which my objections to the scheme were based—a scheme, I may observe, founded upon no military necessity or advantage, and advocated, most erroneously in my opinion, as an economical arrangement.

The native army, which forms at least two-thirds of our military force in India, was organised, speaking generally, upon the pattern of all European armies. Each regiment had a lieutenant-colonel and two majors; a captain and two subalterns to each company : these were all Europeans. In addition to these, there were two native officers to each company, holding ranks equivalent to that of captain and subaltern. Their rank was given them as a reward for faithful service as soldiers and non-commissioned officers, and not with the least intention of conferring upon them any of the powers of the rank which they respectively held; and I may safely say that in the Madras army the native officers thoroughly realised their position, and, as a rule, had not the least desire for further promotion, or for higher responsibility. In time of war it had been usual to add to the strength of the native army by raising irregular bodies for temporary service. Young and active officers, having a good knowledge of the native language, and of the habits of the particular people among whom they were going to act, were *selected*, from among the captains generally, and, with the aid of a subaltern or two, were authorised to raise bodies of irregulars, well fitted to act on the flanks and rear of a retreating army, or to encounter other natives when brought into line. It was the effective services of some of these bodies which suggested the preposterous scheme of making the whole native army irregular. I say preposterous, because it is, in fact, self-contradictory. The scheme, as proposed, takes out portions of the system upon which the irregular bodies were formed, and strives to graft them upon a different stock altogether; and in carrying out this absurd anomaly of a regular army irregularly organised, it strikes at the root of the very principle upon which the irregular system was based, namely, that of the *selection* of officers qualified to command and to lead these bodies into action. The necessary result of the system, submitted to me for my opinion, was that there would be in Madras a regular native army with six officers to a regiment instead of twenty-six, that these officers would be all old men, principally field-officers, lieutenant-colonels, and majors; that there would be no subalterns to replace these when they retired, or were expended in action.

The opinion of every military man whom I have been able to consult is conclusive as to the fact that the efficiency of a regiment depends upon the presence of a due proportion of European officers. Soldiers require to be *led* : they will follow readily whenever and wherever they see their officers willing to lead, but they will rarely go forward when the latter merely indicate the road, and are not prepared to show the way along it. The officers, in the best armies, must go in front. If this be the case with Europeans, how much more necessary must it be with the native soldier. He is fighting for a Government which he, in common with the great mass of his country-men, cannot but look upon as alien and intrusive ; he is acting, in all probability, against men of the same race as himself, speaking the same language, professing the same religion, and this a religion altogether at variance with that of his masters and employers; he has prejudices (as we term them) of caste, which interfere with the performance of his duties in various ways : is it likely, then, that he can be trusted to act with a smaller proportion of European officers than is usual? I shall, of course, be told that irregular bodies have acted very well with but three European officers to a regiment. I do not doubt the fact, but I altogether deny the correctness of the inference. These bodies acted well because they were *irregular altogether*—because they were commanded by special officers thoroughly up to their work, and hampered by no rules, no articles of war, no necessity for courts-martial : they were few in number, and were placed in positions where the officers might look for distinction and promotion if they did their duty well; and, as regards the men, I think it will be found that no very stringent rules were laid down, or at all events acted upon, as regards plunder.

I have said that the officers would soon be all old men—field-officers in fact, and the following return will show what the tendency of the system must be : —

	January 1, 1863.	March 1, 1873.
Lieutenant-colonels	7	30
Majors	104	87
Captains	167	162
Subalterns	71	70

Three months made twenty-three majors lieutenant-colonels, and six captains majors.

The plain and simple truth is that the attempt to convert a whole army into a *corps d'élite* must necessarily fail. The work of an army, like the work of every other profession, must be carried out by *average men*. We cannot afford to get rid of officers after they have arrived at some fixed age ; we cannot afford to dispense with the experience which age gives, or should give ; we cannot afford to dispense with the vigour and activity of youth, the physical energy which scorns fatigue and danger, even though this be unaccompanied with that degree of mental culture which theorists may conceive to be essential to an officer. In an army there is room and work for all, and it would be a fatal mistake so to organise our Indian army as to exclude any of the elements mentioned above. There are, however, considerations, of much more importance than those which may be called professional, to which it would behove the Government to pay the most serious attention. We have become possessed, gradually, of a very large portion of the vast territory of India; we have gained possession of this by means necessarily very distasteful to the former rulers of the country, and to the people generally ; and of these means I may say that they have not been of a character likely to inspire the community with much faith or confidence in us. I have the written admission of Lord Canning that we cannot trust the mass of the Indian community anywhere. We retain our position and supremacy principally by the moral effect produced on the natives by our constant success, and by that energy and determination of purpose which imposes upon the weak inhabitants of India—weak, I say, both physically and morally. We are, even now, but a mere handful of Europeans scattered among millions of natives, and we cannot afford to lessen our number, or to weaken the

European element by which the natives are kept in subjection.

The principle of the proposed change in the organisation of the native army is that of substituting native agency for European. It is proposed to reduce largely the number of European officers in a regiment, and to supply their places with natives, placing these latter in positions of responsibility and authority, making them more efficient than they have been, and selecting them from a higher class. Now our main safeguard during the mutiny was the utter inefficiency of the native officers of the Sepoy regiments; there was not a man among them capable of taking command, or of acting otherwise than he had been accustomed to do. If, however, we submit them to a course of training; if we place them in command of companies, and strive to make them really effective as company officers; if they are to lead their men in action, and thus get knowledge and self-confidence, we shall find that we have raised up a class of men more dangerous than useful. We shall have opened to them prospects which they have never hitherto contemplated; we shall have given them a glimpse of the position to which they might hope to attain were all the rounds of the ladder left free; but we tell them that they must be content with what has been conceded, and that *command* they must not hope for. What will be the result? At present I believe the native officers in the Madras army are satisfied with their position; they have attained the limits of their ambition. Hereafter, however, this will not be the case. The officer who has been raised above his fellows will be discontented when he has reached the conventional, not the natural, limit of promotion; and in proportion as he has been elevated in the scale, and allowed to have influence among the men, so is his discontent likely to produce results of a character which we have not hitherto experienced.

Having thus rendered our native officers more discontented, and at the same time more effective, what do we propose to do with the European element? Formerly we had in 200 regiments about 5,000 officers. With these we not only led the regiments into action, but provided for all the military staff employments, and for a variety of others. In fact, out of the 5,000 officers, it is probable that 1,500 were employed upon other than regimental duties. Under the proposed scheme, the number of officers performing military duty will be 1,200 : if we take the same number as heretofore (say 1,500) for staff and civil employment, we shall have a total of 2,700 actively employed, and we shall lose the benefit derived from the presence of 2,300 men of education and energy, without whom we shall find it difficult to keep the natives in awe. In fact, we dispense at once with more than one-third of the educated Europeans in the country; we lose the services of that number of men, many of whom, from their military training, would be most useful in times of danger and difficulty.

It is not, however, so much the loss of the services of these men that I look upon with alarm, as the moral effect which their departure will produce. We have deprived the Mahometan of empire, and we ask him to sacrifice all his traditions of dominion at our shrine. We turn to the Hindoo, and tell him that he must put on one side his prejudices of caste. We tell both the Mahometan and Hindoo that they must not only submit quietly to the yoke of men hated and despised on every ground, national, political, and religious, but must help us to fasten the yoke upon their own necks; and, while we do this, we strengthen their hands, foster their pride, and hamper and weaken ourselves.

I am quite aware that Lord Canning's wish was to give place and position to what he termed the native gentry, and so to prove to them that their interests were bound up with ours. He looked upon them as a species of feudal nobility, and wished to put power into their hands, under the mistaken idea that they would use that power for the Government, instead of for that which they might consider their own special interest. With every respect for his lordship, I hold this to be a weak, erroneous, and dangerous policy, and one which all history condemns.

Sir Charles Wood, in a letter which I received in the beginning of the year, alluding to the course which he had adopted with reference to the reorganisation of the native army, supported the view which he had taken by the authority of Lord Elphinstone and Sir Charles Trevelyan; and did not hesitate to say that, in his opinion, the irregular organisation for the native army was the best in all ways, military and political, for India. He added to this, it is true, a modest disclaimer, by saying, ' Of course, I may be utterly wrong.' I could not admit that either Lord Elphinstone or Sir Charles Trevelyan were competent persons to deal with a military question, or that their opinion should have any weight when opposed to those of the experienced officers who had condemned the irregular system both in principle and detail. Looking to the fact that I held the experiment to be a rash and a dangerous one, I did not attempt to conceal from Sir Charles my conviction that he was, in respect to his dealings with the native army, utterly and entirely wrong.

Of late years it has become very much the habit to treat professional experience with some degree of scorn, and to believe that, in most cases, a man of ordinary abilities might sit down steadily at his desk, and work out some very complicated social problems, treating them as part of some special science. I mentioned this to Sir Charles Wood, and pointed out to him that war was not a science, but an art, and that to perfect a man in it, and to enable him to express opinions upon it, he should serve a long apprenticeship. I must say that the dealings of the

men of science with matters of which they had no special
cognizance has not been so successful as to justify the
country in trusting them.

To Captain Warburton.

Bangalore, June 27, 1863.

My dear W——,—Thanks for your letter and the port-
folio of ferns, which arrived in safety, and will be a great
addition to my collection. If you have an opportunity
of *purchasing* or procuring a collection of ferns from the
Fiji or any of the South Sea Islands, will you act as my
agent? I will repay all outlay on my account, either by
placing the money to your credit with Cox & Co., or by
transmitting it to you through the Oriental Bank.

Now as to the subject of my last letter. You assume
that the advice I gave you, based upon my own experience, was solely applicable to myself, or to a person
placed in analogous circumstances to those in which I
found myself. A sketch of my career would show you
that you are mistaken, and that the rule I laid down was
one of general application. What, however, I want to
impress upon you is the wisdom of *working*, of gaining
knowledge of every kind. I don't want you to hide your
candle under a bushel by any means, but neither do I
want you to parade it offensively. If you have knowledge people will soon be aware of it, and will be glad to
make use of it. For instance, you are in the midst of a
very peculiar people, placed in very peculiar circumstances. I should, were I in your place, make myself
master of all the circumstances, political, social, industrial,
connected with the country in which my lot was temporarily cast. It would be worth your while to make yourself master of the system of registration of titles to land,
which is peculiar and very simple; ascertain whether it
is effective. You may hear and learn much relative to

the islands in the South Seas, to Australia, &c., &c. Make use of your opportunities, and, what is more, don't trust to your memory; note down everything, even your opinions, in black and white. You may hereafter, when you look back on these records, be rather ashamed to see how hastily you formed, or adopted, such opinions; but the very thought which is necessary for the formation of such is useful; it gives you a habit of thinking, of putting this and that together, of drawing inferences, which is invaluable. I am on a tour of inspection through the central part of my territory. Our mode of travelling is principally in spring carts, drawn by bullocks; fresh bullocks are posted at from five to ten miles apart, and for the Governor they will probably get four, or even more, miles per hour out of them. We travel principally by night; it is too hot to do much by day.

Yours very truly,
W. D.

To Lady C. Denison.

Madras, June 18, 1863.

My dear Sister,—Do you take an interest in Indian architecture and antiquities? I am getting together photographs of many of the buildings, both existing and ruined, and shall be glad to send you some. There is a sameness of form about those of Southern India—I mean about the pagodas; they are all pyramidal—carved and moulded differently, but preserving the same shape. When you get up to Cuttack, or Orissa, near the old Juggernaut Pagoda, the form alters to a sort of oval. There is, however, a sameness of conception and of execution about them, which very soon fatigues the eye. One looks with some degree of admiration at the deep carving of the hardest material; one wonders how the Hindoo could have faced such a solid block of stone, and had courage to commence working upon it; but after a short time this admiration evaporates, and one is tempted to look upon him as a mere laborious copyist, a bad executor of the ideas of others. The longer I stay here, the lower opinion of the native character do I form. People are fond of attributing the vices of the Hindoo to tyranny; they say that oppression has made him resort to the only weapons which he can use; but I very much doubt this. He has been, I admit, ground down by all who have made India their own; but my belief is, that it was the very fact of his poor character— the softness, the cowardice which does, and, I believe, always did, characterise him—that tempted others to make him a prey. I am afraid that the Government is disposed to adopt the cry of ' India for the Indians,' and to attempt to govern by, and through, them. My feeling is just the reverse of this. I cannot trust the Indian—I cannot get the truth out of him; and by leaning on him I should come to grief, for not only would the staff break, but the splinters would run into my hand.

I start for Bangalore to-morrow, and must leave my letter behind me; so good-bye.

Your affectionate Brother,
W. D.

Extract from Journal.

Yelwal, near Mysore, June 30, 1863.

Dearest M——,—I finished my last letter at Bangalore on Saturday. Our Bangalore Sunday was not a very pleasant one. The morning service at church was at seven o'clock, an arrangement which one would be very glad of during the hot season at Madras; but, in cold and cloudy Bangalore, it hardly seemed necessary; and, indeed, the clergyman, Mr. G——, seemed to think it a bad arrangement; but he had been forced into it by the doctors, for everything in Bangalore seems to be conducted with reference to the troops. The service in the evening was at six o'clock, and there was some refreshing singing of good old chants and tunes.

On our return, just as we were going to dinner, we received a telegram from C——, from Mysore, whither he and the rest of the staff had preceded us, saying that the river Cauvery was in heavy flood, and still rising, and that he would advise our not starting till he could let us know that it was falling again. This seemed just the difficulty that used to beset our troops in the old Indian wars—the monsoon rains and flooded rivers; but this particular river has not been so high for twelve years, and I was a good deal disappointed, for I thought it was all over with our expedition. However, between eight and nine o'clock yesterday (Monday) morning, we received another telegram, stating that the river was falling, and that, if we set out at once, we should reach our destination by ten o'clock at night, which would be the best plan, as any further delay would interfere with the Rajah's arrangements for us. Fortunately we were all ready, for we had been packed and prepared beforehand, under the supposition that we were to start at 'skrike' of day, as we should have done but for that first telegram; and as it was, we were off in little more than half-an-hour after receiving the second message. We had a very pleasant journey, like an old-fashioned posting journey. We travelled in Mr. Bowring's carriage, and the Rajah had furnished changes of horses all along the road, and relays of cavalry escort, too; and it was pretty to see, how, at each relief of the escort, the leader of the relieved party used to ride up to the side of the carriage, make a sort of salaam, and utter several words, utterly unintelligible to us; but the whole gesture seemed courteous, and looked like a sort of established form of

farewell, before leaving us to the charge of his successor.
About dusk in the evening we arrived at the outskirts of
Seringapatam, and there we found ourselves surrounded
by a crowd, headed by two or three very voluble men,
who came offering limes and garlands of flowers, and
saying a great deal, of which we understood nothing, but
that they wanted us to stop and get out of the carriage;
and at last it appeared that the Rajah had sent one of his
own carriages there for us. Out we got, therefore, and
transferred ourselves to his carriage, rather a rubbishy-
looking, but a very easy-going one. We crossed two or
three large bridges over the Cauvery, which was still very
high, but not overflowing. I was sorry that we could see
nothing of the town, which I wanted to look at, because
it *was* Seringapatam. However, I hope we shall make a
day of it over there in the course of our stay here. We
reached this place between nine and ten o'clock. This is
Mr. Bowring's official residence, as Chief Commissioner,
a few miles from Mysore. This morning W——, 'with
his tail on,' is gone to pay his state visit to the Rajah,
and the plan is that I am to drive in the afternoon to the
racecourse, and meet him there, in time to see the Rajah
come in state to the races. We were to have dined with
his Highness this evening; but Mr. Bowring, who preceded us here on Saturday, has, by a little skilful diplo-
macy, got us off that; as we were all inclined to think
one of these royal dinners would be enough; and the
great occasion, on which he was most anxious to have us
at dinner, is on Thursday next, his birthday. W—— is
to have his luncheon at the Resident's house in Mysore,
after his meeting with the Rajah, and then to drive back
as far as the racecourse, where I, escorted by Captain
Stewart and Mr. Bowring's secretary, Mr. H——, am to
meet him.

July 1.—We were able to carry out our plans yesterday just according to the programme I sent you. There

was not much worthy of notice in the races; the really interesting sight was the course itself, such an entirely
Oriental scene, though the sport was so exclusively
English. The variety of costumes—the Rajah's motley-
looking troops keeping the ground, and forming guards
of honour and escorts for himself, for W——, and for
me (for, as I came on the ground without W—— and
left it again in a separate carriage, I had a separate and
smaller guard); his elephants, drawn up in a line, with
their tusks and trunks painted; his state car, drawn by
six elephants; officials of all sorts (native) in varieties of
uniforms; one or two Persians, in a sort of dressing-
gown-looking garments, and high, pointed caps (these, I
imagine, were either horsedealers, or in some professional
way interested in the races) ;—altogether they made up a
gay and curious sight. The Rajah himself came on the
ground in a better appointed carriage than any I have
yet seen of his; it had a gilt crown and flag on the top
of it, but otherwise looked tidy enough. His own dress,
except the turban, was rather European than Asiatic; a
dark blue sort of frock coat, white trowsers and English
boots, and a gold lace sash. Altogether the dress seemed
not at all unlike the undress uniform of a general officer,
excepting that he wore a turban; but I was not near
enough to get a good view of him, as he was in his
carriage, or on the ground near it, all the time, and I was
up in the stand. Another small stand near us held all
the Rajah's ladies; but their stand was closed at the
sides, so that they could see without being seen. W——'s
interview with the Rajah in the morning had been very
comical, very ceremonious in its way, and very noisy;
and of the same nature has been the ceremony we have
witnessed to-day, of his return visit to W——. This was
to take place at the Resident's house in Mysore, and
there I also was to receive the visits of all the ladies of
the place; so we drove in there soon after breakfast this

morning, it being about an hour's drive from this place.
Captain Pearse (the Resident) and his wife are old acquaintances of ours : her father has property near Sydney.
About twelve o'clock the guns announced that the Rajah
had left his palace and was on his way ; and in due time
his noisy procession began to make its appearance.   It
was a specimen of ' barbaric pomp,' indeed, but it was *very*
barbaric ; larger than, but not nearly so interesting as that
of the Rajah of Travancore last year : *that* was really in
good taste, after a sort, and most of the Rajah's appointments and surroundings were good of their kind ; whereas
this, to-day, was much more like an exaggeration of the
procession of the Zemindar of Tinnevelly than anything
else—*very* much nearer to the ridiculous than to the
sublime.   He has troops of all sorts, some in red, some
in green, and his body-guard in blue ; elephants, led
horses, quantities of men marching in front of him, carrying spears, with which they eventually file off to each
side of his carriage, and shake them aloft as he passes
by.   The prettiest part is, that in front of his carriage
there walk men waving and throwing up coloured cloths
and shawls before him, with a peculiar and somewhat
graceful wave, which, I always think, is the same kind of
custom that made the people ' spread their garments in
the way' of our Saviour.

The Rajah was in the same carriage as that in which
he came to the races yesterday, but he was dressed in
white, with a fine jewelled scimitar.   I could not see him
well, however, for I was not ostensibly present at the
interview this time.   Mrs. Pearse and I, and two or
three ladies, watched it from a side room, through a
muslin curtain, and the ceremonial was much the same as
at Travancore, W—— handing the Rajah to a sofa, and
sitting there beside him, all the staff and other gentlemen
in a semicircle about them ; a little talk, then a presenta-

tion of garlands and perfumes.[1] The talk was not entirely fruitless; for W——, who has been wanting a sketch of the inside of the Rajah's durbar hall, in which he received him yesterday, obtained leave for Captain Glover to go and make one. 'What! in colour?' said the Rajah, as if he thought a drawing in colour of his hall would be a very fine thing indeed, and as if he was rather pleased with the idea. I have forgotten, after all, to tell you the most absurd part of the proceeding, which is that, just in front of the Rajah's carriage, there come some men, whose supposed business it is to clear the way; and these, when there is no real obstruction, seem to make it a point of honour to get up a *sham* one; and so they go pushing and thrusting and making a show of fighting and forcing a passage, and a perfect turmoil of noise, which continues long after he is fairly inside the house. All through the interview too, there were two or more men spasmodically shouting out in a lugubrious tone, sets of words, which we were afterwards told were some of the great man's titles: 'Father of the sun!' 'Brother of the moon!' &c. &c. As soon as the talk was over, and the Rajah had departed with the same 'pomp and circumstance' that marked his arrival, I received all my visitors; then we had luncheon, and returned here soon after.

July 3.—Oh that pen could do justice to the scenes of yesterday, when we 'assisted' at the celebration of the Rajah's birthday! How I longed for dear P——'s capital illustrating pencil! but even that would not have proved equal to the occasion. W—— began the morning by writing him a note of congratulation, to which, in the course of the day, he received an elaborate reply. We spent the morning quietly here, and at half-past three set out for Mysore, to be present at the birthday review.

[1] I ought to mention one ceremony which we did not observe at Travancore, viz., that as W—— and the Rajah walked up the room together, showers of very small coins were thrown by some of the attendants over and around them.

W—— only drove part of the way, and then he and his staff mounted their horses, to ride on to the ground. I went on in the carriage (accompanied by Spreadborough, my maid, whom we had brought in to see the sights), and arrived on the ground first. Presently came the Rajah, riding a small white horse led by one or two men on foot; and a minute or two afterwards, W—— and his train rode up, W—— in his engineer uniform, which he has taken to wearing on public occasions, and which is much more becoming than the Windsor uniform. The Rajah rode to meet him, embraced him, and then they took up their stations by the saluting flag, the Rajah in the centre, with W—— on his right and Mr. Bowring on his left, and the staff behind them. First, however, they made a digression my way, as the Rajah wished to be introduced to me, to the great alarm of Spreadborough, who squeezed herself into a corner of the carriage, and only just retained presence of mind enough to remind me that we had heard that the Rajah, from some caste prejudice or other, objected to the touch of leather of any kind. I twitched off my glove accordingly, and in the meantime the Rajah dismounted, came to the side of the carriage, and offered his hand to help me out. I stepped out accordingly, bowed, and begged to congratulate his Highness on his birthday, and to wish him many happy returns of it (all which was translated to him by Mr. Bowring), and gazed upon a little wizened old man, with red eyes, and making a sort of mumbling motion with his mouth, as if he were perpetually chewing betel nut, as I believe he really is. He wore the same sort of undress uniform in which he had appeared at the races, and the same turban, but with a necklace of three rows of emeralds and pearls. He is the same person whom we put on the throne as the nearest heir to the old Mysore family, upon the taking of Seringapatam and death of Tippoo. He was quite a child then, but he still remembers the Duke of Wellington (then Sir Arthur Wellesley),

who, it seems, made an attempt to enforce a little education on his young Highness, and used to lecture him
when he heard that he had been idle with his lessons.
After a moment or two of this sort of interview, he bowed
me into my carriage again, and then he and W—— took
up their station as aforesaid, and the troops marched past.
First, the cavalry—very respectable-looking, very well
dressed and well mounted; then the infantry, tolerably
well-appointed at first, but each successive batch decreasing in respectability, till it ended in a sort of Falstaff's
ragged regiment, a regular set of ragamuffins. When they
had all marched past, there was a little manœuvring and
exercising—pretty respectable on the part of the cavalry,
but consisting chiefly, on that of the infantry, in some
rather clumsy volley-firing. There were some artillery with
guns, too, at the corners of the ground, which never fired
a regular salute, but kept banging away at intervals in a
purposeless sort of way, as if the only object was to cause
a certain *quantum* of noise. As soon as all this was over
the Rajah rode up to the carriage again, dismounted, and
went through the ceremony of presenting flowers, &c.
First, he hung a garland on my arm, then presented a
little nosegay, then poured scent on it, and lastly gave me
some betel nut, wrapped up in a leaf; and then he went
through the same form with W——, and W—— with
him, while some of his attendants did the same to all the
staff; only with the gentlemen it is still more absurd,
because the garlands are hung round their necks instead
of on the arm, and at each successive presentation you
have to make a little salaam. When all this was over, we
drove off to the Residency, to dress for dinner, and then
wait till we were told that everything was ready at the
palace for our reception. Then the real comicality of the
business began: all the Rajah's spearmen came to escort
us, and we drove at a foot's pace from the Residency to
the palace, surrounded by these spearmen, and by a very

motley crowd besides, some carrying torches, and some a
sort of wooden frame with candles upon it; and these
last trotted on in happy ignorance of, or indifference to, the
fact that the wind had blown all the candles out, almost
as soon as they were lighted. There were other candles,
too, stuck on frames by the road-side; but, as most of
these either had not been lighted, or had gone out, the
only result was a strong smell of tallow. Very different,
this, from our dinner visit to the Rajah of Travancore,
where the illumination of the road was really beautiful;
but things improved as we arrived at the fort, within
which the palace was situated; for here one or two red
lights were burned with very good effect, showing at one
corner a large elephant, making the regular elephant
salaam, by putting up his trunk to his forehead; at
another, a guard presenting arms, and, above all, the great
square before the palace filled with crowds of people. At
the palace door was the Rajah, still in the same dress, with
a napkin over his hand, and over that a cloth of gold, upon
which W—— put his hand, and thus he was walked up by
the Rajah, I following with Mr. Bowring. But oh! the
places we went through! dirty passages, the floor covered
with shabby pieces of drugget of different colours, up steps
and down; and, oh, the turmoil and noise! Men walking
in front, shouting out the Rajah's titles, and affecting to
move obstructions out of his way; a tall boy in a long
pink dress, just behind him, holding up the end of his
Highness's sword, lest it should catch in his legs and
trip him up: crowds of people of all sorts filling up
the passages, crowds more in the squares below. (The
Rajah's own household is said to consist of 10,780 persons.)

At last we got to the Durbar Hall, and here the Rajah
seated himself, W——, and me; and here we waited
while the rest of the dinner-guests came in and were
introduced to the Rajah by Mr. Bowring. Now we had
time to look about us: and very striking, and at the same

time, truly absurd, was the scene. We were seated on common-looking chairs in a square room, rising to a sort of dome in the centre; the room handsomely painted, all deep red and gold, but disfigured by a number of trumpery-looking pictures hung on the walls; round three sides of the room were seats, on which the guests successively seated themselves, after making their bow to the Rajah, and behind them stood a crowd of native servants. The fourth side was the entrance, and here the noise and clamour had become 'fast and furious.' In front of the door stood two men, waving the cloths, and shouting out the Rajah's titles. On one side of them was a dancing-girl, performing her evolutions to the sound of a common fiddle played by a man standing near her. The door itself seemed besieged by all sorts of people trying to get in: I saw one of our own butlers half forcing his way, half projected into the room by pressure from behind, coming to take up his station among the servants behind the chairs, and others, probably, effected their *entrée* in the same convulsive sort of way. As soon as all the guests had arrived, the Rajah rose and handed W—— out as before, and we all set off again in procession, through more dirty passages, to the old Hall of Audience, where we were to dine. This is the place where the Rajah used to have his throne and receive people officially; but since we English took upon ourselves the administration of his province, and reduced him to an entirely nominal royalty, he has only used it for this sort of state dinner. It is, in fact, a gallery, divided by two long rows of columns, surmounted by something resembling Byzantine arches, very handsome in its own barbaric style; columns, arches, and ceiling richly painted and gilt, the whole a mass of red and gold and gorgeous colouring, and at the centre, near which we sat, four arches joining in a sort of groined work. Two long tables were set in this gallery, between the

rows of columns; a coarse common table-cloth, which
only just covered the table; common, kitchen-looking
chairs; some handsome china plates, some plain white
ones; knives, forks, spoons, and glass very respectable;
rubbishy blue glass salt-cellars. I give you this as a
specimen of the mixture of finery and shabbiness which
pervaded everything. We sat down about ninety in
number—all our own party, all the English residents in
Mysore, and the rest officers and others from Bangalore,
Madras, and other places, who had come up for the races.
Having seen us to our seats, the Rajah retired, and
watched us during the meal from behind a curtain, occasionally sending us a special bottle of sherbet, or some
particular fruit or sweetmeat, on tasting which we had to
make a little salaam towards the invisible Rajah, who, it
is said, always watches the reception of these gifts very
critically. I am afraid we did not get through this part
of the ceremony quite creditably, for W——, between
amusement and discomfort, had by this time got to the
stage of thinking aloud, as he is wont to do when he is a
little uncomfortable; and so the Rajah's benefactions
were received with a very audible ' What is this? What
do you want? Good heavens! I can't eat this! it smells
particularly nasty!' &c., &c., and I, in my vain efforts to
stop him, was at last seized with such a fit of laughter as
I could not suppress till the tears were running down my
face. As soon as dinner was over (there was no dessert)
the Rajah came in again, and W—— and I were removed from our seats at the dinner-table; that is to say,
our chairs were taken away from us there that we might
sit beside his Highness a little way from the table, while
the toasts were being given. Mr. Bowring gave the three
first toasts: the Queen, the Prince and Princess of Wales,
and W——'s and my health, and then W—— returned
thanks and gave the Rajah's health, after which we all
withdrew, W—— handed by the Rajah, as before, to a

place overlooking the great square, where we were to see some fireworks. These were noisy and tiresome enough; but the square itself, with its crowd of spectators, was an interesting sight. After this, we were handed down to another square courtyard of the palace, in the midst of which was a circus, and here we were to see an exhibition of the Rajah's trained horses and elephants. This was much like any other exhibition of the kind, and it concluded the entertainments of the evening. At its close, there was again just the same ceremony of presenting garlands, perfumes, and betel nut, the indefatigable men shouting out the Rajah's praises again every time any one made the salaam in acknowledgment of these gifts, and then the Rajah handed W—— to the carriage, and the spearmen and torch-bearers accompanied us to the gate of the fort. Another salute was fired, as there had been at our entrance, and then it was all over, and we were wending our way slowly and sleepily through the quiet country roads to this place, which we reached at a little after midnight, I thinking that of all the sights or ceremonies at which I had ever assisted, that of a dinner with the Rajah of Mysore was decidedly the oddest.

July 6.—Our doings since I last wrote have been quiet ones, compared with those of the Rajah's birthday. On Friday W—— went to have a private view of the palace, armoury, &c. I was to have gone with him, but was not well enough. However, I hope to make up for it to-day, when I am to pay a visit to the Rajah's ladies, and I shall have an opportunity of seeing what is to be seen in the palace at the same time. On Saturday afternoon we went to the races, and yesterday (Sunday) we again drove into Mysore to church; for there is a very tidy little church there, served by an East Indian (that is, half-caste) missionary. It was but an uncomfortable Sunday, however; for this ten miles' drive to church, and back again in the afternoon, with the interlude of luncheon at the Residency, broke up the day completely.

I was interrupted in my writing this morning by having to get ready for my visit to the palace, and now I have just come back, and will tell you all about it. I was under the delusion that I was going to pay a quiet visit to the ladies, but lo! as soon as we got well into the town of Mysore there was a sudden sound of native music, and presently I found the carriage surrounded by all the spearmen again, and a man at each door with a sort of fan or flapper, and two others with gold and silver sticks: a great elephant, with a man upon him playing kettle-drums, and a tremendous noise altogether; and in this state we drove on to the palace, passing on the way two or three carriages full of ladies, who were taking this opportunity of coming in my train, that they might see the Zenana and the jewels too, and who followed us closely. In the courtyard of the palace there was a guard of honour, and a band playing 'God save the Queen,' as if I had been W——, and at the door was the Rajah in his white dress, and much bejewelled, with his napkin and cloth of gold over his hand, on which I placed mine, and so he handed me up through a wilderness of passages, with every here and there an opening into a fresh one, that looked crowded with people. Mr. Bowring had driven in with me, and Captain Stewart and Dr. Porteous followed in another carriage; but all these gentlemen subsided out of sight soon after we got into the palace, and left me to be handed on to the mysterious regions by the Rajah, the other ladies following, and the attendants walking backwards before the great man, shouting out his titles as usual. At last we reached a little open court or landing-place, crowded with women servants; and crossing this we entered a gaily painted drawing-room, separated from the court only by a row of open arches, and in this were all the ladies. Two principal wives and five inferior

wives sat in a row across the room. They were all
dressed in the same style—viz., a long gown, trailing
below their feet, and over this a sort of gold brocade
shawl.   The gowns were all of some deep colour : one
was of a dark green, embroidered with gold peacocks ;
another, maroon colour, with gold elephants worked on
it ; a third of dark crimson, with small gold fish, &c.   The
shawls were all much alike, and the ladies all had their
heads bare, and jewels in their noses and ears, necklaces,
bracelets, rings, &c.   I shook hands with them all, and
then the Rajah seated me in an arm chair, and beckoned
up five younger women to be introduced to me.   Two of
these were his daughters, the others his grandsons' wives.
These poor girls really looked like a sort of lay figures
for the display of all the jewellery of the palace : they
were literally loaded with it ; and when I expressed a
wish (as I had been told I was expected to do) to look at
their jewels, the Rajah handed me forward again to the
entrance of the room, where there was the best light, and
then made the girls turn round and display themselves.
Such a profusion of jewels I certainly never saw.   They
all had an ornament on the back of the head, which
ended in a long pendant down their back, formed of
diamonds, rubies, and emeralds, great massive necklaces,
earrings, nose jewels, armlets, bracelets and rings, formed
chiefly of diamonds, pearls, and large emeralds, with
a good many rubies too ; but these, like all native
jewellery, are so badly cut and set as to have more the
appearance of pieces of coloured glass than jewels, though
they really are genuine.   After I had duly admired all
this, the Rajah led me to my seat again, and we went
through the usual ceremony of the garlands, nosegays,
&c.   Then I shook hands with the wives, who were all
great fat women (I believe fat is considered rather a mark
of beauty,) and the Rajah handed me back through the
wilderness of passages to the Durbar Hall, where we met

all our gentlemen again. There we sat down for a little
while, and went through another ceremony of garlanding,
and then the Rajah retired and left us to see his palace;
but first, just after he left the room, his prime minister
returned and threw a gorgeous-looking shawl over the
shoulders of Spreadborough, whom, to her great delight,
I had brought with me, and who had been in a state of
great wonderment over the masses of jewellery. The
effect of the shawl was almost bewildering; she half-
laughed, looked a little frightened and shocked at seeing
herself in such a blaze of red and gold, and then said in
an enquiring tone, 'Sure to goodness I may take it off
again?' Once set at ease on this point, she soon recovered
sufficiently to beg Mr. Bowring to convey her acknow-
ledgments to the Rajah, and then viewed her present
with great complacency. On examination, it was found
to consist of two shawls tacked together; and I am told
that they are always given in pairs. Both are red, with
a very deep border of gold, much too gorgeous ever to be
worn, but worth looking at as curiosities. Well, under
the guidance of the prime minister, we went to see first
the golden throne, on which the Rajah only sits once a
year, at some great festival which takes place in October.
It is handsome in its way, with a set of silver steps leading
up to it, and surmounted by a canopy fringed with pearls,
with long strings of pearls hanging down at the sides. The
vacant seat of the throne was now occupied by a little
jewelled peacock. I wonder what these peacocks mean,
for I have read of them before as appendages to Eastern
thrones. It was handed about to us all to look at, but I
confess I did not think it was very much like a peacock
after all. Next we went to the library, which is all composed of manuscripts written on palm leaves, very neatly
arranged and kept, some of them, I dare say, worth fer-
reting into by Oriental scholars and antiquaries. Our
next move was to the armoury, which contained many

curious old weapons neatly arranged, but somewhat rusty
and dirty. While we were there I was informed that the
Rajah's grandsons had come to make their salaams to me,
and straightway there appeared four young men, with
whom I exchanged bows and shook hands, and then they
walked off. When we left the armoury it was raining
hard, and it became a question whether I should wait till
the shower was over; but as we passed back through the
long room in which we dined the other night, I caught
sight of the unfortunate troops still on duty in the courtyard, and I thought it would be better to get away at
once, and release them from their attendance in the
pouring rain. Moreover, just outside this room there was
the Rajah waiting to hand me to the carriage again, so
we went away at once, and it was well that we did, for
the rain lasted more than an hour, so it would have been
of no use to wait. Mr. Bowring, who is skilled in the
native languages, managed very soon to dismiss the escort
of spearmen, who were also, to our concern, running
along by us in the rain, and we drove to the Residency,
had our luncheon there, then returned here and found
that W—— had come back before us from his visit to a
Government establishment at Hounsour.

July 7.—I must finish my letter to-day, for we hope to
start at six o'clock to-morrow morning for Seringapatam
and the falls of the Cauvery; these two objects will
occupy two days, so that we hope to get back to Bangalore on Friday. I am not sorry to bring my letter to a
close, for I am almost afraid you will weary of the
length of it; however, one does not see an Eastern
palace, harem and all, every day, so I could not but make
my account rather long.

To Colonel Harness, R.E.

Falls of Cauvery, July 9, 1863.

My dear Harness,—I left Madras for Bangalore on June 23, and after remaining there a week inspecting the barracks, &c., I started for Mysore, and, thanks to the Rajah, who posted horses for me all the way, we got to our journey's end (eighty-four miles) in twelve hours. Of course a good deal of my time was spent in paying and receiving visits of ceremony from the Rajah, an old man of seventy, who was replaced on his father's throne by us, after the death of Tippoo, upwards of sixty years ago. The Rajah is a kind-hearted, good-natured man, not by any means wanting in ability, and, had he received the advantage of education, such as was enjoyed by the Rajah of Travancore, he would have established himself in the heart of India, and made Mysore a powerful kingdom; but his good nature led him to lavish money upon favourites, and he was unable after a time to pay us our tribute; we therefore took upon ourselves the management of his territory, and retain it still, although the debt is paid off, and there is a balance of a million in the Treasury to the credit of the Rajah. This sounds unfair, and is unfair, but it is the necessary consequence of our system of intermeddling. So far as the people are concerned, it is certainly better for them that they should be well treated by us than ground to dust by native officials.

I will not say anything of the Court of the Rajah : you have seen enough of these people to conceive the mixture of pomp and absurdity, of finery and filth—the utter incongruity of all their arrangements. I went to a review of the Rajah's troops on his birthday. I cannot say much for their appearance as soldiers. As they marched past there was a fair proportion of well-drilled men, but the tail of the column was of a rubbishy description ; it was composed principally of spearmen, the heads of whose

spears were some thirty inches in length. These spearmen would be awkward people to deal with in rear of a
wall. It is said that in an assault upon a mud fort in
southern India, no fewer than thirteen officers were killed,
and the troops beaten off by them. A spear with a head
thirty inches long would be a formidable weapon either for
the defence or attack of a breach. The fact of thirteen
officers having been killed tells against the irregular formation of the army; it shows, in the first place, that officers,
in India, as elsewhere, must go to the front—must *lead*,
and therefore the more there are the better. It shows,
in the second place, that a rush at a place defended by a
few brave men is a rash act. Half-a-dozen shells would
have made a hole in the wall, and disheartened the defenders; the rush might then have been made with some
chance of success.

Yesterday, on my way back to Bangalore, I stopped at
Seringapatam, and went to look at the breach through
which we forced our way into the fort or citadel. The
fort is placed at the upper end of an island in the Cauvery.
The works follow the outline of the island, having but a
poor, irregular bastioned trace, badly flanked. There is
a sort of *fausse braie* at the edge of the water, with but a
low scarp, while in rear of this is a bastioned trace, with
a scarp from twenty-five to thirty feet in height. The
river at the point of the island may be from 400 to 500
yards wide, but the main body of water goes down the
north side of the island, occupying a channel of from 800
to 1,000 yards in width. It is evident that a good deal
of confidence was placed in the river, which at present is
rolling down a great body of water; in the dry season,
however, it is fordable nearly everywhere.

The spot selected for the breach was a badly flanked
face of the bastion at the salient angle of the work; the
scarp was of hard stone for about a height of twelve feet;
above that it was of brick, but this brick was carried back

for a thickness of eighteen or twenty feet. In the gorge
of this bastion was a lofty earthen cavalier, with a command of at least twenty feet. It would seem that a
battery was placed on the opposite side of the Cauvery for
the purpose of breaching this badly flanked face, while on
the opposite side of the main river a ricochet battery
was erected for the purpose of keeping down the fire of
the bastion and cavalier.

The effect of the breaching battery was, first, to beat
down the wall of the *fausse braie*, and to expose the
whole of the brick and stonework of the scarp. The
fire was then directed upon the brick portions of the
revetment, and enough was soon brought down to make a
steep slope up to the top of the stone portion of the
scarp, but the thickness of the brickwork, and its quality,
which is excellent, made it impossible, at the distance of
the battery, to cut through the scarp, and the breach was,
in fact, a slope of rubbish for a height of twelve feet, and
then a broken face of a brick wall, not quite vertical, but
nearly so. The breach was left just as it was, with the
single exception that the rubbish at the base had been
cleared away. I got down by stepping from one projecting brick to another, but to get up again would have
been a very difficult matter, had there been resolute men
at top. The truth, however, is that the men were natives,
and the columns of attack, which forded the river in
face of the fire of the whole front, had shaken their self-
confidence, and I have no doubt had sent a detachment
to the right and left to clear the parapet of the *fausse
braie*, so that there was, in addition to the force at the
foot of the breach, a prospect of an attack both in flank
and rear. I have a strong conviction that Tippoo had
intended to lead a body of troops by a sally port some 200
yards from the breach, to attack the storming party in
flank, and that the detachment which had moved down
the *fausse braie*, finding the sally port open, had forced

its way in. Tippoo was wounded there, and was killed some 100 yards in rear. The look of the breach has strengthened my opinion of the advantages of a revetment such as I wrote to you about some time ago; namely, a thin skin of a scarp wall, with counterforts eighteen or twenty feet in length, and within eighteen inches of each other; in fact, a revetment *en décharge*; and if the spaces between the counterforts were filled in with concrete, it would be right difficult to form a breach. The *fausse braie* was an absurdity; a steep glacis to the water would have covered the foot of the wall, and have made it almost impossible to breach it.

The Cauvery is a fine river during the south-west monsoon. The bridges over it in this neighbourhood are made in a very peculiar way. The rock in the neighbourhood is gneiss, which can be split into long blocks. Three rows of these, some twenty or twenty-five feet in length, and about eighteen inches square, are placed on end in the rocky bed of the river, about ten feet apart from centre to centre, in the direction of the length of the bridge, and about eight feet apart in the width. On the top of these uprights a sort of capstone is notched down, and on these capstones a lintel is placed, projecting some eighteen inches on each side of the bridge. On these lintels a set of blocks of gneiss are placed, in contact with each other, stretching over the space between two piers, and on these gravel is spread, forming the roadway. The most curious-looking thing in these bridges is their irregularity. As the upright stones have to be let into the rocky bed of the river, and notched well into this, it is a matter of necessity that the line of the bridge must follow that of the outcrop of the stone, and accordingly the bridge meanders about across the river in the most irregular manner. There is an advantage, however, in this kind of bridge, in that the destruction of a few of the piers, which is occasionally caused by an accumulation of timber against them, merely carries away sufficient of the bridge to let the timber pass, and this is easily repaired during the dry season. I will send you by the next mail a minute of mine on the subject of the organisation of the Engineers. I am going to send a copy to Sir John Burgoyne, for the purpose of enabling him to bring this subject under the consideration of His Royal Highness the Commander-in-Chief.

Yours very truly,
W. D.

To Sir Charles Wood.

Bangalore, July 12, 1863.

My dear Sir Charles,—You do not like to adopt my opinion of the natives of India. I should be really glad were I able to look more hopefully to their future—could I see in them the elements of improvement. Hitherto education has done but little for the Hindoo; it has not developed him intellectually so much as it has lowered him morally. The truth would seem to be that, their religion being purely formal, and having no connection with anything moral, or, I may rather say, having an intimate connection with the most brutal forms of immorality, is not operated on by that which tends to develop the intellect. The educated Hindoo does not believe in Brahma or Vishnu, but he avails himself of the licence which the profession of such a religion permits, or rather encourages. He lives entirely for the present, and uses the power which knowledge gives him to make that present as pleasant as possible.

I have had a letter from Sir William Hooker, enclosing a memorandum on the subject of 'Colonial Flora,' and pointing out the scantiness of the encouragement given by the East India Company towards the development of the natural history of this great country. Would it not be as well to redeem India from this disgrace, and to hold out encouragement to those who have laboured in the cause of natural science, and inducements to others to follow upon the same track? There is a very wide field open here, but few who attempt to cultivate it.

Yours very truly,

W. D.

To Lady Charlotte Denison.

Oossoor, July 23, 1863.

My dear Sister,—My last letter finished off, I think, the account of our visit to Mysore. We took leave of the Rajah on the race-course, and the next day we started after breakfast on our way back to Bangalore. We stopped at Seringapatam to examine the breach through which the Highlanders forced their way into the place, and, as the breach was nearly in the same state as when the assault took place, we were able to form a good idea of the difficulties encountered by the storming party. I went down from the top, and felt that a very slight poke would have sent me from top to bottom, had I been climbing up. We went from the breach to see the tomb of Hyder Ali and Tippoo. It was built by Tippoo as a sort of family mausoleum. It is square, with a broad stone verandah all round it, the pillars of which are black marble. The basement of the building is of granite, well wrought; the roof of the verandah of blocks of granite; the upper part of brick, covered with plaster, and the dome is the same. There are four doorways, one filled up with a handsome grating of black marble, very well wrought, the others enclosed by heavy doors of rosewood, inlaid with ivory. Hyder, Tippoo's mother, and Tippoo are buried inside; each tomb or sarcophagus is ornamented with flowers, which are freshly gathered every day; when we were there, this ornamentation consisted entirely of roses, placed all along the exterior lines of each

tomb, so as to mark out its shape; and a lamp was kept
constantly burning in the chamber in which these three
tombs were placed. The graves of others of Tippoo's
family are in the verandah and outer court. The whole
place is very well kept up, 50l. a month being paid by the
Government for various items, charities, &c. From the
tomb we went to Tippoo's summer palace, which was put in
full repair by order of Lord Dalhousie. The palace itself
is a quadrangle of about 80 feet wide, with a central hall,
and rooms on the sides, below and above; the whole is
most gorgeously, or perhaps I should rather say richly,
painted, gold being lavishly used in the decorations.
While these are confined to arabesques, nothing can be in
better taste, or more beautiful; but, when natural objects
are represented, such as birds, &c., want of perspective
and of correctness of eye shows itself. I shall try to get
some of the patterns of these arabesques if I can, for they
would, I am sure, be good examples of ornamentation in
colour. We went on about seventeen miles beyond Seringapatam to a bungalow on the road, where we found five
palanquins, with twelve bearers to each, ready for us.
This journey afforded rather a curious specimen of the
manner in which Governors travel in India. The resident
Commissioner of Mysore, Major Pearse, who had arranged
matters for our trip to the Cauvery, rather apologised for
the small amount he had been able to do for us, and
lamented the shortness of the notice he had had of our
intended journey. He had, he said, sent 480 men down
the road to form relays of palanquin-bearers for us; he
hoped *we should be able to manage* with that number; he
was extremely sorry; if he had known a little sooner, he
could have managed a great deal better, &c., &c.

We dined at the bungalow, and got under weigh at half-
past six in the evening, as we had to travel forty miles to
the Falls of the Cauvery, and we found our 480 men
sufficient for us. We seemed to be going across fields,

by no certain or definite path, but we hit our points where fresh bearers were waiting for us, and got to the falls early. The river is divided into two channels by an island, and of course there is a fall in each channel; but these differ from each other in character. In one there is a sheer pitch of 240 feet or thereabouts, with other broken falls roaring to the right of this, and making a very mixed scene; on the other side the river seems to open out above the fall, and to be divided into numerous channels by islands; all these, however, pour down into one central basin, out of the base of which the river makes its exit, so that there were no fewer than sixteen falls in sight at once, some falling sheer over the edge of the rocks upwards of 200 feet, others taking the same depth in a succession of plunges, like natural stairs. I hardly know which of these falls struck me most. We had our dinner at the bungalow at the falls. This is the private property of a native, and he not only permits people to use it, but furnishes them with everything they want without fee or reward. I took down wine, &c., for ourselves, but the owner's wine was put on the table, and we were indebted to him for a good deal of comfort. On the evening of the same day we started back in our palanquins, being told that it was not desirable to sleep at the falls, where fever is said to prevail. We were eleven hours in the palanquins, and got back to the Bangalore road at six o'clock on the following morning. After staying two or three days at Bangalore, where I was laid up by a slight attack of fever, we came on here, where I have taken a house for a few weeks. It is a good castellated mansion, built in and upon the walls of an old fort, by a man who laid out a great deal of money in perfecting all arrangements. The place, within the fort, is pretty enough, but the country round it very bare. There is a constant breeze blowing, the tail of the south-west monsoon, and the weather is cool and pleasant.

L—— and the children will remain here for two months,
at least, but I shall have to make a run to the north,
which will occupy me for three weeks or so.

Yours affectionately,
W. D.

To Sir Charles Wood.

Ootacamund, July 26, 1863.

My dear Sir Charles,—I have just been reading your
speech on the ' waste lands question,' and sit down while
it is fresh in my memory to express my full agreement
with you in every part of the speech, with the single exception of that which relates to the ' permanent settlement.' I have been going carefully into the questions
connected with the Revenue Survey, and I cannot but
feel that the Government will make a great and unnecessary sacrifice of revenue if it establishes a permanent
money rent or assessment. To a *permanent grain rent,*
representing a fair proportion of the crop. I have no objection at all. I would leave to the tenant or occupant
the enjoyment of the *whole* of the increase which might
be due to improvements in his system of cultivation, to
the outlay of his capital, or the application of more
labour; but I should deal unfairly by the rest of the community were I practically to reduce his rent by consenting
to take three bushels of paddy instead of four bushels, on
the ground that the price of the three bushels was. owing
to the rise of price, equivalent to that of the original four
bushels which represented the Government share of the
produce. You have no conception of the great increase
in the value of every kind of produce since 1852. The
mean of the last ten years gives an increase of upwards of
50 per cent. over the mean of the previous ten years; and
the last year, which was a favourable one for the ryot,
there having been plenty of rain, shewed a steady increase
beyond the average. I see no chance of a reduction of

price ; the demand increases faster than the supply, and the causes which have created this rise of prices are still in operation.

Yours very truly,

W. D.

To Sir Charles Wood.

Herior, on the road to Bellary, August 12, 1863.

My dear Sir Charles,—I have just crossed the Huggry river, ten miles below the site of the proposed Mauri Canwai reservoir. The bridge across the river has 15 arches of 15 feet span, or 225 feet water-way. On one occasion a flood came down, clear over the parapet of the bridge ; but now, in the middle of the monsoon, there is only one foot or nine inches of water in the river, and this for a width of 90 feet. The average flood level, as shewn by marks in the piers of the bridge, appears to vary from the present level to about four feet, though there is evidence of one flood up to the springing of the arch, about ten feet above this level.

The Irrigation Company and the Mysore Board of Works have each got a man measuring the water passing down the river. It will be amusing to see how their returns agree with their estimate of the discharge of the river.

There is a good deal of cotton passing down this road, not only from the northern talooks of Mysore, but also from Dharwar. It seems that the merchants would rather send their cotton 250 miles by bandy, and 136 by railway, to Madras, than 100 miles by road, to Sedashegur, or than 160 by road from Dharwar to Sholapore, and 260 miles by rail to Bombay. The cause I believe to be the cheapness of bandy transit. The road from Bellary to Bangalore, and from Bangalore to the railway, is bridged and in good order.

Bellary, Aug. 13.—I was a little premature in reporting

the good condition of the whole of the Bellary road, the rain having had a very damaging effect upon the last 30 miles into Bellary ; for nine months, however, out of the twelve, the road is in reality very good. Nothing could be more barren and more melancholy-looking than the country from Herior. We passed over twenty-seven miles of a bare gravelly plain ; to the right and left of the road we could see nothing to break the outline of this dreary expanse ; from distance to distance we caught sight of a tank, with a little patch of green under it, but these were few and far between. A tahsildar told me that 70.000 acres were planted with cotton this year ; two-thirds of this amount had been substituted for some other crops.

I have been discussing several local questions, one of which is of great importance to the town and district. I allude to the proposal to bring water from the upper Toombuddra to irrigate the upper talooks, and to secure a supply for the town. This is one of the schemes suggested by some of our officers, and taken up by the Irrigation Company ; but, to tell you the honest truth, I do not like to see these companies executing work which ought to be done by the Government, for the benefit of its own tenants. The Nabob of Kurnool is shut up in the fort at Bellary ; he has been incarcerated forty years. He was convicted (upon circumstantial evidence) of having murdered his wife, on our side of the river, and was deprived of his territory and shut up by us. He was a scoundrel, of course : I mean, he had no conception of moral obligation. He was cruel, as most Indians are who have power placed in their hands ; but I do not know that he was any worse than his neighbours.

Yours very truly,

W. D.

To the Speaker.

My dear Evelyn,—I left Oossoor on Monday, drove to
Bangalore, dined and slept there, and started for this
place at eight yesterday morning. The country, for the
first thirty miles from Bangalore, was bare of trees, but it
was all green, there having been plenty of rain to push
forward the crops. The upper tanks also were quite full,
and the lower ones with a good quantity of water in
them, and this adds much to the look of the country, for,
upon every water-course, dams are erected, from distance
to distance, and every drop of water is utilised. The
crop, on irrigated land, is generally paddy or rice, but
here and there sugar-cane. On the upland, a small grain
called raghi is grown in drills, at about six inches apart in
the drill, while at about four feet six inches apart, that is,
the width of the drill, a row of a sort of bean, which produces the Gingeli oil, is sown—a bad practice, but the
ryots have an idea that, by so mixing the crops, they
make certain of getting something out of the land. The
latter part of my route to Bellary was through a dry and
barren-looking tract, a bare gravelly plain extending to a
range of hills in the distance on each side. Bellary is the
head-quarters of a division of the army ; about 2,000 men
are quartered here. There is a curious old fort occupying the bottom, sides, and top of a rocky hill, which on
one side is a mere mass of boulders of all sizes, on the
other a smooth rock of gneiss.

Kurnool, August 22.—We annexed this country some
twenty or thirty years ago. The town is Mahometan,
the country Hindoo. In passing through the country,
one is struck by the appearance of the villages ; every
one is either enclosed with a wall and ditch, or has a
strong central tower. This is pretty good evidence of
the state of the country previous to our occupancy. One

would be apt to think that the feeling of security which now prevails would lead people to draw a favourable contrast between their present and their late rulers; but I do not believe that such is the case. To say nothing of the difference of colour, language, religion, &c., I have an idea that, although each individual ryot cannot but feel himself to be better off than he was, yet there is, with regard to many, if not all, some little sore where we have rubbed against him, and which, though small, is always irritating him.

The rise in the price of every article of produce has been very great; and, consequently, the people who depend upon small payments in money are very badly off. The gate of the yard of the Collector's house, where I am staying, is daily besieged by fifty or sixty old women, whose prayer is that I will fix a maximum price on rice. It is of course impossible to blame these poor creatures: their native Government would either have done this, or, by some equally foolish and arbitrary process, have made some individual merchant supply food gratis; and, just on the other side of the river, the Nizam is in the habit of acting as they wish me to do.

I went up on the 20th to visit the works of the Irrigation Company. These consist of a dam or anicut on the Toombuddra, and a channel leading from this, which brings the water of the floods at a high level, and distributes it over a great extent of country. The river is now in flood; it is, on an average, 1,000 yards wide, and is rolling down a body of thick muddy water, seven or eight feet deep, but during the dry season this wide bed is a mass of sand, with a small stream meandering through it. These periodical rains, while, from their amount and certainty, they secure some return to the cultivator, are a great evil in many respects; the ground is necessarily left untouched during many months in the year, and thus there is a species of enforced idleness which, while it accords well with the character of the Hindoo, is sure to perpetuate its weakness, and destroy all habits of steady industry. My feeling is that the people are deteriorating, and that we have, to a certain extent, been the cause of this. We have destroyed their native manufactures, have put a stop to the development of native talent, and are fast bringing them down to the condition of producers of raw material. I do not like to see this. I would willingly, if possible, raise and stimulate the native to exertion, give his mental power better scope for action, and hold out rewards for such action ; but I confess that I do not see my way to this. However, I must finish this. I leave on Monday to return to Oossoor.

Your affectionate Brother,
W. D.

To Sir Roderick Murchison.

Arrantipore, August 25, 1863.

My dear Sir Roderick,—I am resting during the heat of the day in a bungalow at this place, being on my way from Kurnool, where my territory joins that of the Nizam, to Bangalore, and may as well spend a portion of my few hours' rest in writing to you. This is not a pleasant journey. The distance is only about 240 miles, and yet it will take three days' and three nights' constant travelling in a bullock transit to get over it. Had I not got a lift of thirty miles this morning in a carriage drawn by horses, I should now have been jogging along, semi-baked, at the rate, at the utmost, of four miles per hour. I shall have travelled about 600 miles by this kind of conveyance by the time I get back to Bangalore. There is a great sameness of character throughout all the country which I have seen ; there is a trifling local difference at Kurnool, but this does not extend far. The hills are masses of rock, generally gneiss covered with boulders ; the most marked feature being the constant occurrence of large boulders balanced, like rocking-stones, one on another. I send you a sketch of two which struck me specially, but every hill has a dozen. In No. 1, the top stone was at least thirty feet in length, while that on which it rested was not six feet long. The stone standing on two legs in No. 2 was full twenty feet in height, while the legs were about ten feet in length.

No. 2.

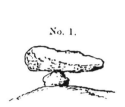

No. 1.

Now I want you to give me a plausible explanation of the mode in which these stones got placed so curiously. The hills are bare of soil ; in fact, they rise out of the dry plain, looking as if they had been washed clean of all earth. A force capable of denuding the hills would, one would think, have destroyed the equilibrium of these balanced boulders. I have said that the rocks at Kurnool are different : there the rock on one side of the river is a clay slate dipping about north-east at a small angle. About a quarter of a mile from the river the contractors for the work of the Irrigation Company are quarrying a bed of limestone, both for building materials and lime, which is curiously contorted. Close to the road the beds appear to be nearly vertical ; at fifty feet from this there is an anticlinal axis which would seem to dip to the south-west, and there is apparently another at about thirty or forty feet from this. The sketch below will give you a better idea of the section than my description.

Road   SECTION OF QUARRY, LOOKING NORTH.

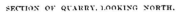

The limestone seems to be devoid of fossils; at least I could not see any. It is crystalline in texture, conchoidal in its fracture, burns into good lime, and, though brittle and difficult to work, makes very good building stone. You have heard of 'cotton soil,' I dare say: it is a black soil, as sticky as birdlime when wet, cracking and gaping when dry; the subsoil in some places appeared to be a stratified rock tilted at a high angle, and composed of quartz and feldspar, the latter black in colour. So much for the soil. Above this everything is bare; no trees are to be seen, and for nine months it presents a very barren aspect. The villages are always either enclosed by a ditch and a wall, or have had a central tower or fortalice. This shows pretty well what the state of the government must have been before we *annexed* the country. Every man's hand was against his neighbour, and the ruler was a predatory ruffian a little stronger than his neighbours. Still I am by no means certain that the great body of the people relish the change from the ruffianism of their native rulers to the orderly legal proceedings of their present masters. The merchants and money-lenders feel more secure, it is true, but even with these there is a sort of conviction that the road to greatness, which their wealth formerly opened to them, accompanied as it was with the risk of the bowstring or dagger, was a more exciting road to travel; there were more prizes then than now; it was a sort of lottery in which a man staked his life against the chance of being able to tyrannise over others. Now his life was not worth much; these Eastern people do not value life as we do, and he staked it readily. They are a curious people: the longer I live among them the less I like them: their bad qualities come before me constantly, and it is but seldom that I hear of their good ones.

Bangalore, August 27.—I am comfortable, and in a better humour than when I wrote the first part of my letter; still, however, I do not think that I can modify the last paragraph. I do not like the people. They are tyrants, bitter tyrants, to those below them; sneaking, abject slaves to those above them: they are cowards, and consequently lie without hesitation, in fact, instinctively. They have marvellously little honesty, and not much sense of honour which might serve as a substitute. People say that it has been mis-government which has made them such as I have described; but in my opinion they have always been such as they are now, and have therefore invited oppression. However, I will not thrust these opinions down your throat at the close of a letter. I am a great believer in breeding and blood: more of our qualities are hereditary than we have any conception of. I do not therefore relish Darwin's *crosses*, which would, in my opinion, spoil the breed, and make a very bad man out of an indifferent monkey.

Yours very truly,
W. D.

To Sir Charles Wood.

Oossoor, September 19, 1863.

My dear Sir Charles,—If you in England are suffering from the deficiency of cotton, we in this part of the world have not escaped scot-free. You have bought up the cotton, and I cannot attempt to estimate the number of spinners and weavers here who have been thrown out of work by inability to procure the raw material, but there must be many thousands. These are suffering also from the rise in the price of food, which is, of course, locally influenced by the transference to cotton of a large portion of the land formerly devoted to the growth of millet and other grain crops. They suffer, too, more than Englishmen, for as they form a 'caste,' they cannot turn their hands to other work. It is wretched to see these poor people prostrating themselves before me, and craving me, as the representative of the 'Nabob,' their old ruler, to do for them what he would have done, namely, order some wealthy man to furnish food to the supplicants. Hitherto the largest portion of the profit arising out of the rise in price of cotton has gone into the pockets of the merchants and speculators; but this year will show a different state of things; the ryots have become sensible of the value of the cotton crop, and are standing out for their fair share.

I have as yet only seen extracts from the report of the Sanitary Commission : from these I should infer that the members had trusted too much to averages, as a means of eliminating numerical errors. Did you ever read ' Buckle's History of Civilisation '? He there proves, to his own satisfaction, by means of statistical facts, that marriage in England has nothing to do with the affections of the parties, but is solely dependent upon the price of wheat. This is an instance of the absurdities into which we may be led by following statistics too closely : the fault of medical men is their tendency to generalise upon too few facts.

I have alluded in former letters to the clumsy system of native farming. I went yesterday to the remount depôt for the purpose of witnessing a match between one Englishman with a scythe and twenty-two women (women always reap in India) with the small sickle which is used to cut every description of crop, hay as well as corn. The women were instigated by the promise of a *rupee* (about a penny for each), and worked as I never saw natives work before; they therefore beat the man with the scythe, but he certainly would have beaten sixteen working at this racing pace, and would probably have beaten twenty ordinary workers. This will give you some idea of the loss of labour in agricultural work. It is true that the man with the scythe was an Englishman, but a native soon learns to use it, as I have seen in my own garden, and he would be physically equal to half an

European. So one native with a scythe would do the work of ten, or say eight, natives with sickles, and were he paid at double the usual rate, the labour of six men or women would be saved by the use of a proper tool. Colonel Thompson showed me a native ploughing, and he drew as straight a furrow as anyone could desire to see. Pray take this as a corollary to my request about agricultural implements. I shall supplement it by an application for *tools* as soon as I get down to Madras.

Yours truly,
W. D.

To Mrs. Des Vœux.

Madras, October 4, 1863.

My dear J——,—We got here yesterday at 11 A.M., having left Oossoor at six the evening before, and travelled all night in transits, getting early in the morning to the railroad, where a special train was waiting for us. A short time before we left Oossoor we went to visit an old tumulus which had been opened. It was about seven miles from our house, on a narrow stony ridge between two small valleys. The one which had been opened was covered with a large stone slab 14ft. by 12ft. by 19in., and weighed full twenty tons. How the people got it there it is difficult to say. There were several tumuli upon the same ridge, and I agreed to pay for the labour of opening another, which we did at a cost of 16s. 6d. We found it to consist of a sort of square box enclosed by slabs of split gneiss about six or seven feet long, four broad, and from six to nine inches thick. The space within was filled with earth well rammed. Some clever fellow had been beforehand with us: he had got in by knocking a hole through one of the side stones big enough to admit his body, and he had taken whatever there was to take, leaving only some broken earthen chatties or pots. The superintendent of the remount depôt has caused several of the tumuli to be opened since our departure, and has found some which had not been disturbed, containing bones and weapons, spear-heads, and swords of iron.

We have made a good many improvements both here and at Guindy. Here we have levelled and improved the grounds about the house, and made a fresh entrance under some banyan trees, which give it the effect of an avenue.   Your affectionate Brother,

W. D.

This alteration of the entrance gave rise to a little scene, which affords a droll illustration of one phase of native character—viz., the total want of perception, not only of the value of truth in itself, but of the importance which we attach to it; and the consequent tendency, on all occasions, to give the answer which they imagine will be most agreeable to the questioner, rather than the true one. This new approach passed so close to the rear of the bungalow occupied by one of the aides-de-camp that he believed himself in some danger of being visible to passers-by while at his bath or performing his toilette; and, under the influence of this idea, he sent his servant to walk by the house and let him know if he could see him from the road. The man, unable to conceive any motive for such a request but one of personal vanity, shortly returned with the assurance that 'master looked beautiful!'

It is scarcely necessary to add that it was found, on more accurate observation, quite impossible to see into the bungalow from the approach.

Extracts from Journal.

Madras, October 6, 1863.

We drove yesterday, in the cool of the evening, up to Guindy. That charming place really has very nearly approached perfection, and is almost like a bit of fairy-land. The beautiful Victoria Regia was in bloom in its tank, which will have to be enlarged to give full scope to all the great leaves.

October 14.— This morning I have witnessed the sight I have been wanting to see—viz., the first burst of the north-east monsoon. It is the only monsoon we get much of in Madras, and it is supposed to begin on the 15th of October, so we missed its first onset last year by not being back from the hills. For the last three days I have been watching clouds collecting in that quarter, and yesterday evening, for the first time, the wind shifted into the north-east very quietly and gently; but, quiet as it was, it was the forerunner of an immense change, for this morning we opened our eyes on a complete atmosphere of mighty rain. It did not come in, as I expected, with a roaring gale; on the contrary, it was quite calm : there was only thunder and this wonderful rain, and *such* rain ! the whole air was darkened with it as if it had been a mist ; but it really was rushing, roaring torrents, which lasted for several hours, and soon converted our ' compound ' into a swamp. There was something grand in it ; and little George, to whom a shower of rain is an event, came running to my room to beg me to look at it. It is curious to see how that child admires rain, and gazes at it as a sort of phenomenon. This morning we have parted with Captain Glover, who has had to give up his appointment with us in order to rejoin his regiment, now that it is going on war service to New Zealand. He is a great loss to our party here : so seriously good and right-minded, so kind and warm-hearted, and so amusing and agreeable; and he, I believe, is as sorry to leave us as we are to part with him.

October 19.—After some days of heavy showers at in-tervals, the north-east monsoon has at last burst upon us in great force. All last night, in waking intervals, I was aware of a continuous roar of mingled wind, surf, rain, and thunder, with vivid lightning ; and this morning revealed to us a very stormy sky, and *such* a tumbling surf as made us resolve that, rain or no rain, we would struggle down

somehow to the beach in the evening to see it in all its
grandeur. At about eleven o'clock the 'danger signal'
was hoisted at the Fort to warn all ships in the roadstead
to put to sea, for the Madras roads are a most dangerous
place during the north-east monsoon gales. During the
latter part of the morning, therefore, my bedroom windows became a point of most tempting fascination, and I
am ashamed to say I wasted a good deal of time there
watching the ships one after another clawing off, as well
as they could, from the dangerous neighbourhood of the
surf, and plunging out to sea, rolling and pitching so
heavily that it almost made one sea-sick to look at them.
About two o'clock the fort began firing guns at five
minutes' intervals, to enforce the warning to all vessels to
put to sea; and as soon as luncheon was over, we all
hastened to the upstairs verandah, to watch the struggles
of the poor ships which had not been wise or fortunate
enough to take the first hint of the flags. It was very interesting. One or two we thought were on shore, or in
the very act of drifting on, as they tried to start; but at
last they all got away, except two. W—— had received
a message to the effect that one of these, the 'Punjaub,'
was drifting on shore, and when we got upstairs we saw
her masts apparently close to the Fort church. At last
curiosity overpowered us, and we thought that on a day
of such heavy clouds there could not be much to fear from
the power of the sun, and why should we not, then, go
down to the beach at once? so we ordered the carriage,
sallied forth, and drove along till we came nearly
abreast of the unfortunate 'Punjaub,' which was lying in
the surf literally within a few yards of the shore, just
under the fort. Her crew were coming on shore one by
one along a hawser, which was stretched from the stern
of the ship, while a group of catamaran men were diving
through the surf to assist them. Each man clawed along
the rope till he came to the line of surf, where the rope

descended till he touched the water, and then he let himself drop into the great wave, and was instantly clutched by these catamaran men and helped on shore. It was really a fine sight to see these men plunge through the surf; diving just under the advancing wave and coming up on the other side of it, all ready to receive the shipwrecked men as they dropped. I waited till we saw one man, who could not swim, hauled along the rope in a sort of bag, or sling; and then I came home, as it was beginning to rain again, and we did not like keeping the servants out in the wet; but W—— remained out himself, and has just come home with the news that all the people are safe out of her. The ship is being lifted in by the surf closer and closer, and I believe she will be almost dry by morning if the sea goes down at all.

To Sir Charles Wood.

Madras, November 7, 1863.

My dear Sir Charles,—Has a doubt ever crossed your mind of the benefit which the public service derives from the system of competitive examination? If such a doubt has not suggested itself, pray have a little conversation with some of the men whom you are about to send out as civil servants to India. Don't take an university man, but some of the stray diamonds which are picked up rather promiscuously. If there is one quality which is more required in India than elsewhere, it is that which makes a man a gentleman. I do not mean that a civil servant should be perfectly *au fait* of the usages of society, but he should respect himself, and be specially courteous to others. I am decidedly of opinion that some *selection* of candidates should be made. It will never answer to ring a bell at the corner of the street and ask all passers-by to come in and fight for their dinner, even though the contest be intellectual. For my own part, I should like to see a really good examination of selected men, without any competition at all. I want to have thirty or forty really good men, but I don't want to know, at this early period of their career, which is considered to be the best of the lot. Competition introduces and fosters cramming, and I believe this to be positively injurious to both the intellectual and moral qualities.

Yours truly,
W. D.

To Sir Roderick Murchison.

Madras, November 8, 1863.

My dear Sir Roderick.—Many thanks for your letter: it was a lucky day, to be marked with a white stone, when I first commenced my correspondence with you. I am glad that you find something in my letters worth notice, for I feel sometimes as if I were exchanging '*greenbacks*' for gold. Your account of the doings of the Duke of Northumberland is very interesting : it is very pleasant to see a man make use of his wealth in the way the Duke is doing ; no one grudges him one sixpence of an income which is spent in such a manner. Your '*Lord and Pearl of Princes*' must be rightly named if he has the varied qualifications enumerated by you. You may take my word for it, however, that he is a very rare pearl, and you might dredge in vain throughout India for an oyster which would turn out such an article. It is lucky for us, probably, that it is so, for our tenure of the country would be very shaky were such men common. I hold, however, to the straightforward, dogged perseverance of our English nature (I will not call it obstinacy, though it is closely allied to it) to enable us to hold India against all the Hindoos that ever were or ever will be born, and I look upon the idea which the doctrinaires are so fond of pressing upon us, that we are acting as tutors to teach the Hindoos to govern themselves, as a piece of sentimental trash, good enough for Exeter Hall, but too absurd to be uttered in the House of Commons. To return, however to our sheep, though he be but a black one. You say he is a Buddhist. How does he manage to feed and worship? Does he carry his little pet idol about with him? I had a well-educated Hindoo in my council, and I heard that he was seen, on one of the hottest days of last summer, stripped to the waist, fanning a stone idol with all his might. Now my experience of educated Hindoos, which I admit is not very extensive —I mean, of course, of men who have some knowledge of *our* literature—is, that they have thrown overboard everything in the shape of belief in their idols, but have not taken up any other belief: they are, in fact, worshippers of themselves; and my friend who was fanning the idol, I have no doubt, had some object to gain which was worth the labour; he was imposing upon a Brahmin, I dare say.

A Hindoo drama on the value of truth must be a curiosity, looking to the fact of their habitual disregard of it in real life. What do you think of Trevelyan's scheme of competitive examination? I dislike it. It may have the effect of getting a few first-rate men into the public service, but it is no guarantee for the ability of the great body. The work of the world is done by men of average abilities, and the Government wants, we will say, thirty of these. By the competitive examination it gets thirty men who go tailing away from A, who gets 7,000 marks, to X, who gets 1,500. I would rather establish a sufficiently high standard, and take care that everybody came up to that, than introduce the system of competition, which holds out an excuse for cramming, a practice most injurious to both the intellect and the morals of the men who are subjected to it.

Yours very truly,

W. D.

CHAPTER XXIII.

DEATH OF LORD ELGIN—ASSUMPTION OF THE OFFICE OF GOVERNOR-GENERAL — WAR ON THE NORTH-WEST FRONTIER—ARRIVAL AT CALCUTTA, AND FIRST DAYS THERE — PROPOSITION TO THE COUNCIL TO RESCIND THEIR ORDER FOR THE WITHDRAWAL OF TROOPS FROM THE FRONTIER—PROTEST OF SIR CHARLES TREVELYAN — MINUTE EMBODYING THE REASONS FOR THE PROPOSITION—FORWARD MOVEMENT OF TROOPS—SUCCESSFUL RESULT—POLITICAL AGENTS AT THE SEAT OF WAR—OBJECTIONS TO THE REMOVAL OF LOCAL CORPS FROM THE CONTROL OF THE CENTRAL GOVERNMENT—GALLANT CONDUCT OF ENSIGN SANDERSON—ETIQUETTE AT CALCUTTA—APPOINTMENT OF SIR JOHN LAWRENCE TO THE GOVERNOR-GENERALSHIP—HOUSE OF A WEALTHY HINDOO—REMARKS ON THE GENERAL WORKING OF THE SUPREME GOVERNMENT IN INDIA—GANGES CANAL—BREEDING OF HORSES FOR MILITARY PURPOSES.

LORD ELGIN had decided to call together the Legislative Council of India at Lahore towards the end of 1863, and at the same time to collect a large body of troops at that point, forming a sort of camp of instruction. He left Simla, where he had passed the hot season, and moved across the difficult mountainous district which lies between that place and Lahore. The fatigue, however, of such a journey was too much for a man in his state of health, and he was taken so seriously ill at a place called Dhurrumsala as to be compelled to halt there, and, after lingering for about a fortnight, he died at 2 A.M. on November 20, the proximate cause of death being disease of the heart.

On November 10 I received a telegram from the private secretary, to the effect that Lord Elgin had directed him to communicate to me the fact of his danger, and from that time I received nearly daily accounts of the progress of the disease, till, on the 21st, I received information, both from Dhurrumsala and Calcutta, of its fatal

termination. These telegrams were sent to me because
by the 51st clause of the India Council's Act, providing
for cases in which a vacancy in the office of the Governor-
General might take place unexpectedly, the senior of the
Governors of the presidencies of Madras and Bombay was
authorised to act as Governor-General until the vacancy
could be filled up by the arrival of a successor. I then,
as being the senior, had to assume temporarily the functions of Governor-General, and the following narrative,
illustrated by letters to my family and others, will give a
sufficiently detailed account of the character of the duties
I had to perform in the six weeks, or thereabouts, during
which I officiated as Viceroy, and of the opinion which I
was able to form of the working of the system of the
Indian Government generally.

On November 13, in addition to the usual telegram
giving an account of the state of Lord Elgin, I got another
in cipher from one of the secretaries of Government,
informing me that the work in his department was getting
in arrear, and asking me whether, in case of Lord Elgin's
death, I proposed to proclaim myself at once as Governor-
General under the 51st clause of the Council's Act.

I did not at all like this mode of ignoring the existence
of Lord Elgin, who, for aught I knew, might recover; and
I therefore replied to the effect that I did not intend to
proclaim myself as Governor-General, but that, should
Lord Elgin's disorder terminate fatally, I should proceed
with as little delay as possible to Calcutta, and there
assume the government. I should not have attempted to
carry on the work of the government of India through
the medium of the telegraph, even in quiet times; still
less, then, did I wish to plunge into the troubled waters
of Calcutta politics with nothing better than telegrams or
letters to guide me. Telegrams I did get, both from Sir
Hugh Rose, the Commander-in-chief,* and from Colonel

* Now Lord Strathnairn.

Durand, the Foreign Secretary, bearing upon the state of things on the north-west frontier, and these showed me that matters were not by any means in a satisfactory position. To Sir Hugh Rose I replied by asking him to give me full information as to the particular evils which required to be remedied, and to let me know whether my presence at Lahore would in any way strengthen his hands. To Colonel Durand, who sent me a list of questions which required speedy consideration, I gave directions to let me have a distinct *précis* of all the matters relating to each of these, so that, on my arrival at Calcutta, I might have some notion of the questions with which I should have to deal. I got from Sir Hugh Rose a telegram, on the 25th, saying that it would strengthen his hands most materially, and be of the greatest benefit to the public service, if I were to proceed to Lahore as soon as possible, and he promised me a full and frank expression of opinion upon the existing state of things on the frontier. The effect of this telegram was to decide me to make my way up to Calcutta with as little delay as possible. I had intended to have gone up by the mail steamer, which was expected in about the 28th, but under the circumstances I thought it better to start at once, and I embarked on the 26th on board the 'Arracan' Government steamer, taking with me only my military secretary and an aide-de-camp, as I heard that I should be able to avail myself of the services of the officers on Lord Elgin's staff.

Before I embarked I received a letter from Colonel Durand, and another from Colonel Adye, Royal Artillery, both dated from the camp near Lahore, and written, of course, previous to the death of Lord Elgin, but the former clearly anticipating such an event. From this letter I gathered that the principal cause of the visit of the Governor-General to Lahore was a wish to control the military operations in the north-west against the Sitana

fanatics. ' I say the most important ' (I quote the letter),
' because these operations having been forced upon Lord
Elgin, much against his will, by the aggressions of the
fanatics and their allied tribes, and by the pressure of the
Punjaub Government, anxious to free its frontier from this
irritating sore, the Governor General was determined to
circumscribe the sphere of action within manageable
limits, and not to accede to Sir Hugh Rose's views, which
were all in favour of a regular campaign on a large scale,
under his own guidance, early in the ensuing spring.'
The letter from Colonel Adye gave, as will be seen, for I
copy the whole of it, a sketch such as a clear-headed
military man would draw of a state of things coming under
his own observation, without troubling himself about
causes or motives other than those of which he was
cognizant. It will be the more interesting as showing how
two accounts of the same events may vary, not so much
when the writers deal simply with the facts, as when
they begin to draw inferences from these, and to form
opinions as to the wisdom of the policy pursued. Colonel
Adye says :—

'The frontier question has suddenly assumed rather a
serious aspect, and, as far as I understand, the state of the
case is as follows. The whole of our north-west frontier
is shut in by high mountains, which are inhabited by a
wild, lawless set of tribes, men who only agree in one thing,
which is that they will never leave off cutting each
other's throats, unless there seems a chance of cutting ours.
Various desultory expeditions have been made during the
last few years against these tribes ; but although they are
badly armed, and without discipline, they are brave and
warlike, and their country is so mountainous and difficult,
and so destitute of roads, that it is no easy matter to
punish them. They manage, therefore, to cause us as
much loss as we do them. Being a dangerous frontier, it
is, as seems usual in this country, guarded by a force

which is altogether independent of the Commander-in-chief, with the exception of the one station of Peshawur; in fact, the Governor of the Punjaub has this force at his disposal, and every now and then enters into a little war on his own account, and, in this instance, seems to have burnt his fingers. Some distance to the north-east of Peshawur, there is a tribe which has been harbouring fanatical Mahometans from the plains, including, I believe, some of our old sepoys; and, as they have been troublesome, it was resolved to make a rapid expedition over the Indus into their mountains to punish them. To the Punjaub force were added the 71st Highlanders, and a battery of artillery, the latter carried on elephants, in addition to the mule mountain batteries of the Punjaub force—say 6,000 of all arms. The rebels whom we are anxious to punish inhabit Sitana, and the Mahabun mountain. In order to catch them, a force under Colonel Bright was posted at Derbund, whilst the main body, under Chamberlain, leaving Peshawur, made its way up the Umbeyla Pass behind the mountain. Little is known of the country, and the pass proved longer and far more difficult than was supposed, and the transport of supplies and ammunition was a tedious affair. The Sitana fanatics, therefore, were not so thoroughly surprised and surrounded as was intended. Another result of our unexpected appearance at the head of the Umbeyla Pass was, that we were in close proximity to the fastnesses of the Boneyr and other hill tribes, who, taking alarm, lost no time in attacking us in the most vigorous manner, and have continued to do so almost daily ever since; so Chamberlain, by all accounts, stands intrenched at the head of the pass, perpetually attacked night and day by the Sitanas and Boneyr people, who have also been joined by the Swats, a very powerful tribe still further to the north. These people make rushes at night, charging up to our guns, and, although badly armed, show the most determined courage, and have already inflicted severe loss upon us. We have had several officers killed; in one action there were 80 casualties among the men, and in another about 110, and to-day (Nov. 11th) a rumour has arrived of further fighting, and that two officers of the 71st are killed. Chamberlain cannot well advance, for fear of losing his communications, and to retire would look like a defeat; consequently, I believe, he is standing still, and waiting for reinforcements. It is said that the Momunds, and other tribes about Peshawur, are up, and the whole frontier is in excitement. Regiments and batteries, which had just begun their march to the camp of exercise here (Lahore), are hurrying on by forced marches upwards. Telegrams are flying about, there is all the bustle and excitement of a war. We began, intending to make a small excursion against a few fanatics, and, instead of that, are fighting with others with whom we have no cause of quarrel, or, at all events, with whom we had no intention of coming into collision, and we may find ourselves soon in a state of war along the whole frontier; for, of course, all these people have a certain amount of sympathy with each other. Before the expedition started, Sir Hugh Rose pointed out that the season was late (for snow falls in the mountains in November), that to march European soldiers through a difficult country, where no food is to be got, would necessitate careful preparation, and ample means of transport, &c., &c.; but his views were not listened to, though I believe Lord Elgin, for the most part, agreed with him; and therefore the Governor of the Punjaub began his little war, which is rapidly developing into a big one. Whether the present state of the frontier is influenced by the recent events in Cabool, I am not able to say.'

The actual state of things on the frontier, on the 20th November, as sketched in Sir Hugh Rose's telegram, was as follows: General Chamberlain did not ask for reinforcements; his statement was that he only needed to be supported, kept in supplies of stores, ammunition, &c., and that the corps which had suffered most should be relieved, in order to enable him to tire out the enemy, and overcome all opposition. He had sent all his sick and wounded to the rear, and had established free communications with the plains.

I got a telegram from Sir Bartle Frere, the Governor of Bombay, on the 26th, and I took the opportunity, after answering his telegram, to write to him explaining the motives which induced me to throw upon the President of the Council, Sir Robert Napier,* the responsibility of acting as Governor-General till I could get to Calcutta, and I brought before him one or two matters upon which I wished for his opinion, as will be seen by the following letter, written just before my embarkation for Calcutta.

To His Excellency Sir Bartle Frere.

Guindy, November 26th, 1863.

My dear Sir Bartle,—I got your telegram this morning, and have replied to it. I did not wish to assume the office of Governor-General at once, as Durand telegraphed to me that there was much business of importance pressing upon the Government; I therefore telegraphed back to him that I should not assume the government till I came to Calcutta, and that any pressing matter had better be referred at once to the President of the Council. I should have remained here a few days longer, as one of my children is ill; but Napier pressed me to come up, and Sir Hugh Rose says that it is very desirable that I should come to Lahore, which request is backed by Durand, though, I imagine, upon grounds differing very much from those upon which Sir H. Rose's request is founded, so I have made up my mind to go *at once*. And now I want to say a few words as to the relation between the

* Now Lord Napier of Magdala.

general and local Governments. You may, perhaps, be aware that I pressed upon Lord Canning the advisability of drawing a clear and well-defined line, separating the functions of the one from those of the others. I was desirous of giving to the Governor-General everything which could be said to have any application to more than one Presidency ; but I was equally desirous to retain for the decision of the local Governments, everything local and municipal. The late move of the Public Works secretary has induced me to reiterate these views strongly to Sir Charles Wood ; indeed, in my private correspondence with him, I have always done so; but now I pressed it upon him in a minute accompanying the despatches on the subject of the public works. I should be very glad to be made acquainted with your views upon this subject. The whole system of government at present is in such an unsettled state, that a representation emanating from us might very possibly have a beneficial effect in modifying the present system. I am writing in haste, but will do so more fully when I get to Calcutta.

Yours very truly,
W. D.

The following letter to my wife will give an account of my voyage to Calcutta, and of my meeting with one of the secretaries of the Government at the mouth of the Hooghly.

To Lady Denison.

Steamer 'Arracan,' November 29, 1863.

A very melancholy 'silver wedding-day,' dearest. I am not spending my Sunday or the anniversary of my wedding-day as I could wish, but I can at all events say to you, dearest, that not for one single hour of the last twenty-five years have I ever regretted the day that made you and me one, not merely in name but in reality, one in our affections and our hopes both here and hereafter. I have used a cold expression in saying, 'I have never *regretted*'; for years I have not failed to bless and thank God daily for having given to me a wife who has been truly a help meet for me, who has aided and assisted me upon the narrow path which leads to life eternal.

I began my letters for the December mail yesterday, and shall keep on writing, as I shall not have much time, I suspect, when I get to Calcutta. Time here passes slowly, almost as slow as the steamer itself. However, the weather is fine and the sea smooth. The church service this morning was performed by the captain in a manner which shewed that he was utterly unused to it, as indeed I heard afterwards. He dashed into the first lesson, immediately after 'Oh come, let us sing,' &c.; after the first lesson he read the Psalms, then the 'Te Deum'; after the second lesson he read the several prayers for the Queen, &c., then the Thanksgiving, and then took up the Litany. I am glad, however, that my presence induced him to have service, for some of the officers spoke to H——, regretting his habitual neglect of the practice.

November 30.—We had a better run last night, and may, if the wind would but moderate a little, see the sandheads to-day. I have been working hard at the geography of Upper India, and have been this morning studying the immediate vicinity of the seat of war, thinking how we might best manage to avoid fresh extensions of boundary, by making our present line secure—so secure as to defy aggression. Hitherto we have always pleaded the necessity of extension for security; but extension brings weakness; it lengthens lines of communication with the heart of the country, and brings us nearer to our enemies. I should strongly deprecate any extension of our external boundary; in fact, I would gladly narrow our territory were it not that such a step would produce a bad moral effect ; however, I must hear more before I can come to any definite opinion.

December 2.—We got to Saugor yesterday afternoon, and found there a small steamer with Mr. Bayley the civil secretary, Colonel Whish, and another officer on board. This morning I transferred myself to the small, but fast, steamer, which is to bring me up by half-past three o'clock. The 'Arracan' will not come up till the evening. We were obliged to anchor yesterday afternoon on account of the tide, and the officers from the small steamer came on board, and brought me a variety of telegrams, letters, and papers. The telegrams were mostly from the camp, and gave a better account of our position. I hope to find a telegram from you at Calcutta. God bless you, dearest.

Yours affectionately,
W. D.

The papers brought down by Mr. Bayley comprised the whole of the correspondence on the subject of the move against the Sitana fanatics. I had time to go through it all, and to make notes of the prominent features, while on my way up the Hooghly ; and the conclusion I drew from the perusal of the whole was, that it was very impolitic to meddle with these hill people at all. Their country is very difficult; they are a bold and warlike race ; we have nothing to gain, and everything to risk, in attacking them. This, I felt certain, was Lord Elgin's opinion ; for, though he yielded to the pressure brought upon him by the Punjaub Government, he insisted strongly upon the necessity of imposing a very narrow limit upon the action of the force sent into the country. It is, however, very difficult to chalk out lines of operation for a military force, and it is impossible to impose a limit upon its action. Of course, after the event, people found out that all the difficulties which were encountered arose out of the fancy of General Chamberlain to move by one route in preference to two, that this brought him into contact with the Boneyrs, &c., &c. In my opinion, however, it was most unfair to throw upon the executive agent the responsibility which necessarily arose out of the scheme itself. General Chamberlain took the route which seemed to him, as a military man, most likely to secure the full results of the move; and if this line of march was likely to produce injurious results *politically*, he should have been warned of this by the Government. It is not fair to throw blame upon a man who has acted well and bravely under very difficult circumstances, or to shift the responsibility off the shoulders of the Government upon those of the generals in command. As far as I was able to make out from these papers, there had been a good deal of politico-religious agitation among the hill tribes; prophecies had been uttered, and encouragement given to those nearest the frontier by promises of general support; and the effect was that one might as well have put one's hand into a wasp's nest, with the fancy of being able to withdraw it intact, as to have meddled with any of these tribes without stirring up the whole confederacy. The feeling with which I rose from the perusal of these papers was that we ought never to have meddled with such waspish neighbours.

I could not but think, too, that the Commander-in-chief had been improperly kept in ignorance of the steps which it was proposed to take; and that the communications between the Military Secretary to the Government of India and the Commander-in-chief had not been sufficiently frank and open; while comments were made upon his opinions, which, considering his rank and the position he held, could hardly fail to be annoying.

The most startling fact of all, especially when taken with reference to the report made by General Chamberlain of his position and prospects not more than ten days previous, was the morbid fear which seemed to have influenced the Government of the Punjaub, and the Military Secretary to the Government of India, making the one propose, and the other recommend, the withdrawal of the troops ; while the members of the Council at Calcutta, partaking of, or influenced by, this alarm on the part of the originators of the movement against the tribes, had backed up the recommendation by a statement to the Commander-in-chief that the object of the Government was to withdraw the troops, as soon as it could be done without loss or discredit.

I could not conceal from myself that such a declaration on the part of the Government must very much enhance the difficulties of my position ; that it would appear presumptuous in me, a mere acting officer, to set up my opinion in opposition to that of all the officers of the Government, who might be supposed to know very much more of the circumstances which had induced the Governor-General to make this movement against the tribes than I could possibly be cognizant of, and who ought to be better informed as to the state of the frontier, both within and without our boundaries, than I could possibly be. Still, I felt convinced that nothing could have happened during the short interval which had elapsed since General Chamberlain had made his report, to justify such a cowardly policy, which, if acted upon by the Commander-in-chief, would at once bring the whole of the tribes upon us. I therefore made up my mind at once to press upon the members of Council the advisability of reversing the order given to the Commander-in-chief, and, should they not agree to do so, to act upon my own authority, and direct the Commander-in-chief to make a forward instead of a retrograde movement.

Having finished reading all the papers laid before me, and having made up my mind as to the course to be pursued, I had time to look about me, and to recal what I had seen on my way up to Calcutta in 1861.

The following letter will give an account of the formalities of my landing and assumption of the government, as also of the effect of my address to the Council, on the day but one after my arrival, pressing upon the members the reversal of their direction to the Commander-in-chief.

The substance of my address was that it was unfair to the Commander-in-chief to throw upon him the responsibility of deciding whether the wishes of the Government could be carried into effect without loss or discredit. I then pressed upon them the necessity of keeping in sight the object for which the move into the hill country was ordered by the Government, and stated my opinion that the troops should be directed to act upon the offensive as soon as possible.

To Lady Denison.

Government House, Calcutta, December 2, 1863.

Dearest,—Here I am sitting in the Governor-General's office, having been duly sworn in, installed, and gazetted. I am very thankful for the good news in your telegrams; let me know when it will be safe for S—— to move, and I will send the 'Arracan' for you. I think you might spend your Christmas here; that is, you might leave Madras on the 18th, and arrive here on the 24th, or earlier, if you like. Now for our doings since I closed my last letter.

We paddled, or rather screwed, away in our fast boat, the 'Celerity,' amid a great number of ships, and, at the end of Garden Reach, spied a long range of low houses, apparently floating in the middle of the river, and hanging on to a buoy. These, as we came nearer, transmuted themselves into, first, a long, low steamer, to which was attached a sort of bungalow, and astern of this a tail of

long boats properly manned. When we got near these
we anchored. One of the boats then came alongside and
carried us off to the bungalow, which was really a floating house containing several rooms. The steamer then
started with us in tow, taking us about half a mile
further up the river, abreast of a landing-place near
Government House. We transferred ourselves again
into one of the boats, and pulled in to the landing-place,
where a crowd of people was collected, and I was received by the port officer, who handed me into one of
Lord Elgin's carriages. I was driven at once to the
Government House, and was received at the bottom of
the large flight of steps by Mr. Cecil Beadon, the Lieutenant-Governor of Bengal, Sir Charles Trevelyan, Sir
Robert Napier, &c. Thence we moved into the council
chamber, and I took the oaths and my seat.

Thursday, December 3.—When we went to breakfast
this morning, I found the rule of 'speak when you're
spoken to, do what you're bid'—a very good rule as applied to children—in full force with the officers on the
staff; they kept silence religiously till I addressed them,
and then answered monosyllabically. You may imagine
that if I thought this an unpleasant state of things when I
was in Calcutta in 1861, with Lord and Lady Canning to
converse with, I found it perfectly insufferable when I
was the sole speaker of the party; I therefore set Henley
and Stewart to work to explain to the other members of
the staff, that the state of my lungs was not such as to
admit of my going through a cross-examination of them
all at every meal, and that it would be much pleasanter
to me if they would act just as they would do at the
table of any other gentleman.

Friday Evening, December 4.—I have been too busy to
write till now. The fresh air of the morning makes me extend my walk, so that I have but little time before breakfast
for private letter-writing, and the rest of the day is taken

up by business. The Council met to-day, and I pressed upon the members my views of the proper policy to be pursued on the north-west frontier. I carried a majority of the members with me, and I hope the result will be the speedy restoration of peace, on conditions such as will justify the move we have made in attacking these people; though I think it would have been better had we made no move at all; it is useless to make enemies where you cannot hope to make subjects. My business, however, was to make the best of a bad state of things, and this, I trust, I have done. Having settled this, we decided that, under existing circumstances, it was not desirable that the Legislative Council should meet at Lahore, and they all agreed with me that my presence at Lahore was unnecessary; so here I shall remain till you come up, at all events. I almost doubt whether it would be worth while to bring up books, &c., for, as I find that Lord Elgin sent by the Bombay mail of the 12th, notifying his state, and suggesting the appointment of a successor, it is probable that my tenure of office will not be very long.

Sunday, December 6.—Went to church this morning at St. John's, close to the Government House. Went in a carriage with an escort of cavalry, was met at the door by two mace-bearers, and handed to a seat large enough for three, raised one step above the floor, with three large prayer-books, very high stools, &c. I propose for the future to dispense with the escort, also with the mace-bearers, and to have the big books exchanged for some more portable. I dislike particularly all attempts to carry one's dignity into church: there we are, or ought to be, all on a level.

December 10.—My life here is monotonous enough. I am out of bed a little before six, get on horseback and have a gallop round the meïdán or esplanade, going, generally, to look at the race-horses which are taking their gallops at that hour. There is usually a heavy fog resting on the low ground, and this, I suppose, has given me a cold. When I return home I dress, read, &c., and, if I have any time before breakfast, write letters : breakfast at half-past nine. This is becoming a pleasant meal, as we have more conversation. From ten till five, exclusive of luncheon, I am pretty steadily at work. I am going, however, to concentrate and distribute my work better. At present boxes come pouring in upon me at all times, and from all departments ; and I am interrupted when reading one paper by the advent of another on a different subject altogether. In the afternoon I either walk, ride, or drive. I have made one or two attempts to get beyond the meidân for a ride, but have always been driven back by finding myself on a dusty road.

Yours affectionately,
W. D.

I mentioned the fact that the majority of the Council, on the meeting on the 4th, had adopted my advice as to the movement in advance. Sir Charles Trevelyan, however, did not concur with the majority, and he availed himself of his right to record the reason of his dissent in a minute which was embodied in the proceedings of the Council. I was then compelled to place upon record the reasons which induced me to adopt the view which the Council had affirmed, and these will be seen in the following minute.

Minute.—' Sir Charles Trevelyan has recorded his objections to the course adopted by the Council in modifying, at my instance, the instructions given to the Commander-in-chief relative to the withdrawal of the troops from their position at the head of the Umbeyla Pass. I should, under ordinary circumstances, have submitted to the Council a minute embodying my reasons for pressing the matter on their notice ; but the urgency of the occasion was too great to admit of any delay. As, however, the policy of the decision of the Government has been questioned, I think it but due to myself, and to the members of Council who agreed with me, to place on record the reasons which induced me to adopt the view which has been affirmed by the Council.

' The following brief recapitulation of the circumstances connected with the movement of troops into the mountainous country beyond the Indus will be a necessary preface to what I have to say.

' At the urgent request of the Lieutenant-Governor of the Punjaub, Lord Elgin consented to allow a body of 5,000 men to move into the country around the Mahabun mountain, for the purpose of destroying, if possible, or at all events of driving to a distance, a horde of fanatics who had reoccupied Sitana (from which they had been driven in 1858), and who were in the habit of making inroads upon our territory, and robbing and murdering the merchants whom the hope of gain might tempt into such a dangerous neighbourhood.

' The proposition, as laid before Lord Elgin, was very distinct and definite. The force was to be divided into two columns, one of which was to march on one side of the mountain, and another on the other side, and it was anticipated that the whole operations would not occupy more than thirty or thirty-six days, from October 10 to the middle of November, after which the mountains were said to be covered with snow. General Chamberlain, a well-known and distinguished officer, was selected to command the whole force, the object of which was, *I assume*, clearly explained to him ; at all events, if not, it ought to have been.

' General Chamberlain, in the exercise of a discretion most properly, and indeed necessarily, vested in an officer in command of such a body of troops, chose to keep his men together in one body, and to move up the Umbeyla

Pass in rear of the Mahabun mountain. He made his way to the top of that Pass, and encountered there, not merely the fanatical occupants of Sitana, but also strong bodies of mountaineers of different tribes, who attacked him in the most vigorous manner, and who have, in point of fact, as yet barred any forward movement of the troops, have occasioned us a heavy loss both of officers and men, and have practically set us at defiance.

' As soon as the Government was aware of the resistance encountered by General Chamberlain, reinforcements were moved to the front as expeditiously as possible, better means of transport for stores and ammunition provided, arrangements were made for the conveyance of the sick and wounded to the rear, and every means taken to place the force in a position to overcome the resistance it was encountering.

' While these steps were in progress, the Lieutenant-Governor of the Punjaub, taking alarm, in the first place, at the, *by him*, unexpected results of the incursion which he had recommended, and, in the second place, at the drafts made upon the troops occupying the Punjaub, whose presence he supposed to be necessary for the maintenance of peace and good order, pressed most urgently the withdrawal of the force. Colonel Norman, the military secretary to the Government of India, in a memorandum dated November 20, anticipated most disastrous results if General Chamberlain were allowed to remain at Umbeyla, and suggested his withdrawal to the plains, where the Government would have time to prepare for future operations. The Government, yielding to these pressing instances, conceded to the wish of the Lieutenant-Governor, and gave directions, on November 26, that the troops should be withdrawn " as soon as it could be done without risk of military disaster, or without seriously compromising our military reputation."

' While, however, these messages were moving backwards and forwards, events were progressing. The troops at the head of the Pass maintained their position, causing serious loss to the enemy, who were consequently getting disheartened; reinforcements were moving up; the troops which were intended to form the camp at Lahore were rapidly approaching the scene of action; better means of conveyance for stores and ammunition had been provided; the threat of snow proved to be a delusion; and the fears of the Lieutenant-Governor of the Punjaub that risings would take place in consequence of the removal of troops to the frontier were seen to be groundless.

'Such was the state of things when I landed at Calcutta, and, such being the case, I felt myself compelled to ask the Council to modify the instructions previously given for the withdrawal of the troops. I did not think it necessary to comment upon the original proposition of the Lieutenant-Governor of the Punjaub, or to express an opinion as to the policy of meddling with these warlike tribes. I did not, as a military man, express an opinion as to the mode in which it was originally proposed to carry this aggressive movement into execution, or hint a doubt as to the wisdom of dividing a small force into two columns, neither of which would be able to give the least assistance to the other. It has been assumed, somewhat gratuitously, that the operation, as originally schemed out, was quite simple and easy, involving only a march through a rough district, to which little or no resistance would be offered; and the blame of the failure of the plan has been, in my opinion, most improperly and unfairly thrown upon General Chamberlain. I mention these circumstances merely for the purpose of expressing my opinion that they have been improperly imported into the discussion. What the Government had to consider was the simple fact that a body of troops, ordered (whether wisely or not is nothing to the purpose) into a district for a specific purpose, had been resisted and prevented from executing that

purpose; had sustained some loss, but was now in a
position to overcome all resistance, and to carry out the
spirit of the original instructions, and very probably the
letter; and that, under a different and a much more unfavourable state of things, it had been induced to order a
retrograde movement of the troops, which order it was
now requested to reconsider.

'My opinion was, and is, that the withdrawal of the
troops from what had proved to be merely a defensive
position would be considered by the mountain tribes as
equivalent to a victory on their part; and, although I did
not doubt the possibility of withdrawing the troops without loss, I yet felt convinced that the moral effect on our
troops of such a move would be of the worst possible
description.   I was, and am, of opinion, that a movement
in retreat would probably bring about all the financial
difficulties so vividly described by Sir Charles Trevelyan,
for the certain result would be such a series of aggressions
on the part of the mountain tribes, elated by their supposed
success in causing us to retreat, as would compel us to
make a more serious attack upon them in the course of
next year for the purpose of asserting our superiority.
Upon the grounds, then, both of policy and economy, I
consider the instructions given to the Commander-in-chief
to be right and proper; and while I am disposed to maintain this opinion, irrespective altogether of what the local
authorities may think, yet I may observe that the Lieutenant-Governor of the Punjaub, who is quoted by Sir
Charles Trevelyan as an advocate for the immediate withdrawal of the troops, would seem by the latest telegrams
to press most earnestly for an immediate advance.'

I was able, on December 10, to report to Sir Charles
Wood that we were in a position to make our movement
in advance.   The Government having, previous to my
arrival at Calcutta, thrown the responsibility of directing
the movements of the force upon the Commander-in-chief,

I was not in any way disposed to take this responsibility off the shoulders of one who, from his position, was the only proper person to bear it. As a military man, I had, of course, opinions upon such matters, but I should no more have thought of insisting upon the adoption of my ideas by the commander of a body of troops, or even of obtruding, unasked, these ideas upon him, than I should have thought of discussing a question of law with the Chief Justice.

On the 12th, news was received from the seat of war to the effect that the chiefs of the Boneyr tribe had come in, and were disposed to make their submission; but it seemed that they were not willing to agree to the terms proposed by us, so in a day or two a forward movement was made. The position occupied by the mountain tribes, a very strong one, was attacked and carried, the defenders being driven from their commanding point into the plain country below, leaving 300 men dead on the field. A day or two afterwards the forward movement upon Umbeyla, the village on the north side of the range below the Pass, was continued. The troops were attacked while on their march by a strong body of the fanatics, who, rushing in upon our men sword in hand, carried their standards into the middle of the leading regiments of the columns, so that the fight became a hand-to-hand conflict. We lost fifty men; one officer was killed and four wounded, but the assailants were routed, and a couple of hundred killed. This settled the whole affair. The tribes made up their mind that they could not compete with us, so they sent to ask for a cessation of hostilities, agreeing to all our demands, one of which was that Mulkah, the stronghold of the fanatics, was to be destroyed. This they accordingly did, some of our officers having been sent to witness this closing scene of a drama which, while it disturbed our financial arrangements, has probably taught us a lesson as to the folly of interference with

these tribes, and at all events has read them a lesson
which they will not forget for some years. Before I
allude to other subjects which came before me at Calcutta,
I may as well finish my account of those which were
brought specially under my notice during the progress of
the campaign in the north-west.

The telegram announcing the desire of the Boneyrs to
come in and make their submission contained also a proposition from the political agent with the army that the
general in command should be directed to carry out
whatever he, the aforesaid agent, might fancy or recommend. I had, in other letters to the Secretary of State,
dated a few days before the receipt of this, remarked that
a good deal of the difficulty of campaigning in India was
created by the 'political agents.' These men, very often
officers of no high standing in the army, are apt to think
that the possession of a small amount of local knowledge
entitles them not only to express opinions on military
matters, but also to control the action of the military
authorities. They do not make the general in command
acquainted with the facts which their position enables
them to ascertain, but, reasoning upon these, they strive
to get practically the command of the force, while they
repudiate the responsibility attaching to this; and they do
not hesitate, as in this instance, to apply to the highest
authority to grant them powers which no general in his
senses would allow them to exercise. Several instances
of this craving for power came under my notice. The
agent, communicating with his superior (the Commissioner
or Lieutenant-Governor, as the case may be), complains
of the conduct of the officer in command, asks for additional powers, feels confident that if these are vested in
him he could quiet the country in a week, and so on. I
was obliged to administer a severe rebuke to one officer
who acted in this way, and I pressed upon the Secretary
of State the advisability of directing that all the corre-

spondence of the political agents, when in camp, should be submitted to the general in command. That officer ought to be cognizant of the character of this correspondence, and it might be better that he should have political as well as military power invested in him when the operations are extensive. Had I remained in the position of Governor-General for another month or two, I should have acted upon my own opinions, merely reporting the fact to the Secretary of State, but under the circumstances in which I was placed I could do nothing but make recommendations.

Another matter which I brought strongly before the Secretary of State was the impolicy of leaving the command of local corps, such as that of the Punjaub Irregular Force and the Nizam's contingent, in the hands of civilians. Lord Elgin found that the control of the Punjaub force made the Lieutenant-Governor there, to a certain extent, independent of the Governor-General. He had the power of so employing his force as to bring about a state of things which compelled the supreme Government to act in a manner the very reverse of that which a sound policy would have dictated. I gathered from what I read and heard, that the principal reason for maintaining this anomalous state of things was that it secured a large amount of patronage to the Governor-General. Much stress has, I know, been laid upon the advantage which the possession of such patronage gives to the head of the Government; but for my part I am inclined to dispute this. I never found that the dispensation of patronage helped me in the least, while I am certain that it led me occasionally into difficulties. In reality it is but a system of political bribery, such as is carried on to a great extent by those who profess the highest principles of political purity. Whether, however, my view of patronage, or the more ordinary one, be correct, there can be no doubt that the application of the latter in a way which leads to such an anomaly as that of placing the army, or any part of it, under the command of a civilian, must be erroneous.

It is but right to state that my mode of proceeding did not meet with the approval of Sir Charles Wood. He told me that he differed very much from the views which I seemed to entertain, and that the whole story gave him the greatest pain and annoyance. That such should be his feelings with respect to the origin of the war is not surprising, but with this I had nothing to do. I had from the time that I first heard of it expressed my opinion that it was unwise and impolitic. As a military man I had not hesitated to affirm that the scheme involved a grave strategical blunder; but, as soon as I had power to act, I had pressed upon the Government the adoption of a course which had brought matters to a satisfactory termination.

Lady Denison to F. G. Denison, Esq.

Guindy Park, Madras, December 12, 1863.

My dear Frank,—I had not time to write to you by the last mail, and I minded it the less as I knew your father was writing: he would tell you that the event we were expecting when I last wrote—poor Lord Elgin's death—had come to pass, and that he (your father) was, in consequence, on the point of starting for Calcutta to assume the office of temporary Governor-General. He sailed on the 26th of November and got to Calcutta, and assumed office there on the 2nd of this month. I could not go with him on account of S——'s illness; but we are anxious to join him as soon as possible, and he was to have sent the 'Arracan' steamer for us; now he has telegraphed to us that the vessel has to be sent to Moulmein first, so I almost doubt our being together again by the new year. I had a letter from him last Sunday, and it contained one very sad piece of news, which I have since seen confirmed in the papers—namely, that amongst those who have fallen in one of the skirmishes now constantly taking place on the north-west frontier is the younger of the two Sandersons. This news has cast a cloud over us all, for we were all fond of him on his own account, besides our sympathy for his poor mother and brother. Your father's letter could tell me nothing beyond the bare fact of his having been killed in action; but the other day I found in one of the newspapers a letter from an officer at the seat of war giving an account of his death, which is really a noble one, and shows what a stout, gallant heart there must have been in that small fragile-looking body. It appears from this account that two companies of his regiment (the 101st) were at an outlying picquet under the command of a Major Delafosse, and that a fierce attack was there made upon them by such overwhelming numbers that the officer at the head of one company of the 101st absolutely quailed and retreated with most of his company, 'but,' says the account, 'Delafosse bravely held on with his company, and the subaltern of the other—Sanderson—and Dr. Pile, until at last further resistance was hopeless. Pile and Sanderson lay dead, together with twenty-six of his company of fifty men.' Thus it would seem that this noble boy held on with his commanding officer even when deserted by his senior officer and many of the men. Is not this good? and is it not a comfort to think that our dear little friend should have done his duty so nobly.

—

To Mrs. Stanley.

Government House, Calcutta, Christmas Day, 1863.

My dear Mrs. Stanley,—I can hardly wish you a merry Christmas, but I can and do wish you a happy Christmas and New Year. Happiness is for the grave man what merriment is for the youth; and the older one gets, I think, the happier one gets, for one becomes more thoroughly

satisfied to place oneself in God's hands to do or to suffer
as to Him seems best. You will have heard, I have no
doubt, of the event which has brought me up here. On
the death of Lord Elgin I succeeded to the office of
Governor-General *pro tempore* till a successor was appointed, in virtue of my position as senior of the two
Governors of Madras and Bombay. I have now been up
here for a month by myself. I left Lady D—— to nurse
S——, and I am in daily expectation of her arrival with
the rest of my belongings. As you may suppose, however, Christmas is anything but merry to me, for I lack
the sound of my children's voices, and the merry laugh of
childhood, which is so cheering to my ear and heart. You
will naturally expect to hear somewhat of my new
position, and of the people by whom I am surrounded. I
think I must have given you my impression of Calcutta
when I was here in 1861 with Lord Canning, and I see
no reason as yet to alter the opinions then formed. There
seems to be less sociability than there is at Madras, less
cordiality among people themselves, and more stiffness
and etiquette in their relations with me. This, however,
is, I think, to be attributed to the governors, not to the
governed. It seems to me that people here have always
had a tendency to the opinion that we, the governing
race, must submit to the etiquette of the people whom we
rule; that we are bound to make all sorts of display, and
to try to overpower the native by convincing him of his own
insignificance. We accordingly surround ourselves with
a sort of atmosphere of etiquette, forgetting that, when we
have done our best, the most miserable of the zemindars,
or petty nobility, can, and does, beat us hollow on the
ground of outward magnificence. He comes up to see me
with elephants, horses, dancing-girls, &c., is covered with
jewels from head to foot, is dressed in cloth of gold while
I sit quietly in a black coat and waistcoat, and, though I
have a guard about me, aides-de-camp in uniform, &c.,

make a very inferior show. My feeling is rather the reverse of the Calcutta one. I look upon myself in my plain clothes as the representative of the earnestness and power of the *Englishman*, and I consider that I lower myself by attempting to compete with the native race. Government House is a large mass of building, consisting of a central block which contains dining-room, ball-room, drawing-rooms, &c. on two floors, and four wings in which family and staff reside. This looks out upon the esplanade—the only place on which one can either walk, ride, or drive. The consequence of this is, that one's life is most monotonous. I ride in the morning, and take two turns round the racecourse: in the evening I do the same thing, only I extend my ride by a turn in the ring—a sort of oval drive round a garden in which there is a band, and round which the carriages collect.

Yours truly,

W. D.

To Mrs. Des Vœux.

Calcutta, December 27, 1863.

My dear J——,—I am spending but a lonely Christmas here in this great rambling house. I long for a child to romp with; but, instead of that, no sooner do I open my door than up start four or five men in scarlet dresses, who are waiting my commands, and if I move about the house, one of them is sure to follow me. Poor Lord Elgin said that he felt like what he could imagine a lunatic would feel with his keeper always close to him. It is not etiquette to go out without an aide-de-camp, and when I ride or drive, an escort of cavalry follows me; while in Government House there are, heaven knows why, sentries at the bottom and top of the staircase. It looks very much as if I was under watch and ward, only I find that I can pass these sentries, and go out if I like.

December 31.—I got a telegram this morning, notifying the appointment of Sir John Lawrence, who will be here on January 10. I stay here to meet him, and shall then take myself off to Madras with as little delay as possible. Bating the difference of pay, Madras is a far pleasanter place than Calcutta, and my houses there are four times as comfortable as either this house, or the one at Barrackpore. Here I am shut up in a town mis-named, most woefully, 'the City of Palaces,' with nothing between these so-called palaces, and the river, but a large green plot, on which I can either walk, ride, or drive: there is a vast compound of villanous smells pervading the whole space; how can one, then, expect to escape disease of the liver? I long for a good hearty laugh to clear my lungs; as it is I cannot muster more than a whimper.

January 5.—The ' Nemesis,' with Sir John Lawrence on board, has arrived at Galle. I may look for him here on Monday.

January 10.—The Bombay mail leaves to-day, so I will close this, and write again when I get to Madras.

Your affectionate Brother,

W. D.

To Lady Denison.

Government House, Calcutta, December 31, 1863.

Dearest,—I stopped writing because I was in daily expectation of hearing that you had started. I now begin again, and shall send this by the first conveyance, because, by a telegram I have just got, I find that my tenure of office here will be shorter than I expected. Henley came to me this morning, bringing me a telegram from Sir Bartle Frere, informing me that Sir John Lawrence had been appointed Governor-General, and would be here on the 10th. My first thought was, ' How lucky it was that you had not started;' my second was a mixed one : I was glad to get away from Calcutta, but I grieved over the loaves and fishes. However, this very soon wore away, and I can say now that my feeling is almost one of unmixed pleasure. How I do look forward to the time when we can sit down together and have a regular talk.

January 1, 1864.—A happy New Year to you, dearest! I got your telegram this morning, and am very glad that you are not disappointed. I am not in the least sorry. The little bit of love of mammon which acted upon me yesterday has vanished, and I feel the happier that I shall be with you again, please God, about the 16th or 17th.

I went yesterday to pay a visit to a rich Hindoo, the owner of house property in Calcutta. He lived in the centre of the native town, and the access to his house was through the filthiest of filthy lanes. In one of these lanes there was a handsome gateway, opening into a sort of court, or rather garden. Lions and other figures marked the roadway, and among these were stalking about cranes and ostriches. The house was a very large one, forming a quadrangle; the court in the centre was full of statues, shrubs in pots, &c. The rooms on the ground floor on two sides were show rooms, as were those on three sides above. A magnificent verandah on both sides kept off the sun. The rooms themselves were full of tables, on which were placed bronzes, statuettes, &c. &c. Statuettes filled the corners, the walls were covered with pictures, and it was evident that a very large sum of money had been expended in various ways. In the courtyard were cages for birds, of which there were many of great value: the owner had been in correspondence with the late Lord Derby, and had got specimens from all parts of the world; *but*, the place was covered with dust—the bronzes and statuettes had not seen a duster for a long time; the plants in the quadrangle had their leaves brown instead of green; the temple of the idol which was in the yard looked very rubbishy— he would have been covered with dust had he occupied his seat; the buildings for the animals and birds were

out of repair, &c.; all this, not from want of means,
but from an incongruity of mind, a tendency to display,
without care for that harmony of the whole which makes
display pleasing. I have no time for more, but look forward to be with you again before long, and am not a little
pleased to think that our separation is drawing to a close.

Yours affectionately,

W. D.

Sir John Lawrence landed on Tuesday, January 12,
1864. A large crowd was collected to see the procession from the landing-place to Government House, and
Sir John was loudly cheered.

I had a long talk with him on sundry matters on the
following day; told him what I had done, and what I
had left for him to do. I gave him, according to rule,
the two dinners which the out-going Governor gives to his
successor; but I did not remain to receive the two which
he was to give me in return, so we parted at the landing-
place with a request on my part, and an engagement on
his, that he would write to me, whenever he had anything
to communicate, in the plainest and simplest English.

The result of my short experience of the working of
the Government at Calcutta was a conviction that there
was great room for improvement; that it was slow in
decision, and slower still in action. Lord Canning had
distributed the business among the different members of
Council, retaining for himself a specific portion. This
arrangement, while it relieved the Governor-General from
a great amount of labour in looking into petty details,
was defective in that there was hardly any check upon
the action or inaction of the members of Council. Ordinary business which required but little thought was
got through rapidly; but questions involving a good deal
of consideration were apt to slumber in the pigeon holes
of the office for months, and to come out unhatched at

last. I mentioned this to Sir John Lawrence, and told him that I had schemed out a plan, by which the Governor-General would have before him, weekly, a return of the state of business, showing what subjects were awaiting decision, and where they were delayed. This, however, was but a minor evil ; a much greater one arose out of the tendency on the part of the Commissioners and Residents at the courts of the native states, to make their position appear to be one of importance, and consequently to thrust upon the Government, through the Secretary for the Foreign Department, a mass of petty details relating to the internal condition of these states, which could be productive of nothing but annoyance to their rulers, and trouble and waste of time to the Governor-General. I give, as an instance, a sketch of a matter which came before me very frequently, involving a mass of correspondence sufficient to have decided the fate of one of the minor states of Europe.

It seems that the Rance, or princess, ruling over a small territory in the interior, had succeeded in getting leave to make the pilgrimage to Mecca (it seems hard that a sovereign princess should not be allowed to please herself in such a matter as this ; however, it had all been settled before I came to Calcutta). Some questions had arisen as to the management of the government of her country during her absence, and the Resident thought himself called upon to interfere. In the course of this, a request was made by the Rance that she might be allowed to visit England. Here was another subject for correspondence, and letter after letter was poured upon me through the Foreign Secretary, placing in the strongest possible light the impolicy of acceding to the request of the Rance ; but I never was made aware that her Highness had slipped her neck out of the collar, and had got as far as Mecca, till, being thoroughly tired out, I asked where she was, and finding that she had already got halfway to England, I decided that the correspondence should cease, as we had practically no power to prevent her doing what she pleased.

The following letter will show the view taken by me of a matter of professional interest which was brought under my notice at Calcutta :—

My dear ——, —I have an interesting subject to bring before you, one which has caused a good deal of discussion among the engineers here, and which, in point of fact, has been dealt with here more as a personal matter than as one involving some very serious professional questions with reference to both the principle and details of certain classes of works. The Ganges Canal was undertaken for the purpose of bringing water to irrigate the land lying between the rivers Ganges and Jumna ; and as there were doubts as to the possibility of taking the water at different points from either river by constructing dams, or anients, as they are termed here, it was decided to bring the whole body of water required from a point on the Ganges above the district to be irrigated, along the ridge or saddle dividing the two valleys, taking off the water to the right and the left as occasion might require. As a matter of course, the estimate for a canal of such length (upwards of 350 miles), and wide and deep enough to bring down a body of water sufficient to irrigate such an enormous tract of land, was very largely exceeded. It was, however, completed to such an extent as to allow the water to be brought down ; but it was then found that, on striving to economise excavation by adding to the slope of the bed, and consequently to the velocity of the stream, this had been increased to such an extent as to threaten seriously the stability of the work : the banks were worn away, the masonry works undermined, and it became a matter of necessity to lessen the amount of water passing down the channel, while reports were called for as to the state of the works, causes of failure, &c.

This brought out, of course, comments on, and excep tions to, the original scheme. It was stated by one party that the difficulty of establishing dams on the Ganges had been exaggerated. An instance was given where a dam 12ft. high, with a water-way of 2½ miles in width, had been constructed on a sandy foundation, and had stood the test of the annual floods passing over the coping to the depth of 20ft. and 25ft. without requiring much repair. This discussion was going on while I was at Calcutta, and com ments and replies were passing backwards and forwards. A committee of engineers was appointed, I believe, after I left, to decide upon the plan to be adopted, and to form an estimate of the cost of completing the work in a substantial manner. I will not attempt to go into the question of the possibility or impossibility of making a dam across the Ganges. I know too little of the cha racter of the bed of the river, or of other circumstances connected with it, to attempt to 'decide when doctors disagree;' but the fact of a dam of such height and width having been established over a river pouring down such a body of water as the Godavery is a precedent of some value. I may as well, however, having given you this sketch of the existing state of things, say a few words on some of the questions under discussion, to which it would be as well that officers of Engineers, many of whom will have to serve in India, and some of whom may, in all probability, be called upon to work on this very Ganges Canal, should turn their attention specially.

The first question may be stated thus: Is it wise to attempt to combine together, in one, a canal for irrigation and one for navigation? As a general rule, I should say, certainly not. The object of a canal for irrigation pur poses is to pass a given body of water to the spot where it is to be utilised in as short a time as possible, due attention being paid, of course, to the capacity of the soil to withstand the action of running water, and to the nature of the works, &c., required to control and regulate the discharge. For the convenience of navigation, on the contrary, it would be desirable to convert the channel into a series of quiet pools. It would be far better, in my opinion, where the traffic is likely to be large, to go to the expense of making a separate narrow canal for navigation, and to keep this altogether distinct from the irrigation channels, taking water now and then from these, should occasion require it, than to strive to combine the essentials of the two into some compound which would work unsatisfactorily for both. I am by no means sure that the cost of the two, working in the best manner, would be more than that of the one in which the two objects were attempted to be combined.

The next question has reference to the source or sources from which the canal, whether for irrigation or navigation, should be supplied with water. This must of course be determined by local peculiarities; but wherever it is possible it would be better to secure several sources of supply. An accident to the main channel, if there be only one, puts an end to both navigation and irrigation until the damage is repaired; and the large body of water passing through a breach in the bank would render repairs more difficult to execute than they would be were the channel smaller, as would be the case when there are several supply channels. It would also be advisable to seek for sources of supply as near as possible to the land to be irrigated, for the cost of bringing the whole of the water for a district of 350 miles from one point at the upper extremity of the district would be enormous. However, I have given you enough to think of for the time. What has struck me most in the correspondence relative to the Ganges Canal is the strong feeling exhibited between the engineers of Madras and Bengal; it almost seemed as if the locality governed the opinion of those who had to discuss the subject.

Yours very truly,

W. D.

Calcutta, January 4, 1864.

My dear ——,—You will feel an interest in a question which has been lately brought before me. It seems that the subject of the supply of horses for the artillery and cavalry had been under discussion previous to my arrival here, and that some enquiry had been made as to the number and quality of the stock bred at the Government establishments. A return was handed to me a few days ago containing a summary of the operations of the stud depôt at Koruntadha for the eleven years from 1852 to 1862 inclusive; also another return containing a detailed account of the expenditure upon the stud for the year 1862-63, and the number of horses furnished to the service in that period. From this latter return it appeared that 923 horses had been furnished to the troops at a *minimum* average cost of 765 rupees per horse. I say the *minimum* cost, for I cut out all the items of expenditure which seemed to me questionable. Had I included these the cost would have exceeded 1000r. On looking into the returns of the breeding operations it was evident that there had been a steady falling-off in the numbers both of stallions and mares, for of the former there were sixty-seven in 1852, and only thirty-seven in 1862; while of the latter there were 1,850 in 1852, and only 1,018 in 1862. I went fully into the data furnished by these returns, but could not discover any reason for this falling-off, and was obliged to infer that there must be something wrong either in the management or the system.

In making enquiries as to the quality of the animals bred at the stud, I heard, of course, several very contradictory reports. I was told by some that the horses bred were good, hard-working, willing slaves; by others that they were not fit to ride, &c. An inspection of the Calcutta stables, where there were horses of all sorts—Arabs, Australians, and stud-bred—convinced me that these last were animals of a low stamp: they were heavy in the carcase, light in the limbs, their joints small and badly formed. I should have been very sorry to put even my weight upon one of them, and of course could hardly have felt justified in putting the eighteen stone of a light dragoon upon its back. I cannot but think that the Government has made a most egregious mistake in sending out stallions from England; you recollect what a washy, weedy lot were forwarded a year or two ago. No one would be surprised, after looking at these, at the sort of stock of which they have the parentage. The Arab stallion, which stands not more than $14\frac{1}{2}$ hands, when put to a good Australian or English mare, becomes the sire of a fine animal, with many of the good qualities of both parents. It has the clean sloping shoulders of the Australian, and stands from $15\frac{1}{2}$ to 16 hands high; it has the good head of the Arab, the good hard bones and hoofs of the sire, is well ribbed up, and has a good hind-quarter. I have had, as you know, many specimens of these in my possession both in Australia and India, and I never had reason to complain of one of them: they were well up to my weight, which is no trifle; they carried me well through and over everything, and I ride hard. Their legs are always clean, they never throw a splint; and though, now and then, if bred in India, they showed a tendency to the shuffling walk of the Arab, which brings him down on his nose occasionally when walking, yet this was the exception, not the rule; they generally bent their knees and pasterns well, after the pattern of their Australian parent, whose first hint of the propriety of this is given a few days after its birth by a hard rap on the shins against a log in the bush.

I commenced importing *mares* from Australia on the ground that this extended our range of choice of animals, and that by so doing I was introducing the rudiments of a better description of stock. I would much rather see a hundred or so strong, well-shaped, three-parts-bred mares from Australia or England imported annually than the twenty or thirty washy thorough-bred stallions which are of no use to the Government or the country.

I was sorely tempted the other day when going round the stables at Calcutta by a beautiful thorough-bred chestnut mare, well up to my weight, and fit to go across any country. I resisted the temptation, however, and it was just as well that I was so self-denying, for I heard that the man who had bought the animal, for, I think, 2,000 rupees, had at the end of the week offered 10*l.* to any one who could ride it; it was an inveterate buck-jumper.

Yours very truly,
W. D.

CHAPTER XXIV.

RETURN TO MADRAS — OPINIONS AS TO ORIGIN OF SO-CALLED FLINT
WEAPONS—WATER RATE—FINANCE MACHINERY—WANT OF SURVEY OF
FRONTIER—IRRIGATION WORKS—WANT OF STATISTICAL INFORMATION—
DEATH OF CAPTAIN GLOVER—CINCHONA PLANTATIONS—ACTION OF FORESTS
ON RAINFALL—TOILSOME WALK AFTER SAMBUR—KILLING A TIGER—
LETTER TO THE MAHARAJAH OF TRAVANCORE—IRRIGATION COMPANY—
VISIT FROM TODAS AND KOTERS—WYNAAD—NATIVE ARCHERY—RETURN
TO GUINDY—CYCLONE AT MASULIPATAM—LETTER TO THE RAJAH OF
TRAVANCORE.

Lady Denison to F. G. Denison, Esq.

Guindy Park, Madras, January 13th, 1864.

MY DEAR FRANK,—Unless your father has written to you
by this mail, you will wonder to find me still writing from
hence; for, of course, I expected to have been at Calcutta long before this, but now I am not going there at
all. You never heard of such a succession of impedi-
ments as there were to our voyage. I think at the time
of my last letter to you things must about have arrived at
the point at which the Government steamer 'Arracan,'
which was to have been sent for us, had been diverted to
take some convicts first to Moulmein, at the urgent request
of the Bengal Government to your father, which he
thought it right to comply with. Having accomplished
this service, the 'Arracan' came here for us, arriving on
the 21st of December; but in the meantime a new difficulty had arisen about some Government stores of gun-
powder which were to be conveyed from hence to
Calcutta, and for which no conveyance could be found, as
the mail and passenger steamers are not, I think, allowed
to take combustible or explosive cargoes on board. At
all events they would not do it; so at last your father

telegraphed to us to give up the 'Arracan' for the powder, and come up ourselves by the mail steamer which was then daily expected at Galle. Then the mail steamer broke down and never got here at all! and the supplementary steamer, which found her in a disabled state and brought on her mails and passengers, did not get here till the 5th of this month ; and in the mean time the Bombay mail had arrived, bringing news that Sir John Lawrence had been appointed Governor-General, and would be out by the very next mail ; so then, of course, it was not worth while for me and S—— and the children to go up to Calcutta, and your father telegraphed to us to stay where we were. The news took us rather by surprise, for we had not thought it possible that a new Governor-General could get out so soon ; nor could he, in fact, if he had only been appointed on Lord Elgin's death ; but the truth was that, at the beginning of his illness, Lord Elgin had telegraphed home his wish to be relieved, and they had acted on it at once. However, your father does not seem at all disappointed at the speedy termination of his Governor-Generalship ; he does not ever place his happiness much in money or honours, so he can do very well either with or without them, and he writes in great joy at the prospect of being with us all again, and you may be sure we, on our side, are equally looking forward to having him here, for we have had on both sides a solitary, unsatisfactory Christmas and New Year.

The mail steamer, with Sir John Lawrence on board, kept to her time very well, and got to Calcutta last night ; at least we presume she did, for a telegram from your father in the evening informed us that she was in the river, and that he himself hoped to start to-morrow. In this case we may hope to have him here by Sunday night or Monday, not sooner, I am afraid, for the 'Arracan,' in which he comes back, is a slow vessel. When she went up with the powder, just after Christmas,

J—— went in her at the head of a band of cricketers; for a challenge had come down from Calcutta to a Madras eleven to come up and play there, and it was a good opportunity for doing so, as it was during the Christmas holidays, and the 'Arracan' was here to convey them. I am happy to tell you that the result was a complete victory on the part of Madras; they beat their opponents by sixty runs, though they had all the disadvantages of being, not a picked eleven, but only the best that could be got together at a few days' notice, of playing on an unknown ground, and having had no time or opportunity to practise together beforehand. J—— will return with your father, of course; the rest of the victorious cricketers will probably be back here to-night by the mail steamer.

To Mrs. Des Vœux.

Guindy, February 3, 1864.

My dear J——,—Here I am again safe and sound, feeling happy at being among my belongings, and with all my comforts about me. I have a conviction that I am at home, while at Calcutta I felt uncomfortable, and as if I were upon a journey, and were tenant of a house for a week or so. I left on the 14th, having inducted Sir John Lawrence into office. I was heartily pleased, however, to think that I had been able to hand over the government to him with an assurance that everything was quiet, both within and without our frontier.

There is a pack of hounds here, and I have generally a gallop about twice a week. We have to get up early, as we throw off as soon as it is light enough to see—about twenty minutes before sunrise. We are always in before eight o'clock, so there is not much chance of our being affected by the sun.

February 6.—Mr. Chaplin, of Blankney, and Sir F. Johnstone made their appearance on Thursday at a ball we gave. They are coming to stay with me while they remain in Madras, which will be only for a few days, as they move on to Calcutta by the next P. and O. steamer. Mr. Chaplin wants to kill an elephant: however, I am afraid he will not have the opportunity, unless he calls in at Ceylon. Several men take advantage of the steamer, and run out here in the cool season, for a month's shooting. Sir Victor Brooke, an Irish baronet, made a very large bag last year, including elephants, tigers, &c. These latter in some parts of the country become a regular nuisance, carrying off cattle, and occasionally men. Last year a reward of 50l. was offered for one in Mysore, which had killed upwards of fifty people. They say that when a tiger has once tasted human flesh he loses his appetite for beef. In revenge, however, for his unnatural taste, a man-eater is sure to become mangy, and to lose his respectable appearance.

B—— and I walked round the park with our guns yesterday, and brought home five couple of snipe, two brace of partridges, one brace of quail, and a hare.

Your affectionate Brother,
W. D.

To W. R. Cornish, Esq.

Madras, February 20, 1864.

My dear Sir,—Mr. B—— has shown me your letter, and I have inspected the so-called 'stone implements' which you sent. These are very similar in form and character to some which Mr. Oldham shewed me a few months ago.

I agree with you as to the probable age of the laterite in, or upon, which you found these specimens. I believe the laterite, which is always, as far as I know, a superficial deposit, to be among the latest post-pliocene formations.

I will now go into the question of what you term the 'genuineness' of the specimens; that is, I suppose, their character as implements or tools *made by man*. So far as

I know, the character of the evidence in favour of their human origin is as follows. Implements of flint, or, to speak more generally, of stone, have been found in connection with human remains in cairns and other places; and there is ample evidence to prove that these stones have been used as 'weapons' or 'implements.' The next step, however, in the chain of evidence is, 'that man made or shaped this tool or weapon;' and the only reason for this assumption seems to be this—that the stone does, in form, resemble articles now in use, which we term hatchets, chisels, &c. The geologists having settled that man *made* the tool found in connection with his bones, then infer, legitimately enough, that, wherever similar stones are found, man must have had a hand in shaping them into forms fittest for use; and, having found quantities of similarly shaped stones in a deposit far below the tertiary strata, or post-tertiary strata, supposed to be coeval with man, they conclude that this supposition is incorrect, and that man is much older than we assume him to be.

I do not think that I have in any way misstated the general chain of reasoning adopted by Lyell and the geologists with reference to these stones.

I quite admit that they are found so frequently in connection with the remains of man as to justify fully the inference that he made use of them as weapons or tools; but *did he make them?*

We are told, in proof of the allegation that he did do so, that the discoverers of similar stones were able to make a pebble into an instrument similar to one found in a cairn. Very possibly. I have no doubt that man could make such tools; but this possibility is no evidence that he *did* do so; and there are many facts connected with the position and numbers of the implements themselves, to say nothing of their irregularity of form, which would induce a contrary belief.

In the first place, the stones appear to be very numerous. You, in the course of a short time, have picked up several, and in the sites mentioned by Lyell a great number of flint specimens have been found. Now, from all we know of savage life, each man is the maker of his own tools or weapons; there is no trace of the existence of any manufacturing establishment among them. Each family makes its own tools, clothes, weapons, &c. If this be the case—and every voyager and historian will vouch for it—who could have made the stores of tools which are said to be scattered about so profusely? Few or none exhibit evidence of having been used, and we must therefore suppose the existence of a manufacturing establishment, at which the work, when finished, was allowed to lie about after the expenditure of a good deal of labour upon it. The stones, however, which have assumed the form of tools, are not the only stones which exhibit the action of force upon them. You have sent me one chipped about in various ways, but which could not have been intended for any implement; and I have Oldham's admission that several had been picked up for him by the collector, which were rejected by himself because he could not give a name to them, or imagine a purpose to which they could be applied. I decline, therefore, to admit the validity of the evidence in favour of the assumption that man made these stones into the shape in which they are found. That he saw them on the ground, as you did, that he took them up and made use of them, as you would have done had you been pushed for an implement of the kind, is very probable; and this, as it is the most natural supposition, so it is the one which accords best with all the facts brought under our notice.

I do not wish to enter into any speculation as to the forces which were brought into action to produce the effect now shown on these stones. It is evident that many of them have been rounded pebbles, and I believe that if such a pebble were powerfully compressed, in directions perpendicular to its curved surface, the effect would be to break a material having a conchoidal fracture into some of the various forms we now see exhibited. I should like to try the experiment, and would do so had I an hydraulic press at my disposal. However, I must not prolong my letter. My belief is that man found the stones, and made use of them just as the South Sea Islanders make use of the shark's teeth, or the thorns of trees, &c., as barbs to their weapons; but I do not admit that there is any evidence to prove that he did more with his stone tool than fit a handle to it.

Yours very truly,
W. D.

To Captain Warburton, R.E.

Madras, March 12, 1864.

My dear W.,—I gather from your letter and sketch that we have crept into the enemy's country about abreast of Waingaroa, which is, I infer, Raglan. We have got, however, some distance to make good before we get into the heart of the country by the Taupo Lake. General Cameron is going about his work in the proper way, making roads, opening the country, and securing what he has got by stout works.

I confess that I am sorry for the Maories. I advised Gore Browne in 1857 to place them on the same footing as the other subjects of the Queen; to divide their country into provinces, and to give them the power of settling all their own matters in their own way. A couple of thousand pounds per annum, spent in giving a salary of 300l. per annum to each of the three presidents, and of 50l. each to twenty of the subordinate chiefs, would have saved us all the expense and disgrace of these two wars, and made the country prosperous and the people happy. Now we have made it impossible for the white man and the Maori to live together, and the latter must go to the wall, that is, must be swept away. It is a sad termination to a people who had commenced the task of civilisation so promisingly.

The Government has got itself into a difficulty with reference to the amalgamation of the Engineers, and I do not see any way out of it; neither, am I sure, does the Secretary of State or the Commander-in-Chief.

As regards special service; do you fit yourself for it and it will come to you, take my word for it: let yourself be known for a hard-working, active, intelligent officer, and you will find many that will seek for you. It is better to be sought after than to seek.

Yours very truly,
W. D.

To Sir Roderick Murchison.

Guindy, March 8, 1864.

My dear Sir Roderick,—Your Hindoo friend may be an exception, may have an unfeigned love of truth, may even have been a martyr to this love; but you may depend upon it, if that be the case—which by the way I very much doubt—he is a phœnix, more rare by far than a black swan. I do not put the least faith in the statement that they were, at one time, a truth-loving people, and have been made liars by oppression; the character is bred in the bone and is indelible.

My administration of the Indian Empire did not last long, but I was able to put an end to the war in the north-west, and to hand over the government to Sir John Lawrence with an assurance that all was peaceful both within and without our boundaries. I found on my arrival at Calcutta that the Government having been persuaded by some of its subordinate agents to undertake a *small war*, and having met with stronger resistance than it anticipated, had lost heart, and

had given orders to the Commander-in-chief to withdraw
the troops; that is, they were prepared to admit that
the mountaineers had had the best of the battle so far.
This I strongly objected to, and I urged upon the Council
the necessity of eating its words, and of directing the
Commander-in-chief to move forwards and act on the
offensive, instead of confessing his weakness by withdrawing the troops. This was done, and the result was
that two days' fighting finished the business, frightened
the mountaineers, restored to our troops the prestige of
victory, and secured us peace. My feeling is that we
have acted unwisely in stretching our frontier beyond the
Indus: a marked line of boundary should be established
between civilisation and barbarism ; the two ought not to
be brought into too close contact. As to attacking these
Affghan tribes, it is the height of folly. They are fine, bold
fellows, very like your Scotch borderers in old time, with
very much the same tastes and propensities—they quarrel
with one another, cut throats, &c., but will always join
against an enemy from without. They are like the Highlanders whom Baillie Nicol Jarvie declared to be sure to
join in the long run against 'a' civilised folk that wear
breeks on their hinder ends, and hae purses in their
pouches.' I should propose to maintain an efficient
border police, well backed up by a military force, and
to enact a stern border law. I should hang, as a matter
of course, every man whom I found *armed* within my
boundary ; but I should take especial care never to cross
the frontier line, and if my people chose to do so, they
should do so at their own risk. We have everything to
lose and nothing to gain by such petty incursions as we
have just made : we have roused a hornet's nest, and
have shown the inmates that they have very effective
weapons to use against us.

Yours very truly,
W. D.

To Sir Charles Wood.

Guindy, March 16, 1864.

My dear Sir Charles,—I have been at work upon the drainage and water supply of Madras : these will be some of the first questions which will come before the Sanitary Commissioners. The risk we run is that crude and hasty theories will be adopted as general principles, and be acted upon without due allowance for local peculiarities. I send you a copy of some memoranda of mine on the subject of the 'Water Rate.' The correctness of the view which I have taken has been exemplified by the conduct of the ryots in the Godavery district, many of whom have thrown up their land because the charge for water was too high ; I don't mean generally too high, but too high for their particular quality of land. I feel certain that the old system, of valuing land by the crop which it produces, is the simplest and best ; it is fairest both to the ryot and to the Government.

Yours very truly,

W. D.

To Mrs. Des Vœux.

Guindy, April 5, 1864.

My dear J——,—This is our spring as well as yours, and although the whole of our trees are, so to call, evergreens, they all get a new suit of clothes at this time of year, dropping their old leaves and getting a fresh set in a few weeks, and the whole face of nature is changed, and looks happy and joyous. When, however, I say the whole face of nature, I must except a large portion, for the surface of the ground, instead of being green, as with you, is burnt up, and as brown as the road : we have to wait for our grass till the autumn. Still, however, it is a pleasant time of year ; the trees are not only in leaf, but in flower, and the whole air, as I walk about in the park, is perfumed with various scents. I am getting on well with my garden; the passage between my room and the drawing-room is filled with flowers in pots, and, having three stephanotus, and two pergolaria odoratissima, you may imagine how sweet it is. I delight in the pergolaria, and am using it as a creeper in a variety of places. My orchids too are beginning to do well, and next year I shall have them in the verandah and about the house, showing magnificent spikes of flower, and lasting in bloom for a long time.

April 14.—There is rather a gap between the beginning and end of my letter, but one's life here is not very eventful. I do my best to amuse the people, and I think I succeed well, for all seem to reckon upon me as the leader in all sorts of amusement. We had a paper chase the other day on horseback, which gave great pleasure. Thirty-six people came to luncheon, and at four o'clock two of my staff started off as hares. We had a round of about ten or eleven miles, and sent them home well tired and well pleased.

I had a narrow escape in the morning, having been run away with in my carriage going down to Council, and upset. However, I sat quietly in the middle of the carriage, holding on by the straps on both sides; so, when the smash came, I held on by the upper strap, and all the inconvenience which I suffered was from the wrench given to my left shoulder by the shock of turning over.

To Sir John Lawrence.

Guindy, April 10, 1864.

My dear Sir John,—I cannot think that our finances are in such a state as to require any petty economies. I can quite understand Trevelyan's anxiety to make a great show of a surplus in order to enable him to propose the reduction of taxation; but, upon my word, when you look fairly into the question, I think you will agree with me that there are few countries in the world where taxation presses less upon the people than in India. With good management there will be a steady increase in the land revenue, and in every other branch of our income. If, however, for the purpose of making a show of reduction of expenditure, and especially of our military expenditure, we sell this thing and that, and decline to maintain our forces in a proper state of efficiency, we shall find ourselves at the beginning of another war in no condition to carry it on effectively. Last year we sold off our steamers and transports, and the result was that we had to pay 50l. per man for the transport of troops to New Zealand, simply because the ship-owners and merchants knew that we were entirely in their hands. This year we are going to sell more steamers, and shall be left altogether at the mercy of the steam companies.

Yours very truly,

W. D.

To T. Sutherland, Esq., Rangoon.

Madras, May 19, 1864.

Sir,—I have to acknowledge the receipt of the drawings of your hulling mill and turbine, and of your letter expressing your willingness to give me any information I may require upon subjects connected with machinery and engineering.

I should be glad to obtain from you such definite information regarding the work of this turbine under different falls—the quantity of water required per horse-power under each of a series of falls; the velocity of the first mover, which is, I suppose, the prolonged axis of the turbine itself—as would justify me in applying the machine to a variety of purposes. I want a pump to lift water about 100 feet, and I can get any fall I like within the limits of from forty to sixty feet. I want to work a saw mill in the forest where I can always get water; the quantity will be small, but the fall great; but as there are many parts of the country where no water is to be found, I should like to utilise the power of the wind for the purpose of raising water from wells to irrigate land. In one district of this Presidency there are upwards of 20,000 wells, and with many of these a pump worked by a self-acting windmill would save an immense deal of labour, and would, if shown to be successful and decently cheap, soon commend itself to the natives: a powerful pump is not wanted. I suppose that ten acres might be watered from one well, and this would be equivalent to about 1,550 pounds raised per minute from a depth of, say, twenty feet, which would be equivalent to a horse-power. This would be the maximum. I take 5,000 cube yards as the amount of water to irrigate an acre, and this quantity is distributed over the whole season of, say, three months. I suppose the pump to work ten hours per day. With many thanks for the information you have given me,

I remain, &c.

W. D.

To Sir Charles Wood.

Madras, May 19, 1864.

My dear Sir Charles,—You say, very truly, that neither the Government nor any of its officers knew anything of the ground over which the troops had to move to the attack of Mulkah; they knew nothing of even that portion which was within our own territory.

I wrote to Sir Hugh Rose when I was steaming up the river, and asked him whether there was in existence a military report on the frontier, and was told that he knew of no such thing. And when I enquired at Calcutta, from the survey officers and others, I found that no such thing had ever been thought of. Now I recollect, some five-and-thirty years ago, looking over a French report upon the Rhine frontier, drawn up with great care, noting down every feature of the ground which could be of service to the officer in command of a force, either advancing or retreating through that country; and I think it would be very desirable that the Government should be in possession of a similar report for the whole of our trans-Indus frontier. This is the only portion of the whole of our frontier by which an enemy of any importance could attempt to attack us, and we ought to have a thorough knowledge of every position which it affords for defence, or any advantages which it may present to aid a forward movement.

I am afraid, from what I see in the papers, that we are likely to have some trouble in the north-east, now that we have settled the north-west. The Bhootan people have frightened Eden into signing a treaty conceding certain matters to them. I don't know the extent of his weakness, but the Government can never dream of carrying the treaty out. These embassies to and treaties with a people which has nothing to be called a Government, are merely traps. The breach of a treaty, which is sure to be broken ten weeks after ratification, can always be brought up as a ground for hostilities. It would be far better to maintain a strict border law, to hang every man found *in arms* on our side of the frontier; the borders would be desolate, but we have more land already than we know what to do with.

Yours very truly,
W. D.

To Sir Charles Wood.

Madras, May 26, 1864.

My dear Sir Charles,—I have got returns of the cost of our three principal irrigation works—the Godavery, the Kistnah, and the Pennaar or Nellore works.

The first has cost 360,000l. or 370,000l., and will cost

about 200,000*l.* more; it irrigates at present 650,000 acres, and will irrigate about 450,000 more. The cost has therefore been about 11*s.* 6*d.* per acre, and will be, when the whole is completed, about 10*s.* per acre.

The Kistnah has cost 240,000*l.*, and will cost 370,000*l.* more; it irrigates 200,000 acres, and will irrigate 300,000 more; it has cost 24*s.* per acre, and will eventually cost about 22*s.*

The Pennaar has cost 100,000*l.*, and will cost 10,000*l.* more; it irrigates 30,000 acres, and will irrigate 7,000 more; it has cost 30*s.* per acre, and will eventually cost 27*s.* 6*d.* This latter work has cost more than the others because the dam was placed too near the sea. Had it been placed near the spot where the river issues from the hills, the work would have cost more, but ten times the quantity of land would have been irrigated. Even here the work has paid itself, the return being at the least 6*s.* per acre, or one-fifth, or 20 per cent. upon the cost. It would always be good policy in the Government to borrow money for works of this kind : it might set apart a portion of the revenue as a sinking fund, so as to pay off the capital in a few years; while the indirect return in the shape of money put into the ryots' pockets would soon make itself felt in the extension of cultivation.

Yours very truly,
W. D.

To Mrs. Des Vœux.

Madras, May 29, 1864.

My dear J——,—It seems to me that you in England are all afflicted with a sort of periodical fit of insanity : with some it takes the form of professed admiration of Shakespeare, while others fall down and worship that very small lion Garibaldi. I am told that one lady framed and glazed a glove which Garibaldi had touched, while another had actually gone on her knees to him. I do not think that I should have partaken of either phase of this madness, but there is no telling. I most certainly should not have followed Garibaldi, for I look upon him as a mischievous fellow—just the sort of person who is pushed to the front in order that others may reap the benefit of his courage. In India we cannot get up steam enough for hero-worship, although we have a good many small people, heroes in their way, to whom we erect statues. This tendency to try and immortalize people in brass or in marble is becoming almost an evil of which the police should take notice : the thoroughfares will very soon be blocked up by statues. I came upon them at Calcutta in the most extraordinary places, and even here I have two which block up a crowded thoroughfare. I suppose posthumous fame has its attractions, for we see many who strive for it, and many more who strive to perpetuate the memory of some friend or relation ; but I had all this knocked out of me years ago, partly by reading the life of Lord Metcalfe, who worked for fame from the beginning of his life, and reached high places and honours, but whose name is now absolutely forgotten ; and still more by the conviction of the utter worthlessness of such a motive to action.

We have had a cool season at Madras, but no rain. I went to Guindy yesterday, and found my garden doing well, owing to constant watering. My Victoria Regia has seeded itself to such an extent that I have hundreds of plants, which I am going to spread about in every direction. The orchids which I got from Burmah are doing well, but it is a little too hot for those from the hills. What a pity it is that we cannot generate cold as we do heat. We are all well, and have arranged to go to the hills about the 4th or 5th of July.

Your affectionate Brother,

W. D.

To Sir Charles Wood.

My dear Sir Charles,—I have been trying to pick up
facts as to the longevity of the natives, their physical im
provement or degradation—in fact, statistics of popu
lation; but, of course, I only get vague opinions. These,
however, appear to point to a decrease in the length of
life, caused, as said by some, by the habit of breeding
in and in, and by a mere sensual indulgence of the
appetites.

My informants say that men are now obliged to marry
not only within their caste, but within their family, and
that they marry much earlier than they used. All this
may be true, or may be false, but it points to the necessity of acquiring some definite information as to vital
statistics; and I think it would be as well that we should
commence a system of registration of births, deaths, and
marriages as soon as possible.

June 8.—The mail came in yesterday, and I got your
letter. You have mistaken my meaning as regards the
comparative merits of military and civilians; but I did
and do maintain that, for military work, the former are
the proper authorities. As regards the operations in the
north-west, they were suggested by civilians, interfered
with by civilians, and the only wonder is that they terminated so well. This they would not have done had I not
put an end to the meddling of the civilians and placed the
matter in the hands of the military.

To Sir John Lawrence.

Madras, June 20, 1864.

My dear Sir John,—I congratulate you most sincerely
upon the safety of Lady Lawrence, and upon the addition
to your family.

I have always taken to myself the saying of the Psalmist, 'Lo, children and the fruit of the womb are an heritage and gift that cometh from the Lord: happy is the man who hath his quiver full of them,' and have found it literally true in a variety of senses; so I can and do congratulate you on the addition of another arrow to your quiver.

Many people say that with children come cares. Perhaps so; but with children come thousands of pleasures. From the very day that we can take them in our arms, even to that when we may have to place them in their coffins, and even after that, they are a help and a blessing to us; and I can hardly believe that a man not a parent can comprehend the blessed meaning of that which we learn from our Saviour—that God is our Father.

I have given directions that, unless in cases of absolute necessity, the rail is to be kept clear of all burial-grounds near Trichinopoly. This place is the head-quarters of a sulky and fanatical Mahometan population; but they have so few to back them that I do not apprehend any risk of an *émeute* among them. With the new railroad to Trichinopoly we should be able to pour in troops upon them so speedily as to put down any disturbance immediately. It is, however, far better that we should not give them any just cause of complaint.

I will do my best to keep clear of any increase of police expenditure. It is a very hard service for officers: I have now upwards of 25 per cent. on sick leave. I think, however, that we are working ours very satisfactorily. My inspector-general, Robinson, is a first-rate man, not only as regards his thorough acquaintance with the police system, but his zeal and energy in looking after his subordinates and working out all details. The result of his energetic working is that the gaols are filled to overflowing. This was the result in England also of the introduction of the new police; but in a few years we shall find the preventive action will begin to tell, and the gaols will be emptied again. It would not be wise, therefore, to calculate upon the maintenance of the present number of prisoners, and to erect gaols to contain them: we had better make temporary arrangements for working the surplus, which we might do with advantage.

Yours very truly,
W. D.

To Sir Charles Wood.

Madras, June 17, 1864.

My dear Sir Charles,—I see that Hawkshaw agrees with me, that, if light railways are to be made, they should be worked by animal power. This was the opinion I expressed in New South Wales, and the reasons are stronger in favour of it here. I am completing some old papers of mine on the subject by adding a chapter on India, and I will send it to you when finished.

June 27.—I had letters from New Zealand by the last mail. It seems that the pah which we failed to storm was situated on a hill; it had been breached, and the naval brigade and three or four companies of the 43rd were ordered to storm the breach. They moved up to the attack very steadily, and forced their way in without much difficulty; but as soon as they were inside a terrific fire was opened upon them; the officers were shot down. My poor friend Glover was leading, and was shot through the head at once, and the men, in spite of every effort to retain them, retreated in haste, leaving the dead and wounded officers behind them. Lieutenant Glover tried to carry off his brother, thinking that he was only wounded, but he was so severely wounded in the attempt that he died in a few days. The soldiers have got to appreciate the character of the war, and say that they are sent to bolster up a land-jobbing speculation.

I tried in the last war to persuade the military autho-

rities that it was a piece of folly to storm a 'pah.' The
Maories hold on till they are seriously attacked, and then,
as we come in at one end, they, having done as much
harm to us as possible, go out at the other. We ought
to take a leaf out of Cæsar's book, and when we have
three or four hundred men in a pah we ought to enclose
them. They are not provisioned for a siege; the pah is
as often as not on a hill having no water within the line
of palisades; so that in a few days the garrison would be
obliged to capitulate, or to make a rush to escape, when a
ditch or parapet with a few trees felled in front would
detain them under fire long enough to cause a very serious
loss, if not to compel them to surrender.

Yours truly,
W. D.

Lady Denison to Mrs. Stanley.

Madras, June 28, 1864.

My dear Mrs. Stanley,—Before this reaches you, you
will have seen the newspaper accounts of that terrible
battle in New Zealand, and will know that Captain
Glover and his youngest brother were both killed. The
news has been a real grief to us. I think I know few
people who made themselves so generally beloved as
Captain Glover has done, and it is quite nice to see how
people here think and talk of him, and how his death
has been a general blow to Madras; while to us, of
course, it is the loss of a real and intimate friend, and
from his having lived in our house so long, it is almost
like one of the family being gone, in respect of the many
little matters in and about the house with which the recollection of him seems connected. We were, of course,
anxious to hear all the particulars we could about him,
beyond the bare fact which the telegram conveyed, and
we have got all the details by this mail, in a letter to
W—— from Colonel Carey, the Adjutant-General in
New Zealand. From this letter it appears that Captain

Glover was one of the leaders of the storming party, and had made his way at the head of his men well inside the enemy's 'pah,' when he was shot through the head and died instantly. His poor brother, thinking and hoping that he was only wounded, tried to carry his body off, and was shot himself in so doing, and as the event proved, mortally wounded. He lingered, however, for two days, and, I am afraid, suffered a great deal; but then died; and the two brothers were buried together in the mission burying-ground near the camp, along with all the others (a fearfully large number) who fell in the same battle. It is a sad story, and I am afraid it was a bad business altogether; for there seems little doubt that the officers, who all behaved heroically, were not supported as they should have been by their own men. As regards Captain Glover himself, the details are just what one could have wished to hear. As far as human eyes could see, his life had been so good a preparation for an early and sudden death, that its suddenness only gives one the satisfactory conviction that it must have been painless; and one cannot but be glad that he fell during the early part of the action, before the repulse which befel our troops, and which must be a grief to the very few officers who survive. The two brothers were so devotedly attached to each other, that one could just imagine one of them losing his own life in the effort to save the other.

Yours affectionately,

C. L. D.

To Mrs. Stanley.

Woodlands, Ootacamund, July 14, 1864.

My dear Mrs. Stanley,—Our cinchona experiment is working admirably; we propagate from 20,000 to 30,000 plants per month, and are preparing and planting out land rapidly. The plants like the soil and the climate, and private individuals think so well of the prospect of profit as to be willing to pay us sixpence per plant for the purpose of planting out. Now sixpence per plant is about 15l. per acre, to say nothing of the probable loss in planting; in fact, it will be nearer 20l., so that, what with purchasing the land, clearing and preparing it, the cost will not be short of 30l. per acre. Bark, however, will be worth three or four shillings per pound, and in three or four years the yield would be at least 200 lbs. of bark to the acre, which at even two shillings per pound would give 20l. I think, therefore, the speculation would be a good one, and I have no doubt that a great many people will go into it. The difficulty will be to find labour enough. People imagine that India is overflowing with population, the fact being that we have not labour enough to cultivate our own soil. We do this, it is true, in a slovenly way, and I am trying to introduce machinery which will set labour free. This, however, will be a long process, for I have a curious set of people to deal with. To revert to cinchona. At present we cannot make use of quinine in the hospitals to the extent which would be desirable; not so much on account of the expense, as of the scarcity of the commodity. When we have got our hills well covered, we shall be able to extend the use of this febrifuge, and this will be an immense blessing to the natives. I hear of villages actually depopulated by fever.

To Sir Roderick Murchison.

Ootacamund, July 29, 1864.

My dear Sir Roderick,—Thanks for your letter. I am glad that you have decided to remain as President of the Geographical Society. I should have voted for any arrangement which would have been required to retain the right man in the right place. I shall read your views as to Africa and its inhabitants with a good deal of interest. I am at present corresponding with Dr. Schertzer

of Vienna on the subject of his ethnological views. He
is engaged in drawing up the report of the Austrian
voyage of discovery, and I furnished him with a variety
of matter relative to the Australian and Indian population. He differs from Darwin and Huxley as to man's
antecedents, but is disposed to adopt some German views
as to various centres of creation, and to repudiate Adam
and Eve. It occurred to me, a month or two ago, to try
how Bunsen's and Lyell's speculations as to the antiquity
of man would harmonise with any reasonable views as to
the progressive increase of the race ; and I found reason
to believe that the chronology of the Bible, and the fact
of the Deluge, would agree better with the state of the
existing population as to numbers, than any of the theories
of a prolonged residence upon earth, or of different centres
of creation, would do. For instance, if we assume that
the population doubles itself in 100 years—only half the
rate at which we are progressing, in spite of our Irish
exodus—we shall find that in the first thousand years the
population increased from two to about two thousand : in
the second thousand years the two thousand became two
millions ; in the third thousand it became two thousand
millions ; in the fourth thousand it became two million
millions, and so on. Now we require such an event as
the flood to sweep away sixteen or seventeen terms of
this progression, and even then we should find that the
theoretical population would be about ten thousand times
as numerous as the real population. Famines, pestilences,
wars, the sweeping destruction of nations by the Jews, by
the Eastern kings, by the Romans, by Attila, &c., will
make, of course, shrewd gaps, and reduce the numbers in
particular terms of the progression ; but if we assume
four centres of creation, we shall have to multiply the
numbers given above by four ; and if we suppose, with
Bunsen, that man has been 20,000 years upon earth, we
should be puzzled to find standing-room for the present

population. We ought to have some evidence of his existence in the remains of his bones, looking to the number which must have been placed under the sod.

I have been discussing a question relative to the action of forests upon the rainfall, with reference to the very dry character of a great part of our plain country, and have arrived at the conclusion that the Government ought to take energetic action to remedy a state of things which has a most injurious effect upon our agriculture. I think I must have mentioned to you the curious fact that the south-west monsoon, that is, the rainy part of it, stops at a specific line in the middle of a plain, which line is marked by the existence of jungle on the rainy side, while the dry side is bare of trees. I at first attributed the presence of trees to the rain, but I am now disposed to look upon the jungle as the cause of the rain, not the effect of it; for I have been told that, just in proportion as the belt of jungle is cut away, so does the line of rain retreat. When one comes to consider this, the reason is plain enough : the cleared ground is exposed to the action of a vertical sun at the solstice, and a heated stream of air ascends from it, converting the rain into vapour, which is carried off by the prevailing winds, and falls into the Bay of Bengal. The desolation of a great part of the East, Palestine, Edom, Assyria, &c., may, I think, be traced to the causes which are now in operation in India, and which I wish to neutralise.

Colenso insists upon the existing state of the Sinaitic desert as a proof that the Israelites could not have passed through it, could not have found fuel, &c.; but, in truth, the existing denuded condition of the country, coupled with the fact that there is evidence of the action of torrents, where there is now hardly a dribble, is the best possible proof of the correctness of the story of the exodus. The wood required for the use of a couple of million of people during a period of nearly forty years would have covered the flanks of the mountains, and have been used without stint. That there was wood we know, that there is none we know; where there was wood there was rain, where no wood exists there is no rain. A proper consideration of meteorological phenomena will afford an explanation of many of the anomalies which puzzle us when we view them with reference only to the existing state of things.

I am getting the benefit of the south-west monsoon. I have been up here little more than three weeks, and have only had one day without rain. We are high (7,500 feet) and in the clouds, where we get our provision of water in the shape more of mist than of rain ; but twenty miles from this, and a couple of thousand feet lower down, the rain has been very heavy, fifty-seven inches having fallen in the month. I am looked upon here as a water-god, a sort of Jupiter pluvius. The native, when I ask him if he has had a good monsoon, says, 'by your favour we have had rain.' This is meant by them as a delicate piece of flattery, but my gorge rises at it.

Yours very truly,
W. D.

To Mrs. Des Vœux.

Ootacamund, August 5, 1864.

My dear J——,—We have been here for more than a month, and have had only four days without rain. Still we have made our way out, both on horseback and on foot. I have had two special wettings in an attempt to get a day's shooting.

Can you imagine the cold being sufficient up here to kill people ? It is, however, the case. The coolies from the low country, with cotton wrappers, and a blanket which covers their head, their legs and feet being bare, frequently die from exposure to the wind and rain. They seem to get stupified, just as a man does when exposed to intense cold, and will lie down and die within a few hundred yards of shelter. A man, the other day, carried, for about a couple of miles, one of his coolies who was just giving in. The temperature at this time of year is seldom below 60°, but the wind and the rain together make a very chilly compound.

Lady Denison to F. G. Denison, Esq.

Ootacamund, August 22, 1864.

My dear Frank,—I am afraid I have not much to tell you from hence to make a letter lively. We are in the midst of torrents of rain, according to the usual fashion of Ootacamund; but we really had a few fine days at the beginning of last week, which were very enjoyable. Thinking the monsoon must be nearly over now, we are beginning to plan a few excursions for next month. The present idea is to start on Tuesday, the 30th (to-morrow week), for Pycara: a party of twelve. The plan is to spend the remainder of that week between the Pycara waterfall and Neddiewuttum—a very beautiful place in the neighbourhood—returning here on Saturday, and the following week going out again to Makoortie Peak. This last expedition is the one I am most anxious for, for I have never seen that Makoortie Peak view, which is said to be such a glorious one. We attempted it when we were last up here, but there was such a mist when we got up that we could see nothing.

Last Thursday we gave a ball, the only way we could devise of doing the needful in the way of hospitalities to the people of Ootacamund, as our rooms in this house are quite too small to admit of our giving dinners. It was ball-giving under difficulties, as you may suppose; for, of course, the rooms here, being too small for dinners, are also too small for balls, so we had to give it in the bungalow occupied by the staff, where there are two rooms opening into one another—small, indeed, for the purpose, but larger than our own, and altogether the most convenient we could get. The floors were very rough, and had to be planed and smoothed, and old Chinniah, the butler, danced up and down them nearly all day to see if they were getting smooth enough. Then it rained in torrents all the afternoon; and, though it cleared a little in the evening, it was very wet everywhere, and we had only the B——'s palanquin carriage in which to get down to the bungalow in detachments, for we only brought one pair of horses with us, and a stupid native coachman managed to throw one of them down the other day and break one of his knees, so he was *hors de combat.* However, in spite of all these difficulties, the ball went off very fairly well, and people in general seemed pleased.

Your affectionate Mother,

C. L. D.

To Mrs. Des Vœux.

Ootacamund, August 25, 1864.

My dear J——,—I propose to finish off my three months on the hills by a visit to a district called Wynaad, which is on the top of the Ghauts, though 2,000ft. or 3,000ft. lower than the mass of hills upon which we are perched. This district is principally occupied by coffee-planters, who, being for the most part Englishmen, are always grumbling that the Government does not help them, though we are spending much more money upon them than we get from them. I want to stop their mouths if possible. This journey I shall have to make principally on horseback, and I do not look forward to it with any very pleasant anticipations, as I shall have to ride between 250 and 300 miles. Of course, the people whom we talk to on the subject have always some story of wild elephants and tigers that we are to meet. There is rather a good story of an elephant meeting a man and his wife, who were coming up a narrow path in palanquins; they, of course, trundled quickly out of their palanquins, which the elephant destroyed; but, when he had passed, all their goods were found correct, except a large box of Holloway's pills, which it is supposed the elephant must have swallowed. A rider has been added to the story: that the elephant was found dead a few days after, in consequence of the severity of the dose: but this is mythical.

Pycara, August 31. We came out here with a party of fourteen altogether, two of whom are in the bungalow and the rest in tents, with the intention of seeing the waterfall, the cinchona plantations, &c., and having a little shooting. We were just starting for the waterfall when a man came in and told us that a tiger had killed a buffalo and a pony about a mile and a half from our camp. We went to the place and found that there were two tigers: one of them, after being fired at from above, came down towards the spot where B—— and I, with a Colonel Hamilton, were posted. He was sneaking away down the river, when I caught sight of him. I hit him with my first barrel, when he turned, growled savagely, and made at us, but I fired my second barrel and crippled him, and B—— and Hamilton finished him, but he took a great deal of killing. I am very glad that I have killed one, but I am more and more convinced that no one ought to encounter a tiger single-handed.

September 2.—We went yesterday to visit a cinchona plantation, which has been established about three years, and I was very much struck with the growth of the plants during the last two years. Several, put in two years ago, being then yearling plants about 15in. to 24in. high, are from 8ft. to 10ft. in height. The experiment has been a very successful one, and in a few years we shall beat the South Americans out of the market. This success is principally owing to our gardener, Mr. McIvor, a Scotch man. I relieved him from control and superintendence, and made him answerable for the success of the scheme, and the result is certainly most satisfactory. Were I a young man with a few thousand pounds I should decidedly become a cultivator of cinchona on these hills: they are very healthy, and the profit from cinchona cultivation will be very large, if a man would look after it himself. Many men, however, buy tea and coffee plantations, and place them in the hands of agents, expecting to receive large interest for their money, but the agent swallows up the whole of the profits.

Ootacamund, September 6.—We returned here on Saturday, having a perversely fine day for our ride back.

I am going to have another ' out ' to-morrow, to visit Makoortie Peak—the great lion of the place.

Your affectionate Brother,
W. D.

To His Highness the Maharajah of Travancore.

Madras, August 29, 1864.

Your Highness will be pleased to accept my congratulations upon the birth of the first of the new generation in your family, and my best wishes for the health of both mother and child.

Your visit to Kuthalum must have given you great satisfaction, but I am more interested in the remarks which you make on the subject of utilizing the water of the second fall. I am very anxious to see the forces which nature places at our disposal in India made use of for productive purposes. Hitherto both wind and water have been allowed to waste their energies, while man has been tasked to do the work which might have been better and more economically performed by these natural agents.

In Travancore water-power is available to any extent. Saw-mills, spinning and weaving machinery, mills for hulling rice and preparing it for exportation, and, in fact, for a hundred other useful purposes, might easily be established. I have sent to England for a variety of agricultural implements, among which there is a steam plough, and I hope to prove to the ryots, and to the agricultural population generally, that by the use of better implements their crops will be improved, and their profits larger. I should wish to see more attention paid in the schools to instruction in mechanics; that working implements should be exhibited in action to the scholars, so as to produce an impression on their minds and memories that there are means by which results may be arrived at such as man could not hope to perform unaided by machinery. My object is to enable you to utilize a large amount of power which is lying dormant in Travancore. Wages are rising daily, demands are being made upon India with which she will be unable to comply, unless she avails herself of the knowledge which the pressure of circumstances has matured in England and America, and this leads to the employment of other agencies than man.

Of course, all progress of this kind must be very gradual; but educated men, like your Highness, are well aware of the kind of preparation which is required to fit the minds of people for the changes which must take place, and in which your position fits you most especially to take the lead.

I trust that you will excuse me for writing thus to you; but I feel so great an interest in the development, through native energy, of the resources of the country, that I do not like to let an occasion slip of pressing my views upon any whom I may think likely to aid in carrying them out.

Believe me to be your sincere friend,

W. D.

September 5, 1864.

My dear Sir, I am afraid that you must make up your mind to encounter all the difficulties arising out of the increased cost of labour difficulties which press hardly upon all departments of the Government, and from which, therefore, the Irrigation Company cannot hope to be exempted. The rise in the price of labour has its origin in too many causes to admit of the application of local remedies to the evils which it creates—evils, by the way, which have their counterbalancing advantages. The railways are one of these causes; the works of the Irrigation Company another; the great extension of public works another; the rapid increase of cultivation another; emigration another. The remedy is to be found not in diminishing the demand for labour, but in increasing its efficiency; in applying mechanical expedients to enable one man to do the work of half a dozen; in utilising the power which nature has placed at our disposal; in making more use of animal power, &c. &c.

The principle which the Government has affirmed, with reference to the emigration question, is the right of the native of India to carry his labour to any market which suits him, and it most certainly will not modify this to meet a difficulty which is, but to a very slight extent, due to the exercise of this right by the natives. I do not quite comprehend the course of action which you have submitted to the Directors of the Irrigation Company, and which you say they have sanctioned. That you will act wisely in concentrating your efforts upon the upper portions of your present work—that is, upon those between the Toombuddra and the Pennaar—I am quite disposed to admit; as these portions are, in the first place, likely to be most remunerative, and as they are, in the second place, essential to the efficiency of the lower portions of the work : but you must recollect that your contract embraces all the work from Sunkesala to the sea ; and you must understand that the Government, whilst it does not wish to hamper the action of the company in its efforts to carry out the work to the best advantage, is not in any way disposed to ignore the contract which has been entered into, or to allow the company to leave undone any portions of the work, on the ground that such are not likely to prove remunerative.

Yours very truly,
W. D.

To F. G. Denison, Esq.

Croormund, September 10, 1864.

My dear Frank,—Our Makoortie trip has proved a failure. I am writing now at the Croormund bungalow, as we are preparing to return to Ootacamund. We intended to come out on Wednesday with a party of sixteen, seven ladies and nine gentlemen ; but it rained too hard. It was finer on Thursday, so we started, but were caught in the rain before we got to our camp. We had a very merry party, however, in the evening, and decided to be up at four on Friday morning, so as to get up to the top of the peak betimes. At a quarter to four I looked out and found that it was raining; however, it was too late to make any change then, so we started. Our first difficulty was how to get across the stream just below the bungalow, which was over the saddle-flaps. We first proposed to carry the ladies over in a chair ; but it was suggested that the elephants which had brought out the tents might carry us over, so we decided to try. They had no howdahs, but only the pads, so there was not much to hold on by.

Your mother and I and two others went over first, and I never was in such a fright. The elephant kneels down, and one gets on his back easily enough ; but when he gets up, he lifts his fore-quarters first, and one has a great tendency to slip over his tail. Then his motion is a sort of rolling gait, very like a boat in a short sea ; and when he lies down to let you get off it is almost worse than when he rises up, for he brings his hind-quarters down, bending what would be the hock of a horse inwards instead of outwards, so that his leg from the stifle is flat on the ground. In one instance, the animal, instead of kneeling properly, rolled over on one side, so that two ladies had to be pulled off backwards. We were amused at seeing one of the men belonging to the elephants, sitting far back on one of them, and pulling up the creature's tail behind him, to keep himself from slipping off. In spite of our early move, we found, when we got to the river, that the whole of the upper part of the valley was enveloped in mist, so that it would have been a piece of absurdity to attempt to get up the peak. We went back, therefore, to breakfast, and a party went off to beat some sholas, but they saw but little game, and came home wet and tired.

We have had some very good sport with the hounds. We go out twice a week at half-past seven, and are in generally by ten or half-past. The other day we must have ridden upwards of twenty miles.

A party went out shooting yesterday and brought home three hinds ; they missed one or two fine stags. B—— made a very pretty shot at a stag running across him, and killed him dead.

September 23.—We had an exhibition of the Todas and Koters, two of the tribes of these hills, yesterday, at the Commander-in-chief's house—146 of the first and 89 of the second. They brought with them a strong smell of garlic, which rather overpowered some of the visitors, of whom there were many. I sent them away pleased enough, giving half a rupee to each of the men, and a

quarter of a rupee to each of the women and children.
There were two very fine old fellows standing upwards
of six feet high, and with very good features. I am going
to have them photographed.

Your affectionate Father,

W. D.

A visit from these Todas and Koters was an annual
occurrence during our stay on the hills. Their chief
object, of course, was to obtain the above-mentioned
dole with which our interview concluded; but before
this was given to them, they used to entertain us with
their national dance. That of the Koters consisted in
whirling round, first with one arm raised, and then in a
contrary direction, holding up the other arm ; but, as
their dress was rather remarkable, consisting of a long
white robe (usually very dirty), covered with patches of
red, arranged in peculiar and cabalistic-looking forms, there
was a kind of weird and witch-like look about the whole
—a something between the dervish and the sorcerer—
that, but for the extreme dirt, would have given a kind of
quasi-dignity to the performance. The dance of the
Todas consisted merely in slightly raising and advancing
one foot, and hopping slowly upon the other, each hop
being accompanied by a peculiar grunt; their dress, too,
was less strange than that of the Koters, consisting simply
of a blanket thrown over the shoulders and reaching to
the knees, which garment, *it is said*, is never changed
or taken off till it drops to pieces from actual age ! The
hair of the Toda man is worn in a kind of thick mat on
the top of the head; that of the women is dressed with
some care, in long and shining ringlets round the face,
and reaching down to the neck. The Todas, however,
are much the finer people of the two ; they are stronger
and more muscular than the Koters, and there is some-

thing of an independent dignity and fearlessness in their manner which contrasts most favourably with the cringing servility of the Hindoo in the plains.

To Mrs. Des Vœux.

Manantoddy, September 30, 1864.

My dear J——,—I may as well explain my date before I commence my story. Manantoddy is the central town of a district called Wynaad, inhabited principally by coffee-planters, who, having complained to me bitterly of various grievances, have, to a certain extent, compelled me to pay them a visit. The mode of travelling, on horseback, did not lead to any very pleasant anticipations on my part; and I started on the 26th at 2 P.M., not in the best of humours, for a ride of seventeen miles to my resting-place for the night, with the prospect of a wetting. However, matters turned out better than I expected : we escaped the rain, and found our bungalow fairly comfortable. Our Tuesday's journey was rather a formidable one. We were to start at seven, to get down a descent of about 2,000 feet; then to meet a deputation of planters, and to ride on about fifteen miles to breakfast. We started to walk down the ghaut, and soon found that our four miles of descent lengthened out to five, six, seven and a half : in point of fact, it was upwards of six miles, and this elongation of our walk made us behind time with the deputation ; this, however, did not matter much. We said our say, had a cup of tea, and then pushed on along a new road as fast as its character would permit. We had been warned that we must keep our eyes about us, for that the road was rotten in several places, the ants having made excavations which were likely to let us in, and give us a fall. However, by careful riding, we got on to our breakfast place, which was a tent pitched upon a grassy knoll, and did ample justice to our fare, as you may imagine, having ridden and walked twenty-one or twenty-two miles. We intended to have remained at this place for some hours, and then to have pushed on when the sun got low; but about 10 o'clock the clouds collected and it began to rain, so we decided to start at once, and try to ride out of the rain. We therefore sent on our tired horses, and, mounting fresh ones, made our way as fast as we could to our resting-place for the night, which was a bungalow with tents round it, at a place called Sultan's Battery; Hyder or Tippoo having established a post here, in a move which they made against the Zamorin of Calicut on the coast. I wish I could give you an idea of the beauty of the scenery, both generally and specially. The road wound round hills, giving us peeps of the range of mountains we had left, and showing us, from different points of view, detached hills with rugged and irregular outlines: the country was clothed with timber generally, but the hills had beautiful grassy patches of the most vivid green. Then the forest itself was not like an American one, a mass of trees and underwood, but had much more the look of an English park: here and there a mass of wood, then a grassy glade, with beautiful short turf dotted about with clusters of bamboos, whose feathery foliage rose to the height of fifty or sixty feet, and whose outlines are most beautiful and graceful. Then the wild flowers were lovely; the trees, shrubs, and creepers were just bursting into bloom after the monsoon. The butterflies, by hundreds, were flaunting about, of colours such as you never saw or dreamt of in an extra-tropical climate. Our journey, therefore—barring the rain, out of which we managed to ride—was very pleasant, and a good sponge with warm water made me feel quite fresh, notwithstanding a walk of upwards of six miles and a ride of twenty-eight or twenty-nine. We stopped at Sultan's Battery all Wednesday, in order to give our men and horses time to get forward. In the

afternoon we had a party of the wild tribes, who keep
much to the bush, to exhibit their archery. They put
up a bottle at twenty yards, and I gave a prize of two
annas (3d.) to whoever hit it, and four annas to the one
who broke it. Their bows were made of bamboo, strung
with vegetable fibre; arrows also of bamboo, some
headed with sharp iron like the pointed blade of a knife;
others, with which they shoot birds, had a broad head,
widening gradually from the shaft, with a hole in the
middle in which a bit of stone was placed. I was not
much impressed with their skill. I was struck, however,
with the muscular power exhibited by men whose frame
was slight, and their limbs by no means well clothed with
muscle: their bows were very stiff, and I found it difficult
to bend them to the extent which they do with apparent
ease.

On Wednesday evening it rained hard, continued to do
so all night, and when I got up at a quarter before six it
was still drizzling. We had intended to have ridden on
some thirteen miles to breakfast, but, looking to the state
of the weather, we decided to breakfast before we started,
and to ride straight through, taking our chance of the
heat. A tent is not a pleasant tenement under a burning
sun, even though it be double, with a space of some three
feet between the inner and outer tent, as they all are
here. We started at ten o'clock, and rode through a
country more beautiful than that which we passed through
on Tuesday. We had three rivers to cross, upon rafts
made of bamboos, which just carried me and my horse,
the water even then coming up over the raft. The rope
which was stretched across the river, and by which the
raft was pulled across, was made of twisted rattans;
these grow to a length of from 60ft. to 80ft., and make a
very strong rope. We did our twenty-four miles, including these crossings of rivers, in about six hours, and
were glad to find ourselves under a good roof.

Lackady, October 4.—We rested at Manantoddy, Friday, Saturday, and Sunday, being comfortably lodged in a bungalow belonging to the deputy collector. I had to receive and answer an address, to dine with the settlers, to write several letters, &c., so the time passed away quickly enough. We had service in the house on Sunday, at which several settlers attended. On Monday we started to ride thirty miles to this place—Lackady—at the head of a pass down to the low country. We passed through a country differing very much from that which we had seen on our former rides; the forest was closer, but there were occasional openings which made beautiful pictures. We came across the tracks of several wild elephants : these come lumbering down the hills to drink at the brooks at the bottom, and leave their marks upon the road ; they will be gradually cleared out as the country gets cleared. This morning I breakfasted with the settlers, received a long grumbling address, gave a written answer, and then had a long talk with them, which ended satisfactorily, for we parted very good friends. It is raining hard, everything feels damp, and I shall not be sorry to get down the ghaut into the low country to-morrow.

October 6.—We started at six yesterday morning and walked seven miles down the ghaut, through a dense forest, out of which we only got a peep occasionally. The vegetation, however, was truly tropical ; here and there the road was strewed with wild nutmegs, the mace good enough, the nutmegs themselves without any taste. A merchant of Calicut sent home a large cargo of them one year, for which he got a good price ; he tried the same trick the next year, and found that they would not pay the freight.

From the bottom of the ghaut we rode nine miles to breakfast, and I was then driven in to this place (Calicut) by the Collector, Mr. Ballard, at whose house I am staying. I am now writing in the verandah in front of my room in my dressing gown, the temperature being that of an orchid house. We move on by rail to-morrow, picking up L—— and the rest of the party on the road.

Madras, October 12. We started from Calicut on the afternoon of the 7th, reached Beypore in time for the special train, which took us 100 miles to Coimbatore in three hours ; found L—— and all our belongings waiting for us. Slept at Coimbatore that night ; set off at 8 A.M., and got to Madras at a quarter to 6 P.M., having gone 306 miles in nine hours and three-quarters, including fifty minutes given us for luncheon ;—fair going. Formerly it would have taken seven or eight days of bullock transit.

Your affectionate Brother,
W. D.

To Sir Roderick Murchison.

Madras, October 31, 1864.

My dear Sir Roderick,—I want to get from you an explanation of some phenomena connected with the gneiss formation. The Government is making a new ghaut or pass down the hills from Wynaad to the coast, and a couple of companies of sappers are at work upon the upper 500ft. of the ghaut, which has to be cut out of a solid mass of gneiss. The face of the hill where the men were at work is very steep—say from 75° to 80° ; this, however, is not the dip of the gneiss, but the plane of a section across the strata which stand at much the same angle, shewing the plane of stratification in parallel lines of black and white on the face of the hill. Here and there we came upon veins of quartz crossing the planes of stratification ; and these, producing no dislocation of the strata, nor exhibiting any evidence of having acted upon the edges of the narrow lamina of the gneiss, would almost seem to have been deposited at the same time, or even previous to the gneiss. I assume gneiss to be an aqueous deposit; to have been at one time horizontal, or nearly so; to have been tilted up ' somehow '—how deponent sayeth not. How and when came the quartz vein in the position shown below?

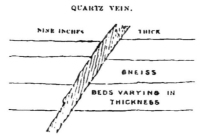

QUARTZ VEIN.

Yours truly,
W. D.

To Mrs. Des Vœux.

Madras, November 8, 1864.

My dear J——,—I think I mentioned the cyclone at Calcutta, which had done so much damage, in my last letter. We have had a repetition of it on this coast, about 200 miles to the northward, at a place called Masulipatam. The damage done to the town has been very great; it lies low, and the wind brought the sea upon it, the water being two or three feet deep in the streets. With the rubbishy houses built of mud, of course the destruction was great, and I am afraid the loss of native life was great also. I only heard the account yesterday evening as I was going out, when I was called upon to sanction an outlay of 3,000*l*., to clear away the ruins and bury the dead. Just about the change of the monsoon is hurricane time here. I hope they have blown themselves out by this time, and that those dear to me, either coming out or going home, may encounter nothing of the kind.

Your affectionate Brother,
W. D.

To Captain Warburton.

My dear Warburton, – Many thanks for your letter, and the account of the loss we sustained in our attack on the Gate Pah. I was deeply interested in getting at the truth of this affair, for I lost in the two brothers Glover, who were killed, two very good friends. The elder brother had been on my staff ever since my arrival in India, and quitted it, like a gallant fellow, to go with his regiment to New Zealand. It is useless to speculate as to the cause of the panic of the 43rd and the Naval Brigade, unless for the purpose of drawing instruction from it ; but I should say that the failure of the attack was due to the absence of proper support. As a rule, the storming party should be strong enough to overcome all opposition ; but it ought to have a strong support in rear, and to be aware of the presence of such support. The accounts in Jones's ‘ Sieges in Spain ’ of the storming of Badajoz, Ciudad Rodrigo, San Sebastian, &c., and of the assault on the castle of Burgos, are most instructive. At the pah, however, there would seem to have been an inner line of stockade, of which we ought to have been cognisant ; and we ought to have breached the other angle of the work, and have attacked both breaches at once. But the folly was in storming at all. In the Peninsula we were pressed for time ; unless we could take the town in a given time, the chance was that the French would have got together a force sufficient to raise the siege ; but in New Zealand time was no object, and to take the garrison prisoners was a very great object. Altogether, then, it seems to me that our mode of carrying on the war has been marked by no originality of conception, by no proper adaptation of means to ends, and by no proper appreciation of ends. I do not think it will redound to the credit of any of the parties concerned.

I have just returned to Madras from a trip to the hills, which ended in a tour on horseback into a plateau of the Western Ghauts occupied by coffee planters. I never rode through a more beautiful country, one for which nature has done so much and man so little. The bridges over the small watercourses were made of bamboos covered with mats made of split bamboos, while the rivers were passed upon rafts made of bamboos covered with the same material. This is very strong when new, but easily broken when dry. The rafts will carry but one horse and his rider, and are kept in their place by a strong rope made of twisted rattans. Nothing could exceed the beauty of the foliage. The south-west monsoon was just over, everything was fresh and green, flowers coming out, and most gorgeous butterflies flaunting about gave one's eyes quite enough to do. By the way, why don't you take to the study of some branch of natural history? I have always found that, when a tendency to slumber comes over me, which is apt to be the case about the middle of the day, a change of occupation from writing minutes to classifying shells wakes me up at once. Apart, however, from such a motive as this, which you probably will not require in New Zealand, I hold the study of nature to be a very wholesome occupation. There is a calming tendency in it very different from that stirring, exciting feeling with which one deals with man, either singly or collectively.

Yours very truly,

W. D.

To His Highness the Rajah of Travancore.

Madras, November 16, 1864.

Your Highness,—I have lately received from Mr. Brown a description of the series of magnetical observations which he thinks it would be desirable to continue, for a few years, with the instruments already in the observatory : these observations, it would seem, could be made at a very small cost, while their value to science would be great.

Their continuance would involve the maintenance of the magnetic instruments in their present position, and the payment of a small salary to two observers, while the remainder of the instruments might be removed and sold, and the main buildings of the observatory be made available for any purpose to which your Highness might choose to apply them, subject to the condition that the magnetical instruments should not be disturbed, nor the action of the observers interfered with. The matter is one which rests entirely with your Highness. I have only alluded to it as Mr. Brown brought the subject under my notice, and because I thought it would be as well to make the series of observations complete.

I am going to exhibit some new agricultural implements, such as reaping and threshing machines in action, and to compare the results arrived at by working these machines with those shown by the employment of native implements or processes. I think it probable that with some it will be seen that both time and money will be saved, while with others—such as the steam plough, and, perhaps, the threshing-machine—the first outlay and the cost of working may either put it beyond the means of the ryot, or make it incompetent to compete with the cheaper but less efficient native processes.

I know that your Highness appreciates fully the advantages which result from the introduction of improvements in tools and implements; and I will therefore take care that you shall be furnished with the results of the experiments we make. Eventually I hope to be able to exhibit the action of machinery in the districts bordering upon your Highness's dominions, in which case notification shall be sent of the time and place of such exhibition, when the officers and the agriculturists of Travancore will be able to witness the working of the machines, and thus to convince themselves of their usefulness. There is a great store of water-power in the hills at the back of Travancore, which will eventually, I have no doubt, be made available. Even at present I should think that a simple American saw-mill, which would cost very little, might be of much use in bringing the valuable timber of these forests into an available form, such as planks, beams, joists, and rafters, for which a ready market would be found at Bombay. It is a pleasure to me to write on such subjects to one who, like your Highness, has the interests of his people at heart.

I remain your Highness' sincere friend,

W. D.

CHAPTER XXV.

FINANCIAL SUGGESTIONS—BAPTISM OF NATIVE CHRISTIANS—NEW YEAR'S
CEREMONIES—VISIT TO 'THE CITY OF BALI'—CATTLE SHOW AT ADDUNKY
—VIZAGAPATAM—ROMAN CATHOLIC FEMALE SCHOOL—EVENING PARTY AT
THE HOUSE OF A NATIVE—GANJAM—CHILKA LAKE—ASKA—SUGAR FACTORY
—WILD BOY OF THE WOODS—ROMAN CATHOLIC CATHEDRAL AT S. THOMÉ.—
GRAVE AND RELICS OF ST. THOMAS—THRESHING MATCH, NATIVES VERSUS
THRESHING MACHINE—MADRAS A GOOD WINTER RESIDENCE FOR INVALIDS
—PRINCE FREDERICK OF SCHLESWIG-HOLSTEIN—FESTIVAL OF THE MO-
HURRUM—BANGALORE—LALL BAGH—MADRAS IN JULY AND AUGUST—
POINCIANA REGIA—MYSORE CARPETS—NATIVE MODE OF MAKING UP CHINTZ
—CYCLONE—EXPERIMENT WITH MONGOOSE AND SNAKES—VISIT TO CUDDA-
PAH—FAREWELL FÊTE BY THE MAHOMETAN COMMUNITY—DEPARTURE FROM
MADRAS.

Towards the end of 1864 I received a letter from Sir Charles Wood on the subject of the finances of India.

He pressed on my attention not so much the state of the revenue of Madras, as that of the whole of India, and said, 'I am sure that the greatest benefactor to India will be the man who devises some means of raising taxes.'

My reply was a lengthy letter, much too prolix and detailed to find a place here; but as my opinions differed very much from those advocated by others, a brief sketch of them, as an essential part of my vice-regal experience, may not be uninteresting to all, and can easily be skipped over by those who do not care to meddle with questions of finance.

Very soon after my arrival at Madras I wrote to Sir Charles Wood, expressing my belief that Wilson, and, generally, the financiers who had been sent out from England to re-establish the revenue system of India, had omitted to take into consideration the difference between the Indian and the Englishman, and had attempted to apply to the former rules deduced from the experience of the latter.

Four years' additional experience of Indian people had but added strength to the conviction, and furnished me with a variety of instances in which the management of the finances by the imported revenue secretaries had been unsatisfactory. This opinion I did not hesitate to express to Sir Charles Wood, and I pressed upon him the advisability of adopting a system which would harmonise with the traditions and habits of the natives of India. The national difference between the Hindoo and the Englishman is not merely that of colour, or of language; it exhibits itself in every relation of life, and has its roots too deeply seated in the character of the race to be reached or acted upon by any of the specifics which political doctors—may I not say quacks?—are so fond of prescribing.

We hear constantly such expressions as these: ' A fine people spoiled by misgovernment,' and, coupled with this, plans for good government based upon English experience. There cannot be a greater fallacy than this supposed action of a government upon a people. It is the Englishman who has made his government, not his government the Englishman. In like manner it is the cowardly Hindoo who has made for himself the bed on which he has been lying for some two thousand years: the men are the same as they have been, and will be, and as Hindoos they must be dealt with.

Now, as Hindoos, they have always admitted the right of their rulers to the soil of the country, and to an indeterminate share of the produce: their Mahometan conquerors took, nominally, 45 per cent. of the gross produce. They have admitted the right to impose duties both on *exports* and imports; to establish monopolies, such as those of opium and salt; to insist upon payments from individuals for licenses to exercise peculiar privileges, or trades. They have admitted the right of the Government to compel them to give their labour for any public work, upon the mere condition of being fed. Such as they have been they will be; the taxes which they have been used to pay, they, as children of habit, will pay without demur; but they will grumble at, resent, and perhaps resist, any new system of taxation. I have long been of opinion that change in itself is an evil, and that nothing but a clear conception of the benefits to be derived from it, and a conviction that these predominate over its inherent evils, can justify the disturbance which change creates; but if it be an evil even to a changeable people like ourselves, what must it be to the Hindoo with whom habit has become a second nature? Now, of the sources of revenue alluded to above, the land is by far the most productive, as will be seen by the following tabular statement of the revenue of 1864.

			£
Land	.	.	19,440,244
Assessed Taxes	.	.	1,760,000
Customs	. .	.	2,610,393
Monopolies { Opium }		. .	6,359,270
{ Salt }			4,534,693
Stamps	. .	.	1,604,452
	Total		36,309,082

Of this total the land and the monopolies yield 30,334,207*l.*, or more than five-sixths. It is, then, to the improvement and proper cultivation of these that we must look, if we want to add to our revenue. The opium monopoly is a mercantile speculation, and as such is uncertain in its yield; but the salt, as dealing with a necessary of life, is equivalent to a poll tax, without any of the evils which attach to a direct personal demand upon each head of a family. So that our chief dependence must be on the improvement in the land and salt revenues.

The following table will show the distribution of the land revenue among the different Presidencies and Governments, the population of each of these, and the amount per head contributed towards this item of revenue.

	Population	Land Revenue	Amount per head
		£	s. d.
Bengal	40,853,000	4,670,796	2 3
Madras	23,301,700	4,831,402	4 1
Bombay	12,038,113	3,075,534	5 1
North-West Provinces .	30,250,000	4,960,813	3 2
Punjaub	15,467,800	1,952,639	2 6

The land revenue of Madras is equivalent to 4s. 1d. per head of the population, while that of Bengal does not exceed 2s. 3d. Whence this very marked difference? It is due (I believe) principally to the difference of the land tenure. In Madras a very large proportion of the land is held directly from the crown, which stands to the ryot in the relation of landlord; whereas, in Bengal, the land has been to a great extent granted to zemindars, at a fixed and low money rent or assessment, under the idea that by so doing a foundation was being laid upon which a landed aristocracy might be built up, who would have a special interest in the improvement of their estates! This idea is due to Lord Cornwallis; it is known by the name of ' the Permanent Settlement,' and is regarded by most of the civil servants in Bengal as the perfection of administration and financial wisdom. Let us see what it is in fact, and judge, by the results upon the land revenue and upon the condition of the people, whether the praise bestowed upon ' *the Permanent Settlement* ' be in any way merited. What Lord Cornwallis did was to hand over, in fee simple, to zemindars—a set of people analogous to the publicans in the Bible—the whole district, the revenues of which they were in the habit of farming, subject to the

payment of a quit rent equal to two thirds of the then
existing land revenue. That is, he paid these men $33\frac{1}{3}$
per cent. for collecting the existing revenue, probably
twice as much as it would have cost to collect it by
Government agents; he sacrificed the revenue which
would, necessarily, have arisen out of the increased cultivation of the village land; he sacrificed, by making the
money rent perpetual, the very large amount which
would have accrued to the Government from the rise in
the price of produce, whether this might be owing to the
increased demand for such produce, or to the diminution
in the value of money. This is a brief sketch of what
his lordship did, and the difference between the rate per
head paid in Bengal and that paid in Madras, may be taken
as the measure of the monetary loss sustained by the Government in Bengal alone, which is equivalent to about
three millions and a half sterling annually. This, however,
is by no means a measure of the whole loss incurred by the
Government. The revenue in Madras is lessened to some
extent by the existence therein of some of these zemin-
daries, and also by the prevalence of a sort of traditional
feeling in favour of a permanent *money* assessment. I
found that in Madras, owing to the change in the value
of money, caused partly by the discovery of gold in
California and Australia, and partly by the increased
demand, prices had risen at least 50 per cent., and I felt
convinced that, by a careful survey of the country, giving
not only the area of cultivation, but also the average
yield per acre, and by the establishment of an equitable
corn rent, I could have raised the land revenue of Madras
from 4,800,000*l.* to at least 6,000,000*l.*, or to 5*s.* 1*d.* per
head of the population, in which case the equivalent
revenue in Bengal would have amounted to ten and a half
millions. With these convictions strongly pressed upon
me, I submitted to Sir Charles Wood the following
suggestions as to the best mode in which he could enhance the receipts from the land :—

1. That in all parts of India where the permanent settlement had not been established, the permanency of any settlement should apply only to the *corn rent*.

2. That the commutation rate should be determined from time to time on an average of the prices of a given number of years ; say ten.

3. That the proportion of the crop to be taken by the Government should be determined after a careful consideration of returns to be furnished by the collectors.

4. That the water supplied by the Government from the rivers or tanks should be charged according to its value, as tested by the amount of the crop produced by it.

The object of the first suggestion was to give an aspect of finality to the arrangement, so that the ryot might feel secure in the enjoyment of the produce due to any expenditure of capital or industry bestowed upon the land.

By the second he would learn to know the absolute amount of the claim made upon him, and would be secured from the extortion practised upon him, too commonly, by the native officials.

The third is required in order to secure the Government its fair share of the produce of the soil.

While, by the fourth, I get rid of an absurd system of imposing a water-rate : by which, under a mistaken analogy between the occupiers of land in northern Italy and the ryots in India, in their relations to their Governments in respect to the supply of water for irrigation, the system in force in Italy had been introduced into India.

The practice in India, or at all events in Madras, had nearly always been to put a value upon the water in proportion to the effect produced by it on the crop ; but, by the change proposed in accordance with the analogy of the Italian scheme, a fixed sum per acre was charged for water, whether it was employed to produce rice or sugar-cane; whether the land was bad or good; so that the poor soil was over rated, and the rich very much under-rated; and the Government, while injuring many of its tenants, and adding largely to the profits of a few, was itself a very great loser. In point of fact, there was no true analogy between the Government of Italy and India in their relation to the occupants of land. In Italy the Government was the owner of the water; it made the dam and the main distributing channels, and charged as much for the water as the landlords were willing to pay; but, having no interest in the land, it could not claim any share in the crops resulting from the application of the water. In India, on the contrary, or at all events in Madras, the Government is generally the owner of the land, as well as of the water, and is entitled to the profit which accrues both to the constructor of the water-works and the retailer of the water.

I will not attempt to guess at the amount of the land revenue under circumstances altered as they would be were my proposals adopted generally, but an increase of several millions might fairly be anticipated.

The charge now made for salt varies very much in the different Presidencies and Governments. In Bengal it is 1s. 1d.; in Madras it is 8½d.; in Bombay 7½d.; in the North-West Provinces, 4½d.; in the Punjaub, 9½d. These might without difficulty be gradually brought up to the Bengal standard, and an addition would then be made to

		£	s.	d.
the revenue of Madras of . . .		436,906	7	6
„ of Bombay . . .		275,873	8	5
„ of North-West Provinces		1,633,804	3	6
„ of Punjaub . . .		225,572	1	8
	Total	2,574,156	8	11

The remainder of my letter to Sir Charles Wood was filled up with remarks on a variety of details of outlay to which it is unnecessary to allude here.

Extract from Journal.

Guindy Park, Madras, January 1, 1865.

My dear M——,—Many happy New Years to you all, dears, if it please God! This new year has opened very brightly on me, for W—— is much better. To-day, too, the Bombay mail came in, bringing your welcome letters. In fact, I have two mails' letters to answer at once, for the last mail was terribly slow, and only came in the day before yesterday, and I had not time to comment on its contents in the little scrap I wrote yesterday. With regard to M——'s queries as to the baptism of native and half-caste children attending our own and other Christian schools, the 'half-castes,' or East Indians, as they call them here, are all regularly brought up just like English children, and baptized in infancy ; in fact, they receive altogether an European education. Of the native children who attend Christian schools, several are, of course, the children of native Christians, and these are, I suppose, baptized as infants : the others, of course, are not baptized, unless, after due instruction, they themselves express a desire to become Christians, and show, as far as one can judge, evidence in their conduct that the desire is a sincere one, and that they understand what they are about ; even then they would not baptize them under a certain age (sixteen, I think) without the consent of their parents : after that, or whenever it is that they come so near to man's or woman's estate as to be fairly capable of judging and acting for themselves, they would be received to baptism even without their parents' consent, if they continued to desire it themselves, and were considered fit for it. This seems, on the whole, all one can do ; but it is

painful to see how many there are who go on attending a
Christian school, reading the Bible regularly there, and
having it explained to them, and answering questions, &c.,
so as to show that they are acquainted with its main
facts, and yet go away after all without ever becoming
Christians, or, at all events, without professing themselves
such. As to M——'s other supposed case—of a converted
woman in a harem—I really do not know what she would
do, nor am I aware whether the case has yet occurred. I
believe some ladies at Calcutta have made an attempt at
paying visits to the harems and teaching the poor ladies
there to read, shewing them how to do amusing sorts of
work. &c., and trying to awaken a little taste for occupation, in hopes that it may lead to something better by-
and-by ; and it seems a good move ; but I do not know
how far the Mahometan husbands will allow of its being
carried out. You would like to see the little knot of
native Christians at the Mount coming up to the Sacra-
ment : the women all with a red or white muslin scarf
thrown over their heads, like a Spanish mantilla. In
other respects, the Christian native women dress just like
others, and a very pretty, graceful dress it is ; but they
always throw this scarf or mantilla over their heads and
shoulders, in addition, when they go to church; I suppose
with the notion derived from the Epistle to the Corin-
thians, of not praying with their heads uncovered. The
sentences, on giving them the bread and wine, are always
read by the clergyman first in English, and then repeated
over again in Tamil by the native catechist.

January 5.—We have been for the last three days
going through the usual little New Year's ceremonies, and
they are all such an amusement to Mrs. Stanley that I am
quite glad she has come in for a sight of them. On
Monday morning there came up the native aide-de-camp
with his usual New Year's offering of garlands and limes;

then I received, and had to answer, a New Year's letter of good wishes from 'Lady Sharf-ool-oomrah-Bahadoor,' a personage of whose existence I had hitherto been ignorant, as, of course, like other Mahometan ladies, she never appears. This morning W——— is receiving the visits of native gentlemen, for the same purpose ; and, besides this, we have had all the children of the servants, to the number of some hundreds, to receive their usual Christmas dole. This is a very amusing sight. Mrs. Stanley thought it reminded her of a picture of ' the gate alms' in some old convent or monastery. The night before last we went to the official New Year's ball at the banqueting hall, but did not stay there late.

January 7.—Yesterday we went to Madras, for the double duty of receiving visitors and of giving a tea-drinking to the children of the civil and military orphan asylums. This last affair was not quite so satisfactory as I intended it to have been. I meant to have given them a Christmas-tree, by way of wind-up to the amusements, and with a view of sending them away with something that would be a pleasure to them even beyond the actual day ; but the box of presents I had ordered from England did not arrive, so that fell through, and, as we had lingered on till nearly the last day in hopes of it, we had to alter that part of our programme hastily at last, and turn it into a magic lantern, which, being neither very good in itself nor at all well exhibited, proved rather a failure. W———, being a little tired with the afternoon's work, came away just after the children's tea, L——— and I, with the staff generally, remaining to superintend the magic-lantern part of the business.

Lady Denison to ———.

Guindy Park, January 22, 1865.

My dear ———,—The week before last we made a most interesting excursion to a place on the sea-coast, about thirty miles to the southward, commonly called 'The Seven Pagodas,' but more likely to be known to people at home as the remains of the 'City of Bali,' mentioned in Southey's 'Curse of Kehama.' We started on the evening of the 11th, a party of twenty, in ten boats on the canal, which runs down close past the place to which we wanted to go. It was a glorious night, with a full moon; and very quietly and pleasantly we floated down, partly sailing, partly towed by men walking along the banks. The country on each side of the canal was very bare and ugly; but the soft beauty of the night, and the glorious moonlight, made it pleasant. During the evening the party collected in groups in two or three of the boats; but towards the middle of the night all retired to their own boats, where, in the middle of each boat, was a space covered in, and partly curtained off, in which there were beds spread, two in each boat. Thus, partly undressed, we reposed as well as we could during the remainder of the night; and early the next morning we found ourselves at our landing-place. Here, as soon as we stepped out of the boats, we were surrounded by a group of the native inhabitants of the neighbouring village, accompanied by some dancing-girls, who straightway began to dance. In a few minutes, however, palanquins arrived for the ladies, and horses and ponies for the gentlemen, and we all started for our camp, which was about a quarter of a mile off, close to the sea, and very comfortable—two rows of tents, the party lodging two in a tent, except W———, Mrs. Stanley, and I, who had each a tent to ourselves; and at the head of the double row was a large dining-tent, with a sort of bower of bamboos

and palm leaves in front of it, making a very pretty
sitting-room facing the sea. As the sun was not up when
we arrived there, we agreed, as soon as we had each had
a cup of tea, to walk off at once to a beautiful old pagoda
that stood on the sea-shore, very near us, and which we
thought we should have time to see before it got too hot.
I mentioned before that this village is the place to which
the legend of Bali belongs; one of its native names is
Mahabalipoor, which means 'the city of the great Bali;'
and I, for one, am inclined to believe that there is some
foundation for the notion of a submerged city, though we
certainly did not see any tops of pagodas peeping above
the waves; and though one place, a little way out,
where the sea was breaking over some obstruction or
other, was named by us 'Bali's Palace,' I am afraid it
was only a sunken rock. Still, there is this one temple,
so close to the sea that the waves actually dash against it
at high water, and in rough weather; closer, I think,
than anyone was likely to have built it in the first
instance; and, indeed, we are told that twice within the
last twenty-four years the sea has advanced so as quite to
surround it, and twice it has receded again. There are
three of these sea-side temples; but one is in ruins, and
another appears to have been only just begun to be carved
out of a solid lump of rock, and then abandoned. This
one temple, which we went to see, is the centre one
of the three, and is very handsome. It is all carved over,
inside and out, with figures of gods and goddesses, lions,
bulls, &c., and altogether it exactly answers to the description in Kehama of the ancient temples of the city of Bali,
once so crowded with worshippers, now so silent and deserted. We scrambled about it till the sun was well up,
and it began to be hot, and then we walked back to our
camp, bathed, dressed for the day, breakfasted, and
amused ourselves quietly during the hot hours. As soon
as it got cool enough in the afternoon we sallied forth

again, all on horseback this time, except Mrs. Stanley
and Mary S——, who were in palanquins, and rode
through the village at the back of our camp, which is full
of pagodas and rock sculptures. The head Brahmin of
the village, a decrepit old man, with his head somehow
sunk down between his shoulders, and four or five other
natives, accompanied us about, sometimes acting as guides,
when we could make them understand what we wanted
to see; at others volunteering their information thus:
'Tomasha!' pointing in one or other direction as they
spoke. A 'tomasha' generally means a show or
spectacle; but it evidently may be understood as meaning
anything to be seen; for sometimes, with this inviting
word, they got us into some nook or cranny of the rocks,
where there was nothing to look at but, perhaps, a single
rudely traced carving of an elephant, or a peacock, on the
face of the rock. These sculptures up in the village are
of a different kind from the temple on the sea-shore, and,
I should think, of a more modern date. Some are
temples, more or less in ruins; others are excavations—
temples partly formed out of the rock, with all sorts of
Hindoo mythological figures carved on the walls inside. A
portion of the story of Bali is the subject of one of these;
in another is an image of Ganesa, the elephant-headed
son of Siva; and this last is still worshipped by the
village people, and is consequently very black and dirty
with all the offerings of ghee and cocoa-nut oil which
they pour over, or burn before it. I saw one of our poor
horsekeepers turning round to adore this grim, ugly idol
as we passed it. Further up the hill are five very curious
temples, each carved out of a single block of stone: and
in other parts the whole face of the rock is covered with
carvings. Of these, the most curious is that which represents the penance of Arjuna, a devotee, who, in order to
obtain some favour from the gods (a charmed weapon to
destroy his family's enemy, I believe it was), stood for a

month on the tip of his left great toe, with his right leg lifted up, and his hands crossed above his head. His figure is carved on the rock in this attitude; but, what is more unaccountable, some way lower down, on an adjoining rock, there is the figure of a cat on its hind legs, with its fore legs crossed over its head, in manifest imitation of Arjuna up above. What the history of this figure can be it is not easy to imagine: it looks too like ridicule of Arjuna to have been perpetrated by the same authors; but, at any rate, it is a capital caricature of him. We had not time to see all the ruins and carvings that evening, so we returned to our tents, and came again early the next morning to complete our inspection. The curious thing about these carved temples and excavations is, that they are all unfinished; it is as if they had all been stopped suddenly, nearly at the same time. W—— could not help imagining that the place had, at one time, been a sort of school of design, and that the workmen must all have fled from it, either during a Mahometan invasion or some similar convulsion. This was merely a guess on his part; but I have been delighted to find a sort of confirmation of it since in Fergusson's 'Rock-cut Temples of India,' where, in speaking of these Mahabalipoor carvings, he gives two traditions respecting their history. One is as follows: 'A northern prince, about one thousand years ago, was desirous of having a great work executed, but the Hindoo sculptors and masons refused to execute it on the terms he offered. Attempting force, they (in number about four thousand) fled with their effects from his country hither, where they resided four or five years, and in this interval executed these magnificent works. The prince, at length discovering them, prevailed on them to return, which they did, leaving the works unfinished.' Another tradition is, that, during a famine, many artificers resorted hither, and wrought on the mountain a great variety of works during two or three years.

Having finished our inspection, we spent the remainder of the day, as far as the heat allowed, some in sketching, some in trying to copy some of the figures on the Arjuna rocks; Mrs. Stanley and I in a last visit to the beautiful sea-side temple—our favourite. In the evening, after a rather early dinner, we re-embarked in our canal boats, and reached Guindy by six o'clock on Saturday morning.

To Mrs. Des Vœux.

H.M.S. 'Feroze,' January 20, 1865.

My dear J——,—I embarked yesterday morning with the intention of going up the east coast, and of calling at several points: at the first, which was about 160 miles from Madras, I was to land, to proceed forty miles in-land, to be present at a cattle show, &c.; but, having steamed away for twenty hours, I find myself about ten miles from the coast in shoal water, and the captain of the steamer professes utter ignorance of his whereabouts, and will have to wait till twelve o'clock to get his latitude, the probability being that I shall not get into the place at all. The coast is so low, and has nothing to mark it, that I can quite understand the unwillingness of the captain to take a ship of 1,500 tons any nearer upon experiment, and I do not think the visit to be of such importance as to justify me in running the least risk.

January 26.—While we were waiting for the sun, out came five boats from the shore, and we managed to land after a long pull of twelve or fourteen miles. We started off at once in carriages; mine, in which there were four people, was drawn by twelve men harnessed in three rows of four each. These two-legged horses took us about eight miles, where we met our regular team, and pushed on to our dining-place. We left this at twelve o'clock at night to proceed to our destination (Addunky) in palanquins, and reached it by day-break. We have, ever since our arrival, been busy in looking at stock, of which a large proportion has been brought together. There are some very fine bulls, and I am having photographs taken of the prize cattle, for the purpose of exhibiting them in other parts of the country, and of gratifying the owners.

January 28.—I gave the prizes to the successful competitors yesterday, and promised to five, who had each gained two prizes, a special gift of a gold ring. I then started, and drove thirteen miles to dinner, after which we got into our palanquins, and reached the coast by 4 A.M. As it was dark, we all slept on, the bearers having dropped us on the sand, till it was light enough to embark, and here I am, steering northward to Vizagapatam, which I hope to reach to-morrow night.

Vizagapatam, January 30.—We landed here this morning, and were received by the civil and military authorities and a guard of honour. On our way up to the Collector's house, we stopped to visit a Roman Catholic female school, and a large Hindoo school. I was much pleased with the former; the children looked clean and happy, and they sang well. Generally speaking, the children of schools in and near Madras have a nasal twang when they sing. I stay here over to-morrow.

Ganjam, February 2.—I went to an evening party given by a wealthy native on Monday night. The first part of the exhibition was a dance, or rather a set of postures by a number of girls, who accompanied themselves with their voices, and a horrid set of screechers they were. After that, a man sang a hymn of his own composing, accompanying himself on the pianoforte, playing with one finger, like a child picking out a tune. Then we had a man, said to be a well known improvisatore in the district, who played upon a sort of guitar with seven strings, which, as they were metal, made a villanous twang; then we had fireworks, and a good supper. I was heartily glad to get away, having to get up early to reach Bimlipatam, seventeen miles, by breakfast. We drove there across a barren-looking, stony country, which, however, during the rains is green and well cultivated. Bimlipatam is a small town on the east coast, formerly occupied by the Dutch. Several merchants have established themselves in the town, as holding out a prospect of business, and it bids fair to increase in importance. The steamer called for us about twelve o'clock, and we got under weigh for this place, where we landed this morning.

February 4.—We remained at Ganjam the whole of Thursday, and started early on Friday morning to come to Rumbah, on the Chilka Lake. I am now sitting in the verandah of the house looking out on the lake, having a nice breeze blowing upon me. The lake is covered with boats, bringing rice from Cuttack: the hills come down to the right and left steeply into the water, the whole making a beautiful picture. The lake is covered with water-fowl of all sorts, but they are too shy to be got at.

Berhampore, February 7.—We left Rumbah on Sunday night, and, travelling in palanquins, arrived at Aska— about twenty miles—by 6 A.M. The whole day was spent in looking over the sugar factory, and making enquiries. The manager of the factory buys the coarse sugar from the ryots, and refines it ; but he is going to try how he can manage by purchasing the canes, and going through the whole process himself; and I have no doubt that he will succeed, for he is an active, intelligent man, with capital *and brains.* We had a magnificent illumination at night, the whole of the factory buildings being lighted up. There were 10,000 lamps, consisting of little earthenware saucers holding oil and wicks, and, as the night was quiet, nothing could look better. We left Aska at half-past five A.M., and arrived here by eight. I have to hold a levée, and see a number of natives. To-morrow I embark on my way to Madras, and right glad shall I be to get there again.

To Sir Roderick Murchison.

H.M.S. 'Feroze,' January 26, 1865.

My dear Sir Roderick,—I have been looking into M‘Causland's 'Adam and the Adamite,' and cannot admit that his theory will hold water; it compels him to class the 'Turanian race' in India as inferior to the pure Hindoo, who, according to him, is made of the pure porcelain clay of the earth. Precious bad workmen have been at the material, if his theory be correct. I, however, am in the middle of the Telugu or Turanian district, and, I must say, in the presence of a very fine race of men. All the trash talked of the Mongol type is simple bosh, there is not a trace of the high cheek bones of the Mongols. India is full of tribes or septs which present marked differences of face and form, which might suggest the idea of difference of origin, but which would not, if closely looked into, in any way bear out M‘Causland's idea of the plurality of races. There are on the Neilgherries no fewer than five distinct tribes, and the difference between the Toda and the Co-rumba is nearly as great as that between the red Indian and the Hottentot.

Ganjam, February 2.—I arrived here this morning at the limit of my territory to the north, and shall have to travel about for some days to see what is to be seen, and to be seen by those who may want to tell me any stories or make complaints. I have already heard one curious tale, which will interest you. Captain Phillips has charge of a part of the hill country to the west of the district; it is occupied by a wild tribe called Khonds, but who are daily becoming more civilized. Captain

c c 2

Phillips was riding through the bush not long ago, and he saw before him a *curious animal galloping* awkwardly, but fast; he put his horse into a canter and gained upon the animal, but before he could come up with it, it ran into a hut; he followed it, and found a child of about seven years old, who, he was told, had been lost for a long time in the bush, but had been recovered. Captain Phillips examined the boy and found him to have a horny *callus* upon his knees. I will see if I can get some more detailed information as to the boy. This I give only at second hand.

Berhampore, February 7.—I have paid a visit to some large sugar-works, the manager of which, Mr. Minchin, being an active, intelligent man, has not only improved many of the ordinary processes, but has given the natives a helping hand, by showing them how to get some 30 per cent. more juice out of the canes than they could extract by their native methods. We had illuminations and a display of tumblers, dancing girls, &c., in the evening.

I agree with you altogether in your opinion that the action of forces which lifted up the mountains, and produced the great and marked features on the face of the globe, was much more violent than that of which we have at present cognizance, and I believe that it *must* have been the case necessarily. Every force which lifted up the surface of the earth, must, unless we suppose a corresponding depression elsewhere, have added to the cubical space occupied by the fluid or active agent under the surface or skin of the globe, and therefore have lessened to some extent the expansive power within; and every fresh action must have still further lessened the power, if we suppose it to have been a constant, or rather an elementary force, and incapable of recruiting itself. If, on the contrary, we suppose it to be the result of chemical action, or of any process whatever which is going on constantly, I see no reason why it should not vary indefinitely, at one time squirting up a column of water, at another upheaving an island or a continent. I do not see how small forces acting for an indefinite period could explain the phenomena which come daily before my eyes in this country. I have no time for more ; so good-bye.

Yours very truly,
W. D.

Extract from Journal.

Guindy Park, March 25th, 1865.

On Thursday we went to see the Roman Catholic Cathedral at St. Thomé, in which, or rather under which, is the place where the apostle St. Thomas is said to have been buried, he having been killed at St. Thomas's Mount, about four miles distant. The present church, or cathedral, as I believe they call it, though it has little right to the name, does not even *profess* to be more than 250 years old or thereabouts, and I believe it was built by the Portuguese. When we got there, we found waiting for us Mr. Symonds, the Church of England clergyman of St. Thomé, who had promised to ask the principal padre to shew us the cathedral ; and there was the padre also, M. Amaranthe, a dark Portuguese East Indian, or half-caste, who looked intelligent and good-humoured, and spoke very fair English. He shewed us through the church, which seemed tolerably well kept, though with a good deal of tawdry gilding about the altar and shrines ; and then into a sort of back chapel or shrine, built over the vault said to have been the original grave of St. Thomas. The first chapel built over this hole has entirely disappeared, and the bones of the saint are said to have been removed, some to Rome, and some to Milan ; only a small portion of them being left here, which, with some fragments of his clothes, were shown to us, enclosed in a sort of relic case. Two of the other brethren (for there is a small monastery of them at St. Thomé), who were apparently hearing confessions in the church when we went in, joined us just before we

My dear J——,—We had a curious exhibition of agricultural implements last week, and a contest between a threshing-machine worked by bullocks, and the rude mode of threshing and dressing rice practised by the natives. Rice being a grain with a head something like that of oats, the natives take a sheaf or a bundle and beat it against the ground : two blows suffice to loosen 90 per cent. of the grain from the straw ; this is then thrown into a heap, and the bullocks are driven round and round upon it. The natives set to work in a way which you never see tried except on occasions when their mettle is up, and the result was that they threshed their share of the crop in a shorter time than we could do with the machine, and then crowed over us.

Mrs. Stanley has derived great benefit from her trip to Madras, and I have another invalid from Tasmania staying with us, to whom the soft, warm, unchangeable temperature of this place is doing a great deal of good. I believe that Madras would be the best place for invalids from November to April ; I mean for such as wish to fly from the cold of England ; the range of temperature is so very trifling—from 70° to 80° or 85°, and generally from 78° to 84°.

Lady Denison to Mrs. Stanley.

My dear Mrs. Stanley,—I will begin to-day my history of what we have been doing since you left us ; I need not say that we thought of you a great deal, and followed you in mind throughout the day. On Monday the Bombay mail arrived, bringing, amongst other things, three

letters for you, which might as well, I think, have come
the week before. Our own letters were not numerous,
but the accounts pretty good. There arrived also a note
from Prince Frederick of Schleswig-Holstein (who, you
know, was expected here), saying that he was coming by
way of the Seven Pagodas, and hoped to be here on
Wednesday morning. Accordingly that morning the
carriage went down before five o'clock to the canal bridge
to await him, and with it poor Captain McLeod, who had
the pleasure of waiting there till nearly nine before the
Prince's boat made its appearance. Spreadborough is
evidently a little disappointed in her vision of a royal
guest, because, as she observes, 'he does not look the
least like a Prince,' neither does he ; he is evidently a
man who throws 'the Prince' altogether aside, very
wisely, probably, under his circumstances, and is quite
content to knock about the world pretty much like any
body else, with plenty of energy and independence, and
apparently rather liking little adventures, and laughing at
small difficulties.

There was a cobra caught in the park this morning,
and brought alive to the door. How perverse of it not
to have been caught some days ago, when you were wish-
ing to see one!

We have had some *such* evening skies as I never saw,
even here, before : the usual bank of clouds that rises in
the west at this time of the year, but along the upper
edge of it, and just above it, streaks and patches of the
colours of the rainbow—a sort of rainbow edge to the
cloud, *most* vivid, and all the colours, though not the
shape, of the bow. The general exclamation has been,
'Oh! if Mrs. Stanley could but see that!'

Madras, May 30, 1865.

My dear Sir Roderick.—I wonder whether the men who are rummaging after the dry bones of the past ever dream of speculating as to the future of the world, as to the effect of the twists and changes which it is in process of getting from the perpetual stomach ache of which it shews evidence. We hear of calculations as to the quantity of coal, and whether there will be sufficient to last our time ; but, even in these, it strikes me that the speculators leave out one principal element in the calculation—namely, the number of people who burn the coal. They keep in the background altogether the startling fact that in England the population is doubling itself in fifty years. Malthus stated, and very correctly, that the tendency of population is to increase in a more rapid ratio than the means of subsistence : and a little industry bestowed upon working out the results of this startling fact would have led to much the same conclusion that I have arrived at from an analysis of the statistical tables—namely, that the old hypothesis that the world is to last about 6,000 years, is by no means an improbable one. Men increase in a geometrical ratio, and every step of progress in social life ; every check which improve-ment in morals imposes upon the gratification of our passions ; every invention which makes war more expen-sive ; every improvement in medical science (by the way, medicine is not a science, but an art) which adds to the security from the effects of disease ; every step taken by sanitary commissioners—each and all of these accelerate the rate of increase of the population, that is, cause it to double itself within a shorter period. The result will, of course, be that our present 1,200 millions will become 2,400 millions ; the 24 become 48, the 48, 96, with increasing rapidity ; the world will be replenished and subdued, and *then* shall the end be. I am afraid that the end will come before any more of Darwin's species will have time to develop themselves.

I have been looking into Marsh's book upon the action of man upon nature. I think I have mentioned to you one or two very startling instances in which this action has been exhibited in India. These were, it is true, special and local; but I should say that all the southern part of India owes its parched and desolate aspect to the reckless mode in which man has stripped it of its clothing. No chance here of the deposit of a new coal-field. If they who succeed us as tenants of the world are dependent for fuel upon the *débris* of our forests, they will hardly be able to cook their dinners, unless they can arrive at some mode of making the hydrogen of the water available—an event which seems to be prefigured in the old saying of ' setting the Thames on fire.'

A gambling mania, set on foot by the Manchester people, in their anxiety to secure cotton to fill up the gap in the supply caused by the war in America, has swept over the whole of India. The focus, however, has been in Bombay, where every species of company was set on foot, every species of work suggested, not with any intention of carrying these out, but as a plausible basis for a company, and a means of getting shares afloat to gamble with. They say that everybody at Bombay is bankrupt: officers, civil and military, judicial and ecclesiastical. Here we have had the disease in a milder form, and have not suffered much; one or two firms have declared themselves insolvent, but generally we are sound and can pay our way. They tried me the other day with a gigantic scheme for docks, &c., baiting their hook with an engineering bait, which they thought I might rise at; but I was too old a fish to nibble; and when the projector stated that, if I would express an opinion that the work was feasible, he had no

doubt that he could form a company, I told him plainly
that I considered the whole as a humbug. I hope to be
at home at the end of the year. To tell you the honest
truth, I am tired of the people : they are a hopeless race,
hanging upon our hands as a dead weight, which we
strive in vain to lift. I do not think that they have
undergone any change—at all events, for the better—since
the time of Alexander. All talk of educating them, of
fitting them for liberty, of teaching them to govern themselves, is the veriest twaddle. I wonder how the people
who, upon the strength of affinities of language, insist
upon the identity of the Hindoo and the Englishman,
account for the colour of the Hindoo, and other physical
differences? The Hindoo is darker than the red Indian,
and in many cases nearly as black as the African ; his
skin does not blister as ours does, and a new-born infant
is exposed with its head bare to the sun, the action of
which would kill an European child in five minutes.
In fact, he is physically adapted to the climate just as
the animals are, and by the same agency, which is *not*
that of climate, but of something beyond and above it.
Good-bye.

Yours very truly,

W. D.

Extract from Journal.

Madras, June 5, 1865.

Dearest M——,—Owing to the departure of the
Bombay mail so early there will be rather a long interval
before that of the next steamer ; but, nevertheless, I may
as well begin at once, and keep up my journal as regularly
as may be. After finishing our letters on Saturday we
took a ride ; but it was but a short one, for we wound it
up by paying, according to promise, our annual visit to
the body-guard lines during the festival of Mohurrum.
I am not skilled enough in Mussulman lore to know

whether, or how far, this festival ever had a religious character. It was originally, I believe, a sort of annual funereal celebration in honour of two departed heroes — Hassan and Houssein — sons of Ali, the grandsons, I think, of Mahomet; and I believe it is still observed in Northern India as a kind of mournful anniversary, where people go about howling and wailing, and shouting, 'Hassan!' and 'Houssein!' at the top of their voices; but here it has entirely changed its character, and has become a mere merry-making, a sort of saturnalia, in which Hindoos and Mahometans all join, in equal ignorance of what it is about; at least, Spreadborough asked me this morning what it was intended to commemorate, and said she had asked several of the servants, *none of whom could tell*, so she was fain to come to me for an explanation, after all. Our body-guard always dress up and illuminate a tent to hold their sports in on the occasion, and we are always invited to come and look at it; and it certainly is one of the most completely Oriental scenes, and most characteristic of Indian life, that we see here. Unfortunately, on Saturday evening, we were a little too early in our arrival, and the newly-lighted lamps and candles had hardly had time to burn up; so the illumination was dim compared to what it usually is; but still the general effect was pretty. There was, as usual, a crowd of natives outside the tent, and the officers of the body-guard (English) waiting for us, with a little guard of honour, just at the entrance; and we were conducted to a carpeted space inside the tent, at one end of which is a representation of the tomb of Hassan and Houssein, manufactured by the body-guard men themselves out of talc and paper. On each side of this space were seats placed for our party and the officers; and behind us were, what always forms the principal feature in these Indian scenes, the mixed crowd, in all their picturesque varieties of costume. As soon as we were seated, blue lights were burned at the entrance,

and some of the body guard men, attired- or, I might
rather say, *disrobed*—for the occasion, assisted by some
hired performers, came forward and began exhibiting
jugglers' tricks with balls, knives, &c., singing and acting,
and performing gymnastic and acrobatic feats. As an
interlude, they handed round sweetmeats, and adorned us
all with garlands, and poured rose-water and attar of
roses on our handkerchiefs ; and so, having sat there
about half an hour, we took our departure, leaving them
to the noisier sports which, I imagine, succeed, and got
home just in time to dress for dinner. The festival still
continues : to-day, I think, is the last day of it, 'and a
good thing, too,' as Spreadborough observes, for it gets
noisier and noisier as it advances towards its conclusion.
One of its features is, that, amongst the crowds which
parade the streets are sets of mummers, dressed and
painted to look like tigers walking on their hind legs,
with other men behind them holding up their long paper
tails—a most absurd sight, but one which delights George,
who calls it the ' tiger feast' in consequence. Yesterday
(Sunday) afternoon he was with me in the drawing-room
verandah, when the sound of drumming, which is *comparatively* quiet during the morning, began to make itself
heard again in the streets, and drew from him the
question, 'Mamma, do you think the people ought to
make that *tiger music* on Sunday ?' I could only explain
to him that I was afraid the poor people who made it did
not know much about God, or about Sunday either, and
that we must only hope that they or their children would
be wiser in time ; but they *were* sad sounds for a Sunday
evening—so different from the quiet of an English town
at such times. In the course of the night the ' tiger
music,' as usual, got louder and louder, and at last swelled
into such an uproar, accompanied by such a glare of red
light, reflected upon the wall of our room, that I got up
and stepped on the verandah to look out, and really it was

worth it as a spectacle. There was the main street (which, at this point, is only separated from the house by a narrow strip of 'compound,' or pleasure-ground) all in a glare of red and blue light, and a perfect Babel of sound proceeding from it: drums, squeaking fifes, and all sorts of native music; shouts, cries of all sorts, and that kind of general, undistinguishable *roar* which characterises a large excited crowd; and then, over all, the bright, glorious, tropical night, with the grand stars looking so quietly down on the confused scene; altogether, it was a striking sight in its way, and I was half unwilling to go to bed again; but I certainly thought that George's 'tiger music' is not at all a bad name for it.

Bangalore, June 8.—We left Madras at seven o'clock yesterday evening, after an early dinner, and reached Vellore, where we had a late tea at ten. After this, the whole party retired to their different sleeping carriages, leaving us in undisturbed possession of the large saloon carriage, in which we had all spent the evening together, the gentlemen playing at whist at one end of it, the two girls at chess at the other. When they retired we had our pillows in, and made beds of the sofas at each end: but the sleep one can get in a railway carriage is never much, I think, as I am a good deal tired to-day. We got here about half-past five this morning, and found carriages waiting to bring us on to this house, which is a couple of miles from the railway station. The house is a better one, and the rooms more comfortable, than I had expected, from the description; but, unfortunately, people here seem to have built their houses as if the climate had been that of Madras, instead of Bangalore—all open: and the consequence is that there is a raging wind blowing everywhere, which one cannot get out of, and which goes through me, and makes me feel as if I had an incipient cold already. The rest of the party *like* it, luckily.

June 11.—Yesterday W—— held a levée here, which

was numerously attended ; and when it was over we drove down to the ' Lall Bagh,' *anglice*, Botanical Garden,* the fashionable resort of Bangalore, especially on a Saturday evening, when a band plays there. The garden itself is very pretty, and very nicely kept. W—— and I had had a quiet walk in it the evening before, when we had it pretty much to ourselves, and, consequently, could see it to much more advantage than in its crowded state yesterday.

June 20.—Sunday came again to confirm us in the impression that Bangalore Sundays are not nearly as pleasant as Madras ones. The singing is very bad, and the church terribly haunted with eye flies, making it really a difficult matter to sit still ; and altogether we have a great idea of trying some other church, though I do not like wandering about from church to church, as a general rule. I have established two days for receiving visitors here—Mondays and Thursdays—and yesterday I had a pretty continuous stream of them.

June 25.—On Friday evening we took an exploring drive into the country, which served to strengthen our original impression that Bangalore is a sort of oasis in a desert: a green, well-planted place in the midst of a very bare country ; or rather, I fancy, the real difference is, that, just about the cantonment, the trees have been preserved, while everywhere else throughout the province of Mysore they seem to have been cut away for firewood ; and all looked barer than usual just now, because the fields have been ploughed in preparation for the monsoon rains, but not a blade has as yet had time to come up. However, it was a pleasant drive in the soft, summer-like evening.

June 27.—Our last two days have not been very pleasant ones, for the rains have set in just in the usual

* I believe the literal meaning of the word to be ' red garden,' but why it is so called I know not.

Bangalore fashion—viz., the rain always commencing just before the time when one can go out in the afternoon. This would not matter much in a climate like England, where one *can* get out at any time of day; but here, where one cannot go out before half-past five, on account of the sun, rain then, of course, implies not getting out at all, except what little one can do in the early morning. We could not go to church on Sunday evening for the rain, nor out at all yesterday, and to-day it is threatening to be just the same; but we are growing desperate, and shall not give up all hope till the last moment. Fancy, under these circumstances, how irritating it is to be perpetually asked whether I do not find this an *agreeable* change from Madras! I think, however, that I have nearly put a stop to this question by the vehemence of my negatives.

June 28.—I rather wronged the climate yesterday, for it actually *did* clear up after the rain in time for us to have a drive, though the air was somewhat damp and chilly. We went out this morning to see a general inspection of all the troops here: a very pretty sight, as artillery (horse and field batteries), cavalry, infantry (European and native), all were there—about 2,600 men, I think.

July 5.—I had visitors this morning; amongst others, a lady, who gave me a very interesting account of her adventures during the great cyclone at Masulipatam last winter. She was there at the time, and her husband away; and the sea broke into her house, and washed down a great part of it, one of her servants being so injured amongst the ruins that he died a few days after; and she and her children and 'ayahs,' after remaining all night sitting on a table in the centre, or safest part, of the house, in perfect darkness, got, as soon as it was daylight, into two of their great bathing-tubs, and floated away in these to the house of the doctor at the station—the nearest place of refuge.

Bangalore, July 23, 1865.

My dear Sir Roderick,—Many thanks for your letter : it is a great pleasure to have a correspondent whose letters stir up the mud of the mind, the deposit which is too apt to settle down at the bottom of the mental reservoir ; or, to speak in Indian phrase, the tank, which receives the drainage from all sources. I am very glad to hear that you retain your position as President of the Geographical Society. One of the follies into which our American cousins have fallen, is the adoption of the principle of ' rotation in office : ' they look upon office as a *bonne bouche* of which every adult man ought to have a bite. I think that we ought to apply competitive examination to the heads of departments as well as to the unfortunate clerks.

I have been reading Vambery's narrative of his journey through Central Asia, and have been much interested with it. What a country it seems to be, and what a country it might be made if it were in the hands of an educated and energetic people! I was surprised, on looking at the map, at the smallness of the portion of Asia known to us ; and also at the extent of that which has been, either by the action of man, or by nature, left unfit to maintain any amount of population. You may depend upon it that we, the breeding part of the human race, shall soon have to avenge the inroads made by the Huns and others, and to reoccupy the whole of Northern and Central Asia, if the world lasts four centuries longer.

It has struck me that many of the hypotheses pro-pounded of late years, as modes of determining the cause of some specific phenomena, are singularly deficient in probability ; and I have been reading up, latterly, the works published within the last few years on physical science, for the purpose of classifying the so-called discoveries of modern science under one of the three heads : *Facts, or realities ; Theories, or probabilities ; Hypotheses, or possibilities.* You would be startled were you to see the large proportion which come under the latter category ; many indeed are barely possible, and some physically impossible.

You say that, ' without we adopt the theory of some separate creations of man, an enormous period is required to change the white man into the negro, or *vice versâ.*' I do not believe that the white man would ever become black by the operation of the climate, and we have a curious instance in India of the permanence of colour. We have, on the west coast at Cochin, a colony or synagogue of White Jews. Their own tradition says that they have been there 1,800 years, and I believe that there is fair collateral evidence to prove that they have not been there for fewer than 1,400 years. They have intermarried among themselves, or have sought wives for their children among the western Jews, and the result has been a permanence of type ; so that, within eight degrees of the equator, under a tropical sun, they are just as fair as ourselves. Climate has had upon them none of that action which is, in my opinion, erroneously attributed to it. To race, to breeding, to the effects of crossing, I attribute very great influence upon the physical structure, complexion, &c., and also upon the intellectual and moral qualities of men. I have seen a good deal of the world, and have always observed that, where there has been no marked intermixture of races, physical peculiarities and mental characteristics remain constant. Education has no action in altering the type of character : the Frenchman in Lower Canada is a Frenchman, not an American ; the Hindoo of the present day is framed upon exactly the same pattern as the Hindoo of the time of Alexander ; the Greek of the present day is the same animal as the Greek of the time of Themistocles ; the same may be said of every unmixed or only slightly mixed race.   If education does little to modify man, government does less.   As a general rule, it is the people who model the government, not the government the people; and, in cases where the government is that of a conqueror, who may be supposed to act according to his simple will, the result is either an amalgamation of races, and the gradual but certain action of the majority upon the minority, as was the case in England, or the submission of a weak and cowardly people, who may perhaps become more weak and cowardly; but the change in this case is not one of kind, but merely of degree.   Yours very truly,

W. D.

In the course of the summer of 1865 I had a letter from Sir John Lawrence, pressing upon me the necessity of fortifying our barracks and railway stations.   I wrote to Sir Charles Wood, characterising this as a bad and cowardly policy (epithets, by the way, almost synonymous), and asking him to ignore it, as the result would inevitably be to create an impression among the natives that we feared them.   I pointed out that if we attempted to fortify these rubbishy places, we should be compelled to maintain competent bodies of troops to defend them, and should have our men scattered about along the lines of railway, half a company here and half there, exposed to the risk of being cut off, and their arms and stores appropriated by the enemy, instead of having them massed together in bodies capable of acting independently.   Sir John looked to a system of defensive operations; he considered a camp or a barrack, not as the mere temporary residence of a body of troops, but as a sort of stronghold to be defended.   This is altogether a mistake.   What we want in India is a force capable of moving speedily, whose efficiency is multiplied indefinitely by rapidity of movement.   We cannot hamper military operations by thinking of the fate of the few civil servants or settlers whom we may be compelled to leave behind us; the delay which would be caused by attempts to secure the safety of these would be ruinous; we must be content to avenge them.

The plan of dotting the country about with small forts would do nothing but harm; if we are to make our barracks small bungalows for four inmates, to please Miss Nightingale, and then to fortify them and our railway stations for fear of the natives, the immense estimates which have been sent in for military buildings will be largely exceeded, and an increase of the army will be required. If, however, following out sound military principles, our forces were concentrated at good strategical points, and held in readiness to move at a few hours' notice, we should always be able to act on the offensive; should do the maximum of work with the minimum of men, and rule all India with ease, as we should inspire the natives with a wholesome dread of us.

I cannot but think that the tendency of late years to look upon professional questions as subjects which any man of ordinary abilities might be able, without any severe amount of application, to deal with, has been productive of bad effects generally, but specially in military matters. There cannot be a greater fallacy than the tendency to treat professional questions as matters of science. I had to press this more than once upon Sir Charles Wood, who has tinkered the native army in a very 'civil way,' and to point out to him that war was not a science, but an art, to practise which a man should undergo a severe apprenticeship.

Extract from Journal.

Government House, Madras, July 29, 1865.

Dearest M——,— I am afraid there is not likely to be anything to make my letter lively, for mine seems likely to be a very quiet, monotonous life for the present. Greatly did we rejoice yesterday in a Madras Sunday instead of a Bangalore one. We went to church in the morning at the cathedral, in the evening at St. Thomé, as usual. The evening service at St. Thomé is particularly nice, and our drive home was absolute perfection : the moon and stars overhead, the white gleaming surf on one side, and on the other the distant lightning, so far down on the western horizon that we could not see the cloud, only the flashing light, made one of those combinations of glory and beauty that tropical evenings excel in. I cannot but think that people lose a great deal by their determined fancy for rushing away at this time of year to the wet, gloomy hills, under the idea that Madras *must* be too hot to be healthy or agreeable in July and August. It is positively less hot than it was in May, for then we had some days of hot wind, obliging us to shut the house up, whereas now, though it is always radiantly, gloriously bright, there is always a sea breeze, so that we can have all the doors and windows open all day long ; and the still evenings, when the breeze dies away, are as perfect as ever. Moreover, the flowering trees ! The whole place is alive with a grand tree, covered with the most brilliant scarlet flowers, which I have never seen in their full perfection before, because we have always gone away just as they were beginning to come out, whereas here they are now almost dazzling our eyes to look at; the *Poinciana Regia*, I think, is its name.

To Lieutenant-General Sandham.

Madras, August 29, 1865.

My dear Sandham,—The steamer came on Sunday, bringing your letter of July 14. I could not reply to it by the mail which has just gone out, but shall begin writing while I have your letter fresh in my memory. I agree with you as to the length of the course at Chatham; the effect of it is to disgust men who wish to start into practical life, and to get rid of the idea of school; and at the same time to make men presumptuous when they do join the corps, as they think that the smattering they have picked up of a variety of subjects is sufficient to enable them to perform *all* their duties. People now-a-days seem to imagine that one can turn a thoroughly educated man out of school or college, just as a tailor turns out a good pair of breeches: they forget that a man is not worth his salt who is not always learning something.

Another evil we are falling into is that of believing that our clothes will suit all other people, and we set about, in New Zealand, in India, and elsewhere, adapting our form of government, and our principles of action, to nations whose habits, feelings, modes of life, are altogether different from those which we recognise as right and proper. I had been but a few weeks at Madras before I pointed this out to the Secretary of State, and I have never lost an opportunity of pressing the absurdity of such a system; but one feels like a man pulling hard against a stream which he can only just overcome, and which at any sharp turn is sure to beat and drive him back again.

You say you can hardly fancy me as a colonel of Engineers. I can hardly fancy myself doing the duty; still, I have never lost sight of my engineering experience, and all that I shall require will be instruction in the routine of duty. I wish very much to be able to have my say to the Commander-in-chief with reference to the organisation of the corps in India. I have just heard from Colonel Adye, R.A., who is working hard to reduce the Artillery into order. He anticipates, as I do, a large reduction of the corps, and indeed, as regards the Artillery, the necessity of the reduction of the strength of the corps out here has been seen by the Governor-General, who proposes to get rid of a whole brigade of Horse Artillery. I want to avoid a half-pay list, which does infinite harm to the corps, and I should propose to begin at once, and give no commissions for vacancies in the Indian Engineers until we had brought them down to a reasonable strength. I am not satisfied with what I have seen of the corps out here ; nothing will make matters work satisfactorily till we adopt our English system of placing all military works under the corps as part of their ordinary duty, and making a marked distinction between Engineers' work, and the civil work upon which an officer may occasionally be employed, and while doing which he ought to be seconded.

Yours very truly,

W. D.

Lady Denison to Mrs. Stanley.

Guindy, October 23, 1865.

My dear Mrs. Stanley,—Let me begin my letter by answering yours, and thanking you for all your commission-doing, your choice of chintz, &c. I grieve to say, however, that a dire misfortune has happened to this chintz ; *so* dire that I really should hardly have liked to let you know of it, but that the calamity has its ludicrous side, too, and altogether I cannot help telling you about it. I was pleasing myself as I drove up here last Friday, with the idea of seeing the drawing-room, &c., glistening in the new chintz, which had been made up during my absence at Madras. When I got in, however, it struck me that the general effect was somehow rather disappointing, and when I came to investigate matters a little more closely, imagine my dismay at finding that the native upholsterers had, as I conceived, *washed* it all before making up, thereby taking out the glaze and gloss, and reducing it at once to the aspect of old furniture that wants calendering! Really I could have cried with vexation, but yet it was impossible not to be amused, too, when the unlucky upholsterers were spoken to on the subject, with their utter unconciousness of having done any harm. They denied the *washing*, and, I really believe, truly ; but, without the least hesitation, they told, and showed by signs quite as expressive as words, what they really *had* done, which was, to rub the chintz together hard in their hands, near the edges, a sort of *dry* washing process, 'to take the conjee out,' as they said. 'Conjee' means, in general, any preparation of flour, meal, &c. In this case, of course, it meant 'starch,' and was applied by them to the glaze of the chintz. In short, though I was wrong as to the means used, and the extent of the mischief, I was quite right in supposing that they had purposely got rid of the glaze, in order to make their work easier. Indeed, they had not the least hesitation in avowing this, and they quite seemed to think that it was the most natural and perfectly right thing to do under the circumstances

Extract from Journal.

Guindy, October 27, 1865.

Dearest M——,—I am expecting W—— and the rest of the party from the hills this afternoon. Such a luncheon as has been sent up to meet them, at a station with an *unrememberable* name, just on the other side of Vellore, I have not often seen. The old butler brought me the bill of fare for it yesterday, and I was on the point of saying that I thought it rather more than the occasion required, but I was silenced by the old man's remark, 'Captain Stewart say, great many coming, all very hungry!' It is quite true that we have not only our own party to provide for, though *that* is pretty numerous, but there are almost always on these occasions one or two extra people who are glad to take advantage of our special train, and to whom W—— gives a passage.

November 10.—Yesterday, the Prince of Wales's birthday, we had our great official ball in the Banqueting Hall, which properly should take place on the Queen's birthday, only that it is too hot for it at that time of year. The ball was rather thinly attended: Prince Azeem Jah was not there; he sent an excuse, at the last moment, of not being well, or something of that sort; but there are one or two surmises that the real cause of his absence was an affront at a note which W—— had caused to be written to him, to say that, in consequence of his sprained ankle, he should not be able to come down the stairs of the Banqueting Hall to meet his Highness, but would receive him at the door. This sounds simple enough to us, but any such little difference in ceremony is a matter of real importance to the Eastern mind, and this poor old Azeem Jah is specially tenacious of his little privileges and dignities, as is natural, I suppose, considering the anomalous nature of his position, and the struggle in which he is engaged with the British Government, for the purpose of having the ancient dignities of his family restored to him. Old Shurf-ool-Omrah, the native member of Council— the old man who always used to say he regarded me in the light of his *aunt*, appears now inclined to consider me more as his *mother*, for, in the course of the evening, he brought up to introduce to me his son, a vulgar-looking youth, not at all, in appearance at least, worthy of his father, who is really a gentlemanlike old man; and, not satisfied with this first introduction, the old man waylaid us on the steps as we were going away, and again brought up the youth to me, saying, as he did so, 'Your *grandson*, my eldest son !!'

November 25.—I received visitors here yesterday afternoon; the weather was looking threatening then, or, I should rather say, *promising*, for rain was much needed, and anxiously looked for—and we have got a magnificent burst of monsoon at last : torrents of rain, and such a gale of wind as makes me a little anxious about the mail steamer, which arrived at Galle on Thursday, and left it again yesterday evening. This morning we heard the guns from the fort, warning all ships to leave the roadstead, so it is fortunate that the steamer is not due to-day, as her passengers could not have landed.

November 27.—The weather has moderated, but I do not think there is a chance of that poor mail steamer getting in to-day ; indeed, I shall feel very thankful if she comes in safe at all, for she must have had a terrible time of it. I mentioned on Saturday that the ships had been warned off by the signal guns from the fort ; they all got out safely. The gale continued all that day, and all night, with torrents of rain. Some of the gentlemen went to Madras in the afternoon, and on their return reported that the surf was very grand ; the waves, even then, were dashing over the end of the pier. Yesterday (Sunday) morning we thought the storm was breaking : the rain stopped, and the sky partially cleared ; the glass went up, and it looked so promising that we went to church as usual, being overtaken, however, before we got there, by a sprinkle of rain ; but before the service was over the wind came on again in tremendous gusts, with torrents of rain, and by the time we got home the storm raged more fiercely than ever. Soon afterwards, a tree fell near the kitchen, and still the wind and rain kept increasing, and between three and four o'clock one of the casuarina trees, at the other side of the house, was torn up by the roots. The next event of the afternoon was the arrival of a warning note from the astronomer at the observatory, thinking it right ' to forewarn his Excellency of the approach of a severe gale.' (Fancy being told that the severity of the gale is only approaching, when you have two trees down already!) However, Mr. Pogson, the astronomer, went on to explain what he meant by a severe gale; saying that, from all his observations of the barometer, force and direction of the wind, &c., he waited to believe that a cyclone was coming on, the centre of which would, he thought, pass directly over Madras! so he sent this opinion (backed by that of the master attendant) to warn us to secure the doors and windows on all sides, so as to be prepared for the counter-burst of the cyclone, which, after its first burst from the north-east, would, he said, wheel round and come on still harder from the south. W—— sent on the note to our nearest neighbour, Sir Adam Bittleston, begging him to forward it to his neighbours, so as to warn as many as possible. Then we took our measures of defence; all the glass doors were shut, and the wooden shutters closed and bolted on the outside of them, so that we were soon almost in darkness, and obliged to have candles nearly an hour sooner than usual. Of course, going to evening church was out of the question, the torrents of rain would have prevented that, to say nothing of the violent wind; so we sat in the house, which was very hot in its closed-up state. Mr. Pierson coming in to dinner told us of two more broken trees, and of a frightened herd of spotted deer, huddled together near his bungalow, apparently not knowing what to do with themselves. Just after we had closed up the house, I fancied that the wind was lulling; but in the course of the evening it came on again, and about eleven o'clock the wind reached its greatest force, and the expected whirl round to the south took place. The centre of the storm did not, I am thankful to say, pass over us, as the astronomer expected:

it passed to the southward, somewhere about Negapatam, so we only got the skirts of it ; and the only effect of the sudden change of wind, as far as we were concerned, was a thumping and clattering in the north and south verandahs, betokening that something had ' gone adrift ' there. We peeped cautiously out, and found that one of the ' chicks,' or large blinds, had been partly blown away. Some of the men were sent to try and secure it, and were still feebly and ineffectually struggling with it—amidst a great deal of talk, as their manner is—when W—— came up to bed; so he sallied forth to their aid, and, seeing that it was quite impossible to secure the chick effectually, told them to take it down altogether ; but, before they could accomplish this, the wind did it for them, and the chick was blown down bodily. This was our worst : the gale raged on through the night, but, after a time, became not much more violent than I have often heard gales before, and we slept quietly enough, only that I could not help thinking of the mail steamer, and her passengers. Now it is *quite* calm, and we propose to drive down to the beach and see the surf, which, however, is rapidly going down.

November 29.—The steamer arrived last night, all safe, I am thankful to say, but too late to land her passengers, though the mail was sent on shore, so that we got our letters at five o'clock this morning.

December 4.—I am afraid we have by no means heard the last of the effects of the cyclone of yesterday week. Here we only got the skirts of it, which was sufficient to do some damage : two trees were blown down, and our whole bed or grove of bananas was entirely destroyed. All along the roads between this and Madras there are trees blown down, or very much broken, and in Madras itself one of the native infantry barracks and a portion of the hospital were inundated, and I believe one or two native huts were washed down ; but I am afraid the disasters at sea must have been far worse. Very few vessels have returned, and all the coasting steamers seem to come in with reports of having seen and assisted dismasted and otherwise disabled vessels; but there are some that have neither been seen or heard of since the cyclone, and in three of these one cannot but feel a peculiar interest. One has troops on board, one wing of the 60th Rifles, who, poor fellows! had just arrived from Burmah as the storm was beginning, and the surf too high to allow them to land, and they had to put to sea again. Another ship had just arrived from Australia, with a cargo of horses, and had expended nearly all her forage on the voyage. She had to go off again in this state, and it is feared that, even if the ship is not lost, the poor horses will be nearly all dead of starvation before she gets back. The third of the missing vessels is the ice ship, which had only landed a small portion of her cargo, when she had to run for it, and we can ill spare her, for if she does not return we shall soon be without ice.

December 5.—To-morrow, if all be well, we have promised to go up to Cuddapah for the doings there on the occasion of opening the new railway (the railway has been opened and used some little time, I believe, but they waited for the festivities till W—— could come up to be present at them). We do not expect to get back till Friday.

This morning's paper announces that *a* ship with troops, supposed to be the missing one, has been seen, totally dismasted, but in a position which gives good hopes that she may have got into Trincomalee; the ice-ship has actually been spoken, with only the loss of her foremast, so I hope she will soon be back.

December 6.—Our expedition to Cuddapah was suddenly put off, in consequence of a telegram received yesterday by the manager of the railway, announcing that three bridges on the north-west line had been washed away by the bursting of some tanks during the late rains, and, consequently, that all communication with Cuddapah was cut off; so, of course, we stayed our preparations, and the orders for a start were countermanded. I am sorry for the Cuddapah people, who have been in a great state of preparation, and gone to a good deal of trouble and expense for nothing; for though W—— thinks the disaster will be repaired in a few days, it will be difficult for us to find two such convenient days for our expedition as to-day and to-morrow would have been, for December is a very busy month with us. The poor ships that have been missing since the cyclone are beginning to creep in again: the horse-ship has arrived, but with only four of the poor horses left alive, as, besides those that died of starvation, many of the animals broke loose in the storm, and literally kicked and trampled each other to death. Happily, she had landed more than half her cargo before the storm began, so there were only seventeen horses on board when she put to sea again, but the death of thirteen out of these, and the probable decease of three more which are in a very doubtful state from starvation, must be a heavy loss to the owners. The ice-ship is known to be at Pondicherry, repairing damages, but great anxiety is beginning to be felt about the troop-ship, of which there is no certain intelligence. A steamer has been sent out to look for her, and I hope may succeed in finding and bringing her in.*

I have nothing to add, but that we are all well; unless you would like to hear of a small calamity that has befallen us, or rather our gardener, on whose feelings it weighs most heavily. We have got a tame emu, lately imported from Australia; and, as the gardener did not know anything about the habits of this bird, and nearly killed it by

* This troop ship came in just after the steamer had been sent in quest of her: totally dismasted, and having been, for about twenty-four hours, in considerable danger.

cramming it with meat, we made him let it go to shift
for itself about the garden, pacifying his rather alarmed
feelings by assuring him of what we, at the time, believed
ourselves, viz., that it would only graze, and not meddle
with his flowers and vegetables. However, in this we
have found ourselves deceived—it does meddle with the
flowers; but the most cruel blow to the gardener has been
that there was one cauliflower which he actually had
succeeded in nursing into flower, of course a very rare
thing to do in this climate, and over which he was watching with great anxiety, thinking it would just be ready
for our Christmas dinner; and the emu has eaten it!
We do not break our hearts much over the cauliflower,
but it will never do to have all our flowers nibbled at, so
we shall have to rail in a place for the emu, or to turn
him into the park.

To Children in England.

Madras, January 2, 1866.

My dear Children,—Many happy New Years to you all.
This year will be specially happy to me, for I have the
prospect of seeing you all again, and am looking anxiously
for news from England as to the time of the arrival of my
successor. I have secured a passage in the P. and O.
steamer leaving this in March, and, as I stay a short time
at Alexandria, Malta, and Gibraltar, I shall be in England
in May, I hope.

On Saturday we got three mongooses and four snakes,
and turned them into an enclosure, for the purpose of
seeing the mode in which the mongoose deals with
a snake. We had not much sport, however; neither the
snake nor the mongoose seemed to like the thoughts of a
fight. In one instance the mongoose got hold of a snake
by the neck, and gave him a shake, the result of which
was that the snake coiled himself up into a stiff coil, with

his head well hidden in the centre of it, and no persuasion could induce him to put his head out again.

Cuddapah, January 9th.—We came up here yesterday to be present at a fête given by the native inhabitants of Cuddapah on the occasion of the opening of the new railway as far as their town. We left Madras at 10 A.M., and arrived here a little after four, the distance being about 160 miles. We went as far as the Naggery Hills, or that part of the N.W. line which I opened in '61. From thence it was a new country to me, and the aspect was peculiar, if not pretty. We ran along a narrow valley, with bare hills on each side, the rocks of which took very fantastic forms, while the valley was rich and well cultivated. When we got to Cuddapah we were received by the civil and military authorities and a crowd of natives; were placed in carriages, and taken off to the Collector's house, while the rest of the party were accommodated in tents. We rested till it was time to dress for a great dinner given by the native inhabitants of Cuddapah. This took place in the verandah of a house not far from the Collector's, and was rather a tedious affair. Nearly a hundred guests sat down to dinner—all the European inhabitants of Cuddapah, together with a large party from Madras. None of the natives dined with us, but after dinner a body of them came in with an address, which they read. I gave a written answer, which, after I had read it, was freely translated into Telugu by one of the civilians. Then we had some toasts and speeches, and then followed fireworks, for which we adjourned to a verandah at the other side of the same house. This was really the best part of the evening's amusements; the fireworks were very good, and all firework and torchlight scenes are, to my mind, peculiarly effective in this country, owing to the very picturesque groups of natives, in their many-coloured dresses, which they illuminate. When the fireworks were expended, dancing commenced;

here, however, as the ladies were few, and the floor hard and unelastic, they soon got tired; but altogether you may suppose we had had a pretty good day's work. On Tuesday we were all tired. I had to hold a levée and a durbar in the morning, and in the afternoon we drove round the town. All the compounds were filled with magnificent mango trees, which, in their wild state, are certainly the handsomest trees in India. The ground was clean, the crops good, and there was a flourishing aspect about the immediate vicinity of the place, but the hills in the distance were very bare and brown. In the evening there was another dance—a sort of small-scale repetition of the ball of the night before; but we got away a little after twelve. On Wednesday I went in the morning to visit the mission school. The girls seemed to be well taught, as they were under the immediate supervision of the missionary's wife; but as to the boys, it seemed to me that they suffered from the mixture of missionary and schoolmaster, the duties of the mission taking the schoolmaster away too often from the school. We started at twelve on our return home, having, as all agreed, had a very pleasant trip.

To Sir Charles Wood.

Guindy, January 11, 1866.

My dear Sir Charles,—I am sorry to see from your letter to me, which I received yesterday, that your fall has damaged you more than I anticipated. I trust, however, that by this time you are all right again. I came down yesterday from Cuddapah, about 160 miles from Madras on the north-west line of railway. I was asked by the natives to be present at an exhibition of fireworks, and they gave a dinner and a ball to a party of nearly 100. I was well pleased to have the opportunity of paying a visit to this, which is one of the ' ceded districts.' I had seen the other two in '63.

The line taken by the rail did not seem promising; it ran for 100 miles in a narrow valley between two ranges of very bare hills, but opened out near the town itself, and the level portion seemed very well cultivated. The Collector brought before me several of the merchants and ryots, all apparently well-to-do. Here, however, as well as elsewhere, it is perfectly clear that the assessment or rent is very much less than it ought to be.

The Collector submitted a plan for a branch railway which he told me the native capitalists were anxious to undertake. I gave him every encouragement; but I warned him not to allow himself or the natives to be deluded into constructing a locomotive line, at a heavy cost, when a line worked by bullocks would answer every purpose. The promoters of the line to Conjeveram, which is visited by three or four thousand pilgrims annually, have found that the rolling stock required to work an occasional flood of traffic swallows up all profits. It is very difficult, however, to induce an engineer to calculate quietly the cost of working a line of rail; he is always looking forward to an enhancement of traffic, which is pretty sure to take place in England, but which looms but vaguely in the far distance here.

We have just had an outbreak in the north among the Khonds, but have put it down by the police. I will not shock you by using the terms fire and sword, but in dealing with savages any excess of lenity is looked upon by them as an evidence of weakness. I am very glad that we are far enough away from the Exeter Hall fanatics, or they might propose to me to hang my active, useful police officers, as they seem inclined to do to Eyre at Jamaica.

Yours very truly,
W. D.

To Sir Charles Wood.

Madras, February 13, 1866.

My dear Sir Charles,—I got a telegram a few days ago announcing your resignation. I am afraid that your fall has been productive of more serious effects than were anticipated. I trust that the relief which secession from business will give you, and the absence of that mental strain which the management of such a territory as India must necessarily occasion, will set you right again in a month or so.

I cannot close my correspondence with you without thanking you for the kindness you have shown me during my Indian career. I believe that, in my correspondence with you, I may have often expressed my opinions too strongly, but my object was to let you know what those opinions were, without any disguise, leaving it for you to judge of their correctness, and being quite prepared to find that your views and mine differed; but being in no respect desirous to maintain my own opinions in opposition to yours.

I leave this in about six weeks, but as I stop to have a look at the Suez Canal, and also at the works at Malta and Gibraltar, I shall not be in England before the end of May. Trusting to see you in good health in a few months, believe me,   Yours very truly,

W. D.

Extract from Journal.

Guindy, March 12, 1866.

Dearest M——, —On Friday I received visitors here— my last Guindy reception, probably, as we are thinking of going down to Madras on the 20th, and taking up our abode there till our departure. Here is a specimen of the ' march of intellect,' which made its appearance on Saturday: the original was printed on a common invitation card :—

' The Committee of Management for the Entertainment to be given by the Mohammedan Community to his Excellency Sir W. T. Denison, K.C.B., Governor of Madras, and for the presentation of a farewell address previous to His Excellency's departure, request the honor of Lady Denison and Miss Denison's company at a Dinner and Nautch, at the gardens of Azeez-ool-Moolk Bahadoor, Græmes Road, at 7½ p.m., on Saturday the 24th of March, 1866.

' SUMSAUM-OOD-DOWLAH BAHADOOR,

' *Secretary.*'

Do not these names rather savour of the ' Arabian Nights'? an evening entertainment in the gardens of a man bearing such a name! but the ' march of intellect' lies in Mahometans inviting ladies! The next step will be when they bring their own ladies to meet us; and I think that will come, in time, though they are a good way off it yet: and even now there was a curious little etiquette about our invitation. A deputation of these Mahometans came in person on Saturday to invite W—— to this *fête*; but they could not couple L——'s and my invitation with his: it would have been decidedly improper to mention our names in public! so we had to be asked, as you see, separately.

This *fête*, as it was the last, so was it one of the most picturesque, of the festival ' tomashas' which we attended in India. At the hour appointed, we drove through the illuminated garden of Azeez-ool-Moolk, and drew up in front of a wide, open verandah, brilliantly lighted, the effect of the lights being heightened by their being intermingled with suspended globular mirrors.

Upon this verandah stood our hosts, massed together on either side of the central steps. They were mostly dressed in white robes, with red turbans and sashes, though here and there might be seen a slight admixture of other

colours. We were conducted up the steps to a carpeted
space in the back part of the verandah, on which were
placed sofas for the Government House party and other
principal guests; all the chief dignitaries, military and
civil, being also invited; and here the ladies remained
seated, while the address of the Mahometan community of
Madras was presented. In this, as well as in most other
documents of the kind, the Mahometans strive to bring into
view the difference between their own nation and the Hindoos, of whom they were once the conquerors. We are
too apt to take no account whatever of this distinction,
and to confound them altogether, when we speak of them,
under the one general term of ' natives : ' wrongly, I
think ; for, after all, the distinction is founded in fact,
and we unnecessarily wound their feelings by ignoring it. After the presentation of the address, we proceeded to dinner, in a temporary erection at one side of
the verandah. Old Azeez-ool-Moolk conducted Lady
Denison to dinner, while his son, Nazim Jung, who is an
active, rather intriguing man, a sort of politician in his
way, and the presiding genius of the present entertainment, marshalled me in. These two, and a few of the
other leading Mahometans, sat down to table with us,
but partook of nothing, throughout the repast, but a little
fruit, or a biscuit. The dinner itself was served in the
European style, and was rather a tedious affair. After it
was concluded, we were conducted to the part of the
building in which the ' nautch ' was to take place, and in
front of which, to begin with, some brilliant fireworks
were exhibited. This nautch was to be marked by the
introduction of a dance, which is only performed on
special occasions, and which is much prettier than the
ordinary ' nautch.' Eight dancing-girls, all dressed alike,
stood in the centre of the apartment, each holding one of
a cluster of eight ropes, which were suspended from the
ceiling ; and then, with a slow and graceful movement,

passed to and fro, in and out, in such a manner as, by this movement only, to twist the eight ropes into a regular plait through their whole length, and then to untwist them, the whole being done by the dance figure only, without any further application of the hands. These dancers were, of course, the only native females that appeared; but, on some enquiry being made about the ladies of the families of our hosts, we were told, by an European conversant with Eastern manners, that they were sure to be all looking on, somewhere: probably in carriages drawn up in front of the building. In point of fact, though the Eastern lady objects to being seen (and the objection apparently is more on her own part than on that of her lord and master) she has a great notion of seeing; and generally contrives to get her share of any sight or festival that may be going on, in this sort of invisible way. Our part of the entertainment ended with the above-described dance, and we took our leave on its conclusion; all the European guests, I believe, shortly following our example.

To Sir Roderick Murchison.

Madras, March 12, 1866.

My dear Sir Roderick,—Another fortnight will see me on the eve of embarkation for England. I will not, however, lose the opportunity of answering your last letter, and of congratulating you upon the *tardy* acknowledgment of the position which you hold in the scientific world. Better late than never, however.

I will not attempt to discuss geological questions in a letter: nor, indeed, do I pretend to deal with such matters; they come before me only occasionally, and I ask for explanations from those who know more than myself. To tell you, however, the honest truth, I get little satisfaction from the books I refer to. I am quite sick of the term ' philosophy of causation ;' and even ' philosophy ' occasionally stinks in my nostrils, when I see how the term is abused, and how a man is termed 'a lover of wisdom or science,' when, in point of fact, he is doing his best to make science ridiculous by thrusting ill digested '*hypotheses*' down the throats of those who, like young birds in a nest, open their mouths and swallow all that is offered them.

I have read your Birmingham address. I am quite prepared to maintain the correctness of your view of the magnitude of the forces which have been acting on the crust of the earth. Why Lyell and others should insist upon small forces and an infinity of time, when they might just as well draw upon the bank of force, and measure the amount of their draft by the effect required to be produced, is beyond my comprehension. The evidence before our eyes shows every gradation of force from that which disintegrates a bit of sandstone, to that which heaves up thousands of square miles. For my part I am more puzzled to account for the small forces than the large. I can imagine an enormous meridional force sufficient to lift up the Rocky Mountains and the Andes; but I cannot comprehend, either upon Lyell's theory or yours, the mode in which the small contortions are made; as, for instance, in the new gneiss of India; or how the crystalline limestone, described in a former letter, got rolled up into such a peculiar form. However, this we will talk about before long. I have a *fancy*—I won't call it either theory or hypothesis—that the world will come to an end before we work out our coal-fields. I base my fancy upon the rapid increase of population. It seems to me that in two hundred years we shall hardly have standing room. Even at present we in England do not feed above one-half of our population : that is, we do not supply bread and meat to more than ten of our twenty millions. What shall we do when the twenty millions become forty? However, the world will, in all probability, last my time, and that of my children, so I need not trouble myself about its future, but look to my own, not here, but hereafter. It is a great comfort to me to find that the '*so-called*' discoveries of science strengthen rather than disturb my faith.

I am reading Palgrave's 'Arabia:' he deals more with the men than the country they inhabit. I can back up his assertion as to the fatuity of the Mahometans, and the curse of their system of Fatalism. Trusting to see you in June, believe me, Yours very truly,

W. D.

Here must close our epistolary recollections of Madras. On the very day of the Mahometan *fête*, above described, March 24, 1866, I received a telegram announcing the arrival of my successor, Lord Napier, at Galle. On the afternoon of that day I, for the last time, conferred degrees at the annual commemoration of the Madras University. On Monday, March 26, my wife had a farewell reception in the grounds of the Government House, at Madras, and I embraced the same opportunity of taking leave of numerous friends and acquaintances, rather than encounter the more formal ceremony of a farewell levée.

Lord Napier arrived on Tuesday, March 27. His commission was so worded as to take effect from the date of my 'death, resignation, or departure;' and I had, therefore, on that morning, previous to his arrival, gone down to the Council, and there tendered my resignation of the government, so that there might be no objection to his installation immediately on his arrival.

On Wednesday, March 28, we sailed for England, and, though the reception on the previous Monday had been the ostensible parting with our Madras friends, their kindness did not allow it to be the real one. All those who had, either from official position, or any other circumstance, been more intimately connected with us, were, with their families, waiting on the pier to send us off with their kindly good wishes and warm-hearted farewells, and their hearty cheer, accompanying the parting salute, was the last sound we heard as we left the shore.

It is a blessed thing to return to one's own country after a long absence, and to find, as we did, loving friends to greet us—friends who had never allowed our places in their hearts to be otherwise filled up; but I cannot finish this record of the twenty years' absence from home without thankfully acknowledging that the years so spent have been by no means the least happy of a very happy life. Many an enduring friendship has begun in them; many a kindness been received; many a blessing enjoyed that will ever remain in grateful remembrance; and were it not for the impossibility of having two separate dedications of the same work, I would willingly dedicate these closing lines, at least, to the many friends made in Australia and in India, who will never lose their hold upon our hearts, and to whom these pages may occasionally recal some past scenes of pleasant intercourse.

CHAPTER XXVI.

CONCLUDING REMARKS.

AMONG the subjects brought forward in the foregoing portions of this work are one or two which appear to me to be of so much importance that I cannot but subjoin a few remarks on them in conclusion, by way of moral to my tale, and in order to show how far the opinions I expressed at the time when they were first forced on my notice have been illustrated and borne out by subsequent and still existing facts. These subjects are, first, the relations between the colonies and the mother country; and, secondly, the state and prospects of our Indian native army.

Nine years have elapsed since I left Australia, and fifteen years since I was made an unwilling instrument in working out a change in the form of the government of the Australian colonies. A period so short as this is but a trifling portion of the life of a country; it may, however, show evidence of tendencies on the part of a people or of its Government to carry out in action certain political fancies or hypotheses, the effect of which on the character and happiness of the people may be strongly marked either for good or for evil. I have said above, 'a people or its Government.' I am by no means, however, disposed to limit the tendency to work out political theories to the people and the Governments of the colonies. The changes which were asked for by some of the colonies were thrust upon others; all, whether in a state of infancy or incipient manhood, were treated alike—

were told to manufacture constitutions for themselves; and these specimens of constructive capacity were adopted by the Government of England with so little question or remark, with so little thought of their possible, or even probable, action upon the future of either colony or mother country, as would almost lead to the supposition that the object was to give to these infant states a lesson in constitution-making, which might induce them to think that they were of full age and capacity to manage their own matters, and to set up housekeeping for themselves.

The impression created upon my mind was, as will be seen by more than one of my letters to the Secretary of State, that a feeling was creeping up in England that the colonies were expensive encumbrances. This I did my best to combat. I felt certain that the prestige arising out of the spread of our colonial system, and the extent of our nominal empire, added largely to our actual strength, as well as to our political importance.

I am afraid, however, that a feeling of the kind has got possession of the public mind, bidding fair to produce results as injurious to England as those which were brought about by a similar feeling of petty economy just about a century ago.

The Government in 1769 strove to make the colonies contribute towards the general expenditure of the country, and asserted the right of Parliament to impose taxes on these dependencies. It had courage enough to maintain its opinion by the sword, and was only convinced, after a struggle which lasted several years—which cost many millions more than we could ever have drawn from the colonies had we been successful, and thousands of lives which we could ill spare—that it had acted, both economically and politically, most foolishly, sowing the wind which had produced the whirlwind, changing those who were friends and relatives into bitter enemies.

There is now a similar economical outcry. The colonies, it is said, ought to defend themselves; they have no right to call upon England, the parent state, their mother country, for aid and assistance when they are attacked, whether the attack be the consequence of any action on the part of the colonies, or of the policy of the Government of England; and when the colonies claim to be considered as brethren, as children of one common parent; when they (which they do unanimously) express an anxious desire to maintain their connection with a country which they term their *home*, they are told by the penny-wise and pound-foolish political economists that these feelings of affection ought not to influence them, that they are of full age to judge and act for themselves, and that as soon as they have arrived at the period of manhood, they should cast off the ties which bind them to their parents, act without any reference to the views and wishes of those who have nurtured and brought them up, and think only of themselves. It is a curious circumstance that, while a century ago we were anxious to retain our children under our control, and spent blood and treasure in the effort to do so; now, when these children pray to be allowed to retain the family name, we are anxious to turn them out of doors. The same paltry spirit of economy which made us act so foolishly a century ago is now working, though in a different and more cowardly manner, to produce the same results—the dismemberment of the empire.

Let us, however, enquire whether there are any sound *economical reasons* why we should grudge the outlay of the few thousands of pounds which the colonies (properly so called) cost us annually.

Are we poverty-stricken? So far are we from this, that, while in 1846 the difference between the income and expenditure of the people, making the annual addition to the capital of the country, was twenty millions, now, in

1869, this very difference is estimated by some to amount
to 150 millions, and acknowledged by all not to be less
than 100 millions per annum. Surely we might spare a
small portion of this accumulation of wealth to maintain
a state of things which insures to us a friendly welcome
in every corner of the globe, which guarantees to our
ships assistance and protection at every colonial harbour,
instead of the cold treatment of a neutral, or, it may be,
the active enmity of a competitor in trade and manufactures.

If an individual is wise in investing money in the
purchase of an annuity for his support when old age or
infirmity renders him incapable of helping himself, surely
a nation would act still more wisely in expending a portion of its capital in maintaining a state of things which
may almost be said to insure a perpetuity of the strength
of manhood, and to guarantee the presence of loving and
affectionate children in every part of the world where its
flag can fly.

But in truth it is not in the absence of means that this
outcry against the expense of maintaining our colonies
has its origin ; it is due to that superfluity of wealth which
generates an intensity of selfishness—an insatiable appetite for accumulation, a greed for gain, which looks upon
every halfpenny expended in a manner not reproductive
of money as lost to its possessor.

I hope and trust that no visions of a paltry saving of
expense will induce the Government to adopt such a
suicidal policy as that which has been suggested by the
advocates of economy ; that it will regard the colonies as
integral portions of an empire destined to embrace within
its limits a very large proportion of the surface of the
earth, which should be added to, strengthened, and
developed to the uttermost, in the certainty that every
such addition or development is a source of strength
instead of weakness—of practical economy, as contrasted

with that penuriousness which looks merely to the accumulation of wealth, and not to its employment as a means of promoting the welfare and happiness of others.

State of Indian Native Army—1869.

Nearly four years have elapsed since I left India, and upwards of eight years since I addressed to Lord Canning the memorandum upon the reorganisation of the native army, which I afterwards forwarded, with his lordship's remarks and my comments, to Sir Charles Wood, and of which a copy will be found in vol. ii., p. 56 *et seq.* What has been the effect produced by this so-called reorganisation upon the discipline and efficiency of the native army up to the present date?

The effect, so far as the experiment has gone, is in every way injurious; the native army is less efficient than it used to be, and is steadily deteriorating. This, be it remembered, is not an *opinion*, but a *fact*: it is testified to by officers of all the three Presidencies, speaking from their own experience of the change of tone and feeling among the officers and men of the regiments to which they are attached, and repeating the statements of officers with whom they have been thrown in contact on duty, as to the state of other regiments.

It may, perhaps, be said that this is merely the ordinary expression of dissatisfaction of men with a change of which they have not yet reaped the anticipated benefit; and I have but little doubt that the advocates for the change will assert that the existing evil condition of things is the necessary consequence of the change of system, and has been foreseen and provided for, as no alteration could be expected to produce its full benefit in so short a period as has elapsed since the change was commenced. Let us, therefore, go a little more into detail, and see whether the evils of which the officers complain are mere petty, temporary inconveniences, which will, after a time,

die away, and from the dead roots of which will spring up
efficiency and economy, the latter of which, by the way,
was held out as the *immediate* result of the change of
organisation; or whether they are not the inevitable results
of the new system, which, erroneous in principle, has
been made more actively injurious by the mode in which
it has been carried into effect.

What, then, has been the action upon the European
officers, as a body?

They complain that they are too few in number to
maintain a mess, or to act collectively as a social body:
that they are, therefore, obliged to decline invitations
which they receive, as a body, from the officers of European regiments, quartered in the same cantonment, as
they cannot make any return to such civilities. From
this arises, necessarily, a feeling of dissatisfaction with the
service among the officers of the native regiments, and
something allied to contempt on the part of the officers of
the British regiments, the joint effect of the two being a
want of harmony between the services, which is gradually
drawing them farther apart, lessening, in all probability,
the disposition of officers in the British regiments to serve
in the native regiments, and most certainly injuring the
efficiency of the army as a body.

Next, as to the action upon European officers individually, and their relation with the regiment to which
they are attached. This last, according to the present
system, is merely a matter of chance, or favouritism: it is
in no way, as heretofore, a matter of selection. An
officer now belongs to the so-called Staff Corps; he is
not known as belonging to any regiment; he does not
share, necessarily, in the credit which the regiment has
obtained from its previous service; he has no *esprit de
corps*, for he has no body of which he can feel that he
forms a part. He belongs to the Staff Corps, it is true:
but this is a body without a soul, or, rather, it is an

empty name, meaning nothing. All other bodies in which promotion is dependent on seniority—such as the Artillery, the Engineers, and the old Staff Corps which served with distinction during the Peninsular War—have a proud reality: the credit which is gained by each officer or man becomes the property of the corps, and is reflected upon each individual belonging to it. I may say also that each individual suffers from the misconduct of a member of the corps, and has a direct interest in maintaining the character of the body.

Is this the case with the Indian Staff Corps? No; most certainly not! The praise which officers may gain, while serving with a native regiment, may belong to them individually, or may be shared with the regiment to which they are but temporarily attached, but none of it is credited to the 'Staff Corps.' But are they likely to get any credit? or, rather, are they entitled to any? They have nothing to do with the organisation of the body; they have not raised it, or disciplined it; they are merely attached to it for a time—can hardly be said to lead their men into action, for they are mounted officers with infantry, they do not fight alongside of them. The credit, if there is ever likely to be any credit with such an organisation, belongs to the native officers, who march and fight with their men, who are identified with them, and to whom, in the scheme worked out by the Government, no prospect of promotion or honour is held out. What is the change in the relation between the European officer and the men serving under him? Formerly he was responsible for their appearance and efficiency, but the responsibility is now transferred to the native officer. The effect of this is, naturally, to separate the European officer more and more from the natives whom he commands, to deprive him of the interest which he used to take in the conduct of each individual of his company, and to make the soldiers careless of his approbation, which can have little practical effect upon their comfort or well-being. The native officer, to whom the responsibility of the discipline of the regiment has been transferred, has more required from him, while he has less hope of reward ; he is made more efficient, and has more power of doing harm, while he has less inducement to remain faithful to his colours, or content with his position. It will, possibly, be said that the absence of fellow-feeling between the men and their European officers will be more than compensated for by the closer connection between them and their fellow-countrymen, the native officers. I will not allude to the risk to our dominion in India arising out of such a transference of confidence from the European to the Asiatic officer, should it take place ; it is sufficient to say that as yet it has not taken place. All the accounts received from India, at all events all the accounts received from men who have no interest in putting a false colouring upon the actual state of things, represent the *disorganisation* of the regiments to be on the increase ; they say that the men have no confidence in the native officers, and these latter but little influence over the men, while a general feeling of indifference and dissatisfaction prevails among all—Europeans as well as natives—arising out of the conviction that the change of organisation has been the source of a variety of evils, all of which are felt and appreciated, but from which no one sees a way to escape.

In point of fact, the Government, thinking, as is too commonly the case, that, with the power to deal with professional questions, the knowledge and capacity to treat them aright was necessarily united, caught hastily at the title of ' *The irregular organisation,*' and attributed to the name all the advantages which were in reality due to the talent and energy of the individuals at the head of the irregular regiments. By meddling in this hasty manner with a professional question, of which it was profoundly ignorant, it has broken up and disorganised a very efficient body of troops in the Madras army, upon which it could depend fully; while it has, with the most perverse ingenuity, deprived itself of the power of organising, in case of necessity, bodies of irregular troops, such as, under the direction of men like Jacob, Skinner, and others, did good service in former campaigns.

REMARKS ON THE ORGANISATION OF THE CORPS OF ROYAL ENGINEERS IN INDIA.

I WISH to bring more clearly before my brother officers the peculiar position in which they are placed with reference to their duties in India; a position the action of which upon the future of the corps few, as far as I can judge, seem to realise. The following statement of the views with reference to the constitution of the corps, and the character of its duties, which I pressed upon the Government of India, in 1863, and which I have reiterated during the year just past to the Government in England, will be a fitting conclusion to these volumes.

The amalgamation of the European portion of the troops of the East India Company with the Queen's army seemed at first to be a very simple matter, involving merely a change of name; it has, however, been found more complex in its results than was expected. As regards the Engineers, it has led to a variety of complications, arising out of the mixed character of the duties which the officers are called upon to perform, and these difficulties have kept increasing up to the present time.

Very soon after my arrival in India, I was obliged to enquire into the constitution of the Department of Public Works, which, having been reorganised by Lord Dalhousie, had been placed in the hands of the officers of Engineers, as being, in point of fact, the only persons competent by their education and training to perform properly the duties of the department.

The result of this change was to make the officers of Engineers practically officers of the Public Works; the organisation of the corps was military in name, but civil in substance.

I brought this anomalous state of things under the consideration of the Government in 1863, and I pointed out the injurious consequences which must necessarily result from this sort of hybrid constitution ; the following is a summary of the statement made by me on the occasion.

'The military organisation of the corps of Royal Engineers has been lost sight of altogether. The military duties of the officers have either, as in the case of the Sappers,* been transferred to others, or, as in the case of the construction and repair of military works and buildings, been merged in those of the mixed department of Public Works, which is composed of officers of Engineers, officers of different regiments, and civilians.

'One of the results of this mixture of civil and military duties is the undue enlargement of the corps of Engineers, the strength being calculated with reference to the sum total of its duties civil and military ; the consequence is that the number of officers is far in excess of the military wants of India.

'I am of opinion that this arrangement has not worked economically as regards the outlay of money, or satisfactorily as regards the service of the public ; but whether economical or not, satisfactory or unsatisfactory, the system cannot be maintained for any length of time under circumstances as they exist at present.

'For a few years the Indian Engineers might continue to officiate in their present anomalous condition, but gradually, as their numbers lessen by death and retirements, the vacancies even in the higher ranks would

* The Sappers are not a portion of the corps of Engineers, but are under the command of officers detached from native regiments, or from the Staff Corps.

have to be filled up by officers from England, and the English and Indian systems would necessarily come into collision.

'If we suppose, for instance, the death of a captain of Engineers in charge of some Public Works district—there will be a vacancy in the *department* which will have to be filled up by some competent officer, and there will be a vacancy in the *corps* which will have to be filled up by the promotion of the senior subaltern, and this senior subaltern may be employed in any part of the world. The vacancy in the corps will, therefore, in all probability, have to be filled up by an officer from England.

'Now the officer so sent out will not be able to speak any of the vernacular languages; he may, very probably, be unwilling, at his time of life, to commence the study of a new language, or, if willing to make the attempt, he may be unable to attain the necessary proficiency. He will, however, be entitled to the pay and allowances of his rank, and if he cannot qualify himself for the Public Works Department, he will be, according to the existing system, a supernumerary, with no duties to perform. This, which, in the instance quoted, applies only to a single individual, will practically be the case with an increasing number of officers until the present constitution of the Public Works Department breaks down altogether.

'The simplest mode of remedying this anomalous state of things, and of avoiding the inconveniences which must necessarily in a few years arise out of a system requiring the officers of the same corps to be paid and employed according to two different rules, would be that of restoring to the corps of Engineers in India its military organisation, and of making the arrangements there harmonise with those which regulate the service in England and the Colonies.

'Under such a state of things the construction and repair of all military works and buildings would be placed in the hands of the officers of Engineers, as part of their military duty; while the Department of Public Works would be exclusively a civil establishment.'

This arrangement, which would have had the effect of lessening the nominal strength of a military body, and of requiring the organisation of a fresh civil department, was, as might be imagined, objected to by both the military authorities and the Government—the latter taking its tone from its military advisers; and matters were allowed to continue in a most unsatisfactory condition.

It must be understood that in India the Government is obliged to construct and maintain *all* the roads and bridges, *all* the public buildings, *all* the works of irrigation, great and small; it is the owner, at all events in Madras, of the soil of the country, and is bound to act as landlord.

While I, then, in my capacity of landlord, was anxious to carry out large works of irrigation which would have been a most profitable investment of capital, I was met by complaints on the part of the General Government of the expensive organisation of the department, and was unable to employ an officer to plan these profitable undertakings, because the whole department was fully employed upon its ordinary duties of repairing and main-taining existing works.

Gradually, however, the demand for a larger outlay upon all sorts of works, both military and civil, became overpowering, and an appeal was made to the Government at home for an addition to the number of officers of Engineers. It was proposed to add two battalions to the strength of the corps serving in India, not because the existing strength of the corps was in any way inadequate to the performance of its military duties, but because the number of officers was not sufficient for the additional duties of the Public Works Department.

Two battalions would have given an addition of about 80 officers of all ranks. As however, this number could not be collected at once, it became necessary to employ civilians in the subordinate appointments, and gradually the number of these increased till it exceeded that of the military members of the department.

The subject was brought under my notice early in 1869 in a peculiar way. I am an old Associate of the Institution of Civil Engineers, and was appointed in 1869 a member of the Council of that body. In this capacity I was made cognizant of the present state of the Department of Public Works in India by the complaints of the civil officers, addressed to the Council of the Institution. These gentlemen were dissatisfied with their position; they were socially in a lower scale than the military officers, though employed upon the same duties, and they pressed the Council to bring the subject under the consideration of the Secretary of State for India. The President, naturally enough, made a reference to me, as being thoroughly acquainted with the relative position of the military and civil members of the Public Works Department, and I was very glad to avail myself of this opportunity of pressing upon the Government the conclusions I had arrived at in 1863, which had been strengthened and confirmed by the statements made of the existing condition of the department. I therefore wrote to his Grace the Duke of Argyll, suggesting the expediency of assimilating the duties of officers of Engineers in India to those of officers of the same corps in England and the Colonies; of retaining the purely military organisation, which enables the officers of Engineers to act as an integral part of the army; and of proportioning the strength of the corps to the military work which the officers are called upon to perform; while I modified to a certain extent my recommendation as to the constitution of the Public Works Department, by proposing that it should be organised upon a system analogous to that of the 'Ponts et Chaussées' in France.

Further considerations, and a knowledge of the recommendations which have been made for the purpose of obviating some of the difficulties arising out of the military organisation of the department (recommendations which, in point of fact, get rid of the difficulties by destroying the organisation), have convinced me that it would be more economical in every respect, more for the advantage of the corps of Engineers, as well as for that of the Public Works Department, that a distinct line of division should be drawn between them; that one should have a positive military organisation, while the other should be composed of officers trained specially for the Public Works Department in India, should look to that country as its sole field of labour, should have a recognised social position analogous to that of officers in other departments of the Government, and be entitled to all the advantages which men who have to encounter the risks of an Indian climate have a right to expect. I wish my brother officers to understand that my principal reason for advocating such a change of system as that alluded to above, is the conviction that an attempt to maintain the present anomalous organisation of the corps in India would in a few years have the effect of destroying our efficiency as a body. By it we are practically divided into two sections—one, and that the most numerous, looks to India as its principal sphere of duty; while the character of that duty, and the mode of performing it, is so different from that which prevails elsewhere, as almost to unfit an officer trained in such a school for the performance of the ordinary duties of his position in England and the Colonies. On the other hand, the military duties in India will be distributed among such a very small section of the corps as to deprive the majority of the means of keeping up their knowledge of details which they are never called upon to practise.

It is quite true that an officer who has acquired some

knowledge of civil engineering is in many respects more efficient as a military engineer than one who has not had similar advantages; but this improvement will be purchased at too high a price if, in the process of acquiring it, an officer ceases to be a soldier.

I must now bring these volumes to a close. I have probably sufficiently wearied the patience of my readers by repetitions, and may, perhaps, have incurred the reproach of harshness and presumption by the strength of some of my expressions; but a man is apt to express himself strongly when he feels strongly, and whatever objection may be taken to the force of my expressions, they have, at all events, the claim to be the utterances of one who has earnestly at heart the interests of the corps of which he has been so many years a member, the honour of our common country, and the welfare of those portions of her empire with which it has been his lot to be specially connected.

INDEX.

ABO

ABORIGINES of Tasmania, account
    of, i. 66–72, 103, 104
— Children at Orphan School, i. 78–79,
    81
— Visit from, i. 81, 83
— of King George's Sound, i. 513
— hideous appearance of, i. 513
— of Australia, a hairless tribe, i. 440
Adam's Bridge, ii. 196
— channel through, ii. 202
Adam and Adamites, ii. 387
Adye, Col., R.A., war in north-west, ii.
    292, 294
Anglo-Indian colonization, objections
    to, ii. 112, 113
— an element of weakness, ii. 116, 117
Antiquity of man, inquiry into, ii. 348
Appointment as Governor-General of
    Australia, i. 265
– – as Viceroy of India, ii. 290
Approval of conduct, i. 213–215
Army, Indian, strength of, ii. 37–39
    — native, reorganisation of, ii. 55–
    72, 95, 239, 240, 243
— — reduction of, ii. 72, 82
— — present state of, ii. 429–433
Auckland Islands, government of, i.
    188, 189
Auckland, New Zealand, i. 428
Aurora Australis, i. 471
Avoca, i. 90
Azeem Jah, Prince, ii. 147

BACKWATER, mode of travelling
    on, ii. 214
Ball, under difficulties, i. 61, 62
— at Madras, ii. 146
Bangalore, journey to, ii. 397
— appearance of, ii. 398
— climate of, ii. 399
Bathurst, journey to, i. 323–326, 327
Bazaar, i. 83
Beacon, plan for, i. 191
Becker, Mr., i. 170, 171, 175, 180
Bees, journey stopped by, ii. 186
Bellambi, coal mines at, i. 450
Bessemer process, ii. 136
Black swans, i. 86–87
Blow-holes, i. 234, 451

COL.

Botany Bay, i. 315, 316
Botany of India, proposed work on, ii.
    141
Braidwood, i. 388, 389
Bridge at Perth, i. 197, 198, 202, 203
Broken Bay, proposed trip to, i. 378, 379
Brownlow Hill, journey to, i. 342–346,
    385–386
Bushrangers, i. 22

CALCUTTA, voyage to, ii. 73, 291
    — landing at, ii. 297
— life at, ii. 302, 304
Calcut, journey to, ii. 120
Campbell Town, i. 90
Capital sentences, rule concerning, i. 19
Cataract Glen, i. 60, 61
Cattle-show, ii. 385
Cauliflower, fate of, ii. 414
Cauvery, bridges over, ii. 266
    falls of, ii. 270
Chamberlain, Gen., unfairly dealt with,
    ii. 299
Chatham, course too long, ii. 405
Chinese immigrants, i. 133
Chintz, catastrophe with, ii. 407
Christmas at antipodes, i. 66, 68, 69,
    101, 102, 372, 373
Christianity, action of on natives, ii.
    216, 377
Chupatties, a species of fiery cross, ii.190
Church of England, i. 141, 142, 233,
    252, 253
Church government, i. 173
Church Society, i. 355, 381, 382
Church of Rome, absent from levee,
    i. 459–460
Cinchona, opinions as to site, ii. 156
— value of, ii. 347
— rapid growth of, ii. 354
Clergymen's daughters, school for, i. 360
Coal mines in Tasman's Peninsula, i. 38
— — road to Falmouth, i. 90
— specimens of, i. 108
— – on East coast, i. 120, 153, 154
Colonial Secretary, suspension of, i. 195,
    197
Colonies, relation of to mother country,
    i. 346, 347, 439, 441

Col.

Colonies, relation of to mother countries, ii. 125-128
Competitive examination, objections to, ii. 281, 287
Conversion of natives, effect of, ii. 139
Convict labour, i. 23-25, 41
— females, i. 30
stations, i. 37, 39
— carriages pushed by, i. 38
at Maria Island, i. 41, 42, 104, 105
at D'Entrecasteaux's Channel, i. 86, 87, 104
Convicts Prevention Bill, i. 257
Curious mode of docking ships, i. 87
Cotton presses, ii. 202
— transit of to Madras, ii. 272
— famine, effect upon India, ii. 181, 279
— speculations created, ii. 393
Cuddapah, opening of railway to, ii. 417
Cyclone, Masulipatam, escape from, ii. 399
— to the south of Madras, ii. 409-414

DAIRY Farms. i. 209
Defences, plans for, i. 244, 245, 219, 494
— expenses of, i. 444
Defence of fortresses, how affected by improvements in artillery, ii. 180
Defensive system, a mistake in India, ii. 403
D'Entrecasteaux's Channel, i. 85, 86
Despatch, confidential, publication of, i. 123-130
Destitute Children, asylum for, i. 348-350
Development, Darwin's theory of. i. 495, 496 ; ii. 238
Disturbances in Victoria, i. 216, 217, 263, 264
Doubts Bill, i. 75, 81, 82.

EAGLE Hawk Neck, i. 41
— Life at, i. 231, 232, 234-237
Eclipse, i. 382, 383
Education, i. 56, 161, 217-225, 311
— Bill, i. 84, 85, 89, 90
Electoral scheme, i. 242-244, 460-463
— for Moreton Bay, i. 446, 447, 469
Elephant, docility of, ii. 140
— riding, effect of, ii. 357
Elgin, Lord, death of, ii. 288, 314
Embarkation, i. 3
Embrasures, suggestions for improvement in, i. 464, 465
Engineers, as Governors, i. 194
— employment of, ii. 237
— education of officers of, ii. 169

Geo.

Expenses, organization of, France fails, ii. 123
Factories best situations, selected for Hindoos, ii. 265
Epitaphs, i. 133, 134
Lawyers and Revenues, remarks on, i. 139
Estates, management of, i. 88, 89
Etiquette, i. 56
Etiquette, official, a mistake, ii. 311
Executive Council, i. 13
Exhibition of 1851, contributions to, i. 115, 117, 169, 170, 227

FACT, theory and hypothesis, definition of, ii. 190
Falmouth, i. 91
Farewell addresses in Van Diemen's Land, i. 270, 271
— in New South Wales, i. 508-512
— Levee, i. 273-276
Federal system, i. 261-263
Female Refuge, i. 82, 83, 93
Fern Tree Valley, i. 20-22
Fire in Hobart Town, i. 237, 238
Fitz Roy, Sir Charles, visit from, i. 109-111, 112
Floods in Hobart Town, i. 238-241
— at Parramatta, i. 489-491
Ford, adventure at, i. 200, 201
Forests, action of on rainfall, ii. 340
Freemasons, ball given by, i. 355, 356
French naval officers, i. 336, 337

GAIRSOPPAH Falls, journey to, ii. 122-129
— description of. ii. 132
Galle, sketch of, ii. 28
Ganges canal, remarks on. ii. 320-322
Gate Pah, attack on. ii. 366
Geology of Van Diemen's Land. i. 153, 154
— New South Wales, i. 445
Glover, Capt., death of, ii. 346
Gneiss, question as to origin, ii. 130
— peculiarities of formation. ii. 365
Godavery, navigation of, ii. 84, 96, 97
— irrigation works, ii. 89, 90
— slow progress of, ii. 97
— — cost and value of, ii. 230, 231
Gold, discovery of, in California, i. 136-138
— in Australia, i. 159-160
— effect of, i. 159, 160, 176, 182-187, 192-195, 210, 217, 227, 229, 248
— diggings at the Turon, i. 328-330
— — at Kiandra, i. 492, 493
— reduced yield of, i. 479
— diggers, representation of, i. 268, 269
Good Friday, singular observance of, ii. 167
Gooseberry fool, i. 317

GOV

Government domain and gardens, i. 19, 20
— new house, i. 194
— servants, classification of, ii. 37
— suggestions as to constitution of, ii. 73–78
— of India, slow working of, ii. 225
— — relations between general and local, ii. 296
— comments on working of, ii. 318–320
Govett's leap, i. 432

HAMILTON, i. 88
Hero-worship, folly of, ii. 341
Hindoo unfitted for self-government, ii. 48.
— relation to us, ii. 50, 51
— mental capacity of, ii. 79, 83
— character of, ii. 83, 267
— disregard of truth, ii. 287, 353
— house, visit to, ii. 317
Hobart Town, arrival at, i. 9.
— description of, and scenery, i. 10–18, 20
— return to, i. 64
— harbour of, i. 105, 106
— social state of, i. 107, 108
Holicul Droog, ii. 179
Home legislation, difficulties of, ii. 18
Horses, supply of, for India, i. 429, 430, 437, 438; ii. 185
— breeding establishments in India, ii. 323, 325
Hospitality, i. 207
Hot wind, i. 29, 227, 228
Hunter River railway opened, i. 383
Hunting accident, i. 162
Hutchins school, i. 57

INDIA, troops sent to, i. 434, 436, 438
Indian railways and navigation works hastily undertaken, ii. 84, 85
— government curiously framed, ii. 114
— finance, ii. 370–377
— army, suggestions as to constitution, i. 437
Infant schools, i. 52–55
Insects, i. 373.
Intercolonial differences, i. 377, 378, 486
Irish State prisoners, i. 130–136, 144–149, 151–153, 181, 182, 248
Irrigation, i. 371, 372
in India, money for, to be borrowed, ii. 226
— reservoirs for, ii. 203
— works, cost of, and returns from, ii. 339, 340
— Company, works of, ii. 275.

MAK

JEWS, white and black, at Cochin, ii. 220–222, 401
Jordan, river, i. 28
Jubilee, i. 149, 150
Judges, difficulties with, i. 73 78, 79, 93, 94, 97–99, 134, 135

KANGAROO, i. 56, 130
— Point, regatta at, i. 204–206
Khonds, outbreak of, ii. 418
King Tom, ii. 176
Kirwee, plunder taken at, ii. 178
Kurnool, appearance of villages, ii. 274
— geology of, ii. 277

LABOUR, scarcity of, i. 18
Lake Tiberias, i. 163.
Land, sale of, ii. 184
— price of, ii. 184
Laterite, geological position of, ii. 217
Launceston, journey to, i. 23–27
— events at, i. 58–61
— farewell visit to, i. 258–260
— harbour of, i. 106, 107
plans for sewerage of, i. 380
— swamp, i. 203, 204
Lawrence, Sir John, appointment of, ii. 316
— arrival of, ii. 327
Legislative Council in Van Diemen's Land, old, i. 32, 47, 48, 76, 85, 92–96, 156–158, 208, 241–244
— new, i. 173, 174, 175, 178 180, 184, 193.
— in New South Wales, i. 312
— in India, objections to, ii. 43
— — proposed admission of natives to, ii. 127
License fee to gold diggers, i. 268
Lieutenant-Governor, proposed appointment of, i. 440
Lignite, i. 451

MADEIRA, i. 4, 5
Madras, appointment to, i. 496, 498–507
— voyage to, i. 510, 512–514
arrival at, ii. 26
mode of life at, ii. 30
first receptions at, ii. 30, 31
— climate of, suited to invalids, ii. 390
— departure from, ii. 424
Magnetic observations at Travancore, ii. 368
Mahometans, state of feeling amongst, ii. 42
— invitation from, ii. 419
— fête given by, ii. 420
Makorie Peak, ii. 110, 111

MAN

Man, action of, on nature, ii. 393
Mangosteens, ii. 198
Maories, character of, ii. 3
— refusal to sell land by, ii 7
— tribal rights of, disputed by government, ii. 9, 10
— advice as to treatment of, ii. 8, 9, 14–18
— results of course pursued towards, ii. 19
— mistaken treatment of, ii. 332
Market-place, new, in Hobart Town, i. 230, 235
Mathematics, remarks on study of, i. 216
Meat, supply of, i. 450, 451
Midland Agricultural Association, i. 125–130
Military matters, interference of civilians in, ii. 312
Mint, i. 318, 319, 352
Minute on war in N.W. frontier, ii. 305–308
Missionary societies, action of, ii. 19, 200
Mission, London, schools of, ii. 204
Mohurrum, festival of, ii. 395–397
Mongoose and snakes, battle of, ii. 415
Monsoon, north-east, effect of, ii. 283
— south-west, limit of rainfall of, ii. 131.
Moreton Bay, separation of, i. 369–371, 377, 468–470
Mountain tribes, impolicy of meddling with, ii. 299
Municipal organisation, i. 57, 172
Murder of Mr. Price, i. 384
Mysore, journey to, ii. 248–250
— visit from the Rajah of, ii. 251
— birthday of Rajah of, ii. 253–257
— visit to wives of Rajah, ii. 258
— character of Rajah, ii. 263

NAGGERY, interview with Rajah of, ii. 34
Native hill tribes, archery of, ii. 362
— — Todas and Koters, ii. 359
Natural history of colonies, i. 455, 456, 479
— study of, i. 483
National banquet, i. 358–360
Neilgherries, journey to, ii. 97–102
— description of, ii. 103, 104
Newcastle, i. 306, 307
New Caledonia, i. 446, 465
— grants of land in, i. 442, 443
New constitutions, i. 251, 252, 315, 322, 323, 326, 327
New Norfolk, i. 34, 46
New South Wales, appointment to, i. 254–257
— — state of society in, i. 339, 340

PIT

New year, i. 100
— native greetings on, ii. 157
New Zealand, i. 120, 121, 476–478, 479, 480, 485, 186, 488
- bishop of, i. 353, 355
— mode of carrying on war in, i. 483, 484, 493, 494
— sketch of history of, ii. 1–7
— effects of system pursued, ii. 7, 8
Nizam, contingent furnished to, ii. 151–154
Nobbs, Mr., son of, i. 418, 419, 456, 457, 460, 170, 189
Nomenclature, singular, i. 29
Norfolk Island, i. 394–415, 417, 418, 420–425, 428
Norfolk Island pine, i. 20
North Australian discovery expedition, i. 310, 353, 371, 381
North Australia, proposed colony in, i. 362, 363
North-west railway, opening of, ii. 33
Nutmegs, wild, ii. 363

OBSERVATORY, i. 107
— at Sydney, i. 309
Odd Fellows, society of, i. 265, 266
Official life, commencement of, i. 11
Old Jones, i. 481, 482
Orange gardens, i. 313, 368, 369
Oranges, cultivation of, i. 419, 420
Orphan schools, i. 78–81, 96, 97, 111, 112, 116, 117–119, 265
— at Parramatta, i. 316, 317

PAGODAS, different in form, ii. 246
Pah, folly of storming, ii. 345
Parramatta, question as to domain, i. 375, 377
— visit to, i. 470, 472
Parasitic figs, i. 450
Parliament of N. S. Wales, character of, i. 341, 342, 346, 494, 495, 497
— opening of, i. 350, 351
— prorogation of, i. 383
— dissolution of, i. 507
— attempt to swamp Upper House, i. 435
Patriotic Fund, i, 305, 306
Peace, news of, i. 357
Pearls, speculative purchase of oysters, ii. 199
Permanent settlement, a mistake, ii. 271
Philosophical Society, i. 354
Philosophy, abuse of term, ii. 422
Pitcairn, Mr., correspondence with, i. 267, 268
Pitcairn Islanders, account of, i. 337, 425, 427, 439

PIT

Pitcairn Islanders, arrival at Norfolk Island, i. 360, 361, 363
— desire to return to Pitcairn, i. 418
Police new, effect of, ii. 313
Political agents, improper interference of, ii. 310
— changes, evil of, ii. 150
Pontville, visit to, i. 28
Population of world, rate of increase of, ii. 392
Port Arthur, i. 39, 40, 46
Port Curtis, rush to reported gold field, i. 453, 454
Precedence, i. 35
Preparation for voyage, i. 2
Prince Consort, death of, ii. 158, 159
Public Works, system of, ii. 81
— feeling, change in, i. 164–169, 213
Punch, i. 321
' Punjaub,' wreck of, i. 284
Putrid Sea, i. 135

QUAIL shooting, i. 11
  Queen's birthday, celebration of, i. 43–45
Quilon, illuminated garden at, ii. 215

RACES at Newtown, i. 211
— at Sydney, i. 485
Railways, schemes for, i. 307, 308, 314, 315, 319, 320, 367, 368, 443, 487
Rainfall, proportion of discharged by rivers, ii. 188, 189
Rajah of Wundoor, visit from, ii. 137
Rajah of Poodoocottah, ii. 166
— letter sent to, ii. 192
Rajah of Travancore, interview with, ii. 207
— character of, ii. 208
  dinner with, ii. 209–211
Rajah of Cochin, ii. 219
Ranees of Travancore, visit to, ii. 212
Reduction of expenditure, mistaken, ii. 337
Rent, redemption of, ii. 161
— in corn, ii. 162
Registration of titles to lands, ii. 168
Reports, military, on N.W. frontier desirable, ii. 338, 339
Responsible government, i. 326, 327
— inauguration of, i. 331–335, 351, 352
— progress of, i. 353, 364–367, 368, 369, 467, 468, 472, 473, 475, 476, 481, 487, 497, 498
— a misnomer, ii. 20–21
Road to Launceston, i. 24
Roads, inspector of, i. 23
  in New South Wales, i. 325, 387, 470

TRA

Royal Society, i. 107
Runaway horses, i. 206
Rungasami's Pillar, ii. 183

SANDERSON, Ensign, ii. 313
  Savages, conduct towards, i. 445, 446
Sebastopol, news of fall of, i. 321, 322
Secondary punishment, i. 280–301 ; ii. 227, 228
Sectarianism, i. 55, 56
Sedashegur, voyage to, ii. 121
— proposed harbour at, ii. 85, 121
— works at, ii. 125–127, 129
Seringapatam, ii. 264–266
— tombs of Hyder Ali and Tippoo at, ii. 268, 269
Servants, convict, i. 33
— native, number and quality of, ii. 27, 28
— school for children of, ii. 171, 173, 193
Seven Pagodas, visit to, ii. 380–384
Shells, collection of, i. 457, 458
Shoalhaven, ii. 452, 453
Shooting in India, ii. 106–109, 111
Sisparn Ghaut, ii. 138
Snakes, i. 115
Social arrangements, i. 336
Soil, mode of ascertaining quality of, ii. 233
Stanley, Captain, i. 122, 123
Statistical information required in India, ii. 342
St. Thomas, burial-place of, ii. 389
Stone implements, remarks on, ii. 329–332
Storm at sea, i. 415, 416
Sugar works, ii. 386, 388
Sunday, observance of, i. 198, 199
Survey, trigonometrical, i. 105
Surveying in Victoria, i. 473, 474
Sydney, arrival at, i. 278, 279, 302, 303
— description of, i. 304, 305

TABLE-TURNING, i. 225, 226
  Tableaux Vivants, i. 50–52
Tanjore, visit to, ii. 163, 164
Tappa cloth, manufacture of, i. 107
Tasman's Day, i. 64–66
Thierry, Father, correspondence with, i. 411, 412
Thieves, caste of, ii. 166
Thunderstorm, i. 174, 175
Tiger-shooting, ii. 144, 353
Timber of Van Diemen's Land, i. 106, 113, 114, 143, 155, 156
Tortoise, found in railway cutting, i. 458, 459
Training-school for masters, i. 117
Transportation, i. 14, 27, 62, 63, 64, 158, 159, 160, 161, 162, 211, 212, 214

TRA

Trawling expedition, i. 157, 158
Trepang, preparation of, ii. 197
Trichinopoly, ii. 162, 163
— work in gold and silver, ii. 165
Tumuli, contents of, ii. 281

UNIVERSITY, Sydney, i. 338, 339, 463, 466, 467

VAN Diemen's Land, appointment to, i. 1
— description of, i. 12
— history of, i. 13
— state of in 1847, i. 15–17
— climate of, i. 82
— departure from, i. 276–278
— responsible government in, i. 386
Vocal Harmonic Society, i. 491, 492
Voyage, incidents of, i. 3–9

WAR with Russia, i. 247, 261, 265
— Fast Day on account of, i. 253, 254

WAR

War on N. W. frontier, termination of, ii. 369
Waste land, sale of, ii. 161
Water, charge for, ii. 335
— power, use of, ii. 354, 355
Waterfalls, i. 431, 432
Waterspouts, i. 116, 117
Wedding, Archdeacon M.'s, i. 91
— native guests at, ii. 232, 233
Wesleyans, agency among convicts, i. 138–141
Whalers, race of, i. 180, 181
Wild boy, ii. 387
— cattle, i. 249–251
Wine, i. 314
Wreck of 'Dunbar,' i. 390–393
— of 'Punjaub,' ii. 284, 285
Windsor, i. 430, 431
Wollongong, visit to, i. 447–449
— harbour of, i. 449, 450
Wynaad, visit to, ii. 360–361
— scenery of, ii. 361

YOUNG, Sir Henry, arrival of, i. 270–272

THE END.

LONDON : PRINTED BY
SPOTTISWOODE AND CO., NEW-STREET SQUARE
AND PARLIAMENT STREET

LORD MACAULAY'S WORKS.

Latest Editions now on Sale :—

The COMPLETE WORKS of LORD MACAU-

LAY. Edited by his Sister, Lady Trevelyan. Library Edition, with Portrait. 8 vols. 8vo. £5 5s. cloth ; or, £8 8s. bound in calf.

MISCELLANEOUS WRITINGS :—

Library Edition, 2 vols. 8vo. 21s.
People's Edition, 1 vol. crown 8vo. 1s. 6d.

SPEECHES, corrected by Himself :—

Library Edition, 8vo. 12s.
People's Edition, crown 8vo. 3s. 6d.
Speeches on Parliamentary Reform, 16mo. 1s.

LAYS of ANCIENT ROME :—

Illustrated Edition, fcp. 4to. 21s.
With Ivry and The Armada, 16mo. 4s. 6d.
Miniature Illustrated Edition, imperial 16mo. 10s. 6d.

HISTORY of ENGLAND, from the ACCESSION

of JAMES the SECOND :—
Library Edition, 5 vols. 8vo. £4.
Cabinet Edition, 8 vols. post 8vo. 48s.
People's Edition, 4 vols. crown 8vo. 16s.

CRITICAL and HISTORICAL ESSAYS :—

. Student's Edition, 1 vol. crown 8vo. 6s.
Library Edition, 3 vols. 8vo. 36s.
Cabinet Edition, 4 vols. post 8vo. 24s.
People's Edition, 2 vols. crown 8vo. 8s.
Travellers' Edition, 1 vol. square crown 8vo. 21s.

SIXTEEN ESSAYS, which may be had sepa-

rately :—

Addison and Walpole, 1s.	Warren Hastings, 1s.
Frederick the Great, 1s.	Pitt and Chatham, 1s.
Croker's Boswell's Johnson, 1s.	Ranke and Gladstone, 1s.
Hallam's Constitutional History,	Milton and Macchiavelli, 6d.
16mo. 1s. fcp. 8vo. 6d.	Lord Bacon, 1s. Lord Clive, 1s.

Lord Byron and the Comic Dramatists of the Restoration, 1s.

STUDENT'S NOTES on LORD MACAULAY'S

ESSAY on LORD MAHON'S WAR of the SUCCESSION in SPAIN ; comprising a Summary and Map of Peterborough's Campaign, and a concise account of the Names, Quotations, &c. occurring in the Text. By A. H. Bisley, M.A. Assistant-Master of Marlborough College. Fcp. 8vo. price 1s.

London : LONGMANS and CO. Paternoster Row.

WORKS BY JOHN STUART MILL.

CHAPTERS and SPEECHES on the IRISH LAND
QUESTION. Crown 8vo. price 2s. 6d.

ENGLAND and IRELAND. Fifth Edition. 8vo. 1s.

The SUBJECTION of WOMEN. The Third Edition.
Post 8vo. price 5s.

PRINCIPLES of POLITICAL ECONOMY.
Library Edition (the Sixth), 2 vols. 8vo. 30s.
People's Edition, crown 8vo. 5s.

On REPRESENTATIVE GOVERNMENT.
Library Edition (the Third), 8vo. 9s.
People's Edition, crown 8vo. 2s.

On LIBERTY.
Library Edition (the Fourth), post 8vo. 7s. 6d.
People's Edition, crown 8vo. 1s. 4d.

SYSTEM of LOGIC. Seventh Edition. 2 vols. 8vo. 25s.

STEBBING'S ANALYSIS of MILL'S SYSTEM of LOGIC. Second Edition,
revised, in 12mo. price 3s. 6d.

KILLICK'S STUDENT'S HANDBOOK of MILL'S SYSTEM of LOGIC,
just published, in crown 8vo. price 3s. 6d.

DISSERTATIONS and DISCUSSIONS, POLITICAL,
PHILOSOPHICAL, and HISTORICAL; reprinted from the Edinburgh and
Westminster Reviews. Second Edition, revised. 2 vols. 8vo. 24s.

DISSERTATIONS and DISCUSSIONS, POLITICAL,
PHILOSOPHICAL, and HISTORICAL; reprinted chiefly from the Edinburgh
and Westminster Reviews. Vol. III. 8vo. price 12s.

UTILITARIANISM. Third Edition. 8vo. 5s.

An EXAMINATION of Sir WILLIAM HAMILTON'S
PHILOSOPHY, and of the Principal Philosophical Questions discussed in his
Writings. Third Edition, revised. 8vo. 16s.

PARLIAMENTARY REFORM. Second Edit. 8vo. 1s. 6d.

INAUGURAL ADDRESS at the UNIVERSITY of ST.
ANDREWS. Second Edition, 8vo. 5s. People's Edition, crown 8vo. 1s.

ANALYSIS of the PHENOMENA of the HUMAN MIND.
By JAMES MILL. A New Edition, with Notes Illustrative and Critical, by
ALEXANDER BAIN, ANDREW FINDLATER, and GEORGE GROTE. Edited, with
additional Notes, by JOHN STUART MILL. 2 vols. 8vo. price 28s.

London : LONGMANS, GREEN, and CO. Paternoster Row.